NAPOLEON III

AND HIS

CARNIVAL

EMPIRE

Also by John Bierman:

FICTION
The Heart's Grown Brutal

NON-FICTION
Righteous Gentile
Odyssey

Napoleon III

and his

Carnival

Empire

by

John Bierman

✴

St. Martin's Press
New York

Design by Robert Bull Design

Library of Congress Cataloging-in-Publication Data

Bierman, John.
    Napoleon III and his carnival empire / by John Bierman.
      p. cm.
    ISBN 0-312-01827-4
    1. Napoleon III, Emperor of the French, 1808–1873. 2. France—Kings and rulers—Biography. 3. France—History—Second Empire, 1852–1870. I. Title.
DC280.B53 1988
944.07′092′4—19   87-38236
[B]   CIP

First Edition

10 9 8 7 6 5 4 3 2 1

For Hilary,
as ever,
and for Gloria,
who convinced me that a cat
may, indeed, look at a king.

CONTENTS

LIST OF ILLUSTRATIONS

Endpapers: *Les Ambassadeurs Siamois* by J. L. Gérome; Chateau de Versailles. (Art Resource)

"There is properly no history; only biography."
—*EMERSON*

PROLOGUE

POPGUNS AT DAWN

WINTER HAS ARRIVED EARLY in east-central France. It is not quite November, yet already a light snow dusts the steeples and high mansard roofs of Strasbourg. As the city of the fatted goose sleeps through the night of October 29, 1836, the house of Madame Eléonore Gordon at 17, rue de la Fontaine is snug enough to keep the chill at bay, but inside it nobody is slumbering. Uniforms are being laid out, plans finalized, printed manifestos prepared for posting up, and weapons checked for possible use. At first light a tiny group of exalted idiots will launch an insurrection against the throne of France.

To anyone not of the group, to the proverbial fly-on-the-wall, the appearance of its leader must seem rather less heroic—or desperate—than the madness of his mission would warrant. His body is slightly misproportioned, with a torso a little too long for the legs, while his features fall just a little short of the romantic, with eyes that bulge slightly, a sallow complexion, and a too-prominent nose. As for his demeanor, it is strangely calm and phlegmatic, almost offhand, considering the gravity of the task at hand.

To be sure, the tension is there, roiling beneath the placid surface, but Louis Napoleon Bonaparte has long since mastered the art of self-concealment. Indeed, his manner at all times is so undemonstrative and taciturn that a close acquaintance likes to joke that he makes William the Silent seem like a garrulous fool.

Nor is his taciturnity the only way in which the personality of Louis Napoleon seems far from the conventionally Gallic. For one thing, he speaks his native French with a German accent and has none of the mannerisms of a Frenchman of his age and class. For another, though voraciously fond of the company of women, he has no interest in the pleasures of the palate. Yet to his followers he is the very embodiment of France; for as he claims, and they unquestioningly believe, he is the nephew of and heir apparent to the late emperor Napoleon.

Prince Louis professes, with an appearance of complete certainty, that his lineage and personal qualities have bestowed on him the right—even the obligation—to rule France. And even an outsider who might remain unimpressed by his pretensions, by his name or by his appearance, would be forced to admit that his aura of quiet conviction is oddly compelling.

If the physical characteristics of Prince Louis Napoleon Bonaparte at the age of twenty-eight bring to mind those of Don Quixote, the comparison is not entirely absurd. Like the knight of La Mancha, he is self-deluded, vainglorious, perversely innocent, and willing to pit himself against impossible odds. Where he differs markedly from Cervantes's fictive hero is that he entertains no antiquated notions about knightly honor or feminine virtue. He is a confirmed womanizer and a compulsive conspirator: Don Juan as much as Don Quixote, and Signor Machiavelli as much as either.

This demi-Quixote has his demi–Sancho Panza in the squat form of a humorless former soldier and small-time journalist who styles himself vicomte de Persigny, but whose real name is Jean Gilbert Victor Fialin. It will later be said of this son of a customs clerk that "he resembled a gentleman as chicory resembles coffee." But Prince Louis is not worried by the implausibility of his follower's claim to nobility. What commends Persigny to the Pretender to the throne of France is not his lineage but his quick intelligence, his resourcefulness, and his total loyalty. Whatever else about him might be fraudulent, those attributes are not.

Louis had found his faithful squire eighteen months previously, under circumstances so providential that both men felt at once that the hand of fate must have arranged their meeting. The self-styled viscount, long a fervent Bonapartist, was on a business trip to Baden-Baden and was riding in a hired coach to an assignation with a woman when the driver raised his whip to salute a passing horseman and cried: "Vive Napoléon!"

Surely, Persigny asked the coachman, that was not *the* Prince Louis Napoleon? Indeed it was, the man replied, the great emperor's exiled nephew himself. He often visited Baden-Baden to pursue the fashionable ladies who came to take the waters—and, it was said, to catch a glimpse of his forbidden homeland, just across the Rhine.

Confronted so unexpectedly with the embodiment of his political ideals, Persigny made the coach turn around and catch up with the horseman. Drawing alongside, Persigny jumped down, introduced himself, and declared his fealty. From that moment the lives of the bogus viscount and the problematic prince had been bound together.

Another of the conspirators gathered tonight in the house on the rue de la Fontaine is its tenant, the redoubtable and resplendent Eléonore Gordon, née Brault, a woman in whose existence life and art chase each other's tails so relentlessly that she has long since forgotten where one ends and the other begins.

She rides, she drinks, she swears, she is a sure shot and an expert swordswoman, skills she learned from her late husband, a Scottish mercenary officer in the service of the Queen of Spain. Like a man, the young Widow Gordon takes her pleasure where and as she chooses, and currently she takes it with Persigny, though rumor has it that she also makes herself available to the personage whom she breathlessly refers to as "mon Prince."

However that might be, la Gordon's free-ranging lifestyle, lush good looks, swaggering sexuality, and skill with sword and pistol are only part of her vivid persona; she is also a contralto of just sufficient talent to make an uncertain living as a diva in the opera houses and concert halls of provincial France. And, finally, like her lover Persigny, she is a passionate Bonapartist, burning to devote her diverse talents to the cause.

Professional engagements on both sides of the Rhine have allowed her to maintain a household in Baden-Baden as well as in Strasbourg; passing freely and frequently between France and Germany, she has been able to provide a link between Prince Louis and Persigny on the eastern bank of the river, and the small coterie of French officers of the Strasbourg garrison with whom they have been in contact for some time.

The most senior of these is Colonel Claude Nicolas Vaudrey, commanding officer of the Fourth Artillery Regiment, who has secretly pledged the one thousand men and forty guns under his command to the cause. According to the plan hatched by Prince

Louis and Persigny, the Fourth is to be the vanguard of an army that will march on Paris behind the new Napoleon, gathering numbers all the way, in a re-creation of his uncle's return from Elba in March 1815.

Although he is a veteran of Waterloo, and the Fourth Artillery had been the regiment of the Little Corporal himself, Vaudrey was hesitant when first invited to join the conspiracy. Undeterred, the ever-resourceful Persigny gave his mistress the task of winning Vaudrey over. It had been easy; the old soldier lost no time in begging the well-endowed diva to join him in the dance of the sheets. At first, la Gordon kept him at arm's length. "I will only be his who is for Prince Louis," she said. But she surrendered after Vaudrey replied: "Be mine, for I am his!"

If this exchange, vouched for by Madame Gordon herself, sounds suspiciously like a snatch of rectitative from one of the libretti in her repertoire, that may serve to demonstrate how little she is able to distinguish between opera and life.

Another of the conspirators preparing for action at dawn this day is Colonel Charles Denis Parquin, a maturely handsome man of unmistakably military cast, with a saber-scarred upper lip. Like Vaudrey, he is a veteran of Napoleon's Grande Armée, and more than twenty years the senior of Prince Louis, Persigny, and la Gordon.

Unlike Vaudrey, he has not been lured into the conspiracy by the promise of reward, carnal or otherwise. He is stolid, straightforward, and uncomplicated, and it is clear that only utter loyalty to an ideal, unrestrained by common sense, can have allowed so conventional and unimaginative a man to be part of such a madcap scheme. Parquin can never forget that as a young officer he received a battlefield decoration from the hands of the emperor himself, or that he owes a continuing personal loyalty to the Bonaparte family as the husband of a lady-in-waiting to Prince Louis's mother.

The group of conspirators is completed by a pair of young bloods acting as Prince Louis's orderlies—the twenty-five-year-old comte Raphael de Gricourt, and vicomte Henri de Quèrelles, aged twenty-three—and by Charles Thélin, the valet who has dressed Prince Louis since childhood and will continue to do so until his death.

At 4:30 A.M., while Vaudrey waits in his barracks with four junior officers who have already joined the conspiracy, Thélin begins to dress his master in the outfit he smuggled across the Rhine in a trunk the day before. For his coup against France's pusillanimous citizen-king, Louis-Philippe, the young Bonaparte has chosen to dress exactly as his illustrious uncle had so often done, in the uniform of a Grande Armée colonel— green coat, white britches, high boots, and bicorn hat, with the sash of the Legion of Honor across his chest.

Sartorially speaking, it is a mistake. As an English admirer who once saw him in a similar outfit would say much later, "It did not suit him; he was too long in the body and too short in the legs; the latter were not good."

Some time after five the tiny band let themselves out into the street, leaving footprints in the snow as they make their way through the still-sleeping city to the barracks where Vaudrey awaits them. Prince Louis's first act on arrival there is to promote Vaudrey to the rank of major-general. Then they walk together to the parade ground where the cannoneers of the Fourth are drawn up grumbling in the open square, wondering at the reason for such an early muster. It is 6:00 A.M.

"My friends," declaims Vaudrey, "I have just been nominated general." A ragged cheer goes up. "I will cause forty francs to be distributed to each of you." A more sustained and enthusiastic cheer. "And now, I have to inform you that a revolution has broken out in Paris." An astonished silence, broken by an incredulous babble from the ranks.

Vaudrey raises his hand for quiet. "The King's government has been overthrown," he lies. "A new Napoleon has been proclaimed." And then, turning to the man at his side—until that moment unrecognized by the troops—he declares with a flourish: "I present to you, His Imperial Majesty, Napoleon II."* The astonished cannoneers respond with the show of enthusiasm their commander clearly requires: "Long live Napoleon II, long live the Emperor!" Bewilderment rather than fervor seems the dominant mood.

The Pretender's own address to the men of the Fourth Artillery follows. He is not, and never will be, much of an orator and certainly he lacks his uncle's magic gift for achieving rapport with the common soldier. He speaks in lofty and overblown ab-

---

* An understandable error: Vaudrey was not a deeply dyed enough Bonapartist to realize that the recently deceased Duke of Reichstadt, Napoleon's only legitimate son, was considered by devotees of the dynasty to be Napoleon II, even though he had never reigned, and that Prince Louis should therefore be termed Napoleon III.

stractions rather than taking his cue from Vaudrey and talking sensibly of monetary rewards and promotions.

Indeed, his address follows very much the stilted lines of the manifestos which even now are being posted up around the town by Gricourt and Quèrelles— "I present myself to you with the Will of the Emperor Napoleon in one hand and the Sword of Austerlitz in the other. . . . In Rome, when the people saw Caesar's blood-stained corpse, they overthrew their hypocritical oppressors. . . . But, Frenchmen, Napoleon is greater than Caesar; he is the emblem of the civilization of the nineteenth century. . . ." It is not, alas, the stuff by which rabbles are roused.

Although there exists a hard core of Bonapartism within the middle and lower ranks of King Louis-Philippe's army, as among the nation at large, it is born of nostalgia for past glories rather than of any current political imperative. The France of 1836 is not the France of 1815—defeated, humiliated, occupied, and longing for the return of its charismatic emperor—but a realm where life, especially for the rising middle class, is comfortable enough, even though lacking the glamour and excitement of the Empire.

So, if the men of the Fourth—the majority too young to have memories of the first Napoleon—are willing to do their commanding officer's bidding, it is not with any wild enthusiasm but because they are accustomed to obeying orders, and certainly not because they are electrified by the young Bonaparte's oratory.

The first task of the insurrectionists is to either co-opt or neutralize the potential leaders of resistance—the garrison commander, General Voirol, the prefect, Cloppin d'Arnouville, and the commandant-general of the Department of the Lower Rhine. Accordingly, Prince Louis and Parquin go with twenty cannoneers and a junior officer to Voirol's residence.

The clomping of boots on the landing outside his bedroom brings the general out in nightshirt and sleeping cap, demanding to know what all the hubbub is about. Prince Louis advances on him with outstretched arms, as if to embrace, and urges the general to join his insurrection. Louis Napoleon has been assured by Vaudrey that an old soldier like Voirol will be "unable to resist the sight of you and the imperial eagle." But that proves to be a fundamental mistake. Voirol "repelled these advances with great animation," as his official report of the incident will claim later.

Disappointed but not deterred, Louis and Parquin put Voirol under house arrest, leaving the cannoneers under a young lieutenant to guard him while they go about their subversive business elsewhere. It is a fatal mistake; while the soldiers guard the front of the house and Voirol's bedroom door, the general's aide-de-camp, Colonel de Franqueville, is able to sneak out the back way to alert the rest of the garrison to what is going on.

Not long after that, Voirol manages to persuade his captors not only to let him go but to escort him to the barracks of a regiment which has not been subverted. "The loyal and brave cannoneers [he reported later] attending to my voice and, guided by sentiments of duty and honor, surrounded me and, having mounted my horse, I marched out with them sword in hand and proceeded to the Citadel . . . where I knew I should find a loyal regiment, the 16th of the Line. . . ."

Eléonore Gordon actually sees Voirol leaving his residence accompanied by the men of the Fourth, but assumes that he has joined the rebellion—"otherwise," as she said with some vehemence when taken into captivity later, "I'd have blown his head off."

By now the whole city is awake and in a state of commotion. From their windows, or standing on the sidewalks, the solid burghers of Strasbourg watch in amazement as Prince Louis, his uncle's sword in hand, marches through the streets at the head of the Fourth Artillery, to the crash, thump, and tinkle of the regimental band. Some of the citizens cry "Vive Napoléon!" But others shout in praise of King Louis-Philippe, and some even have the temerity to cry "Vive la République!"—clear evidence that the citizenry of Strasbourg are by no means all, or even mainly, in favor of a Napoleonic revival.

But if Prince Louis notices the absence of unanimous support, he pays it no heed and marches bravely on toward the Finckmatt Barracks, where he expects to recruit the officers and men of the 46th Regiment of the Line. At his side marches a co-conspirator carrying a Tricolor standard surmounted by an imperial eagle—the eagle which is supposed, figuratively speaking, to fly from village steeple to village steeple across France until it comes to roost in the towers of Notre Dame.

At the Finckmatt Barrack gates, the Pretender halts the Fourth and enters, accompanied by Vaudrey, Parquin, and a Lieutenant Laity. They are challenged by a young guard commander who seems to have no idea who the strange fellow in the Bonaparte outfit might be. But he does recognize the artil-

lery officers accompanying him, and so far as he is concerned no
gunners are going to barge into an infantry regiment's quarters
without an invitation.

While he argues with the intruders at the guardhouse, men of
the 46th drift out onto the parade ground to see what all the
commotion is about. The Pretender tries to harangue them, but
with little success. Cries of "Shut up!" and "Impostor!" interrupt the uncertain flow of his oratory. Then Colonel Taillandier, commander of the regiment, comes puffing onto the scene,
accompanied by Voirol's aide-de-camp, Franqueville, who has
brought him news of the insurrection.

Taillandier is a man of brisk decision. He immediately orders
the barrack gates closed, cutting Prince Louis and his small
group off from the men of the Fourth, who are left shuffling and
complaining in the snowy street outside. Then he advances on
the insurrectionists and tells them they are all under arrest.

At his command the interlopers are seized, disarmed, and pin-
ioned. Then, in full view of the regiment, Taillandier contemptuously knocks off Prince Louis's bicorn hat, tears his Legion
of Honor and sash from his breast, rips off his epaulettes, and
tramples all these badges of honor and distinction into the ground.

As he does so, the carillon in Strasbourg Cathedral's 450-foot
steeple tower chimes eight and Voirol rides into view at the
head of the loyal 16th of the Line. Prince Louis Napoleon's first
illegal attempt to claim his birthright is ignominiously over.

BOOK ONE

THE

PATH

TO

POWER

★

"From time to time men are created into whose hands the fate of their country is entrusted. I am such a man."
—LOUIS NAPOLEON

1

AN
UNCERTAIN
PATERNITY

AS IT BEGAN, SO IT WOULD END—IN FIASCO. Between the popgun insurrection at Strasbourg that was Louis Napoleon's first stumbling step on the path to power and the grandiose display of diplomatic bungling and military incompetence that ended his career thirty-four years later, all that differed was the scale.

During the years linking those events he would create a glittering empire, his armies would range the globe from China to Mexico, and he would establish himself as the arbiter of Europe. Only after the fall would France and the world come to realize how utterly implausible he and his imperium had been.

But then, Louis Napoleon Bonaparte was conceived in implausibility: although he would become Emperor of the French very largely on the strength of his illustrious name, he was quite probably not a Bonaparte at all. His mother loathed her husband, fastidiously avoiding sexual contact with him, and young Louis was more plausibly the child of one of her lovers. Which one scarcely matters.

Hortense de Beauharnais was the daughter of the great Napoleon's Empress Josephine by her first husband, who died on the guillotine in 1794. One contemporary describes her in young womanhood as "an exquisite blonde with amethyst eyes, supple waist and harmonious gestures. Her feet were rather too small, her teeth rather too large; but what perfect hands and ivory nails, beautifully kept." Josephine having failed to give him an heir, Napoleon married his stepdaughter off to his younger brother, Louis—much to the dismay of both parties—in the hope that she would bear Bonaparte boys to continue the dynasty.

It was not a good marriage.

Beautiful, spirited, and charmingly self-centered, Hortense was a romantic, a dabbler in the arts, a moderately accomplished pianist, and a composer of pretty songs on the theme of courtly love.* The pettifogging and misanthropic Louis had none of the qualities of his brother, or any others that Hortense could admire, and proved to be a dull, petulant, and increasingly paranoid husband. Worse, he was physically repulsive to Hortense, suffering from a scrofulous right hand which made her shrink from his touch. He was also afflicted with a condition which contemporary accounts discreetly characterize as "rheumatism," but which was probably gonorrhea, the result of an escapade while serving in his elder brother's Egyptian campaign.

Nevertheless, in October 1802, nine months after their marriage, Hortense bore her first son, who was christened Charles Napoleon. Two years later, she was delivered of a second son, Napoleon Louis. The gossipmongers had it that both boys were the sons of the emperor. This was probably a canard. True, Napoleon had always shown unusual affection for his stepdaughter, and after her marriage she made a point of spending far more time with him and her mother than she did with her husband. But though Hortense and her stepfather may well have been lovers, this probably did not occur until some years later.

In 1806, in line with his policy of creating satellite kingdoms throughout Europe, the emperor bestowed a second dazzling gift on his brother by making him King of Holland. This arrangement did not work out any better than the marriage. Louis seemed to imagine that he had been put on the throne to represent the interests of the Dutch rather than those of his brother, and soon Napoleon felt constrained to chide him for the way he discharged both his monarchical and his matrimonial duties.

---

* The best known of these, *Partant pour la Syrie*, which told of a young knight leaving for the Crusades, was in time to become the unofficial anthem of her son's Second Empire.

"Your quarrels with the queen are becoming known to the public," the emperor wrote to him in April 1807. "In your private life you should exercise the mild and paternal qualities you display in government, while in government you should be exercising the rigorousness you show at home. You are treating a young woman as if you were commanding a regiment. . . ."

Despite this sound advice—sent, incidentally, from Poland, where Napoleon was dallying with Marie Walewska—the marriage remained the dismal thing it had always been, although it is only fair to say that no matter what Louis might have done to accommodate his wayward wife, it is unlikely that she could have overcome her physical revulsion for him.

So Louis went on complaining incessantly of her infidelities, both real and imagined, while Hortense continued to spend as much time as possible away from The Hague, which she disliked almost as much for its cold, damp vapors as for the presence of her husband.

In May 1807, the death of her firstborn from a croup compounded Hortense's misery. The following month, still in mourning, she went to take a rest cure at Cauterets, in the Pyrenees, leaving her younger son with Josephine at Malmaison. On June 23—the dates are important—her husband joined her at Cauterets. But it seems to have been anything but a second honeymoon, and on July 6 he left in high ill humor to take the waters at Ussat.

Left to her own devices, Hortense took off on a tour through the mountains with a small retinue which included some gentlemen of her court as well as her ladies-in-waiting and personal servants. On their way through the Pyrenees, Hortense and her retinue were obliged to spend some nights at mountain inns, and nine months later, on April 21, 1808, her third son, Louis Napoleon, was born. Could he have been conceived during her peregrination through the mountains, and if so by whom?

The man most frequently mentioned by contemporary gossip as the putative father was a Dutch admiral named Verhuell, but the record shows fairly conclusively that he was elsewhere at the relevant time. A far more likely candidate seems to have been Eugénie's chancellor, the elegant René de Villeneuve, who, unlike Verhuell, was one of her party in the Pyrenees.

Whatever the case, after returning to Cauterets, Hortense

took it into her head to behave in a most uncharacteristic way: she hurried to Toulouse, joining her husband there on August 12, and—doubtless to his delight and astonishment—allowed him to exercise his conjugal rights. As if making sure that their "reconciliation" would be on the record, she wrote to her brother Eugène, Napoleon's viceroy in Italy, to say: "I am with the king and we are getting on well together. I don't know whether it will last, but I hope so, for he wants to treat me better and you know I have never deserved ill-treatment."

From Toulouse, Hortense and Louis traveled in leisurely fashion, and it seems in a state of continuing conjugal bliss, to Paris, where they were to attend the August 23 marriage of Napoleon's youngest brother, Jérôme, to a German duchess. Once they reached Paris, this suspiciously convenient second honeymoon ended. After Jérôme's wedding, Louis returned to Holland, leaving Hortense with her mother and stepfather in the palace at Saint-Cloud. Louis did not bother to attend the birth of the child, which took place not in Holland but in Hortense's mansion in the rue Cerutti (now Lafitte) in Paris.*

Why did Hortense rush to Toulouse to give herself to the husband she had previously avoided so assiduously? She could, after all, have gone directly to Paris and met him there to put in the required joint appearance at the imperial wedding. Either she had a sudden and unprecedented attack of conjugal feeling or, surely more plausibly, realizing that she was pregnant as a result of an extramarital fling in the mountains, she decided to stifle her loathing in an attempt to make it appear to Louis and the world that he was the father.

It looks suspiciously like bogus evidence of legitimacy that word was put about after the accouchement that the child was four weeks premature—which he must have been if conceived during the "second honeymoon"—and consequently so delicate that he had to be soaked in wine and wrapped in cotton wool to preserve his life. It does not seem that King Louis was fooled. The child bore little resemblance to him; he refused to attend the christening; and not long afterward he wrote to Hor-

---

*Ironically, news of the child's birth was taken to the emperor Napoleon at Bayonne, near the Spanish frontier, by none other than Villeneuve, the possible father. Napoleon was delighted and had his artillery fire salutes all along the frontier.

tense telling her their marriage was through: "My only consolation is to live away from you, to have nothing to do with you, and nothing to expect from you. Adieu, madame, adieu for ever."

It seems possible that Louis believed he had been cuckolded by his brother. When the emperor ordained for the newborn child the given names of Charles-Louis-Napoleon (the Charles was later dropped), King Louis committed what looks suspiciously like a Freudian slip when he wrote back saying that "I will conform conscientiously with the desires of Your Majesty over the given names of *his** son."

The following year, seeking the emperor's permission for a formal separation from Hortense, King Louis asked for custody of his older son only, leaving the younger to the care of his wife. Writing at about the same time to Hortense, he pointedly referred to the younger child as "your son," and in July 1810, announcing his abdication as King of Holland, he referred to the older boy as "our well-beloved son," but to the younger only as "his brother, Charles-Louis-Napoleon."

Perhaps most damagingly, in 1831, after his older son's death while taking part, with his sibling, in a rebellion against the temporal power of the Pope, King Louis wrote to Pope Gregory XVI to denounce the "criminal" action of the boys, adding: "The unfortunate [older] child is dead, may God have mercy upon him. As for the other, who usurps my name, you are aware Holy Father that he, thank heaven, is nothing to me. It is my misfortune to be married to a Messalina who breeds."

On the other hand, in the same month as his letter to the Pope, the ex-king referred to young Louis in another letter as "the youngest of my children." And on the occasion of Louis's first communion in April 1821, he was gushingly paternal. "I bestow again on this solemn occasion," he wrote, "the paternal blessings which I give you in my thoughts every morning, every evening and whenever my imagination turns towards you."

Certainly, King Louis never formally disavowed the boy (although this could have been because he did not want to broadcast his cuckoldry to the world), and on his death he left him

---

*Emphasis added: in French *son*, not *mon*.

his entire fortune (although this could have been because by that time there was no one else to leave it to).

Louis's vacillating feelings toward his youngest son only serve to cloud the issue and are significant principally as evidence of his unstable personality. His suspicions can no more be taken as evidence of the boy's bastardy than his occasional bursts of paternal goodwill can be seen as proofs of his legitimacy. All that can be said for certain about the future emperor's paternity is that it remains shrouded in ambiguity. However, historical judgments being at best a balance of probabilities, it seems more likely that he was not sired by his mother's husband than that he was.

More important, perhaps, than whether Louis Napoleon was or was not of the blood imperial is the fact that the doubts existed and that they were known to Louis Napoleon, along with the ruling circles of Europe. Nevertheless, whatever he felt about the speculation and whatever doubts he may have harbored in private, he never once referred to the matter, either in jest or in anger. Indeed, throughout his life he never expressed anything but a sublime certainty that he was destined by birth to occupy the throne and re-create the Empire.

Still, the worm of doubt about his paternity must have burrowed deep into Louis Napoleon's psyche, manifesting itself in a deep craving, surviving constant rebuffs, for the love and regard of the cantankerous absentee whom he called father. "I would give all my heritage for my father's embrace," he wrote, at the age of thirty-six, to a friend who was attempting to broker a reconciliation between them.

The defeat of the first Napoleon and the occupation of Paris by Allied troops on April 1, 1814, found Hortense at Josephine's château in Navarre, about 50 miles northwest of the capital, with her two young sons.

Josephine was by this time no longer empress, Napoleon having divorced her in 1809 to marry Marie Louise of Austria in the hope, which was subsequently fulfilled, that she would bear him a son and heir. As for Hortense, she preferred to risk capture by the Cossacks than accept her husband's urgent plea to bring the children and flee with him to Italy before the Russian Army arrived.

While Hortense sheltered with her mother and contemplated her next move, she received a letter from Prince Leopold of Saxe-Coburg, who was serving as an aide to Czar Alexander I. The dashing and magnanimous Alexander had persuaded the other Allied leaders that it was best to conciliate the defeated French, and Leopold's letter told Hortense that the czar would very much like to make her acquaintance and that of her "August Mother."

"He would have come to Navarre if it had not been so far away," Leopold added, "and suggests that Malmaison would be a more agreeable place for him to meet Your Majesty and Your Majesty's children." On April 16, Hortense and the czar duly met at Josephine's palace. The grounds were teeming with Cossack troops and at first Hortense was no more than polite, maintaining as she claimed later "a cold reserve . . . in the presence of the conqueror of my country." More plausibly, she was playing hard to get.

The czar, obviously smitten, told her how much he deplored the war and offered his help and protection. Hortense accepted demurely, her continued reserve, genuine or feigned, serving only to make the Russian monarch even more attentive. It was not long before the gossips of the restored Bourbon court were commenting spitefully on the blossoming relationship between Alexander and the stepdaughter of the hated Bonaparte.

Soon the czar was telling Hortense (as she would duly record in her memoirs) that his wife didn't understand him. When he had to go to England on a state visit, he left Paris thirty-six hours early so that he could spend two nights with Hortense at her château at Saint-Leu before crossing the Channel. And amid the hectic round of engagements he found time to write her several intimate letters from England.

As another sign of his favor, Alexander pressured the restored Bourbon monarch, Louis XVIII, into giving Hortense the title of duchesse de Saint-Leu and a pension of 400,000 francs a year. Thus spared the horrors of peace, Hortense and her two young sons survived the fall of the Empire in considerable comfort. The only event to disturb their tranquillity was the sudden death of Josephine from a cold, apparently caused by her wearing too flimsy a dress on an unseasonably chilly May day to attend a reception for her daughter's protector.

Later that year, Hortense received notice from her husband, in exile, that he intended to sue her in the French courts for custody of his older son, Napoleon Louis. Perhaps significantly, he did not ask for the younger, although under French family law he had an unassailable case for custody of both.

Hortense, a doting mother despite her promiscuous behavior, was not too proud to beg the despised Louis XVIII to intervene on her behalf. It must have given the Bourbon king considerable pleasure to tell the Bonapartist baggage, with a show of great constitutional virtue, that he could not possibly interfere with the due process of law.

The case came to court in Paris the following January, and after two months of argument and deliberation the verdict was delivered: Hortense must hand the child over. Only the dramatic return of Napoleon from Elba on March 15, 1815, and his triumphant march to Paris prevented the court order from being executed.

When Napoleon reached the capital and installed himself once again in the Tuileries, Hortense was one of the first to hurry to the palace to greet him. Not surprisingly he received her coldly, having learned of her coziness with the czar. However, he did want to see her children, and the following day she brought them to him. With the two boys he was the jolly uncle, all warm embraces and merry quips; toward their mother he remained cool.

But she was a powerfully attractive and persuasive woman and Napoleon's anger gradually evaporated. The empress Marie Louise had elected to remain in Vienna with their infant son, the Duke of Reichstadt, and, unimpeded by her presence, Napoleon did not allow too many of the Hundred Days to pass before relations between him and Hortense were fully restored. Both in private and in public, Hortense filled the role vacated by Marie Louise and previously occupied by her mother, virtually a proxy empress.

She and the children were present on an occasion which must have left an indelible impression on the mind of the seven-year-old Prince Louis: the ceremony to mark the restoration of the Empire on June 1, 1815.

The Champ de Mars was packed with troops, marching and countermarching to the crash of military bands as their regimental colors were blessed by priests and handed over to them. On the saluting stand beside the emperor, newly confirmed as such by the people's vote in a national plebiscite, stood Hortense and her two sons. Napoleon called upon the troops and twenty thousand civilian delegates brought in from all quarters of the realm to swear their allegiance. And from the dusty plain of the Champ de Mars the mighty roar swelled up: "We swear it!"

Eighty of the Hundred Days had passed by that time. The British and the Prussians were deploying their forces for a new invasion, and Napoleon now moved to forestall them, hoping to destroy their armies in Belgium. On June 11, he invited Hortense and her two sons to lunch with him at the Tuileries before going off on campaign. He was in a jovial mood, confident of victory, and the family stayed until late that evening.*

On his return from the shambles of Waterloo a week later, Napoleon and Hortense had four last memorable days together, she leaving her children in the care of a shopkeeper in the Boulevard Montmartre to be alone with him at Malmaison. He planned to take ship to America and asked her to follow him there with the children. She might well have done so had not Napoleon been captured by the British—his reward for tarrying too long at Malmaison—and exiled to St. Helena.

With the Allied armies once again in occupation of Paris and the Bourbons back in the Tuileries, Hortense felt understandably insecure. She could hardly turn coat a third time. Or could she?

The Austrian commander-in-chief, Field Marshal Prince Felix von Schwarzenberg, commandeered her mansion in the rue Cerutti as his headquarters, but he was gracious (or susceptible)

---

*Many years later, Persigny would put it about that, having a premonition of disaster, little Louis begged his uncle not to go. It is an unlikely story, to say the least, but just the sort of legend the propagandist of a charismatic and authoritarian regime would seek to create.

enough to let her live in a suite of rooms on the first floor where, surrounded by the gallant officers of his staff, she felt safe from royalist reprisals.

But when Czar Alexander returned to Paris he pointedly avoided her, telling mutual friends that he felt betrayed by her behavior during the Hundred Days. Even when Alexander came to the Cerutti mansion to call on Prince von Schwarzenberg, he left without trying to see her. And when she wrote to him, returning his letters but obviously hoping to soften his heart, he replied in cold and formal terms that her conduct had been unforgivable.

At that point, Hortense decided it was time to leave Paris and go into exile. On the night of July 17 she set off for Savoy, then part of the Kingdom of Piedmont. Her estranged husband, who had remained in Italy throughout the Hundred Days, sent word that he expected her to hand over Napoleon Louis in accordance with the order of the French court. Deciding that under the circumstances the child might be better off with his father than with her, she let him go. Now she and Louis Napoleon had only each other.

At the end of November the Allies issued a declaration saying that she would be permitted to live in Switzerland, under the supervision of the Allied embassies in that country, but it was not until the spring of 1817 that she was able to move there, having bought a small castle at Arenenberg in the canton of Thurgau, on the shores of Lake Constance. Later Hortense was permitted to reside also at Augsburg, in Bavaria, where she bought a town house.

Prince Louis would spend the remainder of his childhood and his adolescence in these two locations, except for regular winter visits to Bonaparte relatives in Italy.

He was not a particularly robust child, though he would become a fine horseman and a strong swimmer; nor was he much of a scholar, though he had a talent for sketching and drawing. By general consent he was a charmer, seemingly gentle and timid, but stubborn and resilient beneath the surface.

One of his closest childhood companions was Hortense Lacroix (later Cornu), the daughter of parents in the service of his mother and to whom he was godfather, although she was only a year younger than he. We have the word of Louis Napoleon himself that she was a shrewd judge of character. "I wish you were a man," he once told her, "you understand things so well." Her description of him as a boy may therefore be regarded as authentic.

"He was a charming child," she said,

as gentle as a lamb, affectionate, caressing, generous (he would even give his clothes away to anyone in need), witty, quick in repartee and with the sensibility of a girl; but easily puzzled and intellectually lazy. . . . He had not a trace of arrogance, and would throw himself unreservedly into the arms of the first person he met, overwhelming him with caresses beyond rhyme or reason, so that people said he must have a warm and loving heart. But there was nothing in it; he forgot you as soon as you were out of his sight.

Hortense Cornu was equally aware of another side to her childhood companion—of the "furious Italian passions" that seethed beneath his calm surface. "As a child," she said on another occasion, "he was subject to [violent] fits of anger. . . . While they lasted, he did not know what he said or did." It is clear, however, that Louis Napoleon learned to control those fits. In later life his even temperament was to be a source of wonderment to all who came into contact with him.

At the age of fifteen, Louis dramatically demonstrated another side of his nature, a reckless Quixotry, by diving fully clothed into an icy river on a winter's day to recover the hat of his pretty cousin Marie, daughter of the Grand Duchess of Baden. He did this in response to Marie's challenge that, like all males of his time, he lacked the chivalry of the knights of old. On emerging from the water with chattering teeth, Louis indicated that Quixotry had its limits. "For heaven's sake," he said, "let's have no more talk of chivalry."

Louis's mother ascribed the intellectual laziness mentioned by Hortense Cornu to the inadequacy of his tutor, the affable old Abbé Bertrand. In place of the abbé she hired a more energetic and much younger man, Philippe Le Bas, who quickly forced his young charge's nose to the academic grindstone. Le Bas was a republican and a Jacobin, and certainly no Bonapartist. But he thought the Bonapartes preferable to the Bourbons and, besides, he needed the job.

After a few months of Le Bas's unremittingly virtuous tutelage, Louis was showing a distinct improvement in all subjects. Le Bas even broke him of his dependence on a lighted candle by his bed at night, a habit the frugal and puritanical tutor considered to be bad for his charge's character. After a year Le Bas decided that Louis should go to a school where he would have the spur of competition and learn to get on with other boys. Hortense agreed, and Louis was enrolled as a day pupil in the gymnasium at Augsburg.

It must have been hard for Louis. The language of instruction was German, not his native French, but in his first term he rated fifty-fourth in a class of ninety-four and within a year he was fourth in a class of sixty-six. This dramatic progress was largely due to the efforts of Le Bas, who kept Louis at his studies every evening after school and at weekends, never allowing him to slacken off.

But although Hortense was delighted with Louis's progress, after three years she withdrew the carte blanche she had given Le Bas and began to encourage her son—not that he needed encouraging—to spend more time enjoying himself at riding, hunting, balls, and parties.

At seventeen, Louis moved further from the influence of Le Bas when he was enrolled in the Swiss military academy at Thun, where he specialized in the black art of which his illustrious uncle had been a master: gunnery. Two years later, his functions reduced to virtually nil, Le Bas left the service of the Bonapartes.

How much did his years under the tutelage of Le Bas influence the mind and personality of the young Louis Napoleon? Le Bas could hardly have lasted as long as he did if he had made too much parade of his republican fervor. But it seems clear that some of this—as well as his other advanced ideas—rubbed off on his charge, for Louis Napoleon's domestic politics were always more inclined to the left than the right and even as emperor he would declare himself a republican at heart.

Hortense may have contributed to this vaguely "progressive" mindset; for all her high style, status consciousness, and love of luxury, she at least made a show of social conscience, and while spoiling her sons disgracefully and bringing them up to expect every advantage that wealth and a famous name can bestow, she also reminded them that they were privileged and had a responsibility to those less fortunate.

The great Bonaparte had, after all, come to power on the shirttails of revolution, and the political ideology which bore his name, however authoritarian, did contain liberal and reformist elements. Hortense would underscore this by referring to him as "the Messiah of the people," who "firmly established the supremacy of merit over noble birth." How she squared such egalitarian sentiments with her lavish lifestyle and her conviction that the Bonapartes had an inherent right to rule must remain a mystery. Louis resolved the contradiction by having it both ways. "An aristocrat by birth, I am a democrat by nature and conviction," he said in a letter to a friend.

Together with her recollections of an idealized emperor, Hortense did not neglect to give her son some hard-nosed political counsel. "Never weary of hoping," she abjured him. "Keep your eyes peeled. Look out for propitious moments"—advice he would one day follow to stunning effect. But for the moment he could hardly have expected that both his cousin the Duke of Reichstadt and his older brother would die young, leaving him heir to the Napoleonic legend.

Later propaganda would have it that he knew from his teens that he was destined to be emperor, but the face Louis presented to the world at this time was hardly that of a young man preparing himself for the responsibilities of power. His main interest seemed to be in the opposite sex, and although his mother thought he was "not attractive enough to make the women run after him," that was not the opinion of others.

Hortense's lady-in-waiting Valérie Masuyer noted in her diary that "he has a sentimental, melancholy air that is most interesting," while Louis's cousin, Tascher de la Pagerie, remarked that "his eyes speak eloquently of love . . . he seems to me to have a heart as fickle as it is tender."

It was this air of romantic melancholy that was to win him so much success in the game of love. It softened the frank sensuality of his big nose and fleshy lips, producing an effect that, combined with his pallor and his enigmatic gray eyes, made him magnetically attractive to innocent young girls and experienced matrons alike.

It deceived his men friends, too, into believing that he had not much interest in anything beyond the chase. The future Lord Malmesbury, an acquaintance of his adolescence, would remember Louis Napoleon as "a wild, harum-scarum youth, riding at full gallop down the streets to the peril of the public, fencing and pistol-shooting, and apparently without serious thought of any kind."

It was probably only with hindsight that Malmesbury added that "even then he was possessed with the conviction that he would some day rule over France."

2

THE
ITALIAN
ESCAPADE

IN HIS EARLY TWENTIES, Louis Napoleon could pass for a romantically good-looking young man. The Byronic hero had not yet turned seedy; the long nose had not yet become pendulous; the pale complexion had not yet turned sallow; the dark, curly hair was not yet lank and dull. And although Prince Louis was not particularly robust, he had hardened himself with physical exercise and managed to cut a dashing figure on horseback, where the brevity of his legs was not so evident.

With his youthful looks went the standard youthful illusions, and his mind, when it wasn't on women, was occupied less with his native France then with weak, divided Italy, the focus of so much romantic idealism and poetic longing among Europe's *jeunesse dorée*. The fashionable cause among the sons of the rich and well-born was the liberation and unification of Italy, then a collection of impotent states either ruled by the Pope or under the domination of the Austrian Empire.

Prince Louis knew Italy well and loved it unaffectedly. Many members of the extended Bonaparte family, his father and brother included, lived there, and every year he and his mother would winter in Rome, where they had a wide circle of relatives and acquaintances. Racketing around Rome with his brother and friends of similar age and status, Louis had plenty of opportunity to indulge both his burgeoning sexuality and his developing taste for conspiratorial politics.

The Bonaparte brothers felt particularly drawn to the Italian cause because it had been espoused by their illustrious uncle. They were also drawn to it, perhaps, in adolescent revolt against their parents' connections with the papal establishment. Either or both of the brothers may even have been members of the Carbonari, a radical secret society that was the forerunner of today's revolutionary underground organizations. The Carbonari originated the cell system, by which members are known only to others of their immediate small circle; if the Bonaparte brothers did join the movement, no records would have been kept. But more likely they were sympathizers rather than active members.

In 1830, a year of revolutions throughout Europe, the brothers were initially enthusiastic about the overthrow of the Bourbon monarchy in France, which brought Louis-Philippe of the junior House of Orléans to the throne. They had no gain to expect from the change of dynasty, for neither Bonapartism nor any of the Bonapartes as individuals had been a factor in the French upheaval. They could not return home to be part of what seemed at the time to be a new beginning. But revolution was in the air and, excited by its scent, the brothers were keen to join an insurrection somewhere.

They soon got their chance. While staying with their father in Florence, in February of 1831, they were invited to command units in a revolutionary force fighting papal troops in the Romagna. They readily accepted.

When news of this reached Hortense in Rome, she left immediately for Florence, intending to put a stop to such dangerous nonsense. She arrived too late, finding only a note from Louis: "We have accepted engagements and cannot depart from them. The name we bear obliges us to help a suffering people that calls upon us." Her estranged and ineffectual husband was no help at all, so Hortense set out on her own to drag her wayward boys out of the firing line.

Although forty-seven, she was still a formidable charmer. She went to the British Minister in Florence and persuaded him to give her a passport in the name of "Mrs. Hamilton." Then she headed south to the battlefront, only to learn that her sons had been transferred to Bologna in the north, where the Austrian Army had intervened, at the Pope's request, to crush the revolt.

On the road north Hortense received word that her older son was severely ill with a fever at Forli. And at Pesaro, on the coast above Ancona, Louis Napoleon intercepted her with the shocking news that Napoleon Louis had died of the measles on March 17.

Hortense had little opportunity to grieve. Hearing that the Austrians, having crushed the revolutionaries, were advancing south with her surviving son's name on their list of wanted men, she dragged Louis off to Ancona where her late brother, Eugène de Beauharnais, owned a palazzo. No sooner had they arrived there than Louis went down with the same illness that had killed his brother.

Hortense put him to bed and nursed him. Two days later, while Louis lay in a high fever, the Austrian Army entered Ancona and in an odd repetition of what had happened in Paris in 1815, its commander, General Baron von Geppert, commandeered the Beauharnais mansion as his headquarters. As in the rue Cerutti, Hortense asked for and was given permission to continue to occupy part of the house.

For several days, until he recovered, Louis remained hidden in a bedroom adjoining von Geppert's office, not daring to cough or speak above a murmur. To explain the comings and goings of the Italian doctor who was treating him, Hortense pretended that she herself was ill. Then, when Louis seemed well enough to travel, she coolly asked Geppert for a laissez-passer which would allow her to move unhindered through the Austrian lines.

Once again her fatal charm stood her in good stead. Armed with Geppert's note and her British passport, Hortense set off on Easter Sunday with Louis disguised as a footman and headed west for the French frontier.

On April 14, Louis Napoleon set foot in France for the first time in sixteen years, his mother hoping that if their presence was discovered the Orléanist regime would not, under the circumstances, enforce the ban imposed on the Bonapartes by the Bourbon monarchy. Nine days later they reached Paris, where they took a suite of hotel rooms overlooking the Place Vendôme.

The next day Hortense revealed their presence to Louis-

Philippe, and in a private audience begged him to repeal the law that banished her and her son from France. He told her he was planning to do just that in due course, but meanwhile he would be obliged if she would keep her presence secret and leave for England as soon as possible.

Hortense and Louis might have left the following day had he not come down with a recurrence of his measles, and soon Louis-Philippe was regretting his liberality in not sending them packing immediately. The tenth anniversary of Napoleon's death on St. Helena was fast approaching and demonstrations were expected on the Place Vendôme, right underneath Hortense's hotel window. If the presence of Napoleon's stepdaughter and nephew were to leak out, the nostalgia of the populace might express itself in volatile forms.

Day after day, the king sent his aide-de-camp to visit "Mrs. Hamilton" and enquire when she and her son were planning to leave. Day after day she told the aide that Louis was too ill to travel. They were still there on May 5 when, from his hotel window, Louis Napoleon saw demonstrators lay wreaths at the foot of the column on which his uncle's statue had once stood, and heard their cries of "Vive l'Empereur!" It was vivid reminder of the emotions his family name still evoked and one he would not forget.

The next day they left for England via Calais.

Hortense had influential friends in England, as she had on the Continent, among them the Whig leader, Lord Holland, whose wife kept one of the grandest salons in London, and the Duke and Duchess of Bedford, with their palatial mansion and vast estate at Woburn.

The end of the Napoleonic Wars was now sixteen years in the past, and Holland and Bedford, like many in their party, believed the British had treated the late emperor harshly. There was even a Bonaparte at the very heart of British society— Louis's cousin, Lady Dudley Stuart, the daughter of his uncle Lucien. Hortense and her son were accordingly given a warm welcome. At receptions and dinners given for them at Holland House they met such notables as Lord Grey, the newly re-elected Whig prime minister, and other members of his government.

Altogether, their three months' stay in London was a glittering success and during it Louis was to acquire a lifelong regard for the British. He was particularly struck by their inability to bear old grudges and was warmed when quite ordinary people, discovering who he was, shook his hand and assured him the old enmity was forgotten.

He would also gather fond memories of the many Englishwomen who fell under the spell of his romantic aura. It was not, of course, suspected that anything as mundane as the measles had taken his brother's life and caused Louis to retire from the battlefield; the soldier-prince fighting for the freedom of a subject people seemed a *beau idéal* even to the more experienced of the Whig society ladies he met in the salons of London. Even when Hortense took him away from London and—as she hoped—temptation, he managed to find all the female companionship he wanted in Tunbridge Wells.

As news of their presence in England spread, reaching across the Channel to France, Bonapartist sympathizers began arriving with all kinds of wild plans for the overthrow of Louis-Philippe and the restoration of the Empire. Hortense, thinking—quite correctly—that Louis was not yet mature enough for such activities, discouraged the emissaries as firmly as she could.

Eventually transit visas which had been promised by Louis-Philippe arrived and they were able to set off for Arenenberg via France, reaching home at the end of August.

Back in Arenenberg, where he rejoined the military academy, Louis seemed a somewhat more serious person than when he had set out so lightly with his brother on their Italian adventure six months before. The ruthless ease with which the Austrians had crushed the popular Italian revolt had taught him the limits of idealism. And he was conscious that the death of his brother meant he was one step nearer to becoming the heir of his imperial uncle. Indeed, his childhood companion Hortense Cornu believed that "from the day of his brother's death he was a different man." Until then, she thought, he was lacking in ambition, but after his older brother's demise he felt confronted by a destiny he could not avoid.

In July 1832, he moved a decisive step closer to the throne with the death of the Duke of Reichstadt from consumption at the age of twenty-one. In Bonapartist theory, his uncle Joseph, the former King of Naples and Spain, was now Emperor of the French, and next in line would be the other surviving Bonaparte brothers, ex-King Jérôme of Westphalia, and Louis's father, the ex-King of Holland.

But in practice none of them was in the least interested in claiming the title, wanting only to live out their lives in comfortable semi-obscurity. This meant that young Louis was now in effect the torchbearer of the Bonaparte dynasty and, as if in confirmation of that, the dying Duke of Reichstadt had bequeathed him the emperor's sword. The path had been providentially cleared for him, and Louis could have no doubt that destiny was beckoning.

This gave him good reason to wish to establish himself as more than just a princely playboy. He began to dabble in authorship, setting down his thoughts on Switzerland's political and strategic situation in a book that was part reasoned analysis of his adopted country's political and strategic problems and part Napoleonic diatribe.

If the Swiss were invaded, he wrote, they could rely on the emperor's old soldiers to help them, for always Napoleonic France had led the fight for national independence. "What part of Europe," he asked, "can we pass through without finding traces of French glory? If you cross a bridge, its names remind you that our battalions once carried it at the point of the bayonet." And so forth.

The Swiss liked this kind of thing well enough to make him an honorary citizen, an honor he accepted while stressing that he was not renouncing his French nationality. Three years later, after graduating from the military academy, he published a 500-page *Manual of Artillery*. More a history of gunnery than a technical guide, the book was considered by military experts to be quite a worthy effort. But its publication did not please his father, the cantankerous ex-King Louis, who sent word from Florence of his disapproval.

Young Louis's response expresses all the bitterness and rejection that haunted their relationship: "I receive hard words from you so often that I ought to be used to them. Yet each reproach you address to me wounds me as keenly as if it were the first. . . . Is it fair that when I am always trying to do good, I should constantly be the subject of your reproaches?"

About this time Louis also began, in a tentative fashion, to start the intriguing that would culminate in the bungled coup attempt at Strasbourg, paying frequent visits to Baden-Baden, where he met discreetly with Bonapartist-inclined officers from the French garrison across the Rhine, and talked about a Napoleonic renaissance.

But Louis did not neglect his other major interest in life. In the countryside around Arenenberg he became a well-known figure in his tight-fitting uniform with its tall shako, notorious or admired—depending on one's point of view, or relationship to the lady in question—for his relentless wenching.

As if to prove his claim to be a democrat he cast his net wide, being equally eager to bed the daughters of his mother's friends as the wives of the burghers of Constance—among them the mayor's wife, Frau von Zeppelin—or the servant girls at the local inns. At home, Louis was as attentive to the chambermaids as he was to his mother's dames d'honneur. One of these, Valérie Masuyer, referred to him always in her diary as "my prince" and leaves little doubt about the nature of their relationship.

"Ah, my dear prince," she wrote in her diary after he treated her coldly on his return from a trip abroad. "What has become of those outpourings of goodwill, of friendship, of intimacy, by which you taught me to love you. . . . Poor women that we are, it counts for nothing if we do not remain chaste and pure. . . ." And in another entry, again referring to the princely deceiver: "Men, what a breed! . . . We must be strong to resist them, poor creatures that we are."

There was also a fascinating young widow named Madame Saunier, the mother of two children, who owned a château in the vicinity of Arenenberg. Hortense became alarmed when she realized that, since he could not obtain her favors in any other way, Louis was contemplating marrying her. Hortense was complaisant enough about her son's indiscriminate fornications, but an unsuitable marriage was not to be thought of, and she broke up the affair by sending Louis off to London, weeping copiously and clutching a miniature of his beloved which he wore on a pendant over his heart.

Hortense wrote to him: "Love is like a sickness . . . it is not quinine that will cure it but absence and good sense." In the event, what cured Louis, and in short order, was the attentions of the ladies of London, who soon took his mind off la Saunier.

Not long after Louis's return, he fell in love with another neighbor, Louise de Crenay, the beautiful adoptive daughter of a marquis who had recently purchased a château close to Arenenberg. But Hortense found her unsuitable, too, for her fortune was modest. As before, she put a stop to the affair.

These interventions show how—despite the fact that Louis was no longer a boy, but a man in his late twenties and a captain, to boot, in the Swiss Army—Hortense had not lost the ability to rule his life. She was indulgent when his weaknesses seemed to pose no threat to her plans, but authoritarian when they did, and Louis's compliance suggests an emotional dependence, well beyond the conventions of the time, that may have been a little more than entirely filial.

Valérie Masuyer noticed, for example, that he and his mother spent an inordinate amount of time together, that he embraced her frequently, and that he seemed to become very resentful if any gentleman of her acquaintance became at all intimate with her.

By now, Hortense was convinced it was time for Louis to find a suitable wife and settle down, before he was trapped by a Saunier or a Crenay. "I have no greater wish than to keep you close to me," she wrote, "to see you married to a nice, well-brought-up young woman whom you can mold to your character and who will care for your children. That is the greatest happiness one can wish for in this world."

But a suitable wife was not easy to find: the Bonapartes were not acceptable to the very best families of Europe and the remainder were likely to be unforthcoming when it came to negotiating terms. Then a death in the family drew Hortense's attention to Louis's young cousin Mathilde, the fifteen-year-old daughter of ex-King Jérôme of Westphalia.

When Jérôme's wife, Catherine of Württemberg, died in November 1835, Hortense sent Louis to Stuttgart to offer condolences to his grieving uncle and cousins. Before he left, she made it clear to him that she thought Mathilde might make a suitable match. At first, it seemed that Louis was unimpressed. "Mathilde is charming, but don't think that I am in love with her," he wrote to his mother from Stuttgart. But Hortense, by now in collusion with Jérôme, was determined to persevere. She invited Mathilde to Arenenberg, and the girl stayed a week before traveling on to Württemberg to visit her mother's relatives.

She was a charming young creature, with hazel eyes, a rose-petal complexion, and a burgeoning bosom that promised a ripeness to come. To her, Louis was a Byronic figure, romantic, worldly, mysterious. To him, she was still a child. But by April of the following year, when she returned for a second visit with her father and brothers in response to fresh invitations from Hortense, she had undergone something of a transformation, as adolescent girls sometimes do in a very short time. Mathilde was now an accomplished coquette.

On her first night at Arenenberg she appeared for dinner in deep décolleté; according to Valérie Masuyer, "the Prince was quite overcome and devoured her with his eyes." She added, no doubt with some bitterness, that "with him, the flesh is weak." As the visit progressed, Louis began spending all his time at home just to be with this delectable teen-aged cousin, instead of tom-catting around the countryside after more mature and less chaperoned prey, holding hands and sighing as though he too were still in his adolescence.

"She and the prince were inseparable," Mlle Masuyer would recall. "He sat at her feet and went through all the antics of a man in love." And Mathilde would remember that they "played charades and innocent little games. We kissed each other as often as we could, sometimes furtively, when we could escape the vigilance of my good Mme de Reding [her chaperone]."

On Mathilde's sixteenth birthday Louis summoned a group of singers to serenade her as she sat with him, gowned in white satin and with diamonds and rubies at her bosom, in a boat on Lake Constance. And when Mathilde and her family left for home two days later, she gave him a walking stick surmounted by a golden dog's head as a symbol of fidelity, while Louis gave her a locket with a curl of his hair in it and a ring set with a turquoise forget-me-not.

By this time they were engaged. It only remained to obtain

the consent of Louis's father and for Hortense and Jérôme to work out the details of the marriage settlement. But those negotiations were protracted; even within the Bonaparte family such things could not be settled quickly. And from his home in Florence the ailing and pusillanimous ex-King Louis was uncommonly slow in giving his approval to the match.

If not for these delays Louis might have married Mathilde by the autumn of 1836, as originally intended by Hortense and Jérôme. But Louis the sighing swain was also Louis the Pretender with an idée fixe. By some totally irrational thought process, he convinced himself—or allowed himself to be convinced—that the time was ripe to make his bid for power in France.

So it was that Louis Napoleon came to have an appointment not with a bride and a priest in the chapel at Arenenberg but with destiny, humiliation, and a prison cell at Strasbourg.

3

SCANDALOUS EXILE

AFTER THE ARREST OF PRINCE LOUIS and his co-conspirators at Strasbourg, there was one more scene of the farce to be
played out, and this time the butt of the joke was the lackluster
citizen-king, Louis-Philippe.

As the electric telegraph had yet to be invented, Paris was
linked to the main provincial cities by a line-of-sight semaphore
system. But a dense fog descended just as General Voirol's
account of his victory over the insurrectionists was being trans-
mitted. Consequently, only part of the message got through—
just enough to throw a thorough scare into Louis-Philippe and
his government: "This morning at about six, Louis Napoleon,
the son of the Duchess of Saint-Leu, aided by the Colonel of
Artillery Vaudrey, appeared in the streets of Strasbourg with a
party of. . . ."

All that day and throughout the next, the fog lay over the
land, keeping Louis-Philippe and his ministers in an agony of
suspense. Was the new Napoleon even now marching on Paris
at the head of an ever-growing army, just as his uncle had done
at the start of the Hundred Days?

It was not until the evening of the day after the abortive uprising that Colonel de Franqueville came galloping into the
courtyard of the Tuileries Palace with the conclusion of Voirol's
message, informing the king that, "thanks to the fidelity and
sincere devotedness of our troops, this imprudent young man

was arrested together with his accomplices." One of the relieved Louis-Phillipe's first actions on receiving this report was
to elevate General Voirol to the peerage.

Meanwhile, what should be done with the "imprudent young
man"? His insurrection had been such a fiasco that it hardly
seemed appropriate to allow him the dignity of a trial. In any
event, it would not be wise to make a martyr of one who bore
the name of Bonaparte. The best thing, the king and his advisers
decided, was to spirit him away from the prison at Strasbourg
and quietly deport him—not to anywhere in Europe where he
might foment further trouble, but much further afield.

Accordingly, on the night of November 9, the Pretender was
taken from his cell, put under close guard onto a post-chaise to
Paris, and taken on to Lorient, protesting that he wished to
share the fate of his fellow conspirators. "All the world will
take me for a fool, a self-seeker and a coward," he wrote to a
friend before he was put aboard the naval frigate *Andromède*,
bound for an undisclosed destination. "I had accustomed myself
to the prospect of the first two accusations, but the third is too
cruel."

As Louis was escorted onto the warship, the local subprefect
handed him a purse containing 15,000 francs, part of the funds
for the insurrection, which police had seized in a search of Eléonore Gordon's house in Strasbourg.

With the evening tide, the captain of the *Andromède* sailed
due west under sealed orders; when he reached mid-Atlantic he
opened them to find that he was required to make for Rio de
Janeiro, wait there a month, and then head north for Norfolk,
Virginia, to disembark his passenger on American soil, a suitable repository for such riffraff. France, it seemed, had seen the
last of Prince Louis Bonaparte.

Certainly, Strasbourg had made him the laughing stock of Europe. From Britain all the way across the Continent to Russia,
newspaper editorialists poured out their scorn. The stately
Times of London found his behavior "contemptible" and "ridic-
ulous." The Frankfurter *Journal* called him "a young fool, without genius, without talent, without fame." But the Pretender
remained unabashed. "What care I," he wrote to his mother,
"for the cries of the mob, who will call me mad because I have

failed and who would have exaggerated my merit had I been successful?"

Even a terse letter from his uncle Jérôme telling him the engagement with Mathilde was canceled on account of his reckless behavior (Jérôme had been hoping to get a pension from the Orléanist regime) cast him down only temporarily. Indeed, despite all the time he had during his lengthy, enforced winter cruise to reflect on the reasons for his failure at Strasbourg, Louis failed to draw the obvious conclusions, preferring to believe that only bad luck had robbed him of success.

While Louis was at sea, his co-conspirators were arraigned on charges of high treason—all except Persigny, who had slipped away and escaped across the Rhine when the others were arrested—and it became apparent that Louis-Philippe had sent him to the United States by such a roundabout route merely to keep him incommunicado until the trial was over.

But French public opinion was affronted that the ringleader should be set free while his followers faced the full wrath of the law. There was a great surge of public sympathy in favor of the defendants. Spectators in the courthouse at Strasbourg infuriated the judge by chanting "Acquit, acquit!" when the jury retired to consider their verdict. The jury came back into court after only twenty-two minutes and, blithely disregarding the damning evidence, returned "not guilty" verdicts for all the accused on all the charges.

Bound to show that they were dedicated to the rule of law, Louis-Philippe and his government accepted the decision with as good a grace as they could. And Louis's co-conspirators, just as he had, took their acquittal as a sign of widespread public sympathy not just for their particular predicament but for the cause they represented.

By the time the trial had ended in the acquittal of his accomplices, Louis Napoleon was thoroughly enjoying himself in the United States. Although the Americans were popularly supposed to have no time for titles and even less for failures, he was taken up by New York society and lionized as an exotic and romantic figure.

Among those who offered him hospitality were Cornelius van Schaack Roosevelt and his wife Margaret, the grandparents-to-be of President Theodore Roosevelt. At their Union Square mansion, he met such luminaries as the authors James Fenimore Cooper and Washington Irving. The latter invited the Pretender to his riverside mansion at Tarrytown.

Hospitality of a different kind was dispensed by women of every class and condition; Louis found himself liking America so much that he temporarily forgot his imperial ambitions, and planned a trip through the Midwest with a friend, taking in parts of Canada, too. But a letter from his mother, arriving in early June 1837, forced him to cancel his tour.

Hortense had to undergo an "absolutely necessary" operation, probably for cancer, from which she feared she might not recover. "In case it should not succeed," she wrote, "I send you my blessing. We shall meet again, shall we not?, in a better world where you will come to join me only as late as possible. And you will remember that in leaving this world I regret only you—only your gentle affection, which has brought some charm to my life."

On the back of the envelope, Hortense's physician, Dr. Louis Conneau, had scribbled the words, "Venez, venez!" Louis did not need telling twice. Securing passage on the packet *George Washington*, he sailed for England on June 12. The voyage took twenty-eight days and Louis was in London by mid-July, trying to get a transit visa to reach Arenenberg via the Low Countries and Prussia.

The French government, learning of his presence in Britain, and claiming that Louis Napoleon had given a solemn undertaking to remain in America, believed that Hortense's illness was a hoax to give him an excuse to return. Urgent instructions were sent to Louis-Philippe's ambassador in London to "neglect no means of obtaining exact information on the doings of this young man and his plans of travel."

Like others of the Bonaparte family, Louis Napoleon's uncle Joseph, living comfortably in London, wanted no part of him and refused to help. Louis responded to the snub with an angry note. "I do not reproach myself in the least for my deed," he wrote, "for I have a religion which guides me. . . . Nonetheless, if you were not the brother of the Emperor and of my father I should have every right to quarrel with you."

To his father, in Florence, he wrote: "How sad I am, alone amidst the turmoil of London, alone amongst relatives who fly from me or enemies who suspect me! . . . What have I done to be the pariah of Europe and my family? I have carried the flag of Austerlitz for a few minutes in a French city and offered myself in holocaust to the memory of the captive of St. Helena. Ah, yes, it may be that you blame my conduct; but never refuse me your affection. That, alas, is all I have left!"

In the midst of this misery and rejection, the ever-faithful, ever-resourceful Persigny arrived in London to help his master obtain a transit visa. With his assistance, Louis was able to acquire travel documents from the Swiss Consulate in the name of an American citizen named Robinson.

But French agents were on his tail, and Louis feared they might even try to abduct him. He gave them the slip by driving ostentatiously to Richmond, a favorite weekend resort on the Thames, south of London, with Persigny and all his baggage. After checking into a hotel there, Louis doubled back alone to the city, where he hopped on a horse-bus going to the London Docks and boarded a steamer bound that night for Rotterdam. Persigny followed on with the baggage a day or so later.

When Louis reached Arenenberg on August 4, he found his mother sinking slowly, the doctors having decided the operation was too risky to be undertaken. He stayed by her bed almost constantly until her painful death two months later, aged fifty-four. The pseudonymous Baron d'Ambès, who was at the deathbed with others of her household, recalled the last embrace of Hortense and Louis: "The Prince kissed her lovingly, vehemently, folding her in his arms like a wife or a mistress. Never before had I so well understood the adoring affection he bore her."

Without question, the bonds between mother and son had been unusually deep and strong. For all his cynicism about women in general, Louis had an idealized vision of his mother and her death was a profoundly wrenching experience.

As for Hortense, to the last she was intensely ambitious for her son. Among her many valuable bequests to him was this shrewd political counsel: "Never tire of claiming that the Emperor was infallible. . . . Assert at all times that he made France powerful and prosperous [and] brought to Europe institutions which will never be regretted. If you repeat a thing often enough," she added, anticipating the great propagandists of a century later, "it will ultimately be believed."

Arenenberg contained too many haunting memories of Hortense for Louis to remain there. With her death he closed up the schloss, paid off the staff, and moved to Gottlieben, five miles away.

But with his old associates and supporters gathering round him, and his personal exchequer replenished by the wealth his mother had left, the Pretender was considered by Louis-Philippe and his advisers to be too dangerous to be allowed to remain at liberty so close to the French frontier. Once the official mourning period was over, they astonished and affronted the Swiss by formally and peremptorily demanding Prince Louis's expulsion from Switzerland.

Initially, the Swiss fudged the issue by setting up a committee of inquiry and passing the matter from one department to another in classic bureaucratic style. The French grew impatient, understanding well these delaying tactics, and repeated their demands for the expulsion. The Swiss responded defiantly, going out of their way to give evidence of their high regard for the person of the Pretender by heaping honors upon him.

The affair rapidly escalated from cause célèbre to casus belli. The French moved 25,000 troops up to the frontier, the commanding general of this force warning that "our turbulent neighbours will see for themselves, perhaps too late, that instead of making speeches and insults it would be better to satisfy the just demands of France." French and Swiss newspapers exchanged insults. The Swiss mobilized. Trenches were dug in the streets of border towns. Foreign tourists fled.

It seemed that war was inevitable when, with deft timing, Louis offered as publicly as possible to depart and thus spare Switzerland the horrors of war. "In leaving voluntarily the only country in Europe in which I have found support and protection," he said, "in going far away from those places which for so many reasons have become dear to me, I hope I will prove to the Swiss people that I was worthy of the esteem and affection they have bestowed on me." Across Europe, Louis's nobility was applauded and the bellicose mean-spiritedness of the French government condemned.

When he said farewell to Gottlieben on October 14, 1838, en route for England where he had been promised asylum, it seemed that the entire countryside had turned out to see him off. The road to Constance was lined with well-wishers, while the city itself was packed with people, including no doubt Frau von Zeppelin and other temporary mistresses, waving fervently from curbside and window.

As he traveled through Germany and Holland to Rotterdam, there were similar scenes all along the route. By the time he reached London on October 25, it was evident that the bombastic folly of the French government had elevated him to almost godlike status: the formerly derided Prince Louis Napoleon Bonaparte was the darling of the Continent, and even *The Times* had a good word for him.

Among the entourage he brought with him were, of course, Persigny; the loyal old soldier and Strasbourg conspirator, Parquin; Queen Hortense's physician, Conneau; her secretary, Jean-François Mocquard; Prince Louis's faithful manservant, Thélin; and General Charles de Montholon, who had been the first Napoleon's companion during the years of exile on St. Helena. La Gordon was not among the party; although still a fervent Bonapartist, she had remained in Paris in pursuit of her operatic career and a new lover.

In London society, Louis was again lionized. Not only were his mother's influential Whig friends as hospitable as ever, but now even the Tories were affable, among them no less a Tory than the Duke of Wellington, the victor of Waterloo, whom Louis met at a party given in his honor. As in New York, leading literary figures lined up to meet him, including Edward Bulwer Lytton, Captain Marryat, and the recently elected Tory member of Parliament and fashionable novelist, Benjamin Disraeli.*

---

*In *Endymion,* his last novel, Disraeli characterized Louis as Prince Florestan, who "encouraged conversation though himself inclined to taciturnity. When he did speak his terse remarks and condensed views were striking, and were remembered."

At the Tower of London, the Yeomen of the Guard turned out to present arms for him; at the Bank of England, he was shown around by the Governor; at the Lord Mayor's Show, that worthy pulled down his carriage window to salute him. He joined several select clubs, among them the most exclusive of all, Almack's. He lived in Carlton Gardens, bought his clothes in Savile Row, and hired one of London's leading chefs. He shot pheasant in Scotland, caught salmon in Wales, and hunted foxes in Berkshire. His public appearances were carefully stage-managed by Persigny, who had imperial eagles embossed upon the doors of his carriage. When Louis sat in his box at the theater or the opera, Persigny and Parquin would stand at attention behind him throughout the performance.

Feted and lionized though he was, Louis remained hungry for the approval, if not the affection, of the man he called father. Sending Christmas greetings to the ex-king in 1838, he wrote: "I am always afraid to write to you. For a long time past not all that comes from me has had the good fortune to please you. Suffer me nonetheless at this season to mingle with the good wishes of the polite, the sincere good wishes of a son who only asks his father for leave to express all his love and respect."

In August 1839, Prince Louis was the Visiting Knight at a mock medieval tournament held at the Earl of Eglinton's estate in Ayrshire. Chivalry and the Middle Ages were much in vogue at the time, largely thanks to the popularity of Sir Walter Scott's Waverley novels, and Eglinton had invited leading members of the aristocracy, dressed as knights in armor and attended by squires and pages, to joust with lances and perform other feats of arms in competition for a crown to be awarded by a Queen of Beauty.

Prince Louis—with Persigny, of course, as his squire—cut a fine figure on horseback, wearing a polished steel cuirass trimmed with crimson satin, a visored helmet, and a tall feathered plume. At the grand banquet that night, seated at a table 175 feet long and 45 feet wide, he was placed in a position of honor close to Eglinton, Lord and Lady Londonderry, the Duke and Duchess of Montrose, and Lady Seymour, the Queen of Beauty.

It was, perhaps, the pinnacle of his career in English society, for gradually suspicions about him began to surface. Sought after though he continued to be in certain circles, the highest society increasingly viewed him askance, thanks to the aura of faintly disreputable adventurism that clung to his person, accentuated for many by his tendency to dress rather too lavishly and to pursue the opposite sex rather too avidly. As one debutante of the day recorded: "Society did not view this prince with any too favourable an eye, nor consider him an ideal companion for young ladies."

But while the "best" hostesses struck his name from their invitation lists, Louis remained welcome at the salons of the more raffish, such as Marguerite Lady Blessington and her paramour comte Alfred d'Orsay, the latter an old acquaintance and a Bonapartist whose father had received his title from the first Napoleon.

Like Louis himself, d'Orsay and his mistress were considered more than a little scandalous, as indeed they were. Lady Blessington, a widowed Irish beauty now past her prime, was the author of several somewhat trashy novels, which fact—together with the fortune inherited from her husband and the lavishness of her table—had helped establish her as the center of a notorious literary and artistic circle.

D'Orsay, sometimes called "the last of the dandies," was twelve years her junior and a man of considerable sexual versatility, having been simultaneously her lover and that of her late husband. He also happened to be his mistress's stepson-in-law, Lord Blessington having forced his innocent daughter into marriage with d'Orsay to provide a cover for his own relationship with the Frenchman. This complicated arrangement had Lady Blessington's thorough approval, since it not only gave her a cover too, but also ensured that on Blessington's death—which was not long delayed—she and d'Orsay between them would control all his fortune.

Lady Blessington, her stepdaughter, and her stepson-in-law now lived together in Gore House, her sumptuous mansion in Kensington, though "the virgin bride," as the lovers contemptuously called d'Orsay's unfortunate young wife, was not much in evidence at the glittering dinner parties for which the house had become noted.

The diarist Charles Greville tells us that Gore House was "furnished with a luxury and splendour not to be surpassed; her dinners are frequent and good; and d'Orsay does the honours with a frankness and cordiality which are very successful." He adds the withering put-down: "But all this does not make society in the real meaning of the term." Greville was even more brutal in his comments on Prince Louis, whom he met at Gore House in 1839, describing him as "a short, thickish, vulgar-looking man without the slightest resemblance to his imperial uncle, or any intelligence in his countenance."

But there was more to Louis than that and more to his life in London than wining, dining, and womanizing. He never lost sight of his objective, the throne of France; and while he lived riotously by night, he spent at least some of his days preparing himself for the serious business of power—how to achieve it and what to do with it. Some of this preparation was conspiratorial, some literary.

It was during this period, for instance, that Louis published *Napoleonic Ideas*, a book in which he urged that France should return to the principles of his uncle, which would "ensure equality, reward merit and guarantee order." It was a strange mixture of democratic and authoritarian notions in which Louis asserted the supremacy of the popular will but argued that this would be best fulfilled by a chosen leader answerable, by plebiscite, directly to the people with no intervening machinery of parliament.

The book reviewed the careers of the great leaders of history who had pushed mankind forward, culminating in "The Other," as he dubbed the first Napoleon, a Moses, Mahomet, Caesar, and Charlemagne rolled into one, whose Empire had achieved the highest expression of the French Revolution in mystic union with the people. Though Louis modestly refrained from saying it in quite so many words, the message clearly was that such a union would be recreated when he returned to France to complete his uncle's life's work.

Bulwer Lytton, to whom Louis sent a signed copy, called it "the book of a very able mind; with few ideas, but those ideas bold, large and reducible to vigorous action."

Meanwhile, under the watchful eye of French government agents, Bonapartist conspirators came and went from Louis's house in Carlton Gardens. This traffic, and the attention attracted in France by Louis's book, caused such nervousness in

Paris that the British government was requested to banish him. Louis-Philippe, having driven him from the Continent, now apparently hoped to drive him back across the Atlantic where he could do no harm.

But the British declined to expel him, pointing out that he was staying within the law and that Britain was a traditional haven for political refugees. Thus frustrated, Louis-Philippe's security police hatched a plot to discredit the Pretender.

One day in March 1840, comte Léon Bonaparte, an illegitimate and dissolute son of the late emperor, was released unexpectedly from a debtors' prison in France, given a sum of money, and sent to London with secret instructions. On arrival he wrote to Prince Louis—whom he insolently addressed as "my dearest cousin"—and demanded an interview. When Louis, as expected, refused to see him, Léon challenged him to a duel.

Although dueling was to remain fashionable and acceptable in Europe for some decades yet, the British were determined to stamp it out. For Louis to be caught indulging in this forbidden practice could well lead to his expulsion. When, with Parquin and d'Orsay as his seconds, he met Léon on Wimbledon Common to fight it out, his adversary delayed the proceedings by bickering over whether they should duel with pistols or sabers. While they were arguing, the police arrived, apparently alerted in advance by Léon. The entire dueling party were taken into custody and charged with unlawful assembly. But the plot misfired when Louis was let off with a caution, and Léon returned to France and obscurity, his mission unfulfilled.

It was a cumbersome little conspiracy and the French authorities might well have saved themselves the effort. For it was not long before Prince Louis would deliver himself into their hands anyway, lured by a bait the Orléanist regime had not even intended as such—the mortal remains of his illustrious uncle.

Hoping to recruit the ghost of Napoleon to bolster his own colorless regime, the citizen-king decided in the summer of 1840 to bring Bonaparte's body back from St. Helena and inter it with all due pomp at Les Invalides. With the consent of the British he sent his son, the prince de Joinville, to collect the prize in a frigate named, for some inexplicable reason, *La Belle Poule*.

Hearing of this, Prince Louis and Persigny thought first of hijacking the coffin in the South Atlantic. Then they had what seemed at the time a better idea. They had, after all, long since convinced themselves that the Strasbourg insurrection had been a near miss. So why not try again—and this time schedule the uprising so that Prince Louis would be in power and in Paris in time to welcome the illustrious remains in person?

4

FIASCO
AT
BOLOGNE

IT WAS A BLISTERING DAY IN HIGH SUMMER when Captain Thomas Crowe, master of the paddle steamer *Edinburgh Castle*, tied up at the wharf by London Bridge to board a party of foreign gentlemen whom he was to take across the Channel on a "pleasure cruise." They were evidently doing things in style, for with them they brought eight horses and two carriages, plus several crates and boxes which, Crowe was told, contained liquor and comestibles.

It seemed an excessive amount of sustenance, but the swell calling himself Mr. Rapallo who had arranged the hire of the ship from the Commercial Steam Navigation Company, and who now supervised the loading, told Captain Crowe that there would be about sixty persons in the party and that they were planning to have—how do you call it?—a big blowout on their way to the French coast.

Only a few of the passengers came aboard with "Mr. Rapallo." The rest were to be picked up at various points downstream, first Greenwich, then Blackwall, and finally Gravesend.

It was at Gravesend that the bulk of the party boarded, and Captain Crowe could not help feeling that they were an ill-assorted lot. Some were obviously gentlemen and attended by personal servants, but the rest looked like the sweepings of Soho, jabbering away in Italian and French—languages which Captain Crowe recognized—and Polish, which he did not.

The captain also noted with mild surprise that there were no ladies among them. In his experience a pleasure cruise generally meant just that; but you never could tell with foreigners, and perhaps they were going to pick up their frippet at Ramsgate.

It was now late afternoon and the skipper was anxious to head downstream for the Thames Estuary to catch the evening tide, but one gentleman had not arrived and the others insisted on waiting for him. The latecomer, though at this point Captain Crowe did not know it, was Prince Louis Napoleon, without whom there would have been no point in going at all.

He was delayed because, observing that his house in Carlton Gardens was under surveillance by agents of the French government, he had been dodging around London, hoping to throw them off the scent. Louis-Philippe's security police had got wind that the Pretender was planning something, but they did not know what, where, or when.

Most of Louis's old entourage—Persigny, Parquin, Montholon, Vaudrey, Quèrelles, and Conneau—were there, plus some newer members, such as the marquis Bouffet de Montauban, Count Orsi, and Colonel Etienne Laborde. Then there were what might be termed the foot soldiers who, as Captain Crowe had correctly surmised, were denizens of London's sleazy Latin Quarter, recruited at 40 francs a head. Making a head count, the skipper calculated that he had a total of fifty-six passengers boarded. And still they waited for the fifty-seventh.

While they did so, young Quèrelles dashed off a note to his wife in Paris—"After tomorrow our eagles will have triumphed or I shall have died the death of the brave!"

Up to that moment the eagles had been figurative, but Persigny was in the process of recruiting a specimen of the real thing, more or less. Going ashore to buy some cigars, he had seen an urchin feeding a tame vulture and had purchased it for a guinea, tethering it by one leg to the cross-tree of the mainmast where, looking something like an eagle, it would serve as an appropriate mascot for the expedition.

Finally, at about eight that evening, Prince Louis arrived, satisfied that he had shaken off Louis-Philippe's men. The *Edinburgh Castle* got up steam and, chuffing and clattering, made its way to Ramsgate where, having missed the tide, it moored overnight.

Since they did not want to arrive off the French coast until the small hours of the morning, Prince Louis and his party spent all next day ambling up and down the south coast of England until, after an eve-of-battle feast on the food and drink which "Mr. Rapallo" had brought aboard, they instructed the skipper to head for Boulogne.

Captain Crowe still did not realize his passengers' real purpose. It was not until they were approaching the French coast at about 2:00 A.M. on August 6 that he understood things were not at all what they seemed to be. At this hour his passengers, whom he had thought to be sleeping below, emerged on deck in military uniform and carrying weapons.

The skipper listened in astonishment as Prince Louis identified himself, explained the purpose of the expedition, and gave Captain Crowe his orders. The *Edinburgh Castle* was to drop anchor just off the fishing hamlet of Wimereux, about three miles east of Boulogne, and Louis and his men were to be taken ashore by ship's boat. Then Captain Crowe was to wait until he saw a white flag hoisted at the pierhead at Boulogne before steaming into harbor to unload the horses and carriages.

Three times the ship's boat came and went before all Prince Louis's party were ashore. Two patrolling members of the National Guard challenged them as the last boatload came in, but seemed satisfied with the explanation that they were members of the 40th Regiment of the Line, en route from Dunkerque to Cherbourg, whose vessel had developed engine trouble. Then, about an hour before dawn, Prince Louis and his tiny ragtag army set off across the fields toward Boulogne.

As they entered the city, Louis marched his men up to a guardhouse manned by a sergeant and three sleepy privates of the 42nd Regiment. As the sergeant would describe it later, the Pretender introduced himself, saying: "Good morning, my brave fellow. I hereby make you an officer—march with us to Paris." The sergeant declined the invitation, but Louis and his men marched on undismayed, he twirling his hat on the point of his sword as they headed for the infantry barracks where a company of the 42nd—the entire garrison of the town—were quartered.

At the barracks a lieutenant named Aladenize, who had been subverted by Louis's agents, had taken advantage of the absence of his staunchly Orléanist company commander to assemble the men. Revolution had broken out, he told them, all France was up in arms, and here was he to whom the torch of the great Napoleon had been passed.

The proclamation which Louis began reading to the bewildered troops seems a masterpiece of self-delusion: "Soldiers! Your acclamations when I presented myself to you at Strasbourg are still present in my memory. Nor have I forgotten the regrets you manifested at my defeat. Today, the great shade of Napoleon addresses you by my voice . . ." He got no further. At that point the supposedly absent Captain Col-Puygellier, having returned overnight from leave, appeared on the parade ground buckling on his sword belt and shouting, "Long live the King!"

Col-Puygellier related later that "I drew my saber and advanced among them, but was immediately seized, and particularly my sword arm." Louis Napoleon appealed to him to "be one of us and you shall have whatever you desire." But, the infantry captain said, he replied: "You may kill me if you please, but I will do my duty."

At this point, by general consent, a scuffle erupted between the captain and Prince Louis, who drew a pistol. A soldier darted forward to separate them and the pistol went off, shattering his jaw. Later, Louis would say that the pistol had discharged accidentally. However that may be, the bloodletting signaled the end of his attempt to subvert the men of the 42nd.

Ordering his men to withdraw from the barracks, Louis headed for the Column of the Grande Armée, through streets already plastered with his proclamations—"The ashes of the Emperor shall return only to a regenerated France. . . . The glory and honor of the country were exiled with me; but, Frenchmen, we return together. . . . The dynasty of the Bourbons of Orléans has ceased to reign." And so forth.

On the way to the column they ran into the subprefect, who was hastening to an emergency meeting with the mayor. According to an account in the Boulogne *Gazette*, the subprefect "addressed them most energetically on the crime they were committing and the folly of their conduct. But alas his remonstrances were drowned by their rebellious cries and the standard-bearer struck him in the breast with the end of his staff." It was with wounded dignity, but no more serious hurt, that the loyal subprefect pushed by to continue on his way to the Mairie.

By this time the whole town had been aroused, drums were beating the call to arms, and National Guardsmen were pouring out into the streets to repel what at first was thought to be a British invasion, relations between the two countries being rather tense at that time over the "Eastern Question."

It soon began to dawn even on the self-deluded Louis, that the troops, the Garde Nationals, and the populace as a whole were not on his side. Boulogne had prospered under the Or-léanist regime and was doing particularly well out of the English tourist trade. The good burghers of the town did not want any revolutionary nonsense spoiling their fat years. So it was amid a swelling hubbub of hostility that Louis prepared to stage a heroic last stand at the foot of the column.

It was here that he had intended to present a stunning coup de théâtre, devised by Persigny: the vulture which the latter had purchased at Gravesend had been trained during the voyage to take his food from the brim of Prince Louis's hat. At a given signal, while the Pretender was haranguing the population around the column, the bird was to have been released so that it would alight on his head—an augury the people were sure to accept with superstitious awe.

But there was no opportunity now for such flummery and when one of Louis's young officers, Jules Lombard, tried to hoist a flag on the column, it was snatched from his hands by two angry civilians. At this point General Montholon was seen to bury his face in his hands and exclaim: "My God, how mistaken and betrayed we have been!"

Seeing that all was lost, Louis let himself be persuaded to order a withdrawal to the harbor. This turned to full flight as his enlisted men from Soho took to their heels, starting a general panic. Soon the entire company was fleeing downhill with the National Guardsmen in hot pursuit.

Up to this point only the one shot had been fired, but as Louis and his men, seizing boats in the harbor, began rowing out to sea, the guardsmen opened fire. One of the men in Louis's boat, a Pole, was shot dead. Another was drowned when the boat overturned, tipping them all into the water.

Louis and Colonel Vaudrey swam to a buoy at the harbor

mouth and clung to it. Attempting to board another boat in the harbor, eleven fully armed men of Louis's little army allowed themselves to be taken prisoner by a solitary bather named Guillaume Tutelet. Others had been caught and captured by the National Guard in their downhill flight.

Meanwhile, the *Edinburgh Castle* had been boarded and seized by the harbormaster, Pollet, and twelve customs officers whom he had called out in such a rush that they had no time to put flints into their muskets. Pollet ordered Captain Crowe to make for the harbor and he obeyed. The tethered vulture still sat on the cross-tree.

At the harbor entrance the *Edinburgh Castle* hove to in order to pick up the exhausted Louis and Vaudrey, still clinging to their buoy. A correspondent for *The Times* who saw the bedraggled Pretender being taken ashore in custody reported: "I had a peep at Louis Napoleon. Poor devil! He looked awfully excited. A friend of mine saw a musketball fall close beside him [in the sea]. Had Bonaparte been so shot it would have been the proper end of so mischievous a blockhead." Added the *Times* correspondent: "How a man with 50 men could think of raising an army in this peaceably disposed province I cannot understand. He must have been misled as to the disposition of the people."

Louis Napoleon was permitted to change into dry clothes at the Custom House before being taken with other insurrectionary officers to the Vieux Château, where they were placed under heavy guard. Their incarceration there seems to have been comfortable enough, thanks to the intense sympathy of the local female population for the person, if not the cause, of Prince Louis.

"Women, always tender and generous and sympathising in moments of misfortune," gushed the *Times* correspondent, "have sent to the Prince and his companions all the comforts and luxuries of which they stand in need. Baskets of champagne, burgundy, hermitage, etcetera, have poured in in profusion, nor has there been any lack of fowls, pâtés and fruits of all descriptions."

So ended Prince Louis's second attempt at the overthrow of the monarchy. One is tempted to adapt Karl Marx's famous dictum (composed in celebration of a later and more successful Bonapartist coup) and say that history repeats itself, *both* times as farce.

"This outdoes comedy," commented the *Journal des Débats.* Said *Le Constitutionnel:* "In this miserable affair, the grotesquerie vies with the absurd." Observed *La Presse:* "The son of the ex-King of Holland has no more mind than heart."

But Louis-Philippe decided the joke had to end. After their failure to secure convictions at Strasbourg, the Orléanist regime were determined not to risk another jury trial, so at the end of September Louis and his principal lieutenants were taken to Paris, where they were housed in the Conciergerie and charged before the Chamber of Peers.

Outlining the case against them, Attorney-General Franck-Carré observed that "never did a more foolish ambition meet with a more shameful denouement." Louis, subdued and dressed in black, attempted a dignified response. "I represent a principle, a cause, a defeat," he said. "The principle, the sovereignty of the people; the cause, that of the Empire; the defeat, Waterloo. . . . In the struggle that is beginning, there is but one victor and one vanquished. If you are the victors' men, I cannot expect justice from you, and I will not have your generosity."

Retorted Franck-Carré: "The sword of Austerlitz is too heavy for your feeble hands. The name of the Emperor, understand it well, belongs more to France than it belongs to you." The peers seemed baffled by the bearing of the principal accused. "His countenance seemed to us without expression," wrote General de Ségur, "his glance without fire, his attitude simple, unembarrassed, and even of a dignified firmness, but calm even to impassivity—another singular anomaly, another unexpected contrast with the impatient temerity of his rash actions."

After six days of evidence the peers retired to consider their verdict. Louis-Philippe had wanted a death sentence, hoping to win widespread credit by commuting it, but the peers failed to oblige. Instead, Louis was sentenced to "perpetual imprisonment" in the fortress of Ham, a medieval castle near Saint-Quentin. Hearing the sentence, Louis remarked perceptively enough: "Is anything in France perpetual?"

Persigny, Parquin, Montholon, and Vaudrey were given

twenty-year terms, Orsi and Conneau got five years each, and the rest received lesser sentences. Aladenize, as a serving officer, was sent to a penal colony.

During his trial Louis had received a letter from his father which, while taking him to task for his folly, was not entirely unsympathetic. Louis hastened to reply—another of those letters in which he seems positively to beg for his father's affection: "I have not yet written to you because I was afraid of causing you distress. But today, when I learn what interest you have manifested in me, I come to thank you and to ask your blessing as the only thing which now has any value for me. My sweetest consolation in misfortune is to hope that your thoughts sometimes incline toward me."

Six weeks after the gates of Ham closed behind Louis, the remains of the great Napoleon returned to France. A fortnight after that, amid tremendous pomp and before a vast crowd, the Orléans king presided over the ceremony at which Napoleon's remains were consigned to their monumental tomb at Les Invalides.

And in prison, Prince Louis communed with the ghost of his uncle: "From your sumptuous cortege, despising the homage of some people, you have cast a momentary glance at my dark dwelling and, remembering the caresses which you lavished on me as a child, you have said to me: 'You are suffering for me, friend; I am pleased with you.'"

Existence as a prisoner at the gloomy fortress of Ham, though far removed from Louis Napoleon's lavish customary lifestyle, was not entirely durance vile.

He had three rooms to himself, plus the services of the loyal Thélin who, although acquitted of treason, elected to remain with his master. He had the company of Montholon and Conneau, who were serving their lesser sentences at Ham. And in the evenings the commander of the fortress would join them to make a fourth at whist.

One of Louis's three rooms was a bedchamber, the second he used as a study, and the third he was allowed to fit out as a laboratory. There was another room which he, Montholon, and Conneau used as a communal dining room and where they had their evening card games. There was a government allowance of 7 francs a day—about $40 at today's prices—for each prisoner's food and wine.

Louis was allowed to keep a dog, a little black mongrel whom he called Ham and of whom he became very fond. "No one knows better than I how much the loss of a dog one loves can sadden a man," he wrote in commiseration to a friend during this period. He was permitted to send out for books, periodicals, newspapers, and writing materials. Although his mail was censored, he was able to carry on a voluminous correspondence, and he also wrote a number of articles which—even though some of them were distinctly anti-government in tone—were allowed out for publication.

Equally important for one of his temperament, he was permitted to enjoy the embraces of a local beauty, one Alexandrine Eléonora Vergeot, who lived in a castle gatehouse with her father and was known to the garrison as "la Belle Sabotière" on account of her talent as a clog dancer. She worked in the fortress as a laundress and Louis first noticed her when she came to his room to collect a suit for pressing. During his imprisonment she bore him two sons, whom many years later he would create counts of the Second Empire.

Louis would come to call his fortress prison "the University of Ham," for it was there that he completed his education, having none of the usual diversions to distract him.

He dabbled in chemistry and physics and wrote a treatise on electromagnetism; he researched the pros and cons of beet versus cane sugar, a subject of considerable controversy at the time, and wrote a pamphlet in favor of the former; he studied the feasability of digging a canal across Nicaragua to link the Atlantic and the Pacific and wrote a pamphlet in favor of such a project; he wrote a work of history which compared the policies of England's Stuart kings with those of William III who followed them; he wrote another massive technical tome on artillery; and he studied economics, publishing articles and a pamphlet, On the Extinction of Pauperism.

In all this activity he was unstintingly helped by Hortense Cornu, who acted as his research assistant, looking up sources and authorities for his articles, helping to get them published, and even providing him with the chemicals for his experiments.

"A little copper, zinc and acid, and for several hours I forget my troubles and am the happiest of mortals," he wrote to her on a chilly March day in 1843.

But such moments of content were rare. To another friend in January 1845, he wrote: "The years roll on with a depressing monotony. It is only in the prompting of my heart and conscience that I find the strength to stand up against this leaden atmosphere which surrounds and suffocates me."

In September of that year he received a letter from his father and responded with his customary eagerness. "Yesterday I had the first real joy I have experienced in five years when I received the kind letter you were so good to write. . . . Till then, I was resolved to do nothing at all to leave my prison, for I had nowhere to go, nothing to do. . . . Now a new hope dawns on my horizon, a new object presents itself for my efforts."

It would be naive to suppose that Louis Napoleon's years of study and reflection while in prison turned him into a deep political, economic, and social thinker. "The Napoleonic cause goes to the soul," he wrote to a friend in the summer of 1842. "It stirs vibrant memories. And it is always by the heart, never by cold reason, that one moves the masses." Nevertheless, his pamphlet on the extinction of pauperism attracted a degree of respectful attention.

This pamphlet reflected the ideas Louis had derived from his reading of French socialists such as Louis Blanc and Claude Saint-Simon. It focused on the problem of unemployment, advocating the establishment of agricultural colonies on wasteland to absorb the out-of-work. In theory, these colonies, financed by the state, would not only reduce unemployment but would also provide cheap food for the urban workers and their families. The strong likelihood that wasteland was not likely to be productive seems not to have occurred to Prince Louis.

The pamphlet contained other fanciful utopian notions, such as the creation of an intermediary industrial class of "experts" to be elected by the workers as a buffer between them and the employers. It was dismissed by orthodox economists as nonsense, but naturally impressed the followers of Saint-Simon, while Blanc wrote enthusiastically to the imprisoned prince and eventually received permission to visit him at Ham.

✳   ✳   ✳

Despite all the privileges and comforts he was allowed, Louis complained that he was not being treated as his status dictated. "The government which has recognized the legitimacy of the head of my family is bound to recognize me as prince and to treat me as such," he said in a written protest. And although the governor was amiable and the soldiers who guarded the fortress respectful, security was thorough. To escape—as Louis decided he must do after five years' incarceration had brought no hint of amnesty—would require careful planning.

Another incentive to escape was the news that the ex-King of Holland was very ill and not expected to live much longer. Driven, more than ever now, by the yearning for a sign of his purported father's love and approval, Louis felt an urgent need to visit his sickbed and receive his blessing.

In the spring of 1846, he saw the glimmer of an opportunity. Long-overdue repairs were commenced and building workers were coming into the castle daily; if he could disguise himself as one of them, he might be able to walk out past his guards. Dr. Conneau had remained at Ham to keep Louis company on the expiry of his five-year sentence and was allowed to enter and leave at will. So was Thélin who, not being a prisoner, had lodgings in the village. Both were in on the escape plot.

By careful observation they noted that although the workers' passes were scrutinized when they arrived each morning and went each evening, they often left the castle unchecked during the day to collect materials or tools from a dump that had been established outside. Louis figured that if he could get out disguised as a workman and make his way by coach to Valenciennes, near the Belgian border, he could catch a train there and be across the frontier before his absence was noticed.

First Thélin obtained a passport for Louis, through sympathizers in Paris. Then he got him a set of workingman's clothes. On the morning of May 25, he went to Louis's bedroom and shaved off his master's mustache and whiskers. Then he helped him to disguise himself further by rouging his cheeks to cover the prison pallor and blackening his eyebrows. Next a wig and the plebeian clothing—blue blouse, blue pants, white apron, sabots. To complete the effect, Louis shoved a clay pipe in his mouth and, taking apart a makeshift bookshelf, slung a plank over his shoulder and clattered down the stairs in his clogs.

The plank obscured his face as he passed two guards at the foot of the stairs; other soldiers in the courtyard paid him no attention as he headed for the gate and the drawbridge beyond. The sentry by the gate did not bother to look his way as he walked across the bridge to freedom, and two workmen whom he passed coming the other way took him for one of them. "Ah, there's Badinguet," one supposedly said to the other—providing future critics of the emperor Napoleon III with a satirical nickname.

Thélin had gone on ahead with the dog Ham and, getting rid of the plank, Louis headed for a cemetery two miles down the road where Thélin had arranged to meet him in a cab. From there they rode the 15 miles to Saint-Quentin, where they changed cabs and headed on to Valenciennes.

Meanwhile, Conneau had put a dummy into Louis's bed and told the prison governor that he was unwell. It was mid-afternoon by the time Louis and Thélin reached Valenciennes, where they had to wait two hours for a train. Louis paced the platform nervously, afraid his absence might have been noticed and the alarm raised.

He was on tenterhooks to the last, for—as he told a friend once he was out of danger—"I had determined not to endure the ridicule which is the lot of persons arrested under disguise."

But his luck held. By the time the commandant, turning up for his nightly game of whist, realized that the figure in Louis's bed was a dummy, the prince and his valet were enjoying a celebration dinner in Brussels. The following evening they reached London, via Ostend and Dover, and as Louis entered the Brunswick Hotel in Jermyn Street he bumped into an old friend, Lord Malmesbury.

That night Malmesbury was guest at a dinner where he found himself seated opposite a diplomat from the French Embassy. "I suppose you know Louis Napoleon's in town," he remarked slyly. The Frenchman dropped his fork, leaped to his feet, hurriedly excused himself, and left in a panic.

5

ENTER
MISS
HOWARD

AFTER HIS YEARS OF CONFINEMENT AND SECLUSION,
Prince Louis plunged back into the swim of fashionable London
with voracious energy. The serious-minded scholar of "the University of Ham" was once again the roistering dandy, though no
longer the passably good-looking young man he had been.

Whatever benefits prison might have conferred on his mind,
it had done little for his body. Now thirty-eight years old, he
was flabby from lack of exercise; he had a persistent prison pallor; one eyeball was distended due to long hours of studying and
writing in poor light; and he limped slightly as a result of rheumatism, caused by the damp chill of the atmosphere inside the
ancient fortress walls.

But despite his seedy appearance, his daring escape had invested him with garments of glamour. The fiascos at Strasbourg
and Boulogne were largely forgotten and Prince Louis was seen
not as an aging libertine disfigured by past failures, but a dashing cavalier ripe for fresh adventures. Within a few days of his
return, old friends such as Lady Blessington and the comte d'Orsay were giving "welcome back" parties in his honor and fashionable clubs such as the Athenaeum, the Army and Navy, and
the Junior United Services were honored to accept him as a
member.

His Savile Row tailors, Henry Poole and Co., greeted his return with obsequious smiles and extended tape measures: he

was rapidly refitted with all the most fashionable finery, including a double-breasted frock coat with silk linings for 6 guineas, a Venetian cloth overcoat—also silk-lined—for five and a half guineas, a pair of check doeskin trousers for 50 shillings, and a fancy figured cashmere waistcoat for 38 shillings.

He was entertained once again at Bulwer Lytton's riverside cottage on the Thames, where he renewed the acquaintance of the fast-rising Disraeli and met Charles Dickens, whose novels in weekly serialization were the rage of the moment. He went south to fashionable Brighton to bathe in the surf and wager at the racetrack; he went west to equally fashionable Bath where he rented the best suite at the most expensive hotel and met, among other society and literary figures, Walter Savage Landor, who congratulated him on escaping "two great curses—a prison and a throne." Characteristically, Prince Louis "smiled at this, but made no remark."

He was now, for the first time in his life, quite short of money. The fortune left by his mother had all gone to support the high living of his earlier years in London and to pay for the expensively ill-fated Boulogne invasion. But he continued to spend without restraint. Merchants, outfitters, and hoteliers were willing to extend virtually unlimited credit to titled or celebrated customers, considering it their privilege to serve and their obligation to wait, respectfully, to be paid.

In Louis Napoleon's case, they did not have to wait long: his financial problems were solved by his father's death in Italy at the end of July 1846, when he inherited 3 million francs, a castle in Florence, and another property at Civita Nuova.

Whether the former king died believing that the Pretender was not his son is impossible to say. He may have managed to convince himself otherwise, as the affectionate exchange of correspondence between them in the weeks before his death—and the terms of his will—might suggest. But Louis was unable to visit his dying parent, having been refused transit visas by Belgium and Austria and barred entry by Tuscany.

Whether his father's last letters satisfied Louis's craving for acceptance, we cannot tell. And if he mourned the ex-king's passing deeply, he managed to hide his grief—for the summer of 1846 saw him in more or less perpetual motion, dining and gambling at his London clubs, taking tea at Bath, riding on the

Sussex Downs, attending gala nights at the theater or the opera, gracing the salon of Lady Blessington, paying respectful court to respectable women, and leaping enthusiastically into bed with the other sort.

One of the most fascinating of these was the French actress Rachel, then playing a season at the St. James's Theatre. She was a splendidly outrageous creature, the illegitimate daughter of a Jewish peddler, born in poverty and raised through her talent and vivid beauty to the height of international celebrity. Among the many men of fashion whose mistress she had been were Alfred de Musset and Louis's cousin Count Walewski, bastard issue of the great Napoleon's liaison with Marie Walewska.

Rachel did and said whatever she pleased and didn't give a damn for anyone, including those who might sniff at her origins: "Moi toute juive," she would say defiantly. Her temper was notorious and her promiscuity legendary, which gave a special piquancy to her theatrical performances, for she specialized in tragic and virtuous heroines of the kind who prefer death to dishonor. Louis remained enchanted by her until an incident which occurred during a visit to England by his cousin Prince Napoleon, nicknamed Plon-Plon, Mathilde's younger brother.

Rachel was going off on a tour of the provinces and Louis had decided to go with her, taking his cousin along for extra company. Assuming that Plon-Plon would be content to amuse himself with one of the lesser members of the cast, Louis fell asleep on the train to Birmingham, leaving Rachel and Plon-Plon in chaste conversation. When he opened his eyes a while later, he saw them making love on the seat opposite.

Not wishing to cause a scene, he pretended to go on sleeping, keeping his eyes closed until they had completed their exertions. The next day he returned, with equal sang-froid but without explanation, to London, leaving Rachel and Plon-Plon to work out their mutual passion uninhibited by his presence.

His discreet withdrawal illustrates how, in his phlegmatic way, Louis seems to have been immune to the terrible jealousies that often afflict even the most blasé of libertines. It seems that he was unable to become fixated on a woman once he had enjoyed her, that he had the happy knack of being able to separate amour propre and amour impropre. This gave him a kind of alley-cat invulnerability which, perhaps as much as his title, wealth, romantic aura, and laconic charm (and despite his indifferent appearance), made him so attractive to such a wide variety of women.

None was more immediately and violently attracted than the celebrated courtesan Harriet Howard, with whom Louis was to enjoy the most enduring, satisfying, and rewarding—in every sense of the word—sexual relationship of his life.

He met her at Lady Blessington's, where he was the guest of honor, one summer night in 1846. At the time, Harriet was being hotly pursued by any number of rich rakehells who wanted to take the place of the protector from whom she had recently separated. But from the moment she was introduced to Louis by d'Orsay, she had no interest in anyone else.

Miss Howard, as she was always called in the outwardly discreet demi-monde of early Victorian London, was born Elizabeth Ann Haryett at Brighton in 1823, and brought up at Great Yarmouth, in Norfolk. Her father was a respectable maker of boots and shoes for fashionable ladies in that east coast resort, prosperous enough to send his only daughter to a good day school and to pay for her to take dancing and riding lessons.

She grew up to be an accomplished horsewoman, while nourishing a secret desire to become a Shakespearean actress. But when she made that desire known to her father at the age of fifteen, he exploded with Christian wrath and told her he'd see her dead before he'd allow her on the stage.

At about that time she made the acquaintance of a noted jockey named Jem Mason, who would become winner of the first Grand National in 1839 and who is remembered still in racing circles as one of the finest steeplechase riders ever. She told him of her father's objections to her ambition. Mason, with his experienced eye for a promising filly, offered to take her to London and introduce her to friends of his in the theater. She accepted his proposition and, in the best traditions of Victorian melodrama, became a fallen woman.

She and Mason set up house in some luxury at 277 Oxford Street, and true to his promise he introduced her to his theater friends. Through them she obtained her first part under the stage name of Harriet Howard, by which she was afterward always known. It was not the Shakespearean part she had dreamed of, but an ingénue role in a mildly lubricious contemporary comedy, *The Love Chase*, which opened at the Haymarket Theatre in January 1840. And it was her stunning good looks rather than any great dramatic talent that won her the part; after *The Love Chase* had finished its run, she found that her career had peaked early.

No more parts of any consequence came Miss Howard's way. To achieve celebrity, she had to rely on her equestrienne talents, which she displayed daily in Rotten Row to the admiration of the gentlemen who rode there. She was the first of Hyde Park's "pretty horsebreakers" who were to become such a scandalously delightful feature of Victorian London.

Miss Howard's relationship with Mason was far from happy. He was not even nominally a gentleman, he drank and gambled compulsively, and thought nothing of offering her around to men from whom he wanted favors or to whom he owed money. One of these was a fellow member of the racing fraternity, a wealthy gambler named James Young Fitzroy, who enjoyed her so well that he stole her from Mason. She went willingly enough, having become thoroughly disgusted with Mason's loutish behavior.

By now she was eighteen and by general consent a classic beauty—"an exquisite apparition, full of grace and dignity," as one admirer described her. It was not long before she caught the eye of one Francis Mountjoy Martyn, a major in the Household Cavalry who had inherited a huge fortune from his father, a nabob in the East India Company. Martyn was unsatisfactorily married to an ailing and barren wife, whom he kept out of sight in the country, and to win Harriet away from Fitzroy he offered her everything short of marriage—a splendid house, acknowledged status as his "hostess," and a substantial guaranteed income for life from a trust fund.

Given such terms, plus Major Martyn's dashing good looks and impeccable connections, she could hardly refuse. Very soon they were living together and entertaining lavishly at Rockingham House in St. John's Wood, the leafy suburb where London's most successful courtesans were discreetly embowered. In August 1842, she gave birth to a child who was baptized Martin Constantine Haryett, and Major Martyn, denied a legitimate heir, settled a large fortune in real estate on her to ensure his bastard son's future.

After about five years Miss Howard and Major Martyn parted amicably, family pressure—and perhaps waning passion—having driven him back to his wife. As soon as it became known that she was at liberty, a number of titled gentlemen became keen to acquire her for themselves, among them Prince Louis's old friend Malmesbury and his newer acquaintances, the Duke of Beaufort and the Earl of Chesterfield.*

Yet she was no longer a helpless plaything to be passed from hand to hand, but an independent, sophisticated, and self-confident woman of considerable wealth. She could and did add to that wealth by dispensing her favors judiciously and without commitment to any one admirer; and that was her preferred way of life until she met Prince Louis.

Although disdained by "the best" society as little more than an expensive prostitute, Harriet Howard had a good deal more polish than some of the Pretender's previous paramours. During her years as hostess to the wealthy and well-connected Major Martyn, she had acquired a patina which belied her petit bourgeois origins and the picaresque milieu of stables and betting shops in which she had once moved. She now carried herself with an almost patrician air most suitable to the consort of a prince, and for Louis the combination of hauteur and harlotry was irresistible. He was to remain deeply, though not exclusively, involved with her for the next six years.

They were not able to live together quite so openly as she and Major Martyn had done. For discretion's sake, Louis rented a house at 3, King Street, St. James, while she installed herself at 9, Berkeley Street, just a short stroll away.

At that time, Louis wrote to a friend in Paris that he was delighted to have a home once more after seven years. "I am collecting all my books, papers and family portraits, in fact, everything of value which has escaped the shipwreck." He was also delighted with the domesticity he was able to enjoy at the

---

* The author, historian, and politician A. W. Kinglake—not nearly as wealthy as these noblemen but celebrated for his Eastern travel book *Eothen*—was also one of her suitors. When, some years later, he vigorously criticized Louis Napoleon's policies in his history of the Crimean War, it was perhaps unfairly said that he was motivated by jealousy.

house of Miss Howard, who besides being well versed in the arts of love, had a talent for creating a comfortable and charming home atmosphere.

Had Harriet been more sophisticated about politics she might have scoffed at Louis's political ambitions, as his other English acquaintances were inclined to do. ("He has a thousand good and agreeable qualities, my dear fellow," said one Colonel George Damer of Dorchester, "but on the subject of politics he's as mad as a hatter.") But once she fell under the influence of his anomalous charm she became the most fervent of Bonapartists.

"I am convinced," said Louis, "that from time to time men are created, whom I shall call men of destiny, into whose hands the fate of their country is entrusted, and I believe myself to be such a man." Harriet believed it too and she demonstrated that belief in the most convincing way—with her purse.

Why Louis should have run short of money so soon after inheriting a large fortune from his father remains a mystery, although it is likely that he lost heavily at the races and it is known that he was lavishly generous in providing pensions to old comrades who had fallen on hard times. Whatever the reason, the record shows that in 1847 he was so hard pressed that he got involved in a messy court case over a comparatively measly £2,000 loan. Through this period Harriet kept him afloat financially. And when, following the 1848 Revolution which overthrew the Orléans monarchy, Louis got ready to return to France and make his bid for power, she mortgaged properties to raise the 200,000 francs he needed for the venture.

Was she just a shrewd gambler backing a long shot, as her erstwhile lovers Mason and Fitzroy might have done? Going strictly by the form book, it would seem a very poor bet to wager heavily on a horse that had run so badly in two races and whose best years were apparently behind him. But to Miss Howard, however hard-headed her experience of men had made her, it was more than just a matter of calculating odds; her commitment was total and she put everything she had on Louis to win—heart, head, and wallet.

Even Louis's henchman and future aide-de-camp, comte Emile Fleury, who used to refer to her somewhat contemptuously as "the courtesan," had to concede that, "whether from devotion or ambition," Harriet Howard's support of Louis's cause "lacked neither generosity nor disinterestedness." Beyond question he was the one genuine love of her life, and although he was far from faithful to her, she almost certainly remained so to him, even after he threw her over.

6

THE
MIRACLE
OF '48

HOWEVER FERVENTLY HE BELIEVED IN HIS DESTINY, however carefully he plotted his moves, Louis Napoleon could scarcely have imagined at the beginning of 1848 that he would be President of France before the year was out.

The process that brought him to power began with the revolution that erupted spontaneously in February, catching him and everyone else unawares—from the citizen-king, whom it drove into exile, to the republican politicians whom it swept willy-nilly into office. The socialist Louis Blanqui called the revolution "a happy surprise, nothing more," while the bourgeoisie, according to the novelist Gustave Flaubert, were "stupefied" and "astonished to find that they were still alive."

A series of poor harvests, leading to an acute economic crisis, had contributed to mass discontent with the Orléanist regime. Since the rural masses had no money to spend, the demand for industrial products, especially textiles, fell off drastically. The banks and other financial institutions took fright and severely restricted credit, and the economy spiraled ever downward.

Politically, the prestige of the regime had been weakened by a series of financial scandals and a flabby foreign policy, while resistance to suffrage reform had alienated a large, disenfranchised section of the middle class. Even the thin upper layer of society which had the vote and had prospered under Louis-Philippe was beginning to lose confidence in a regime that Alexis de Tocqueville likened to "a joint stock company all of whose operations are designed to benefit the shareholders." The shareholders might not have cared about the regime's other shortcomings, but when profits declined they began to look askance at the chairman of the board.

Just the same, it took a mishap to set off the train of events which brought down the lackluster monarchy. On February 22, 1848, thousands of Parisians took to the streets to demonstrate in favor of suffrage reform. When a crowd gathered outside the home of Louis-Philippe's prime minister, François Guizot, one of the soldiers on guard there, accidentally or otherwise, fired a shot.

The crowd panicked, the soldiers lost their heads, and in the next few minutes thirty people were either shot or trampled to death. Within hours, barricades went up all over Paris. But, shocked by the initial bloodbath, the army and the National Guard—drawn mainly from the discontented and voteless petit bourgeoisie—either stood by or actively sided with the insurrectionists. The day after his troops refused to storm the barricades Louis-Philippe lost his nerve, abdicated, and fled to England on a cross-Channel steamer with his wife, traveling as "Mr. and Mrs. Smith," and leaving the Tuileries Palace to be sacked by the mob.

As Louis-Philippe went one way, Louis Napoleon went the other, also traveling incognito, accompanied by his associate Count Orsi, and his valet Thélin. The barricades were still in place as his cab made its way from the Gare du Nord to the Hôtel des Princes on the rue Richelieu.

An ad hoc coalition of moderate conservative, liberal, and socialist republicans had already formed a provisional government, pledged to the principles of universal male suffrage and to freedom of speech, assembly, religion, and association. From his hotel Louis sent word to them that he had returned "to place myself under the flag of the Republic," and stressed that he had no ambition except to serve his country.

His assurances lacked conviction. Impetuous Bonapartists were already decorating the walls of Paris with posters bearing his picture and carrying the one-word caption: "Lui!" The new government of France hastened to send back a peremptory message to this impertinent and irrelevant intruder: Would Citizen

Bonaparte be good enough to return to England immediately, since his presence might only serve to make a delicate situation dangerous?

Louis decided not to risk another semester at the University of Ham. It was a bitter disappointment, he said, to find that after thirty-three years in exile, he was still barred from his native land. But such was his love for his country that he would rather leave than risk being the cause of further strife.

To many, it seemed like yet another ignominious rebuff for the hero of Strasbourg and Boulogne. *Punch*, for example, carried a cartoon showing him being measured by a tailor for an imperial robe made of moonshine. But though he may not have realized it at the time, Louis's ejection from France at that moment was the best thing that could have happened to him. The disarray of the provisional government and his distance from the scene of their failures would help make him acceptable to the people of France in a way that his presence among them might never have done.

The rulers of the fledgling Second Republic had come to power so suddenly and unexpectedly that few of them had any coherent ideas about their factional policy objectives, let alone about how to reconcile the divergent interests of left, right, and center.

All the three factions had in common was the republican flag. "Everybody paid lip service to the tricolor [wrote Flaubert], each party seeing only one color in the flag—its own—and resolving to remove the other two as soon as it had the upper hand." So while the right and center did their best to make the revolution as unrevolutionary as possible, the left alarmed its uneasy bedfellows by demanding legislation to relieve the burden of unemployment and poverty.

Initially, these demands met with some success and the provisional government set up a number of so-called National Workshops, a forerunner of the public works projects of other countries and later generations.

But the conservatives and centrists were increasingly haunted by fears of a red tide sweeping over the land. These fears became acute when the mob streamed out of the Paris slums on March

17 to demand the resignation of the provisional government and the setting up of a "Democratic and Social Republic." In the general uproar, it passed almost unnoticed that some of the workers marching under the red banner cried, "Vive Napoléon!"—a tribute to Prince Louis's prison pamphlet on the abolition of poverty. It was a harbinger.

The socialist Louis Blanc, a member of the government, persuaded the mob to disperse peacefully—an act of moderation that would earn him an enduring place in Marxist demonology as the classic example of a social democrat who sells out the proletariat. But this was not how Blanc's center and right-wing coalition partners saw it. By now they were becoming obsessed with preserving the sanctity of property and preventing the horror of mob rule, and hysterically afraid of Blanc and his ilk.

As the tumultuous spring of '48 wore on, the National Workshops became the focus for the fears and suspicions of the right and center. In providing scores of thousands of the Paris poor with a bare living wage in return for often pointless work, these ateliers did grave affront to middle-class susceptibilities. Not only did they violate the sacred laws of the marketplace but, frequented as they were by "riffraff too idle to find themselves real work," they were considered to be breeding grounds for Communist agitation.

The conservative press worked itself into a lather of fearful indignation, seeing "on one side order, liberty, civilization, the honest republic, France; on the other convicts emerging from their lairs to massacre and pillage, members of odious sects with savage doctrines in which the family is only a name and property theft." De Tocqueville saw it rather more clearly: "Society was cut in two; those who possessed nothing united in common greed, those who possessed something in common fear."

Meanwhile, across the Channel in England, the whiff of revolution was creating similar spasms of paranoia among the ruling class. When the Chartists announced plans for a gigantic march on Parliament to demand the right to vote and the alleviation of poverty, the victor of Waterloo was called out of retirement by the government and put in command of an army of 10,000 troops and 17,000 special constables to keep the peace.

Among the Duke of Wellington's foot soldiers in the threatened Battle of Westminster was the nephew of his old adversary, Boney—the self-proclaimed socialist Prince Louis Napoleon. Answering the call for able-bodied men of property to defend law and order, and following the example of his fashionable friends, Louis had signed up as a special constable. He spent April 10, the day of the Chartist march, on duty in Trafalgar Square, but fortunately did not have to use his truncheon on the heads of the workers, for at the last moment the Chartists backed down and avoided a confrontation.

In France, it was time for Europe's first election under universal male suffrage. On April 23, 7.5 million Frenchmen went to the polls and, despite the radicalism of the Paris mob, sent an overwhelming center-right majority—moderate republicans and conservative pro-monarchists—to the 880-seat National Assembly. The radicals and socialists between them won fewer than 100 seats.

The Assembly also boasted three Bonapartist deputies, Prince Louis's cousins "Plon-Plon," Pierre Bonaparte, and Lucien Murat. The Pretender himself, although he could have been a candidate in absentia, wisely kept out of it. Another setback at this point could have destroyed his hopes altogether.

Why did the newly enfranchised French masses vote so massively for candidates of the right? The majority of them were peasants and conservative by nature. They were also politically inexperienced, tending to vote for familiar names, which meant the mainly conservative property owners of their own districts.

But, of course, the election of such a huge center-right majority enraged and alarmed the Paris mob. Demonstrations and disturbances continued to disrupt the life of the capital, and on May 15, under the pretext of demanding French intervention to support the oppressed Poles, radical and socialist demonstrators broke into the National Assembly and manhandled deputies.

Once again, cries of "Vive Napoléon!" were to be heard mixed in with the more predictable socialist rallying cries, for had not the emperor taken France to the aid of downtrodden peoples like the Poles and the Italians? Once again the politicians paid little attention to these precursors of the massive chorus to come.

The month of June brought by-elections for another eleven National Assembly seats, and this time Prince Louis allowed himself to be nominated in absentia as a candidate in six electoral districts. His campaign was masterminded by Persigny, aided by a collection of old faithfuls including Eléonore Gordon, Colonel Vaudrey, Lieutenant Aladenize, and Dr. Conneau.

Because their candidate was abroad the Bonapartists held no public meetings, but relied on placards and other propaganda, such as street songs and pamphlets. The appeal was cast right across the political spectrum, from the patriotic old soldier on the right to the socialist workingman on the left. Prince Louis's name alone spoke to the former, while his supposed socialist sympathies commended him to the latter. When the votes were counted, Louis had been elected in four of the six districts.

For the first time, the moderate and conservative politicians showed signs of alarm. The government moved to have Prince Louis's election declared invalid, opposed bitterly by the handful of Bonapartist deputies who insisted that their man was a staunch republican, fairly elected. The socialists sided with them, and for five days the Assembly debated a socialist motion to censure the government.

Outside the Assembly, socialists and Bonapartists staged noisy demonstrations. Throughout Paris and across the land, passions mounted. Everywhere the debate went on. The name of Louis Napoleon seemed to be on everyone's lips. Though still an exile, and through no particular effort of his own, he was becoming the Man of the Hour.

Then, just at the right moment, he broke the tension—much as he had done in Switzerland when the French government was demanding his expulsion—by sending a message from London regretfully resigning his seat in order to prevent further friction among the people of his beloved country. The effect was immediate. Among the mass of the French people his stock rose to new heights. "'Poléon, nous l'aurons," chanted his followers, sure that his triumphant return could now be only a matter of time. On street corners in cities throughout the land the barrel organs churned out the melody of "Napoléon, rentre dans ta patrie."

But soon another crisis erupted that would temporarily drive the name of Louis Napoleon from Frenchmen's minds. On June 21, the government announced the abolition of the National Workshops. All the men employed in them were either to be conscripted into the army or sent to drain marshes. Within twenty-four hours the barricades were going up again in the working-class arrondissements of Paris.

In a panic, the poet-prime minister Alphonse de Lamartine and his executive declared a state of siege and called on the War Minister, General Louis Cavaignac, a harsh but upright republican zealot, to use emergency powers and suppress the revolt.

Cavaignac proceeded to unleash on his own countrymen all the zeal he had lately displayed in action against the rebellious tribesmen of North Africa. Mustering a force of 50,000 regular soldiers, National Guardsmen, and members of the Garde Républicaine, he launched an assault on the barricaded districts in which hundreds were slaughtered. By the time Cavaignac proclaimed on June 26 that "order has triumphed over anarchy," he had earned the grateful admiration of the bourgeoisie and the undying hatred of the proletariat as "the butcher of the barricades."

How to explain such a savage response by an essentially moderate and well-intentioned government to a spontaneous and rather pathetic revolt by a few thousand undernourished, ill-armed, and poorly organized artisans and workers? In a word, fear.

The middle class had fallen victim to its self-induced nightmares, featuring a recurrence of the Jacobin Terror of the first French Revolution. "In spite of the most humanitarian legislation ever passed in France," wrote Flaubert, "the specter of '93 reappeared and the sound of the guillotine made itself heard in every syllable of the word 'Republic' . . . Conscious of no longer having a master, France began to cry out in terror, like a blind man without a stick or a child who has lost its nurse."

To the grateful majority in parliament, the butcher of the barricades was the nurse they had been looking for, and in the aftermath of the Paris insurrection they happily surrendered power to him; the state of siege remained in effect, making Cavaignac for all practical purposes a military dictator.

While such momentous and bloody events were taking place in Paris, Louis Napoleon was gambling at Crockford's, dining tête-à-tête with the divine Miss Howard, and doing the customary social rounds.

At a grand ball given by the Marchioness of Aylesbury, he ran into the Orléanist refugee comte Alexis de Vallon, who wrote to his friend, the author Prosper Mérimée, that "it is enough simply to see this common little gentleman to realize how vain are the hopes that are placed on him."

In a fine burst of invective Vallon described Louis as "ugly and vulgar, with large mustaches and the eyes of a pig!" As for his morals, sniffed Vallon, "he lives openly, to the great scandal of English prudery, with a fifteenth-rate actress, very beautiful admittedly." Vallon concluded his thoughts on the subject of Prince Louis by commenting that "it would only be necessary for this little pretender to run around the boulevards for an hour in his dark suit and white cravat for his prestige to be destroyed for ever."

Allowing for the prejudice of an Orléanist, and disregarding the invective, it must have seemed that Vallon had a point. Even if Louis's unprepossessing appearance should prove irrelevant, even if his playboy behavior at a time of national trauma should be forgiven, how could he hope to avoid the stigma of his supposed socialist sympathies? Some were even saying that the Bonapartists had instigated the uprising which Cavaignac had lately put down. And if Louis hoped to present himself to the French people as the strong "man of horseback" who could stave off anarchy, that role had surely been pre-empted by Cavaignac.

But the Pretender appeared unconcerned. "That man is clearing the way for me," he told his friend, the impresario Benjamin Lumley, at a Gore House dinner party.

This superbly self-confident prediction began to come true in September when Cavaignac allowed the holding of by-elections for eleven vacant Assembly seats and Louis again let his name be put forward. Buoyed by his success in June, and sensing a tide of Bonapartist sentiment as the government stumbled from one crisis to the next and the economy grew progressively weaker, Louis and his advisers felt they could win decisively.

But it was not enough merely to gain a seat in the Assembly; that would be just a step toward the presidency, and to go for that prize, a considerable amount of money would be needed.

By raising loans in London and mortgaging a property left to him by his father in Italy, Louis scraped together half a million francs. While more than enough to finance a by-election campaign, it was not sufficient for Louis's grand strategy, and it was now that Harriet Howard proved her devotion to the Pretender in the most practical way. She signed over to him the deeds of a valuable property at Civitavecchia, near Rome, and with these he was able to borrow another quarter of a million francs.

Fortified by a large infusion of campaign funds, and unperturbed by the absence of their candidate, Persigny and his staff now flooded the nation with brochures, pamphlets, portraits, and medallions. They bribed journalists to insert favorable items into often hostile newspapers, and they paid street singers and music-hall artistes to perform Bonapartist songs.

These efforts contributed to a sensational victory. Prince Louis topped the poll with 110,752 votes, more than four times the number he had received in June, and his supporters rushed out into the streets of Paris shouting, "Vive Napoléon, vive l'Empereur!"

When the news reached London by the new electric telegraph, Louis packed his bags and departed so hurriedly for Paris that he left his bathwater in the tub. Miss Howard followed him a few days later, when she was spotted on the train to Dover with her jewel case in her lap.

But "the courtesan" was too discreet to flaunt the place she had earned, by her cash and her devotion, at the victor's side; on arrival in Paris she demurely checked into the Meurice on the rue de Rivoli, the favorite hotel of the visiting English gentry, while Louis remained at the Hôtel du Rhin on the Place Vendôme. Only a few close confidantes were aware that the beautiful and stately Englishwoman—surely an aristocrat, for did she not bear the name of one of Albion's oldest ducal families?—was the mistress of Prince Louis.

Cavaignac might well have used his near-dictatorial powers to arrest Louis on his arrival, but wisely refrained. The troops and guardsmen who had been willing to help him put down the mob might not have been willing to turn their guns on countrymen protesting against the incarceration of a popular hero, constitutionally elected. So, on September 26, Citizen Bonaparte took his oath of office as a member of the National Assembly and in a brief speech reaffirmed his loyalty to the Republic.

It did not go down well, for he was no hero to the vast majority of his fellow deputies, whatever the general public might think of him. Above all, he was no orator, and in a parliament where oratory was valued over all, that seemed a fatal deficiency. His speech was stilted, halting, at times inaudible, and his colleagues almost unanimously wrote him off as an incompetent whose star would soon fall.

One of the most charitable assessments was that of the socialist leader Pierre-Joseph Proudhon, who noted in his diary after calling on Louis that "the man seems to be well meaning—head and heart chivalrous . . . otherwise, moderate abilities." Proudhon added: "I doubt very much, once he is closely scrutinized and well known, whether he will make much headway."

Just the same, the moderate republicans who held the majority in parliament were worried enough about Louis's popular appeal to fear that he might beat Cavaignac in a one-man-one-vote presidential election. The National Assembly was busy working out the details of a new Constitution and consequently much of the debate centered on how the president was to be elected.

After a good deal of haggling, agreement was reached on a formula designed to keep Louis out: the election would be by popular vote, but unless one candidate received an absolute majority at the polls, and at least 2 million votes, the choice would be turned over to the National Assembly, which would mean the inevitable election of Cavaignac.

During the debate there had been another proposal even more obviously aimed at Louis: a motion by a left-wing radical that no member of a family that had ever reigned could run for president. In the debate on this proposal, Louis made a speech so inept that the wily Adolphe Thiers, leader of the Orléanist faction, remarked to a colleague that Louis was obviously "a cretin." And the sponsor of the motion rose to declare amid gales of mocking laughter that he would withdraw it since it was clear that Louis could never win an election or threaten the Republic.

But not everyone was taken in by Louis's oratorical deficiencies and the disdain of parliament. The correspondent of *The Times* wrote that although he probably would not obtain thirty votes in the Assembly, "in the country he may have millions."

The presidential election was scheduled for December 10. By mid-November, the Constitution having been approved, the various factions were squaring up. The two main candidates were Prince Louis and Cavaignac. The others were the conservative Lamartine, the radical Ledru-Rollin, and the socialist Raspail. One of the most powerful factions, the Orléanist Party of Order under Thiers, did not field a candidate since they were philosophically opposed to the Republic. "If I should succeed," said Thiers, "I should be obliged to marry the Republic, and I am too honest a fellow to marry such a bad girl." Nevertheless, the Orléanists were eventually to play a pivotal role in the election.

Louis's campaign was again masterminded by Persigny, who, well aware of the Pretender's shortcoming as an orator, scheduled no major speaking engagements for him. Instead, he made extensive use of placards, pamphlets, idealized portraits, and catchy songs. Although a good deal of the press was hostile to Louis, there was the countervailing influence of a rash of heavily subsidized Bonapartist newspapers that had surfaced in recent months, each aimed at a different section of the populace, from conservative to socialist. At the height of the campaign it was reckoned that, throughout the country, 190 newspapers were supporting Cavaignac while 103 backed Napoleon.

Persigny's strategy was novel for those days, when democracy was in its infancy: directly or indirectly, he managed to present his candidate as all things to all men—to the masses a reformer with socialist sympathies, to the bourgeoisie a defender of law, order, and property, to the royalists a decidedly lukewarm republican, to the clericalists an upholder of the Church's ancient rights and privileges, and to all the reincarnation of his idealized uncle. His election manifesto managed to cover most of these bases in a sentence, describing a France where "the unfortunate die of hunger; the laborer is without work; the farmer is no longer able to sell his crops; the merchant is unable to sell anything; the proprietor can no longer collect his rents; and the capitalist does not dare to invest." However, "the nephew of the great man, with his magic name, will give us security, save us from misery."

Crude though it was, this strategy went down well with an electorate that was both inexperienced and unsophisticated. And everywhere in France, Louis had his unofficial, unpaid, and unrecognized agents—the old soldiers who spoke nostalgically of the days of Empire when France stood for something in the world and a sou was worth a sou. The magic of a name, the memory of a golden age would be the most potent political weapons of all.

Other factors added impetus to the Napoleonic bandwagon. Louis's principal opponent, the aloof and awkward Cavaignac, might have been the favorite of the Assembly, but he was not loved by the masses. His remoteness and political ineptitude repelled even many of those who had approved of his dispatch in putting down the disturbances of the June Days. And in the country at large, even in Paris itself, enthusiasm for the lackluster and fractious Republic was decidedly on the wane. Cavaignac was the official standard-bearer of this form of government, while Napoleon, for all his lip service to it, was widely seen to embody the possibility, if only implied, of a return to something more glamorous, more in tune with the deeper sentiments of the nation.

Although Napoleon did not speak at any of the mass rallies organized by the Bonapartists in Paris and the other principal cities, he was nevertheless very much in public view. He engaged in a good deal of mass canvassing, riding through the streets of the capital on horseback to greet crowds in the streets and soldiers in the barracks. He conscientiously attended meetings of his supporters and canvassers, encouraging them to greater efforts with smiles, handshakes, and friendly quips. And every day during the campaign crowds would gather outside his hotel in the Place Vendôme to cheer him and chant: " 'Poléon, nous l'aurons," as he left to attend the Assembly, which remained in session throughout.

Louis Napoleon's steady progress toward victory accelerated dramatically a week before polling day when, after weeks of indecision, the Party of Order announced its support—albeit less than wholehearted—for his candidature. Faced with a choice between Cavaignac and Louis, Thiers finally urged his party to throw its weight behind "the cretin" as the lesser of two evils because "he will be our instrument, whereas Cavaignac would be our master." To a colleague who continued to express misgivings, Thiers offered the reassurance that "we will give him [Louis] women and we will use him."

The Party of Order's announcement of support was quickly followed by a similar statement issued by an imposing roster of 150 leading Legitimists. Napoleon was now assured of backing from all points of the political compass.

Nevertheless, Cavaignac's camp continued to believe they could stop the Bonapartist bandwagon, given the requirement for a minimum of 2 million votes and an absolute majority over all the other candidates combined, failing which the choice of president would revert to a National Assembly certain to prefer their man. According to the estimates of the Cavaignac camp, a little over 3.5 million voters were likely to cast their ballots, and Napoleon, they believed, could hardly expect to accrue 2 million votes from a turnout of that size.

But psephology was in its infancy, and the actual results proved to be very different. When the final count came in, after a vote which passed off peacefully throughout the country, it staggered even the optimistic Bonapartist camp: 5.5 million votes for Louis Napoleon, 1.5 million for Cavaignac, and the other candidates nowhere. Louis had scooped up three quarters of all the votes cast, winning an absolute majority in sixty-two of the country's eighty-five departments, including all the Paris arrondissements, and topping the poll in all but four.

No doubt, Louis Napoleon would have won the election without the endorsement of Thiers and the Orléanists. But he might not have won a majority so overwhelming that, even in the moment of victory, he and his inner circle could start looking beyond the mere presidency of a pie-crust republic to a role far grander—to imperial robes and a crown, rather than a frock coat and a silk hat.

The decision to support Louis's candidature was to prove the gravest miscalculation of Thiers's long career in politics. As he would say some years later: "France made two mistakes; the first when she accounted Louis Napoleon a fool, the second when she took him for a genius."

7

THE PRINCE-
PRESIDENT

WHEN CITIZEN BONAPARTE TOOK HIS OATH of office as first President of the Second Republic on December 20, 1848, he added a few words of his own. "I shall regard as enemies of my country," he told the National Assembly, "anyone who shall attempt by illegal means to change what France herself has established."

Less than three years hence, with sudden and brutal efficiency, he himself would be the one to smash with a single blow the governmental structures which France had chosen. But for the time being, the charade of Republic had to be played out. And Louis Napoleon was by no means the only one for whom a charade was all the Second Republic amounted to.

To the dismay of those socialists and radicals who had convinced themselves that his heart was with them, and ignoring the moderate republican majority in the National Assembly, he appointed a cabinet of Orléanist monarchists of the Party of Order and Bourbon monarchists of the Legitimist Party. It was an absurd situation, made possible by an ineptly drafted Constitution: a republican legislature, a royalist executive, and an imperialist president.

However, as an earnest of his honest intentions Louis made his official residence not at the Tuileries—where the Bourbons,

"The Other," and Louis-Philippe had lived and where rumor had said he too would choose to reside—but at the Elysée Palace. Louis's old Bonapartist comrades, such as Persigny, Conneau, Vaudry, Fleury, Laity, Montholon, Mocquard, Thélin, and others, were installed there in official posts analogous to senior appointments in the White House of today.

One notable absentee from this list of beneficiaries was the fading diva, Eléonore Gordon, now in her forties and distinctly overblown. She had been fond of proclaiming, hands clasped over ample bosom, that to her the cause of Louis Napoleon— "my prince," as she called him—was "so noble, great and holy that it is my religion." But in the politics of the day, now that Louis was in power, there was no role a woman could play, even one as forceful and devoted as la Gordon, unless it were the backstage role of mistress.

She had never sought that position, however. At the trial of the Strasbourg conspirators, when asked by the judge if she loved Louis Napoleon, she had replied, "Politically, yes," but that sexually, "he produces on me the effect of a woman." That comment, if reported to Louis, must surely have rankled.

Now la Gordon, demanding her just reward for past services, was a shrill and importunate, if minor, embarrassment to the presidency, and when Louis tried to pay her off with a paltry pension of 4,800 francs she stormed into the Elysée demanding justice. Thélin, who controlled the privy purse, doubled the pension and saw her off the premises. Within weeks she fell ill and died. Her funeral expenses—720 francs—were paid out of the privy purse.

Persigny in office remained a combination of Sancho Panza and eminence grise, controlling access and patronage, rather like a present-day White House chief of staff, and advising the president on political strategies. Fleury's post as master of ceremonies was also influential, if only because ceremonial would be such an important element in Louis's quasi-imperial presidency. And because the playboy side of Louis's character had still to be catered to, the post of social secretary was likewise more influential than it sounded. This went to a distant cousin, comte Félix Bacciochi, with whom Louis had caroused around Rome in his youth. Bacciochi would quickly come to be known as the Palace Procurer.

But the most important member of Louis Napoleon's inner circle, next to Persigny, was a comparatively recent adherent— his illegitimate half brother Charles, comte de Morny. Morny, born secretly to Hortense when Louis Napoleon was three years old, was the issue of her love affair with the dashing and inconstant comte de Flahault, himself the illegitimate son of Talleyrand. Louis Napoleon was not even aware of Morny's existence until after his mother's death and the knowledge came as a considerable shock to him. Nor did the two sons of Hortense ever meet until the presidential election campaign of 1848, when Morny—by now an influential man of affairs—came forward to support his half brother.

Up to that time, Morny had never been a Bonapartist. Indeed, until the 1848 revolution, he had been an enthusiastic Orléanist. Despite this, and the living affront to the idealized memory of his mother which Morny represented, Louis Napoleon was drawn to him and, recognizing his valuable qualities, admitted him to a position of great intimacy and influence from which he was to play a pivotal role in his half brother's presidency and in the affairs of the Second Empire to follow.

In personality they had much in common. Morny had received his title from Louis-Philippe after military service in North Africa, had gone into business and made a fortune speculating on sugar beet, and was currently—and quite openly— the lover of the Belgian Ambassador's independently wealthy wife. He was elegant, clever, stylish, ruthless, and slightly shady, exactly the kind of adventurer who, blood ties or no, would tend to be drawn into Louis's inner circle. Before long, he was a rival to Persigny for the president's ear.

And then there was the Princess Mathilde, Louis's cousin and former fiancée, now an imposingly attractive twenty-nine-year-old, legally separated from the dissolute and sadistic Russian Prince Anatole Demidoff to whom her father had married her in 1840.

Mathilde was the center of a circle of prominent writers and artists and, like her brother Plon-Plon, a standard-bearer of "advanced" liberal ideas. Bearing her no grudge for the dissolution of their engagement after the Strasbourg fiasco, and perhaps seeing her as an aid to the progressive image he wished to maintain, Louis made her his official hostess. And he appointed her father Jérôme, a spiteful dotard, no doubt, but the last living link with the Great Emperor, to be Governor of the Invalides and custodian of his illustrious brother's remains.

Although Mathilde would claim after Louis's death that he asked her again to marry him but that she refused, the truth seems to be that by now and henceforth Louis's attitude toward her was entirely platonic. He remained close, in every sense, to Harriet Howard, whom he had installed in a house located only a stone's throw from the Elysée. Harriet seems to have accepted the fact that she could not expect to be at his side on official state occasions, and if she felt any jealousy at seeing Mathilde in that position, she took care not to show it.

In the way the French have of appearing both discreet and overt at the same time, Louis's relationship with Miss Howard had become widely known, to the detriment of neither. Frenchmen were appreciative of their president's good taste and high style in bringing such a beauty back with him from England. No one with such an eye for woman flesh, they told each other knowingly, could be the cretin certain politicians had made him out to be.

Sharing her new home at 14, rue du Cirque were Harriet's son by Major Martyn and Louis's two sons by "la Belle Sabotière," Alexandrine Vergeot, who had consoled his lonely years in the fortress at Ham. Merely by passing through a door in the wall of the Elysée Palace grounds, Louis could reach this domestic and sensual refuge and, getting away from the cares of office, enjoy the pleasures of family life like any comfortable bourgeois.

Not that he allowed the pressures of the presidency to weigh too heavily on him. According to Victor Lanjuinais, a member of the cabinet at this time, he was lazy and disliked the drudgery of government. On a typical day, Lanjuinais told a British economist, the prince-president would rise at ten, take two hours to dress and breakfast, then spend an hour on state papers. Between one and three in the afternoon he would preside over a cabinet meeting before going to ride in the Bois de Boulogne with Miss Howard. By the time he returned to the Elysée he would have to start dressing for dinner, after which he would either attend or give a reception or spend the evening in the rue du Cirque or with some other woman friend.

The account may contain a degree of bias, for Lanjuinais held his post as Minister of Agriculture for only five months, when Louis sacked the entire cabinet. But numerous other sources agree that throughout his career Louis had little taste for concentrated work. Hortense Cornu described him as "exceedingly indolent and procrastinating . . . everything wearies him. He gets up bored [ennuyé], he passes the day bored, he goes to bed bored." In this frame of mind, he tended to nod off when required to attend to such tedious detail as state papers. He preferred to devote himself to the broad picture, leaving the hard work of government to others. His main function, as he saw it, was to think big, make contacts, and show himself off to the people.

He made sure that the people of the provinces, not just Paris, saw him and that he said the right things in the right places. In staunchly republican areas, he stressed his devotion to the Constitution; to the prosperous bourgeoisie he spoke of order, property, the family; in deeply religious districts the free-thinking Louis stressed the central role of the Church; in working-class areas he spoke of social justice and hinted at his continued attachment to the ideas of Blanc and Saint-Simon. He was prepared to risk being heckled, even jostled, and learned how to neutralize hostility with a well-turned quip or well-rehearsed gesture.

At Saint-Quentin he handed out 20,000 francs to distressed workers and hospital patients. "My sincerest and most devoted friends," he said, "are not to be found in palaces but in cottages, not in rooms with gilded ceilings but in the workshops and fields."

At Rouen, when an old soldier of the Grande Armée tried to kneel before him, Louis lifted him up, saying: "A soldier should kneel only to God or to fire at the enemy." At Lyon, a socialist stronghold, he walked with only a small escort through a working-class district and when accosted by a woman whose husband was serving five years for subversive activities, ordered the man's release.

At a town hall banquet that night Louis recalled an occasion when "The Other" had told the people at Lyon that he loved them. "It would be presumptuous of me to say the same, but I hope you will allow me to say, from the bottom of my heart,

'People of Lyon, I beg you to love me.'" The response was immediate. "Yes, we do love you!" chorused the audience.

Such journeying about the country, made possible by the fast-growing network of railway lines that was spreading out from Paris, was an entirely new phenomenon in European politics. Unveiling a monument here, opening a waterworks there, laying the foundation stone of a town hall somewhere else, Louis enhanced and consolidated by his undoubted personal charm an image of kindly authority, sagacious yet approachable, and with a twinkle in the eye.

The twinkle was personified by Miss Howard, who frequently accompanied him on such trips. She would be chaperoned by Bacciochi or by Mocquard, Louis's *chef de cabinet*, and his wife, but the cognoscenti knew the truth, and with a smile and a wink applauded their president's taste and savoir vivre—except for one individual on one occasion.

This occurred on a visit to Tours, where Louis and his immediate entourage were lodged for the night in the mansion of one Monsieur André, who was both a puritan and a Protestant. André was taking the waters in the Pyrenees at the time, but when he returned to learn that his house had been stained by the sin of presidential concupiscence, he sent an indignant protest letter to Prime Minister Odilon Barrot. "Have we returned to that epoch when the king's mistresses proclaimed the scandal of their lives throughout the cities of France?" he asked.

Barrot, a fellow puritan, passed the letter on to the Elysée Palace, where Louis reacted with uncharacteristic heat. "If M. André really thinks . . . that his house has been soiled by the presence of a woman who is not married," wrote Louis to Barrot, "then I pray you tell him from me that for my part I sincerely regret that a person of such pure devotion and high character should have happened by chance to visit a house where the ostentation of bombastic virtue without any Christian spirit reigns under the mask of religion."

Added Louis: "How many women a hundred times less pure, a hundred times less devoted, a hundred times less forgivable, would have been received with all possible honors by this M. André if they had husbands behind whose names they could have hidden their guilty love affairs?"

Given Louis's normally slow fuse and laconic style, and his

cynicism about women in general, his long and heated riposte to André seems remarkable. A man of his temperament might well have shrugged off the incident as unimportant, taking it as an affront to himself rather than the woman in question. Instead he defended her with, for him, a rare passion, the tone of his letter suggesting an almost chivalric attitude toward his mistress. Perhaps he genuinely loved her.

No such prudery as André's was shown by Lord Normanby, the British Ambassador, who was shrewd enough to invite his countrywoman to embassy receptions. His example was followed by others in the diplomatic corps who wished to be on good terms with the President of the Republic. And although she could not formally accompany him on state occasions, Harriet often managed to be present nonetheless, and to make sure she was noticed. For instance, the maréchal de Castellane noted in his diary on June 21, 1849, that he saw her that day in a box at a spectacular military review and that "her beauty is most remarkable."

But Princess Mathilde would never receive her. It could hardly have been on moral grounds, for Mathilde was openly living in unwed bliss with comte Alfred-Emilien de Nieuwerkerque, who shared her passion for the arts and presided jointly over her salon. Nor could it have been on the grounds of superior lineage, for she was fond of saying that had her uncle, the first Napoleon, not made himself emperor, "I should probably be selling oranges on the quay at Ajaccio." Some complex and unconscious motive of jealousy, a remnant of her long-ago infatuation with her cousin, may be the best explanation for her hostility to Miss Howard.

Because Harriet was frequently seen out with the three little boys who were now part of her household, word soon got about that they were all the children of her liaison with the president. Harriet never contradicted the notion and it was believed all the way up to the level of Odilon Barrot, who would note in his memoirs that she "even had several children by him." She showed equal affection for all three, whom she called "my beloved boys."

Louis's well-known liaison with Miss Howard, his all-round reputation as a bon viveur, and his taste for lavish balls and receptions at the Elysée only enhanced his popularity at all but the highest levels of society, from the historian François Guizot, who noted approvingly that he "loves [Miss Howard] more than many others, though he loves many others too," to the anonymous Paris cabbie who told the correspondent of the London *Times:* "He's a gay dog. I love him, how I love him! What a difference from those little men of the Provisional Government!"

The balls and receptions were a reflection of the imperial style with which Louis was already starting to swathe the austere frame of the Republic. "Fêtes, concerts, banquets, and balls are becoming so numerous, are given on so large a scale and attract such crowds as to almost require the daily labours of a minister for that department alone," reported *The Times.*

At the Elysée there was a regular series of fortnightly balls attended by up to three thousand guests at a time. Upper-crust Paris vied vigorously for invitations, not excluding some of those aristocrats of the Faubourg Saint-Germain who had been wont to disdain the Bonapartes in general and Louis in particular as vulgar arrivistes.

Two vast galleries—one 120 feet by 40, the other 90 feet by 30—were given over to the dancing, each decorated in yellow and crimson damask, the guests glittering in their jewels and finery under massive chandeliers. Often the crush was so great that traffic on the boulevard outside was completely jammed and arriving guests would take an hour or more to reach the door.

More and more frequently, Louis was being described not as "the President of the Republic" but as "the Prince-President." More and more it became de rigueur to address him not as "Your Excellency" or "M. le Président," but as "Monseigneur" or "Your Highness."

It seemed to many that in all but name the Second Empire had arrived already.

Two major issues dominated the confused, complex, and febrile politics of the sickly Second Republic: the Red Menace at home and the Italian Question abroad. One overlapped with the other and both were manipulated by Louis for his own ends. Just the same, he might never have succeeded in his bid for absolute power but for the fact that by the time the Republic was fifteen months old only a minority of the National Assembly, and of the country as a whole, had any attachment to republicanism at all.

When elections were held for the 750 seats of the new Assembly in May 1849, royalists of one kind or another won an overwhelming majority. The moderate republicans were virtually wiped out, returning only 80 deputies where before they had held 500 seats. Two hundred seats were won by the republican radicals and socialists whose joint parliamentary caucus was known as "the Mountain." Orléanists of the Party of Order won four hundred fifty seats, the Bourbonists of the Legitimist Party won fifteen, and the Bonapartists won five—showing the extent to which the massive popular vote for Louis had been for the man, not the party.

The republican left and the republican center were barely on speaking terms. To the moderates, as to the rest of the Assembly, the Montagnards were dangerous reds. They and their adherents throughout the country were considered a threat to the very life of the nation—all the more so since the election results showed that the crimson stain had spread beyond the industrial slums of the big cities to the hitherto unsullied countryside. The Dordogne, Lot-et-Garonne, Var, and the Basses-Alpes, among other rural areas, had succumbed to the virus of "democ-soc," as democratic socialism was known in the political jargon of the day.

This development, coinciding with an industrial recession and a downturn in agricultural production, only heightened the fears of the center and right that Red Revolution was waiting in the wings. Whether Louis believed this, too, or whether he merely exploited their paranoia for his own purposes is not certain. Whatever the case, constitutional guarantees of freedom of speech, assembly, and the press were soon being submerged under a wave of repression.

Hundreds of individuals were arrested for uttering slogans or singing songs considered to be subversive; newspapers presenting any viewpoint to the left of center—or ridiculing the president—were prosecuted and impounded, their editors and writers fined and jailed; clubs and debating societies were raided by the police and gendarmerie.

In fact, all forms of collective activity were deeply suspect—trade associations, friendly societies, co-operatives, clubs, even informal café discussion groups. The barbers of Paris and other big cities did a roaring trade as men who feared they might be thought to look socialistic had their long hair and beards lopped off.

Conservative reaction to the perceived threat from the left was also manifested in an education bill which, in effect, put the school system under the control of the Roman Catholic Church. Behind this legislation lay the belief that secular schoolmasters throughout the country were spreading evil socialistic ideas among the young. Only an educational system firmly based on the teachings of the Church, it was held, could inculcate a proper respect for order, property, and the family.

Paranoia peaked after March 10, 1850, when by-elections were held to fill twenty-one "Red" Assembly seats whose incumbents had been barred after mass anti-government demonstrations the previous summer. Eleven of those seats were now held by "the Mountain," but although this meant a net gain of ten seats for the conservatives, the right considered the result alarming: it showed that the pernicious doctrines of socialism still flourished in the land. There was panic on the Bourse and a run on the banks. And in the Assembly, Thiers called on members to disregard the Constitution and disenfranchise "the vile multitude."

In fact, it wasn't necessary to disregard the Constitution. A loophole in it allowed the Assembly to impose a three-year residential qualification which reduced the total electorate from 9.6 million to 6.8 million. Most of those who lost their votes were working men most likely to back socialist or radical candidates (though opponents of the bill wryly pointed out that it also disenfranchised the prince-president himself).

Louis, who for twenty years had proclaimed universal suffrage to be one of his most sacred principles, could have opposed the bill but chose not to, even though the Bonapartist deputies—including "Plon-Plon," General Montholon, and Edgar Ney, son of the first Napoleon's great field marshal—did.

Parallel with these domestic developments, and to a certain extent impinging upon them, ran the highly charged issue of French military intervention in Italy.

In the autumn of 1848 revolutionaries in Rome, under the leadership of Giuseppe Mazzini, had seized power and sent Pope Pius IX fleeing to the Kingdom of Naples. From there the Pope had issued an appeal to the Catholic powers of Europe to send troops to suppress the revolution and restore him to his throne.

For Louis Napoleon, support for Italian independence had long seemed to be as fundamental a tenet as universal suffrage. But in April 1849, when it became expedient to do so, he betrayed the cause by sending a 9,000-man expeditionary force from Marseilles to Civitavecchia to occupy Rome. It was an intervention that was to bedevil his career to its end.

Louis's ostensible purpose was to protect the Romans from the Austrian and Neapolitan armies which were marching on Rome in response to the Pope's plea. His real object was to preserve French influence in Italy by ensuring that it was "the Church's oldest daughter" and not some other power that put the Pope back onto the throne of St. Peter. And of course, there was the rationale that this policy would greatly strengthen his position with the Church in France and its millions of devout adherents—no matter that such intervention was in violation of the spirit if not the letter of the Constitution, whose preamble pledged France "never to employ its forces against the liberty of any people."

But on the outskirts of Rome the French Army, under General Nicolas Oudinot, suffered an unexpected and humiliating defeat at the hands of 4,000 ragtag Italian volunteers led by Giuseppe Garibaldi. At first, Louis tried to hide news of this setback from the public; but when the truth inevitably became known, he released to the press the text of a bombastic message to Oudinot expressing regret at the "unforeseen resistance" by Romans who should have welcomed France's "benevolent and disinterested mission." Added the president: "Our military honor is at stake. I shall not allow it to suffer the slightest injury. You will not lack reinforcements."

On June 3, after a breather for fruitless negotiations, Oudinot resumed his attack on Rome, bombarding the city with cannon-fire from a hilltop position and killing one thousand of Garibaldi's volunteers who tried repeatedly to storm his emplacements. Four days later, opening the new National Assembly session, Louis asserted that the Roman people would have allowed friendly French forces to enter Rome to protect them from the Austrians if Garibaldi had not arrived earlier, seized the city, and launched an unprovoked attack on Oudinot's men.

The deputies of "the Mountain" utterly rejected this version of events, denounced the French intervention as unconstitutional, and moved for the impeachment of the president. When this motion was defeated, the radical leader Ledru-Rollin appealed to the people to defend the Constitution "with arms if necessary" by removing the president and his ministers from office.

Louis Napoleon took this as a call to insurrection, and when unarmed demonstrators took to the streets the next day, the government declared a state of siege. Seventy thousand troops had been brought into Paris and the protest marches were swiftly and brutally broken up and dispersed. In Paris and Lyon many demonstrators were killed and hundreds arrested. Ledru-Rollin and other deputies of "the Mountain" fled the country to avoid arrest.

On July 3, after weeks of relentless bombardment followed by fierce hand-to-hand fighting, Rome surrendered to Oudinot. Mazzini fled to England and Garibaldi escaped with four thousand of his men to fight another day. The Pope, reluctant to return to Rome until he was sure it was quite safe, sent three cardinals on ahead to make sure all traces of liberal insurrection had been stamped out.

In Paris, Louis protested that he "did not send an army to Rome to smother Italian freedom." But that was how it looked to most of Europe and to the Italian revolutionaries who, in due course, would seek their revenge.

The Italian intervention, like the curtailment of the franchise and the suppression of free speech and assembly, left the country torn and polarized. Yet somehow the prince-president managed to float above the fray. To Frenchmen of the left he appeared to be a restraining hand on the excesses of the conservatives, while to those on the right he appeared to be the guarantor of order, property, family, religion, and the honor of France.

In this he demonstrated the crucial advantage he enjoyed over the blinkered traditionalists and self-satisfied bourgeois who dominated the Assembly, filled the cabinet, and considered him to be a mere passing phenomenon. By contrast with them, and for all his limitations, Louis was a thoroughly "modern" politician—adventurous, shrewd, and demagogic—with an instinctive understanding of populist dynamics.

The conservatives thought they would be rid of him in May 1852, when his constitutionally unrenewable term of office expired, and that in the parliamentary elections due at the same time the restriction of the franchise would enable them to win a big enough majority to dismantle the Republic and restore a monarchy more to their taste than one headed by a Bonaparte.

What they did not realize was that by tampering with the franchise they had more or less legitimized in advance the coup d'état which even then Louis Napoleon was planning. "When they are hanging over the precipice I shall cut the rope," he said in a letter to Hortense Cornu.

In their blindness, the conservative politicians had failed to notice the warning signals provided by Louis's readiness to ride roughshod over both the Assembly and the cabinet. Yet he hardly bothered to hide his intentions and his contempt for both.

At the end of October 1849, when he dismissed the Barrot government, replacing it with a ministry of equally conservative but considerably more pliable hacks, he told the Assembly: "The name Napoleon is a complete program in itself. It stands for order, authority, religion, the welfare of the people at home, the dignity of the nation abroad."

8

BLOOD
ON THE
BOULEVARDS

IF ANYONE WAS IN A POSITION to foil Louis Napoleon's plans and prevent the coup that was widely expected sooner or later, it was General Nicolas Changarnier, commander of the army and of the Garde Nationale in Paris. Deeply conservative, and a Legitimist to boot, Changarnier had little love for the Republic and even less for the prince-president.

Arrogant, overbearing, and plain-spoken, Changarnier scarcely bothered to conceal his contempt for Louis, whom he considered a fool. He once told a confidant that the prince-president reminded him of "a melancholy parrot." On another occasion, during a cabinet meeting—but while the president was momentarily out of the room—he compared Louis with Thomas Diafoirus, the mountebank doctor in Molière's *Le Malade Imaginaire*. On yet another occasion he said that if the president defied the will of the National Assembly, "I will have him taken to Vincennes [prison]."

All these remarks, and others of a similar nature, were soon repeated to Louis, who was under no illusions about how things stood between them. Yet on the surface they maintained the closest of relations. Changarnier spent a good deal of his time at the Elysée Palace with the president, they often rode side by side on state occasions, Changarnier sometimes accompanied

Louis on his trips to the provinces, and Louis invested him with the Grand Cross of the Legion of Honor.

Changarnier was popular with the well-to-do for his no-nonsense way of dealing with socialist agitation. The bourgeoisie regarded him, as they had Cavaignac, as "the broom of the boulevards"—the man who would keep Paris cleansed of radical refuse. Confident of the support of the National Assembly and the public, Changarnier considered his position unassailable and had no qualms about crossing Louis's path.

This he did in no uncertain way in December 1850, when he issued an order of the day forbidding the troops to make political demonstrations or shout slogans while on parade. This edict was intended to put a stop to the troops' habit of crying "Vive Napoléon!" or even "Vive l'Empereur!" while being reviewed by the prince-president. Like the conservative deputies, Changarnier was increasingly concerned at Louis's popularity with the troops, which derived not just from his personality and lineage but also from his practice of providing chicken-and-champagne lunches for the officers of the Paris garrison and wine and sausages for the enlisted men.

Louis appeared to take Changarnier's calculated defiance with equanimity, even inviting him to the Elysée to tell him how much he valued his services. Emboldened, Changarnier went one fatal step further, issuing another order of the day instructing the army to disregard orders from any civilian authority and to obey instructions only from their own superiors.

What was this? The army was not to accept orders from the Minister for War or the president? Louis indignantly dismissed Changarnier for his effrontery and replaced him with General Bernard Magnan, a man on whom he could rely.

Changarnier's dismissal precipitated a parliamentary crisis. The Party of Order moved a censure motion against the government which was carried by 417 votes to 278. But the Assembly could not dismiss the president; Louis merely fired his cabinet and formed a new one of equally compliant hack politicians and civil servants.

Changarnier remained a general without an army and the public remained quietly acquiescent. After all, the Paris mob was not going to turn out on behalf of the general who had put down the disturbances of June 1849 with such ruthless efficiency; and Changarnier's admirers among the propertied classes were not the kind of people to take to the streets.

Seething over this demonstration of their impotence, the deputies were able to get their revenge when, the following month, Louis asked the National Assembly to vote him an extra 1,800,000 francs to cover his expenses. He was feeling the pinch badly; the 1,200,000 francs a year he was already receiving was not enough to pay for his lavish entertaining and gift-giving, even though the year before the Assembly had voted him another 2,000,000 francs to make up the deficiency.

This time the Assembly were pleased to turn him down, deputies pointing out that the first Napoleon had managed on half a million francs a year, while the President of the United States got by on a mere 125,000. And why should they be expected to help the prince-president to subvert the army by providing the wherewithal for him to pay for their picnics?

In debt and anticipating further heavy spending to expedite his future plans, Louis was forced to borrow. He negotiated a 500,000-franc loan with Baring Brothers' bank in London and got the promise of half a million more from the Spanish dictator General Ramón Narváez, who was currently visiting Paris. But his most generous benefactor was again Harriet Howard, who mortgaged some properties in London and even pawned some of her jewelry to raise the remaining 800,000 francs he needed. Louis cut down on his spending to a certain extent, but made sure that the Paris garrison's weekly blowout was not diminished or interrupted.

Louis had another request to make of the National Assembly at this time and again they turned him down. He proposed a revision of the Constitution to enable him to run for a second term, coupling this with a proposal for the restoration of universal male suffrage. He must have expected that the Assembly would refuse him on both counts, and perhaps made the request primarily to establish in the public mind not just that he wished to remain in office but that he had spared no effort to do so constitutionally and in accordance with the people's wishes.

The Assembly's rejection may have seemed to Louis to provide the moral justification he needed to set in motion his plans for a coup. But first he needed to strengthen his position among the top echelons of the military, for although there was a good deal of Bonapartist sentiment in the army, this was still concentrated mainly among the lower and middle ranks, and the great majority of the generals were either republicans, Orléanists, or Legitimists.

In his search for allies among the army brass, Louis's attention was drawn by Morny to an obscure but ruthlessly effective brigadier-general in North Africa. Leroy de Saint-Arnaud was a hard, merciless, and overwhelmingly ambitious man of the far right, as zealous in putting down Arab insurgents as he was in dealing with the socialists and radicals who were deported to Algeria for their part in the disturbances of June 1849. Cautious soundings indicated that he would be willing to join a conspiracy to overthrow the Constitution in order to "save France from the Reds."

But he was, after all, only a brigadier, and could scarcely be appointed to a senior command over the heads of dozens of superior officers. A providential uprising in the Algerian province of Kabilya during May 1851 gave Louis the opportunity he needed to push Saint-Arnaud to the front of the stage. He sent him to crush the revolt, which Saint-Arnaud did with such speed and ferocity that within six weeks he had become a popular hero, permitting Louis to bring him home, promote him to major-general, and give him a senior command in the Paris region. From then on Saint-Arnaud was his man.

During the tense summer of 1851, Louis made a final attempt to persuade the Assembly to revise the Constitution, supporting his case with a monster petition bearing almost a million and a half signatures.

By now many prominent conservatives had become convinced that to allow Louis a chance at a second term might be the least of several evils and there was a considerable body of opinion in favor of the resolution. While the debate raged, fears of a coup d'état were openly voiced, but Changarnier assured the deputies that this could not occur, for the generals of France would remain loyal to the Assembly and the Constitution. "Delegates of France," he declaimed, "debate in peace!"

When the motion finally came to a vote after six weeks of debate, it was narrowly lost, 446 deputies voting for and 278 against, which was 97 short of the three-quarters majority required for a constitutional amendment.

That was the signal for Louis's inner circle to begin the staff work for the coup. Headquarters were set up in a mansion owned by Bacciochi in the rue du Faubourg-Saint-Honoré. The principal plotters were Morny, Persigny, Mocquard, Magnan, and Saint-Arnaud, whom Louis appointed Minister of War when he reshuffled his cabinet in October. For discretion's sake, if for no other reason, Louis himself did not take part in their meetings. How actively he was involved in the planning has never been ascertained; later, Morny would boast that "without me there would have been no coup."

As autumn turned to winter and the new session of the National Assembly got under way, the political atmosphere became feverish. The coming year, 1852, when both presidential and parliamentary elections were due, was widely seen as a year of terrible destiny in which France might either slide into bloody revolution or revert to the rigidities of the ancien régime.

Increasingly, Frenchmen yearned for a middle way, and increasingly Louis Napoleon appeared to be the pilot to steer them between the rocks. If the Assembly would not give him the opportunity to do it legally, then the country would be in his debt if he showed the courage to act extra-legally. The air was full of talk of an impending coup and much of that talk was approving. Finally, Louis Napoleon fixed the date: December 2, the anniversary of the great Napoleon's coronation as Emperor in 1804 and of his victory at Austerlitz in 1805. The code name for the coup was Operation Rubicon.

On the evening of December 1, the conspirators went to great lengths to be seen in public and behaving normally. The prince-president gave his weekly Monday evening reception at the Elysée Palace and conversed with his guests on such mundane matters as slum clearance and railway branch lines. Persigny, Mocquard, Saint-Arnaud, and the Paris police prefect, Charlemagne-Emile de Maupas, were also present.

Morny went to the Opéra Comique to see Limnander's *Bluebeard's Castle* and found himself sitting next to Cavaignac. The general's enjoyment of the opera would surely have been muted had he realized that his neighbor, already designated to be Minister of the Interior, would have him arrested before dawn. During the interval Morny was overheard telling a lady that although he had no idea what was in the offing, "if there is a clean sweep, madame, you may be sure that I will be on the side of the broom handle."

After the opera Morny went to the Elysée Palace where the president, temporarily deserting his guests, had a brief final meeting with his fellow conspirators in his study. It was over by 11:00 P.M. The conspirators solemnly shook hands, and Morny went on to the Jockey Club, where he played several hands of whist before leaving.

In the small hours of the morning Maupas's men began working their way through a list of seventy-six prominent citizens who were to be arrested. Among those hauled out of their beds and taken off to Vincennes were a number of radical and socialist leaders and, on the right, Thiers and four generals, including Cavaignac and Changarnier.

The police detail that came to arrest Changarnier found him in his nightshirt with a pistol in each hand at the door of his apartment, but he surrendered without a fight. Thiers, recovering from a momentary panic as police burst into his bedroom, tried a mixture of threats, blandishments, and jests to avoid arrest, but ended up—like the others—in the Mazas Prison. There, one of the arrested politicians remarked philosophically to General Lamoricière: "Well, General, we would have liked to put him [Louis Napoleon] in here, but he has beaten us to it!"

While the arrests were being carried out, parties of police took over printing works throughout the capital to supervise the production of tens of thousands of copies of a presidential proclamation which were run off and posted up before daybreak on virtually every wall in Paris. At the same time, troops fanned out through Paris and other major cities in the pre-dawn darkness to occupy strategic sites such as telegraph offices, railway stations, and town halls.

They even took over church belfries to prevent bells being rung as a warning to the populace, and occupied National Guard barracks, where they commandeered the drums that might be sounded to muster the guard to defend the Republic. In Paris, troops also occupied the quais along both banks of the Seine and threw cordons around the Place de la Concorde, the Palais Bourbon, the Tuileries Gardens, the Champs-Elysées, and other locations where the citizenry might gather to protest. By the time the capital awoke, the first phase of the coup was complete.

On their way to work Parisians could see the troops and read the president's "appeal to the people," which alleged a conspiracy by Thiers, Cavaignac, Changarnier, and others to stage a coup against him and overthrow the Republic—a coup he claimed to have forestalled by acting first.

Describing the National Assembly as "a theater of plots," Louis said: "It attacked the power I hold directly from the people; it encouraged every evil passion; it endangered the repose of France. I have dissolved it and I let the people judge between me and it." To that end, he said, he had revoked the law of May 15 and restored universal suffrage, under which the people would be invited to vote in a referendum for or against a new Constitution.

This Constitution would provide for a single-term presidency of ten years, with a cabinet responsible to the head of state, not to parliament. A Council of State composed of "the most distinguished" citizens would draft laws for submission to a legislature elected by universal suffrage, while an appointed upper chamber would act as a check on the lower house, safeguarding the liberties of the nation.

If the people wanted a weak government, the proclamation said, they should vote "No," in which event Louis Napoleon would stand down. But if they believed in the cause of which his name was the symbol and wanted to save France and Europe from anarchy, they would vote "Yes."

In a similar proclamation to the army, Louis laid heavy emphasis on the Napoleonic mystique. "Soldiers, I do not speak to you of the recollections attached to my name. They are engraved on your hearts. We are united by indissoluble ties. Your history is mine." The army was to hold its own referendum on the coup within forty-eight hours.

At mid-morning, three hundred indignant deputies converging on the Palais Bourbon were turned roughly away by the cordon of African chausseurs. The legislators hurriedly found another meeting place in the mairie of the 10th Arrondissement, where they passed a resolution deposing the president and declaring the supremacy of the National Assembly. Before they could disperse, the army turned up in force and showed its respect for their supremacy by carting them all off to jail.

Meanwhile, Louis put on a glittering show of strength and self-confidence, emerging from the Elysée Palace at 11:00 A.M. to ride through the streets on a magnificent black charger, flanked by ex-King Jérôme and General Saint-Arnaud. Fleury, Magnan, Ney, and Flahault followed him, while troops of cuirassiers and lancers rode ahead and behind, roaring "Vive Napoléon!"

The cavalcade clattered along streets lined with infantrymen to the Place de la Concorde, past the Tuileries, across the Pont Royal, past the Palais Bourbon, and thence back across the Seine to the Elysée. The correspondent of *The Times*, who witnessed this brilliant display, noted that the president was "received with respect but without enthusiasm," and that "Vive la République!" was the only cry he heard from the crowd.

Meanwhile, Paris went about its normal business. Shops, banks, offices, and restaurants were open as usual, and on the surface at least the populace seemed to be generally satisfied that the president had done what was necessary. "To say that Paris is not agitated would be absurd," observed the *Times* correspondent, "but so far as I have perceived and heard from others I do not see that the agitation is of an angry nature." And that night, he reported, "Paris was so tranquil that the troops were ordered to return to their quarters."

But the tranquility was deceptive. On Wednesday, December 3, trouble began in the republican districts of the city, where barricades went up and soldiers were pelted with paving stones. This activity was limited, scattered, and on a fairly small scale. The great majority of the workers had no great love for the Assembly, which had tampered with their precious right to vote. Morny and Saint-Arnaud were disappointed. It seems they wanted "the Reds" to put on a display more worthy of their mettle. So they recalled the troops to barracks, hoping to lure the enemy out into the open.

The tactic succeeded. On Thursday, December 4, the streets of the republican districts were crowded with demonstrators, though still not on the scale of February 1848 or the following June. Morny and Saint-Arnaud waited for the barricades to grow bigger and more numerous and then sent in the troops. The

"Reds" were poorly armed but the barricades were formidable. Artillery was brought up to pound them into rubble before the infantry went in with rifle and bayonet.

While plebeian blood was being shed in the faubourgs of Saint-Antoine, Saint-Martin, and Saint-Denis, the *beaux quartiers* appeared little concerned about what was happening only a mile or two away. On the grand boulevards of central Paris, the restaurants and sidewalks were crowded. Law-abiding people had been warned to stay off the streets and not to impede the work of the military, but in this part of town there seemed to be nothing to fear.

The *Times* man reported that "the scene bore the semblance of a carnival and the passage of the military a pageant which attracted the attention and excited the cheers and applause of the populace." Other eyewitnesses, however, heard some defiant shouts of "Vive la République!" and occasional insults. Clearly the mood of the bourgeoisie was mixed and the shouts of opposition to the coup may have made the young and untried troops nervous.

Shortly after lunchtime an enormous column of infantry, cavalry, and artillery—estimated by one observer to number "at least 50,000 men"—was moving along the boulevards toward the battlegrounds to the east. Suddenly, a shot was fired from a building on the crowded Boulevard des Italiens. Thinking they were being sniped at, the troops panicked and began firing indiscriminately.

"It was an appalling sight," reported the *Times* man, "and in a few minutes the eye beheld nothing but two walls of flame" as the troops poured round after round into the buildings on both sides of the street. Said the correspondent of the *Morning Chronicle:* "The carnage was dreadful. To one house at the corner of the rue Bergerel there were carried not less than 35 dead bodies, besides those carried elsewhere; and it may truly be said that among this mass of victims there was not a single insurgent."

Enraged soldiers, hunting for supposed snipers and maddened by the sound and scent of their own musketry, smashed their way into buildings, often firing as they went. One building on the rue de Gramont housed the select Union Club, frequented by retired military officers and sedate diplomats. The soldiers threatened to kill an ancient general who ordered them out and might have done so, but for the intervention of their own officer who recognized the old warrior and ordered a hasty withdrawal.

Above the fashionable—and crowded—Café Cardinal, troops broke into a famous music shop, killed an employee, and took the proprietor and his family prisoner, keeping them and others "penned up like beasts" before releasing them hours later. They ransacked another fashionable eating and drinking place, the Café Anglais, smashing most of its furniture and driving the clients out into the street.

On a street corner, innocent bystanders were shot and bayoneted after a butcher's boy cried "Vive la République, à bas Napoléon!" A British officer and his wife, on holiday in Paris, threw themselves to the floor and crawled under their bed as troops poured fire in through the windows of their apartment on the Boulevard Montmartre.

One building on the Boulevard des Italiens from which the troops believed they had been fired at was completely demolished by point-blank artillery fire. The shooting went on for almost two hours, until General François Canrobert arrived on the scene and managed to get the troops under control.

By that time the fighting in the republican districts had also died down with the total defeat of the "Reds." Altogether four hundred civilians—working-class insurrectionists and innocent bourgeois spectators alike—were killed that day for the loss of twenty-seven soldiers. Saint-Arnaud issued an order of the day congratulating his troops: "You have preserved the country from anarchy and pillage and saved the Republic."

In the provinces, resistance to the coup lasted longer. Peasants in parts of central, southern, and southeastern France generally under the direction of middle-class intellectual agitators—schoolteachers, lawyers, and the like—kept the army and National Guard busy for a week before their sporadic disturbances guttered and died out.

But overall, and overwhelmingly, the people were in favor of the coup. When the referendum was held on December 21 and 22, 7.5 million Frenchmen endorsed Louis's action, with only 650,000 opposed. As Karl Marx would comment: "The idée fixe of the Nephew was realized because it coincided with the idée fixe of the most numerous class of the French people," by which he meant the peasantry and—coining a new term—the lumpenproletariat.

True, there had been no time for the opposition forces to mount a campaign against Louis Napoleon; true, their newspapers had been suppressed and their public meetings banned under state of siege regulations; and true, there had been widespread intimidation and here and there some falsification of returns. Nevertheless, contemporary observers and historians alike agree on the whole that the results were a genuine expression of the national will, however misguided.

Right across the political spectrum, from socialist to Legitimist, a majority seemed to believe that Louis Napoleon's coup had saved France from something far worse. Despite the massacres on the boulevards and barricades of Paris, he had demonstrated once again his mesmerizing ability to seem to be all things to all men—to the workers, the man who had socialist sympathies, who had locked up the hated Cavaignac and Changarnier, and given them back the vote; to the well-to-do, the man who would crush the Reds, preserve property, and maintain public order; to the devout, the man who would champion the Church, defend the family, and protect the Pope.

Even as stern a critic and passionate a socialist as Pierre-Joseph Proudhon—father of the phrase "Property is theft"—believed that Louis Napoleon would now "inaugurate social reform by his decrees," and felt able to write: "I will forgive him his coup d'état and will give him the credit for having made Socialism a certainty and a reality."

Not all the prince-president's critics were so forgiving, however. In Belgium, where he had fled with dozens of other republican notables, Victor Hugo dashed off a white-hot indictment entitled *Napoléon le Petit*, in which he accused the new dictator of "murdering civilization in its sanctuary" by deliberately ordering the massacre of December 4. Later, after moving to the Channel Islands, Hugo would continue to produce a torrent of polemic, "his Muse . . . mouthing her detestation on the doorstep of the Empire." In his 1853 poem *Les Châtiments*, Hugo portrayed a Napoleon "ruined by debauchery, dull of eye/ Furtive, pale of feature,/ This thief of the night, who lights his lamp/ By the sun of Austerlitz." As for his courtiers, they were "hyenas, jackals, wolves."

Hugo has been called the greatest French poet and novelist of his century—perhaps of any century—and was undoubtedly a figure of towering moral authority. Yet the very shrillness of his tirades against Napoleon blunted their impact and revealed him to be more passionate than precise in his judgments. Certainly, on the matter of the December 4 massacre, neither Hugo nor anyone else has been able to produce any evidence that Napoleon was directly culpable. Indeed, all available testimony is to the contrary. "The firing was not ordered by anyone," swore Canrobert, and that appears to be the truth.

Moral responsibility, of course, is something else. Morny and Saint-Arnaud, in spoiling for a fight and ordering such massive military intervention, clearly bear a heavy burden of guilt. Napoleon, too, as prime mover of the coup, must take his share. Although he never uttered a public word of remorse or repentance, he may have been betraying a guilty conscience when, on hearing of the referendum results, he said: "More than seven million votes have just absolved me." Many years later his widow would recall telling him that he "wore December 4 like a hair shirt." "Yes," he replied, "it is always on my mind."

Whatever the truth of that, the post-coup killings remained an indelible blot on Louis Napoleon's escutcheon, and as a result many of France's best minds turned their backs on "the man of December," to the considerable detriment of the Second Empire. Victor Hugo, for one, remained in voluntary exile until the collapse of the Empire in 1870.

On New Year's Day, 1852, Louis Napoleon decreed a *Te Deum* at Notre Dame and in every cathedral and church in France. He moved from the Elysée to the renovated Tuileries Palace, and he ordered the republican slogan removed from the national emblem and from all public buildings. "Liberty, Equality, Fraternity," said Marx, gave way to "infantry, cavalry, artillery."

Louis Napoleon was now absolute monarch of France in all but name and the formalization of that state of affairs was only a matter of decent interval. First came the new Constitution, drawn up in reckless haste by a commission of "eminent jurists" appointed by the prince-president himself. When they failed to meet the ten-day deadline he set them for this task, he gave them another twenty-four hours and they presented him with their final draft on January 12, 1852.

The Constitution, giving him a ten-year term of office and making him responsible not to parliament but directly to "the people," empowered the president to appoint and dismiss ministers at will. It gave him similar power to appoint and dismiss the members of a Council of State, senior civil servants who would initiate and draft all legislation. The Legislative Body, to be elected for six years by universal suffrage, would merely have the right to accept or reject, without amendment, the laws presented to it by the Council of State.

A third chamber, the Senate, consisting of archbishops, generals, admirals, and anyone else the president chose to nominate, had no legislative function beyond the ability to veto any laws that might appear contrary to property rights, religion, morals, or to violate the sanctity of family life. The Council of State and the Senate, whose members were appointed for life, were to meet in secret, and although the proceedings of the Legislative Body would be open to the public they could not be reported in the press.

If the Constitution Louis Napoleon had overturned was a prescription for impotence and futility, the one he now hastened to promulgate was a blank check for dictatorship. But he never cashed that check in full. Instead, he would exercise the enormous powers he now possessed with a good deal of restraint, for paradoxically he was an essentially mild-mannered man, fanatical only in his belief that he was born with the right to rule.

It may be that, as some have said, he was too indolent to be vindictive and too faint-hearted to reject a personal plea for leniency. But he could prove stubborn in his resistance to those who, like Morny, would urge him to be more ruthless and draconian than he felt desirable or necessary.

For example, 27,000 political prisoners were being held in the aftermath of the coup, and if Morny had got his way the great majority of these would undoubtedly have been banished, jailed, transported, or executed in short order. But Louis, possibly feeling some guilt over the December 4 bloodbath, insisted that their cases be investigated individually, and in every district a three-man commission of civil servants was set up to carry out this task.

Although this form of justice was not exactly finely tuned and was based solely on a cursory examination of each detainee's dossier, it did result in the prompt freeing of 12,000 prisoners. Of the remaining 15,000, some 900 were ordered to stand trial, 5,000 were released under police supervision, and the rest were sent without trial either to penal settlements or to unconfined exile in the colonies.

Louis Napoleon personally ordered the release of Cavaignac, Changarnier, Thiers—who had been languishing, ironically enough, in the fortress at Ham—and most of the three hundred other deputies arrested on the day of the coup. A handful of "dangerous" deputies of "the Mountain" were sent to Devil's Island in Cayenne, while Thiers and a number of conservative deputies were banished to more congenial parts, like England or Switzerland.

For the next eighteen years of Napoleon's rule it was a similar story of draconian laws, interpreted and applied with unexpected liberality. For although the wholesale destruction of central police records during the Siege of Paris in 1870, and by the Paris Communards later, makes it hard to be categorical, it seems clear that Napoleon was a far less repressive figure than republican propaganda after the fall of the Empire would have us believe.

His political police apparatus, for instance, was inherited from earlier regimes and does not seem to have been augmented significantly. Surviving correspondence found in provincial prefectures shows that the Ministry of the Interior held the departments to "a strict and slender secret funds budget," and that many prefects protested against what they regarded as "politically foolish parsimony."

Only the two largest cities, Paris and Lyon, seem to have had permanent secret police establishments, and although the destruction of records makes it impossible to gauge the size of the Paris establishment, Lyon is shown to have had only between six and ten full-time agents. To these must be added a considerable number of paid and unpaid informers, but their reports were by no means always acted on by the police, since it was common knowledge that denunciations were often made for personal or commercial reasons.

Nor, it seems, were the police of the Second Empire espe

cially heavy-handed. The *Journal des Commissaires de Police* regularly urged its readers not to be over-zealous, enjoining them to know "when it is better to overlook than to punish"; to see that individual rights were "scrupulously respected"; to make arrests only "under legally prescribed forms"; and to refrain from "denial of justice" and "illegal violence." Undoubtedly, abuses did occur during the Second Empire, or there would be no cause to caution against them. But that such injunctions should be published by the official organ of the police commissioners suggests an outlook by no means entirely hostile to the principles of civil liberty.

Then there were the press regulations promulgated shortly after the coup. These gave the government sweeping powers to prosecute editors and journalists and to shut down publications which printed articles deemed to be insulting to the head of state or damaging to public order and morality. But control of the press was never as heavy or complete as the regulations allowed.

In fact, incomplete evidence suggests that the newspapers had an easier time of it during the Second Empire than under earlier regimes. Between 1852 and 1867, only about one hundred prosecutions were brought against newspapers—fifty-one of them in Paris. A far more frequent practice than prosecution was for prefects to have informal chats with editors, in which they would offer "friendly advice." The custom of giving or withholding government advertising and subsidies was another oblique way of exercising control.

All this is not to suggest that the Second Empire, up to the time of its gradual liberalization in the mid-1860s, was anything but frankly authoritarian. The arrest, detention, and exile of thousands of potential enemies of the regime under administrative order following the coup, and again following an attempt on Napoleon's life in 1858, would have been unthinkable, for example, in Britain at that time.

But such draconian action was taken only at times of high tension, and a general amnesty in August 1859 freed most of the detainees and brought most of the exiles home. It is perhaps instructive that while the regime's opponents on the left characterized the police as ruthlessly efficient, its critics on the right accused them of weakness and timidity. Louis Napoleon's dictatorship was more kid glove than iron boot.

In this context, it is significant that less than two months from the day of the coup, Morny resigned as Interior Minister. The ostensible reason was his disagreement with Louis's action, on the advice of Persigny, in expropriating the holdings of the Orléans family—a move that shocked the property-owning classes.* But there were deeper reasons. Morny clearly wanted to be a good deal more severe in his response to potential opposition than Louis thought wise. In addition, he had been feuding bitterly with Persigny, whom he despised as a humorless dolt. The last straw must have come for Morny when Louis removed the police from his control by creating a Police Ministry and putting Maupas in charge of it.

Despite his resignation, Morny remained high in the prince-president's esteem. Morny went back to his business affairs, perhaps with relief, and there was no long-term damage done to his relationship with his half brother, who later appointed him president of the Legislative Body.

With absolute power seized, established, and sanctioned by popular vote, an essential coda had to be played: the fulfillment of the Bonaparte legend demanded that its embodiment be a monarch, not a mere president. So in the ensuing months the proto-public relations man and arch-Bonapartist Persigny drummed up a campaign to transform the sorry vestiges of Republic into the triumphant trappings of Empire.

From the outset he had been urging Louis to proclaim himself without delay, but the latter preferred a cautious approach, not because he feared an adverse reaction in France but because he judged it unwise to alarm the great powers of Europe. However much they might applaud his squelching of the radicals and socialists and welcome the stability he promised to bring to France, the old enemies of the first Napoleon were unlikely to be enthusiastic over the enthronement of a third.

---

* Parisian punsters dubbed this action "le premier vol de l'aigle" (the first flight/theft of the eagle). But Louis put the Orléans fortune to good purpose, using it to set up a social welfare fund to alleviate the effects of urban poverty.

But Louis's caution evaporated as petitions inspired and organized by Persigny came in from all parts of the country, calling on him to take the imperial title. When he went on an expertly stage-managed, triumphal tour of the South in September, he was greeted everywhere by cries of "Vive l'Empereur," "Vive Napoléon Trois," and everywhere deputations of prominent citizens begged him to wait no longer.

Still, Louis feigned reluctance and humility. At Lyon he said he had not decided in which role he could best serve the interests of France. "If the modest title of President could facilitate the mission entrusted to me," he said, "I should not, out of personal ambition, wish to change that for the title of Emperor."

At Bordeaux a few days later he conceded: "It seems that France desires a return to the Empire." But with an eye to the great powers, he added that he must address the concerns of those who feared that Empire meant war. "The Empire means peace," he declared. "It means peace because France desires it, and when France is content the world is at peace."

During his tumultuous progress back to Paris, the enthusiasm for Empire reached a well-orchestrated crescendo. When his train pulled into the Gare d'Orléans in mid-October, the station and the streets leading to the Tuileries were festooned with imperial banners and triumphal arches already proclaiming him as Napoleon III.

As he rode his chestnut charger from the station to the palace, alone and well ahead of his escort, military bands played his mother's tune, *Partant pour la Syrie,* which was to take the place of the *Marseillaise* as the anthem of the Second Empire. It seemed that all Paris had turned out on that perfect Indian summer's day to cheer him home.

At a theatrical gala a few nights later, Louis's former mistress, the splendidly outrageous Rachel, approached the presidential box and, gazing adoringly upward, her fine eyes glistening in the spotlight's glare, she declaimed a breathtakingly sycophantic ode composed by the director of the Comédie Française, Arsène Houssaye, on Louis Napoleon's own theme of "L'Empire, c'est la paix." The audience responded with wild enthusiasm.

It took but a matter of days for the Council of State to draft a law killing off the Second Republic and creating the Second Empire, for the Legislative Body to approve it, and for the Senate to rubber-stamp it. Meticulously democratic to the last, the beneficiary of this legislation submitted it to the people for their approval and the people welcomed it overwhelmingly. The referendum vote was 7.8 million in favor to a quarter of a million against.

After that, Marianne could never claim that she had been raped: she had, in fact, surrendered eagerly to the Napoleonic seducer, as if the illegality, chicanery, and outright butchery which accompanied the coup had been nothing more than a little boisterous foreplay.

On yet another December day, December 2, 1852—the anniversary of the first Napoleon's coronation, of Austerlitz, and of his own coup d'état—Louis Napoleon signed the decree establishing himself as Napoleon III. It was a bitterly cold day and men of the Garde Nationale, on duty outside the Hôtel de Ville where the deed was proclaimed, danced a can-can to keep themselves warm. It was an extraordinarily appropriate way to mark the birth of Napoleon's *fête impériale*.

BOOK TWO

IMPERIAL

HEYDAY

✶

*"Ce n'était pas un empire comme il faut, mais
nous nous sommes diablement amusés."*
—Comte Emile Fleury

9

CHERCHEZ LA FEMME

MONTHS BEFORE HE ASSUMED THE TITLE OF EMPEROR, Louis Napoleon began searching for a wife to match his new status—one of royal blood, and sufficiently young and healthy to ensure the continuation of the Napoleonic line.

He was enough of a realist to understand that he could not expect to marry into one of the front-rank royal families of Europe—the Hapsburgs, say, or the Romanovs—so, setting his sights somewhat lower, he sent Fleury to the court of the Grand Duke and Duchess of Baden to ask for the hand of their seventeen-year-old daughter, Princess Carola of Vasa.

Carola was sufficiently keen to become Empress of the French to volunteer her conversion to Catholicism in order to expedite the marriage. But her parents had deep reservations about Louis Napoleon's character and long-term prospects, and after a three-month delay informed the prince-president that she was already promised to Prince Albert of Saxony.

It looked like the most calculated kind of snub, but Napoleon took the setback in his stride and after due consideration tried again. This time the object of his attentions was Princess Adelaide of Hohenlohe-Langenburg, a nineteen-year-old niece of Britain's Queen Victoria. Again a response was delayed; as before, the young woman was quite excited at the prospect of becoming Empress of the French, but the disparity in ages, the difference in religion, the chronic instability of France, and the suitor's reputation as an opportunist, adventurer, and vulgar Lothario all gave rise to parental misgivings.

When Napoleon's suit eventually was rejected, Victoria wrote to Adelaide's mother to express her relief. "I feel your dear child is *saved* from *ruin* of every *possible* sort," she wrote. "You know what *he* is."

Harriet Howard was outraged and wounded when she first learned of her lover's efforts to find a wife. It seems that she had seriously believed he might reward her love, loyalty, and financial support by marrying her. She reproached him bitterly when she heard of his overtures to the parents of Princess Carola, storming out of the palace at Saint-Cloud, where she had a ground-floor apartment, and returning to her house on the rue du Cirque.

But Napoleon pursued her with assurances that whoever he might marry she would remain his mistress and first in his affections, and eventually she became reconciled to the idea that for dynastic reasons he must join himself to "some hideous German princess with big feet."

Their reconciliation was advertised in the most public fashion at a ball at Saint-Cloud in August 1851, when she made her reappearance on his arm. As they danced together, Louis became so overwhelmed with passion that—as the old gossip Horace de Viel Castel noted in his diary—"at about half-past ten the Prince retired with her to *rest* for half an hour" before returning to the ballroom.

Confident that her carnal grip on Louis was as firm as ever, and determined to stake out her territory as official mistress if not empress-to-be, Harriet began to behave more assertively than had been her habit. As Fleury noted, "her attitude changed somewhat. She became more exacting with regard to ceremonies and excursions and had now lost some of her accustomed reserve." And when, in October, the prince-president attended a gala night at the opera, accompanied by Princess Mathilde, Viel Castel recorded that Miss Howard was there, too, "seated in a grand box and smothered with diamonds." Her presence, sniffed Viel Castel, "makes a bad impression."

Certain courtiers, including Mathilde, and of course Parisian high society, began to mutter that Miss Howard was getting above herself, especially when she gate-crashed a court ball at the Tuileries in December. It had been one thing for her to dance with the prince-president at an informal summer ball at Saint-Cloud, but quite another for her to intrude upon a state occasion, especially since the president was now the emperor. Fleury, for one, was "astonished" by her presumption, if smitten by her "radiant" appearance and "duchess-like bearing."

"From that evening," he wrote in his memoirs, "Miss Howard showed herself in her true colors, those of a grand courtesan whose ambitions had to be foiled at any price." Besides creating a domestic scandal, her flaunting of her relationship with the emperor might reach the ears of the Hohenlohe-Langenbergs, who had yet to announce a decision on Louis's request for their daughter's hand. However, wrote Fleury, "the bad impression created by the royal mistress's appearance was courageously noted in the report of the Prefect of Police. It was a weapon in our hands. . . . It had to be cleverly used. I undertook this task. . . ."

But if Fleury was concerned about Napoleon making a proper dynastic marriage, he should have been worrying less about Miss Howard than about a Spanish beauty who had recently appeared on the scene. And if Miss Howard was concerned about keeping her hold on her lover, so too should she have been.

Eugénie de Montijo, the twenty-six-year-old Countess of Teba, had previously met Louis Napoleon in March 1849, when she and her mother, visiting from Madrid, were invited to one of the prince-president's weekly receptions at the Elysée Palace. Louis's ever-roving eye had noted her Titian hair, flawless complexion, and splendid bust as she stood in line waiting to be presented and, instead of merely accepting her curtsy and passing on, had stopped to chat.

Perhaps a little nervous, and anxious to make a good impression, the young countess said she had been hoping to meet the prince-president ever since hearing about him from one of his most ardent female supporters.

"Oh," said Louis Napoleon, "and who might that have been?"

"Madame Eléonore Gordon," she replied.

The words were scarcely out when she realized she had made a faux pas. La Gordon, whom she and her mother had met the year before at Pau, in the Pyrenees, had been their house guest in Madrid, but it seemed that the mention of her name was not welcome in the Elysée Palace. The prince-president's smile froze and he turned to the next person in line without further comment.

But Louis Napoleon was not the man to let pique banish lust. The young Spanish beauty had intrigued him, and a few weeks later he sent her and her mother, Doña Maria Manuela, an invitation to dinner at Saint-Cloud. The two women turned up in their best finery, expecting to find themselves among dozens of other guests at a semi-formal occasion. Instead, they found a table laid for four in a small hideaway in the park surrounding the château. The fourth dinner setting was for Bacciochi, whom Doña Manuela, if not her daughter, must have known was called "the Palace Pimp."

Louis Napoleon, never one for drawn-out mealtimes, made short work of the food and wine and, rising to his feet, proposed a stroll in the moonlit park, offering Eugénie his arm, while Bacciochi did the same for Doña Manuela. The prince-president's intentions seemed obvious and Eugénie, alarmed at the prospect of an al fresco assault on her virtue, turned to etiquette for protection.

"I said to him," she recalled many years later, " 'Monseigneur, my mother is here,' and stepped aside to show him he must offer his arm to my mother. He did so without wasting another word and I took Bacciochi's arm. . . . I do not believe [Louis] was very pleased about that evening. He certainly thought it would turn out differently."

The invitation was not repeated. But by the autumn of 1852, when the Montijo women were again in Paris, it seemed that Eugénie's two offenses had been either forgotten or forgiven. If only because of their impeccable connections, she and her mother were invited to join a large number of guests for a five-day hunting party at Fontainebleau. And this time, Louis Napoleon's smoldering lust for her burst into flame.

On the first day, Eugénie took the field for a stag hunt riding an Andalusian thoroughbred and wearing an outfit which must have been suggestive to the prince-president of savage southern passions lurking behind a cool facade. Her turnout inspired a fellow guest to this breathless description:

Her dainty figure was well defined by a closely buttoned habit; the skirt was long and wide over gray trousers. With one of her tiny gloved hands she held the reins, while she used the other to urge on the excited horse with the aid of a little riding whip, the handle of which was set with real pearls. She wore patent leather boots with high heels and spurs. She sat her horse like a knight and despised the saddle ordinarily used by ladies. . . .

Eugénie's skill and daring in the saddle exceeded even her sartorial panache. She led the field all the way and was first in at the kill. When Napoleon galloped up to congratulate her, she accepted his plaudits with downcast eyes and a blush, inflaming him even further with her piquant combination of equestrian swagger, provocative dress, and virginal modesty. That evening he sent her a huge bouquet and the next day he made her a present of the horse she had been riding. The court tongues began wagging furiously and bets were placed on how long it would take the prince-president to bed the Spanish beauty.

Such speculation, which even found its way into the dispatches of the British, Prussian, and Austrian ambassadors, was heightened when word spread among the guests at Fontainebleau of a supposed exchange between Napoleon and his fair quarry the following day.

The men had been out hunting without the ladies, a group of whom were leaning over a balcony adjoining the palace chapel when the men clattered back with their bag. Raising his hat to the women, but with his eyes riveted on Eugénie, Napoleon called up: "How can I reach you, mesdames?" Before any of the others could answer, Eugénie called down: "The only way, Monseigneur, is through the chapel."

The riposte seems just a little too neat for the story to be anything but apocryphal. Just the same, within ten weeks of that supposed exchange, Eugénie, by holding fast to her virginity, did get Louis Napoleon into the chapel—or, to be more precise, to the high altar of Notre Dame—where, said *The Times* in a waspish allusion to Samuel Richardson's impossibly virtuous heroine, "the imperial Pamela received her reward."

Virginity? Though worldly, an outstanding beauty, and well past marrying age for her time, the twenty-six-year-old Eugénie undoubtedly went on her honeymoon intacta, as a brief history of her childhood, youth, and young womanhood may indicate.

Her father was Don Cipriano Guzmán y Palafox y Portocarrero, comte de Montijo y Teba, a man whose family history was as resonant as his name. Her mother, Maria Manuela, was the daughter of an expatriate Scotsman, William Kirkpatrick of Dumfries—an exporter of Spanish fruit and wines and also the U.S. Consul in Malaga—and his rather colorless Belgian wife.

Unkind rumor has it that, well before her marriage, the ravishing Manuela became versed in the ways of the opposite sex through helping to entertain her father's wealthy customers in a "clubroom" adjoining his business premises. However easy her morals undoubtedly were in later life, this story of youthful promiscuity may be a malicious libel, for it seems unlikely that a grandee of Spain—even one as liberal-minded and unconventional as Don Cipriano—would have asked for the hand of a woman to whose name that kind of scandal attached.*

As it was, the permission of the King of Spain had to be obtained before a foreign commoner could marry a grandee. To establish the antiquity of his blood lines, Kirkpatrick produced documents to show that he was descended from the barons of Closeburn and thence, via Robert the Bruce, back into the mists of Scottish prehistory. "Very well, then," said the king, "let the noble Teba marry the daughter of Fingal."

Except for the social advantages to be derived from membership of one of Spain's most ancient families, it is difficult to understand why the worldly and frivolous Manuela should have wanted to marry the austere and gloomy Don Cipriano. It was not as though he was rich, for as the younger of two sons he had inherited only a tiny share of the vast family fortunes and estates on the death of his father. And while he may have cut a romantic figure in a melancholy way, the briefest of conversations would have revealed him to be a humorless political ideologue.

As an officer in Napoleon's army, Cipriano had lost his right eye and received serious arm and leg wounds fighting for the liberal ideals of revolutionary France in the Napoleonic Wars.

---

* Though it should be noted that Cipriano's elder brother, Eugenio, did marry a notorious harlot who had been the mistress of his cousin.

He had, in fact, fired the last artillery salvo in the defense of Paris in 1814, and when he returned to Spain after the Hundred Days it was to a distinctly frosty reception from his Bourbon monarch, King Ferdinand VII.

Marriage to the lively Manuela in 1817 did nothing to brighten his temperament or lessen his political ardor, and when revolution broke out in 1820 Don Cipriano enthusiastically supported the insurrectionists, who set up a liberal government. But three years later the French invaded, suppressed the revolution, and restored the reactionary Ferdinand to the throne.

Only his ancient lineage and the fact that the head of the family, his elder brother Don Eugenio, had remained loyal to the king saved Don Cipriano from execution. Instead, he was thrown into the grim prison of Santiago de Compostella and remained there for eighteen months before being allowed out to live, under stringent house arrest, with his wife in Granada.

Presumably Don Cipriano was allowed conjugal visits while in prison, for he never questioned the paternity of his daughter Francisca, always known as Paca, who was born at Granada in January 1825. In later years there was considerable speculation about the paternity of the second daughter, Eugénie, but this seems misplaced.

Rumor had it that she was the child of Manuela's lover, George William Frederick Villiers, later the fourth Earl of Clarendon, but all the evidence suggests that the two could not possibly have met until well after Eugénie's birth, which took place during an earthquake on May 5, 1826. At the time Eugénie was conceived, Villiers was in Paris on a Customs Commission and Manuela, under the terms of her husband's house arrest, was restricted to Granada. Besides, Eugénie inherited Don Cipriano's unusual red hair.

Cipriano doted on the two little girls, but seemed to favor Eugénie, who was distinctly tomboyish and who perhaps represented for him the son he would rather have had. She early showed a liking for outdoor pursuits, especially riding, while Paca was a good deal less hoydenish and much more her mother's girl.

There were serious differences of opinion between Cipriano and his wife on how the girls should be brought up. Manuela wanted them to make brilliant marriages and to learn all the trivial acts and graces necessary for that purpose; Don Cipriano, characteristically, wanted them to receive a serious education and a spartan upbringing. By reason of this and other incompatibilities, relations between husband and wife began to fray.

During the years of enforced restriction to Granada, Manuela pined for some big city gaiety and sophistication, and when Don Cipriano's house arrest was lifted in 1830 she began to badger him until, in 1832, he took her and the children to Paris for a vacation. It was there that she met the handsome English diplomat George Villiers, who became a frequent visitor to their apartment, while Cipriano, overjoyed to be back now that the hated Bourbons had been overthrown, revisited the scenes and renewed the acquaintances of his glory days as an officer of Napoleon.

The Montijos returned to Spain after some months and took up residence in Madrid. In the following year Villiers arrived there to take up his new post as British Minister to the Spanish court. Manuela now became his mistress, if she had not been so in Paris. The affair brought to her life some of the glamour she had always longed for and which was so absent from her marriage to the gloomy and impecunious Cipriano.

In 1834 a death in the family removed the cause of Cipriano's impecuniosity, if not his gloom—that of his childless brother, Eugenio, whose passing left Cipriano head of the family and master of its very considerable fortunes. Manuela prepared to enjoy life as one of Madrid's richest and most socially prominent hostesses, but before she could savor her new status, Madrid found itself simultaneously threatened by civil war, plagued by cholera, and torn by mob violence.

One day in mid-July, ignoring a warning to stay away from the windows, Eugénie looked out into the Plazuela del Angel and saw a pair of monks being hacked to death by a mob, made hysterical by the approach of rebel forces and rumors that the clergy had been poisoning the wells. The following day Cipriano decided that Manuela and the children should be evacuated to France, while he remained behind to do his patriotic duty.

In Paris, Manuela settled Paca and Eugénie into school at the Sacré-Coeur Convent, then returned to Madrid, though she might well have remained in the French capital but for the desire to get back to Villiers. She had, after all, little reason to pine for her husband, whose newfound wealth had done nothing to alter his austere and stingy lifestyle.

To add to their differences, as a purely nominal Catholic he was not happy about her having left his daughters under the influence of the Sisters of the Sacré-Coeur. When he and Manuela returned to Paris in July 1835, he had them moved to an avant-garde co-educational school, the Gymnase Normal, Civil et Orthosomatique, which was run according to the principles of the Pestalozzi Institute by a Spanish fellow veteran of the Napoleonic Wars. Both schools left a permanent mark on Eugénie: from the gymnasium she derived an enduring taste for outdoor physical activity, and from the convent a lifelong preoccupation with the outward forms of the Catholic faith.

By now her parents' marriage was foundering, and after three months, Cipriano returned to Madrid, leaving Manuela and the children in Paris. There Manuela resumed her friendship with the author Prosper Mérimée, whom she had met while he was visiting Spain in 1830. It seems that she was not his mistress—"there has never been anything carnal between us," he would assure his friend Stendhal in 1836—but she gave him something of more enduring value than her caresses: the story of a Spanish gypsy girl whom he immortalized in his novel *Carmen*.

Mérimée took a great interest in Paca and Eugénie, helping them with their schoolwork, taking them to art galleries and the zoo, regaling them with stories of Napoleon's glory. He was to remain a family friend and adviser to the end of his life.

He also introduced the family to Stendhal, another enthusiast for the halcyon days of Empire, and he too was captivated by the girls—especially Eugénie, for whom his affection seems almost obsessive. Stendhal was finishing *The Charterhouse of Parma* when he met them, and while correcting the galley proofs took it into his head to insert cryptic coded messages to the sisters in footnotes to Chapters 3 and 26.

In 1837, the sisters' formal education was disrupted again when Manuela took them to England and put them into an exclusive girls' boarding school at Clifton, near Bristol, before returning to Paris for a brief fling with Villiers, who was on leave from his post in Madrid.

Eugénie hated England—the weather, the food, and especially the school, where the other girls called her "Carrots" because of her red hair. She may also by this time have been sophisticated enough to suspect that Manuela had left them in Bristol to be free for her affair with Villiers.

Whatever the case, Manuela brought the girls back to France once Villiers had left and put them into the Pestalozzi gymnasium again. Soon after this Cipriano returned to Paris after an absence of two years and spent four months getting to know his daughters again.

There seems little doubt that Eugénie was genuinely devoted to her father. During their long separation she had written to him often and with obvious longing. "Daddy, how I want to kiss you and how glad I will be on the day when I am with you and see the last of the Pyrenees," said a letter dated January 2, 1837. And three months later she wrote: "I cannot wait any longer without seeing you; why did I come into the world except to be with my father and my mummy?"

Significantly, Manuela did not once write to Cipriano during their two years apart, although he wrote several times to her. He returned home from his last visit to Paris in January 1838, and the next time Manuela saw him, thirteen months later, he was on his deathbed. Learning that he was seriously ill, she hurried to his bedside, for form's sake if for no other reason, leaving the girls to follow on with their English governess, Miss Flower. But Cipriano died before the children arrived.

Doña Manuela's grief was not excessive. It seems she was far more upset by the defection of Villiers, who by this time had succeeded to the title of Earl of Clarendon on the death of his uncle. She had hoped the Englishman would marry her now that she was free, but he had decided to give up his career in the foreign service, return home, and make a more suitable marriage to an Englishwoman to whom he had already proposed by letter.

Bereft of both husband and lover, but left with a huge fortune, Manuela decided it was time to cut loose. There was Miss Flower and a whole army of servants to take care of the girls; from now on she would devote herself to pleasure.

Even in a period when Spanish society was noted for its easy morals, Manuela's conduct soon began to raise eyebrows. The riotous parties she threw in her townhouse on the Plazuela del Angel and at her country house at Carbanchel became notorious. If contemporary gossip is to be believed, she and a circle of women friends of similar age and tastes used to kidnap attractive young men and keep them for their pleasure until they tired of them. An anonymous diarist of the time tells how a friend of his named José Hidalgo suffered this "delightful" fate when he was "a mere stripling."

He was sauntering in the Prado; a carriage suddenly stopped; a man alighted and approached Hidalgo and, bowing and smiling, asked the youth to accompany him. . . . [He] was spirited off to La Granja where he stayed many weeks under the tyrannical governance of Mme de Montijo and a few other fascinating and equally pitiless lady pirates with a handful of other young men who, like himself, after the fashion of Ganymede, had been stolen from their families. One of their pastimes, as recounted by Hidalgo, was for the men to get down on all fours on the floor and for the ladies to straddle across their backs and tilt at each other as mounted knights might do at a tournament.

It does sound rather like typical nineteenth-century pornography and may well be malicious fantasy, but there is at least a germ of truth here, for without doubt Doña Manuela was a very merry widow indeed. Her blatant sexuality could not have remained entirely hidden from her adolescent daughters and it may have much to do with the fact that Eugénie, at least, seems to have grown up with a marked aversion to sex and a deep contempt for men.

In 1842, when she was sixteen, Eugénie fell in love for the first time, and it was perhaps symptomatic of her exaggerated fear of sexuality that she should choose as the object of her affections the somewhat ethereal fifteenth Duke of Alba, a twenty-one-year-old cousin whom she had known as a child.

Alba was enormously rich and possessor of one of the oldest and most exalted titles in Europe. As such he was a more than welcome visitor to the home of Doña Manuela, who was determined to make the best of all possible marriages for her daughters. Unfortunately for Eugénie, Manuela decided that Alba should marry Paca, and whatever the pliant duke's personal preference might have been, she soon pressured him into asking for the hand of the older sister.

When Eugénie learned of this she went into an emotional crisis, threatening suicide at worst and retirement to a convent at least. She dashed off a letter to Alba in which she poured out her adolescent pain and frustration—"my end draws near . . . it is more than I can endure"—and her wounded pride—"I fear ridicule more than death itself.

"My loves and hates are extreme," she wrote.

I do not know which is the stronger. . . . I am a mixture of passions, which are terrible and strong. I fight against them, but ever lose the battle. My life will end miserably in a turmoil of passions, of virtues and follies.

You will say that I am romantic and silly, but you are good and will forgive a poor girl who has lost all those who loved her and is now looked upon with indifference by everyone, even by her mother, sister, and the man whom she loves the most, the person for whom she would gladly have begged alms, and for whom she would even have consented to her own dishonor*. . . . If you have children, love them equally; remember they are all yours and do not slight the love of one to show more fondness to another.

Eugénie seems to have recovered from her emotional turmoil quickly enough, for within a month of her writing that letter we find her in Paris with her mother and sister, shopping for Paca's trousseau. They stayed for over three months and returned to Madrid laden down with an estimated 600,000 francs' worth of clothes, including dozens of dresses and forty-eight pairs of shoes. "The young duchess is thought to be one of the happiest and best-dressed young ladies in the whole world," gushed Washington Irving, the U.S. Ambassador, in a letter to his nieces after Paca's wedding.

After the wedding, as before, Eugénie appeared to harbor no ill-feelings toward her sister. Whatever she may have felt about her mother's role in the affair, she remained deeply devoted to

---

* The idea of Eugénie begging alms on behalf of Alba is only slightly less unlikely than the notion of her surrendering her maidenhood to him, for while he was one of the richest men in Spain he was also one of the least highly sexed.

Paca and on entirely platonic good terms with her brother-in-law, spending much of her time at their home, the Liria Palace.

Doña Manuela's concern now—apart from pursuing her own energetic sex and social life—was to find a suitable husband for Eugénie, but this was to prove difficult to the point of impossibility. After her disappointment over Alba, Eugénie perfected the technique of the high-society coquette, flirtatious and inviting but eventually dismissive of the young men who came to court her, honorably or otherwise.

Reveling in her power to attract, she enjoyed even more her power to reject, and one of those whom she rejected firmly was the young Prince Napoleon, Louis's cousin Plon-Plon, who made an attempt on her virginity during a visit to Madrid in 1844.

By her late teens, Eugénie was a ripe and dazzling beauty. An anonymous admirer described her thus on a visit to a bull fight: "Her slender body is well defined by a costly bodice which enhances her beauty and elegance. Her dainty hand is armed with a riding whip instead of a fan, for she generally arrives at the bull-ring on a wild Andalusian horse and in her belt she carries a sharp-pointed dagger. Her little feet are encased in red satin boots. Her head is crowned with her broad golden plaits interwoven with pearls and red flowers. . . . She is the Queen of Beauty. . . ."

Eugénie's patronage of the cruel and colorful pageant of the corrida brought her the acquaintanceship of some of the leading bullfighters of her day. Gossip had it that she was the mistress of one, known as El Chichanero, but almost certainly she kept the hot-blooded torero at arm's length, just as she did the more suitable young men of the Spanish aristocracy.

According to contemporary accounts, Eugénie was sometimes seen riding through the streets of Madrid bareback, with a cigarette between her lips and her hair streaming out behind her. She was also a frequent visitor to gypsy encampments, where she would twirl and stamp to the wild rhythms of the Flamenco. The contrast between such abandon and the coldness and untouchability she displayed toward the young men she met at home and in the fashionable salons left Madrid high society unable to make up its mind whether she was a slut or a vestal. Today we can recognize her behavior as typical of the compulsive tease, hungry for excitement, desperate for attention, but terrified of contact.

One incident that demonstrates most tellingly her compulsion to flirt with sexual danger comes from her own lips. She described it in her old age on at least two separate occasions, and whether true or false the story seems equally revealing.

As Eugénie told it, she was brushing her hair one night, in semi-déshabille, when she noticed in the mirror that a man was hiding under her bed. Calmly she called out to her maid that she had left her fan downstairs and told her to fetch it, first pretending to write down instructions on where it was to be found. In fact the note said: "Send help, there's a man in my room."

While the maid went on her mission, Eugénie began to taunt the intruder, softly humming to herself while she performed a partial strip-tease, in which she slowly removed her stockings and dangled her bare legs inches from the man's face. It was obviously a risky thing to do, but Eugénie was confident that help was on the way and her confidence was not displaced. Before the man emerged from under the bed to confront her, the servants arrived and seized him.

He turned out to be a much-wanted bandido who said he had broken in not to steal but to catch a glimpse of the beautiful Countess of Teba. Now that he had done so he was content to go to jail, but first he begged a favor: Would the Condesa permit him to kiss her beautiful, dainty feet? Charmed by his gallantry, she allowed him to do so and as they took him away he turned to her and said: "Adios, señorita, I am proud to think that both you and I are Spaniards."

While Eugénie was busy rejecting the advances, honorable and otherwise, of bullfighters, bandits, and bluebloods—including the Duke of Osuna, who ranked even higher than Alba in ducal precedence—her mother was crowning her career as a society trull by becoming the mistress of the new dictator of Spain. This was General Ramón Narváez, "an ugly little fat man with a vile expression of countenance," as Lord Malmesbury called him, and the very prototype of all the Latin military caudillos to come.

Narváez pressured the queen to appoint Doña Manuela to the highly influential court position of Camerara Mayor, which put her in charge of the royal ladies-in-waiting. One of her first actions in this position was to appoint Eugénie a maid-of-honor, but the privilege was short-lived. After a few weeks the marques de Miraflores became Governor of the Palace and one of the first things he did—being an old friend of Don Cipriano's—was to produce a lengthy dossier detailing Manuela's scandalous behavior.

Miraflores made it clear to the queen that either Manuela must go or he would. "For me to remain in my post is impossible as long as the Countess of Montijo remains in hers," he wrote. "Since 1839, when I represented Your Majesty as her Ambassador in Paris, I had encounters as heavy as they were unpleasant with this lady." Despite her connections with Narváez, Manuela had no alternative but to resign, and Eugénie lost her position at court along with her mother.

Shortly after this deeply humiliating experience, Eugénie seems to have fallen in love for the second and last time in her life. The marques Pépé de Alcañices, a wealthy and worldly young man, wooed her with such masterful self-assurance that for once she felt she had met her match. She was waiting all-atremble for his proposal of marriage when she discovered that it was not her he was after but her married sister Paca; he had been using her as a means to gain access to the Liria Palace.

So great was Eugénie's outrage and self-loathing at having allowed a mere man to trick her that she tried to kill herself by crushing a score of highly toxic matchheads into a glass of milk and swallowing them. As she lay in bed refusing to take the antidote which her family thrust upon her, Alcañices burst in and knelt at her side, overcome not by remorse but by the desire to retrieve some compromising letters he had sent her.

When he asked her for them, she rose in wrath, took the antidote, and sent him off, supposedly—but improbably—saying: "Like Achilles' spear, you heal the wounds that you have made." If she was a man-hater already, this incident can only have confirmed her in the belief that, as she would say some years later, "Men, they are worth nothing!"

The Alcañices affair seems to have made up Manuela's mind that she must get Eugénie away from Spain if ever she was to find a husband for her. It was the start of a four-year Grand Tour in which an increasingly desperate mother vainly paraded a resolutely intransigent daughter around the marriage markets of Europe and the British Isles.

Everywhere Eugénie's beauty was acclaimed. "Very handsome, auburn hair, beautiful skin and figure," noted Malmesbury in his diary, after seeing her at a London reception. "Very elegant, very amiable, clever and witty," noted Viel Castel in his diary after seeing her at a reception in Paris. And everywhere she left a trail of suitors whom she had either rebuffed by her coldness or repelled by her self-absorbed intensity and sudden changes of mood.

"She knew how to keep men at a distance and yet encourage conversation," observed the wife of a Madrid banker. "Her mouth was scornful and drooped. But she had a beautiful figure and her eyes slanted *downwards*. . . ." Rather oddly, Arsène Houssaye "found her nose rather forbidding," and was "not swept off my feet," although he agreed she was "most seductive."

Whatever society thought about Eugénie de Montijo, it plainly could not ignore her. Nor, for different reasons, could it ignore Manuela. Growing increasingly loud and desperate as she paraded her desirable but difficult daughter from one elegant watering hole to the next, she was becoming known as the most energetic matchmaker in all Europe and something of a figure of fun.

This was the situation when, in May of 1852, Manuela and Eugénie came to Les Eaux Bonnes in the French Pyrenees and heard all the excited gossip about Louis Napoleon—when would he declare himself Emperor, and when, and whom, would he marry? It may have been at this point that it occurred to Manuela or Eugénie, or both of them, that if they played their cards right there was an outside chance that Eugénie could hook the prince-president who had shown such a lascivious interest in her in Paris three years before.

For the prize of an imperial crown, if nothing less, Eugénie was quite prepared to swallow hard and sacrifice her long preserv'd virginity.

10

EUGÉNIE'S
"BOLD GAME"

LOUIS NAPOLEON HAD BEEN WAITING CONFIDENTLY for the outcome of the referendum on Empire when his infatuation with Eugénie became obvious to all during the Fontainebleau hunting party in mid-November of 1852. When, by now emperor but still infatuated, he invited her to Compiègne a month later, he was awaiting the outcome of another important initiative—his request for the hand of Princess Adelaide of Hohenlohe-Langenburg.

But that was an affair of state, not to be confused with an affair of the heart, and once more the court gossips began laying wagers on how long it would be before the Spaniard was bedded. Once more Eugénie confounded the cynics and disappointed the emperor: there would be no food before grace.

Finding that his customarily direct seduction methods were getting him nowhere, Napoleon seems to have tried the romantic-chivalric approach. "He will go and look for a flower in the woods on a winter night," Eugénie wrote to Paca, "tearing himself away from the fire to go out into the wet in order to satisfy the caprice of a woman he loves."

The fascinated courtiers, ambassadors, and other guests were transfixed by the spectacle of the lecherous emperor's transformation into a parody of a moon-struck adolescent. The house party lasted from December 17 right through Christmas until the 28th and hardly ever did Napoleon seem to leave

Eugénie's side—except, alas, at bedtime. At all other times he was there, sitting next to her at table, strolling with her through the formal gardens, riding with her in the forest, dancing with her in the ballroom, sharing his box with her at the palace theater.

The imperial family—Mathilde, Plon-Plon, and their father Jérôme—became increasingly alarmed that Napoleon might do something rash. After all, Jérôme had once predicted that "Louis will marry, if she wishes it, the first woman to refuse him her favors." Napoleon's close circle of advisers were equally alarmed. This Spanish adventuress was scarcely more suitable a wife for the Emperor of France than Miss Howard would have been.

The foreign ambassadors were again mentioning Eugénie in dispatches. Baron Josef von Hübner, the Austrian envoy, wondered in one "when the walls would be breached and when the fortress would surrender." A step or two ahead of his colleague, the new British Ambassador Lord Cowley advised his Foreign Office that "the Emperor is going it finely with the young Montijo," adding that "Her mother is, with the young lady, playing a bold game, and I cannot doubt hopes that her daughter may wear the Imperial Crown. Some of the Emperor's friends are not without apprehension that she may succeed in her intrigues and Saint-Arnaud, the Minister of War, has spoken very openly and strongly to the Emperor on the subject: as if a man in love ever listened to reason!"

While all this was going on the French Ambassador to London, Count Walewski, was proceeding in all innocence with his task of negotiating a marriage between Napoleon and Princess Adelaide, who was currently visiting her royal relations in Britain. When Walewski came to Paris on New Year's Eve to give the emperor a progress report, he was astonished to be told by his cousin: "My dear fellow, I am already taken."

Walewski was aghast. A formal marriage proposal had been made and there was as yet no answer. One could not simply jilt the niece of Queen Victoria, who was also related to half a dozen other royal houses. The emperor must at least wait for a reply from the Hohenlohe-Langenburgs. With a sigh, Napoleon agreed that, yes, he supposed he must.

That night there was a grand dinner and ball at the Tuileries to which, of course, Eugénie and her mother were invited. The court dragons were waiting for them with bared claws. As the guests were going into the banqueting hall, Eugénie seemed about to enter ahead of the wife of the Education Minister, one Mme Fortoul, who protested in a loud voice that she had precedence. Eugénie drew back, pale with anger, and replied: "Go ahead, madame." Napoleon, noticing her distress from his place at the head table, hurried over to Eugénie and asked what the trouble was.

She told him that she had been insulted, and would not come to court again to repeat the experience. He begged her to be calm, promising that soon no one at court would dare to insult her. The implications of that avowal were not lost on Eugénie and her mother: a proposal was imminent.

The next day Napoleon received the news that made it possible for him to make good his promise. It was a brief letter from Princess Adelaide, in her own handwriting but obviously dictated by her parents. She did not feel worthy of the exalted position the emperor had so graciously held out to her, she said, and must regretfully decline his offer of marriage. Now Napoleon was free to propose to Eugénie; but she and her mother were to be kept in suspense for a while yet. Other matters had to be cleared out of the way first—the opposition of family and officials for one.

Napoleon convened an informal meeting of his closest relatives and advisers at the Tuileries. Although what he had to tell them was not unexpected, the family were none the less appalled, particularly Plon-Plon; once Eugénie produced a male heir, he would have no hope of succeeding his cousin. "One does not marry women like Mlle de Montijo, one merely makes love to them," he snorted, conveniently forgetting that he, like the emperor, had already tried and failed to do just that.

Mathilde, too, made little attempt to hide her opposition, begging Napoleon on her knees not to marry Eugénie. Already confronted with the realization that she had thrown away a crown when she allowed her father to break off her engagement to Louis, she could not bear to think that she was about to lose her position as the emperor's official hostess.

Most of the cabinet were strongly opposed, although Morny and the Finance Minister, Achille Fould, were not. The Foreign Minister, Edouard Drouyn de Lhuys, threatened to resign, and Saint-Arnaud warned that the army would be very much against the marriage. Persigny took his opposition underground. Aware of his sovereign's great respect for the wishes of "the people" and of the people's inherent xenophobia, he began to orchestrate an anti-Eugénie campaign by circulating scurrilous pamphlets about her and her mother.

There is also evidence that he inspired hostile editorials which were carried not in the cowed and censored French press but in obliging French-language newspapers across the frontier. One such editorial was carried by the *Indépendance Belge*: "A union with a Spanish lady meets with no sympathy from the nation and can only be the result of personal gratification. The head of a great state like France, anxious to found a new dynasty, should entertain more serious thoughts and higher aims than to satisfy a whim and succumb to a young woman's beauty."

By now Eugénie was the subject not so much of a whispering campaign as a shouting match. "To hear the way in which men and women talk of their future Empress is astonishing," Cowley told the Foreign Office. "Things have been repeated to me . . . which it would be impossible to commit to paper."

While this painfully embarrassing controversy raged, Eugénie and Manuela called in their advisers—Mérimée, their cousin Ferdinand de Lesseps, future builder of the Suez Canal, and the Spanish diplomat Don Enrique Galve, younger brother of the Duke of Alba. Why had the emperor not yet sent his formal proposal of marriage? Should they remain in Paris and endure this torrent of public abuse? Would it not be wiser to make a tactical withdrawal, to Madrid or to Rome?

There was a pressing factor which, perhaps, Manuela and Eugénie did not mention to the three men: they were desperately low on funds. Their four-year odyssey around the spas and salons of Europe had made drastic inroads into the family fortune. They were being dunned by dressmakers and other tradespeople and Manuela had been forced to borrow from her wealthy son-in-law, Alba. If the situation were not resolved very soon, they would have to sneak out of Paris to escape their creditors.

Eugénie, by now feeling thoroughly humiliated, was in favor of leaving, if only in the hope that Louis would be desperate enough to pursue her. Manuela said she should grit her teeth and hang on. Mérimée was afraid that Miss Howard had re-established her hold over Louis. Calve said she should return immediately to Madrid to preserve the family honor. And Lesseps spoke in philosophic vein about the unpredictability of human emotions.

The arrival of an envelope from the Tuileries interrupted this anguished debate. Was it the long-awaited proposal of marriage? It was not. It was an invitation to another court ball on January 12. Now the debate narrowed down to the question: Should Eugénie attend and risk further insults from the social dragons?

Cutting through the opinions of the others, she announced her decision: She would order the most sensational gown, make her appearance, and let her enemies do their worst. If the emperor continued to vacillate after that, she would leave France.

She turned up, deliberately late, on the arm of one of her firmest allies, Baron James de Rothschild, dressed in a stunning creation of ivory brocade trimmed with silver tassels. It was not only the dress that caused a sensation but the fact that she was wearing a wreath of orange blossoms in her hair. In France orange blossoms were usually worn only by a bride on her wedding day, a custom of which Eugénie may or may not have been aware.

She curtsied to the emperor as he sat on the dais with Princess Mathilde and others of the imperial family, before passing on to find herself a seat. Knowingly or otherwise, she moved into the zone reserved for the wives of ministers and other privileged court ladies. As she did so, the wife of Drouyn de Lhuys rose in wrath and informed her in a penetrating stage whisper that this area was out of bounds to a "foreign adventuress" like her.

Napoleon, who had not taken his eyes off Eugénie since she entered the room, saw the encounter, and even though he could not hear what was said correctly deciphered the body language of the two protagonists. He hurried over to Eugénie and conducted her back to the imperial dais, where she was seated at his side. Then when the orchestra struck up he took her onto the floor to dance a quadrille.

As they danced, she demanded an immediate private audience. When the orchestra stopped he led her off the floor and, observed by the hundreds of guests, took her down the corridor to his study.

Eugénie was still pale with fury. She would endure no more such insults, she told the emperor. He had intimated his wish to marry her but had made no formal proposal and meanwhile she was treated like an adventuress and a prostitute. But now she had had enough; she would leave in the morning for Italy. Louis begged her not to. A written request for her hand would be delivered to her mother forthwith, he promised.

Triumphant, Eugénie returned to the dance floor with the emperor. Many of those present correctly interpreted her smile and his ardent attentions as they reentered. "One can say that the marriage was announced at that ball," Baron Hübner noted in his diary.

The opponents of the marriage in Louis's inner circle made a last-ditch effort to change his mind. But the emperor would brook no more discussion. "I do not ask your advice," he said. "I merely state the fact. This marriage has been decided upon and it will be accomplished."

On January 15, 1853, Manuela received the following letter at her apartment on the Place Vendôme:

Madame la Comtesse,
For a long time I have been in love with Mademoiselle your daughter and have wished to make her my wife. I am today therefore asking you for her hand, for there is no one so capable of making my happiness or more worthy to wear a crown.
I pray you if you consent to this proposal not to reveal it until we have been able to make our arrangements.
Believe me, Madame la Comtesse, when I assure you of my sincere friendship.
NAPOLEON.

Manuela had scarcely sent back her consent when another carriage from the Tuileries arrived at her front door. This time it was the emperor himself. In a final attempt to stop the marriage, one of his entourage had told him the rumor that Clarendon was Eugénie's real father. If true this could be more than embarrassing, for Clarendon was about to be appointed British Foreign Secretary.

Was the story correct, Napoleon demanded of Manuela? "Sire," she replied with a show of pained dignity, "the dates do not fit." Napoleon accepted her assurance and withdrew.

That night, in a letter to her sister, Eugénie wrote: "I wish to be the first to inform you of my marriage with the Emperor. . . . He has fought and won." She might more accurately have said that "*she* has fought and *I* have won," for undoubtedly she had her mother to thank for everything. As Eugénie's private secretary, Augustin Filon, would confirm many years later when committing the empress's recollections to writing: "Mme de Montijo [was] responsible for the entire matrimonial campaign and . . . played her game with a boldness which . . . indeed was dangerous in the highest degree."

Throughout his frustrating pursuit of Eugénie, Napoleon had continued to visit his English mistress, either at her apartment at Saint-Cloud or at her home in the rue du Cirque, where she generously allowed him to slake the passions that had been aroused by the virtuous Spaniard.

Harriet knew all about Eugénie, of course, public gossip and private intelligence having kept her up to date on the progress of Napoleon's grand passion. And she understood her lover well enough to realize that, as she said in a letter to an English friend, "if the fair Infanta has not yielded, marry he may." Still, she continued to hope that she might remain the imperial mistress.

But for the time being, in the flush of his unrequited passion for the virtuous bride-to-be, Napoleon was determined to be rid of Harriet. "His Majesty was here last night, offering to pay me off," she wrote to her friend. "Yes, an earldom in my own right, a castle and a decent French husband into the bargain. . . . Oh, the pity of it all! I could put up with a dose of laudanum. . . . The Lord Almighty spent two hours arguing with me. . . . Later he fell asleep on the crimson sofa and snored while I wept."

Quite apart from any sentimental debt he might feel he owed her, the emperor could not dismiss Miss Howard like an errant housemaid. Repayment of her loans presented no problem, now that absolute power had relieved Napoleon of his financial embarrassment. But his mistress also had in her possession scores, perhaps hundreds, of the letters he had written to her during the six years of their liaison, some of them potentially embarrassing if not politically compromising, and she might not be willing to return them for any price.

There was also the possibility that, however resigned to his marriage she might seem to be, she would make an embarrassing public fuss when the engagement was announced.

So Napoleon hit on a plan to recover his letters and get Harriet out of the country at the same time. He told her that her former lover, the gambler and man-about-London James Young Fitzroy, had acquired a number of compromising letters concerning his political activities while in exile and was blackmailing him. He begged her to go to London with Mocquard, his political secretary, pay Fitzroy off, and retrieve the letters.

Harriet does not seem to have wondered why Mocquard could not have done the job without her assistance. Perhaps she was blinded by the hope that the marriage to Eugénie might still be staved off by one more proof of her loyalty, or that at least it would help her keep her position as official mistress. For whatever reason, she agreed to go. Early on the morning of January 22, she and Mocquard left in her private coach to catch the overnight packet from Le Havre to Southampton.

But the packet did not sail. A storm in the Channel kept it in harbor and Miss Howard and Mocquard stayed the night at the Frascati Hotel. At breakfast next morning Harriet glanced at *Le Moniteur*,* the official newspaper, which had just arrived from Paris. There, to her outrage, she read that "a happy event, destined to consoldiate the government of His Imperial Majesty and to assure the future of the dynasty, is about to take place." It was the official news of Napoleon's engagement to Eugénie, announced by the emperor while Miss Howard was on her way to Le Havre in the obvious expectation that she would be in London by the time she heard the news.

---

* Parisians called it *Le Menteur—The Liar.*

Rounding on Mocquard, whom Miss Howard rightly assumed must have been party to the deception, she ordered her coachman to prepare the horses for immediate departure. They headed back for Paris at top speed, Miss Howard alternately weeping and berating Mocquard and his master. En route they broke an axle, which delayed them for several hours. When she finally got back to the rue du Cirque, Harriet found that her house had been ransacked.

The place was in turmoil but nothing of value—not the silver, not the rare china, not the jewels, not the paintings—had been taken; only Napoleon's letters were gone from a locked drawer in the desk in Harriet's boudoir. They had been taken in a police raid, under the personal supervision of Maupas and on the instructions of the emperor.

Of all the correspondence between Miss Howard and Napoleon, a potential mother lode of source material for historians, biographers, and simple students of human nature, only her last letter to him survives. "I could easily have sacrificed myself to political necessity," she wrote, "but I cannot forgive you for sacrificing me to a whim. I am taking your children with me and, like another Josephine, your star."

Napoleon never could handle domestic scenes, so he sent Persigny to confront her and finalize the separation terms. Miss Howard made "a terrible scene," Persigny told an acquaintance. "He sympathized with her and they wept on each other's shoulders. But he was firm and his gentleness conquered her. . . ."

Persigny had always been one of Harriet's friends in court, believing Napoleon would be better off to make a dynastic marriage and keep a discreet mistress rather than tie himself to someone like Eugénie. So he persuaded Napoleon to improve on the terms of separation he had already offered.

Instead of insisting that Harriet should live far from Paris and marry a suitable Frenchman, Napoleon gave her permission to live in the château of Beauregard, near Versailles (which she had purchased the year before with 575,000 francs of her own money), and to marry any Englishman of her choice.

He agreed to give her the title of comtesse de Beauregard, with letters patent allowing the peerage to be passed on to her son, Martin. She was allowed to remain guardian to the emperor's two bastard sons, to whom she was deeply attached. She was, of course, repaid her 5 million francs, with interest. And she was allowed to go to Saint-Cloud to remove her personal property—furniture, portraits, bronzes, and china—from the ground-floor suite she used to occupy.

Having faced down his family, his friends, his ministers, and his mistress, Napoleon now had, for form's sake, to break the news of his impending marriage to his rubber-stamp parliament.

He summoned the courtiers, deputies, and senators to the Tuileries, where in a speech from the throne he reminded them that a succession of foreign princesses had not made good queens of France. However, the union he was about to make was of a different kind—"and therein lies its advantage."

It was not his way to try to elevate his status by "royal alliances, which give false security and often place personal interests before those of the nation," or by "making one's coat-of-arms look older and trying at all costs to interject oneself into the family of kings." No, he declared, he would "candidly accept before Europe the status of parvenu—a glorious title when obtained by the free vote of a great people."

Therefore he intended to marry "a woman whom I love and respect." True, he conceded, Eugénie was a Spaniard, but she was "French in heart and in education," and her father had shed his blood for France. She was also "a devout Catholic," and he had "every hope that her court will be as renowned for its virtues as was the empress Josephine's."

The speech got a mixed reception. By no means every Frenchman was pleased to hear his emperor refer to himself as a parvenu, however accurate a description that might be, and to speak of Josephine's "virtues" was positively laughable. But then, oratory had never been Louis Napoleon's forte, and he calculated correctly that the common people would feel he was identifying with them by calling himself a parvenu and would not mind him burnishing the reputation of his grandmother, who was as popular in death as she had been faithless in life.

News reports of the speech did not stop the scurrilous street talk. To discourage this, Persigny, who had previously been busy encouraging such slanders, announced that the police had orders to arrest anyone defaming the empress-to-be. But bawdy rhymes and songs about Eugénie continued to circulate. The chorus to one of them went: "If the Emperor finds her cherry tonight,/ It will mean that she must have had two."

Even the faithful family friend Mérimée—whom some believed was actually the mastermind behind the marriage*—permitted himself a dubious joke: Louis Napoleon had become emperor by election but Eugénie had become empress by erection, he quipped in a letter to a friend.

---

* Arsène Houssaye, for example, composed an elaborate parable on the whole affair in which Napoleon was thinly disguised as the Emperor of China and Mérimée as an Academician who, "wishing to plan a novel in real life," arranges things so that the emperor meets and falls for an "adorably beautiful" foreign woman. This seems a considerably exaggerated view of Mérimée's role, although certainly he was instrumental in getting Eugénie and her mother introduced to court in the first place through his membership in Mathilde's artistic-literary circle, and certainly he was a constant adviser on tactics as the campaign progressed.

11

THE
MODEL
MARRIAGE

RARELY, IF EVER, has a royal marriage gone ahead at such breakneck speed. Although Napoleon originally intended the wedding for mid-February, the rising crescendo of gossip and calumny persuaded him to get the deed done even more quickly, and the nuptials were rescheduled to take place a mere week from the announcement of the engagement.

The shortness of notice threw Napoleon's court into a frenzy of activity, in the middle of which word arrived from Rome that the Pope would be unable to officiate, as requested, on account of his "great age and infirmities." This snub by the man he had sent an army to protect would rankle with Napoleon for the rest of his life; the Pope was to outlive him by five years.

On the day of the announcement Eugénie and Manuela moved into the Elysée Palace. That night Eugénie wrote a strikingly melancholy letter to her sister Paca who, because of the extraordinary haste, was unable to get to Paris in time for the ceremony.

"This is a sad time," wrote the bride-to-be. "I am saying farewell to my family and my country in order to devote myself exclusively to the man who has loved me sufficiently to raise me up to his throne. . . . I fear the responsibilities that will weigh upon me, yet I am fulfilling my destiny. . . . On the eve of mounting one of the greatest thrones of Europe, I cannot help feeling somewhat terrified."

Of her husband-to-be she said: "This man has an irresistible willpower. . . . He was prepared to risk his crown in order to share it with me. He has no hesitations; he is always ready to stake his future on the turn of a card; that is why he always wins." Even when expressing affection for Napoleon, it was with some ambivalence: "I love him, which is a great guarantee of our happiness. He has a noble and loving soul, but one needs to know him well before one can appreciate this." And the note of melancholy persists: "Soon I shall be alone here and friendless. Destiny always has a sad side to it. For example I, who always long to be free, have put myself in chains; I shall never be alone, never free. . . ."

Was this the letter of a woman about to marry a man she loved? Viel Castel would quote one of Eugénie's court ladies, the marquise de la Ferronays, as saying that "she never loved the Emperor and her heart remained faithful to the marquis d'Alcañices." In apparent confirmation, Eugénie's Spanish friend, the marquise de Bedmar, told Viel Castel that Eugénie said to her on the day before the wedding: "Were Alcañices to claim me now, I would go with him." Although Viel Castel's reportage was often malicious, it was seldom inaccurate.

Even stronger evidence of Eugénie's state of mind, and of her continued hankering for the indifferent Alcañices, was her extraordinary behavior—after receiving the emperor's proposal, but before the matter was made public—in sending a telegram to Alcañices to tell him of the pending marriage. The wire was intercepted by Napoleon's security police who, not yet aware of the emperor's matrimonial intentions, were indignant that some upstart foreigner should make such a presumptuous claim. But when the telegram's contents were made known to Napoleon, he merely grunted: "I know all about that."

What was Eugénie's intention when she sent that extraordinarily indiscreet message? Was she hoping that Alcañices would wire back pleading with her not to go ahead, but to marry him instead? Or was she simply showing the man who had humiliated her that she had landed a much better catch? She never explained her motives to her grand-nephew, the seventeenth

Duke of Alba, whom she told about the telegram in her old age. And whatever her intent, Alcañices did not take the bait. He merely replied with a cool, congratulatory telegram of his own.

The royal couturiers and an army of seamstresses worked round the clock to get Eugénie's trousseau ready in time. Between them they made fifty-four dresses, the wedding gown alone containing 40,000 francs' worth of Alençon lace. Although Parisian high society and the masses alike continued to scoff and sneer at the emperor's choice, presents poured in from all parts of the country and the City Council of Paris sycophantically voted to give Eugénie a diamond necklace valued at 600,000 francs.

Learning that on the same day the council had voted only half that sum for the relief of the destitute, Eugénie sensibly declined the gift and asked for the money to be given to the poor. The imperial family thought she was playing to the gallery, but the gesture improved her image lower down the social scale. Even the socialists were impressed. "Her letter of refusal was simple, dignified and honorable," wrote one political exile, "and such as one could hardly expect from a woman capable of marrying the hideous author of December 2."

The socialists might have been even more impressed—or perhaps merely perplexed—by a passage in one of Eugénie's letters to Paca during that hectic week, referring to "my longing to help the depressed classes, deprived of everything, even the opportunity to work. . . ." Like her husband-to-be, Eugénie had in her youth shown some interest in socialist ideas and her concern for "the depressed classes" may have been a vestige of that time. But as empress, though active in performing charitable acts and good works of a condescending and paternalistic kind, she would show little interest in social reform.

The civil wedding took place in the Salon des Maréchaux at the Tuileries Palace on the evening of the 29th before an audience of one thousand relatives, courtiers, and foreign diplomats. Eugénie looked pale and tired, according to Baron Hübner, but the emperor seemed to be at "the very summit of human happiness."

Eugénie wore a magnificent lace dress with a spray of jasmine at her breast, and around her waist a magnificent diamond and sapphire belt, which had been given to the empress Marie Louise by the first Napoleon. After a brief ceremony, conducted by Napoleon's Jewish Minister of State, the banker Achille Fould, the guests filed past the imperial couple, seated side by side on a dais. Witnesses noted that ex-King Jérôme "bowed as he passed the Emperor, but took no notice of *her*," and that Plon-Plon "bowed to neither one nor the other."

Further down the line, Napoleon's Beauharnais cousin Marie, now the Duchess of Hamilton, whispered to her escort, Hübner: "You will see the scandal I shall make when we get near my cousin." Startled, the Austrian Ambassador asked: "Do you really mean that?" "Indeed, I do," she replied. "In that case," said Hübner, "I beg you to walk on alone," and withdrew his arm from hers. In the event, she lost her nerve and behaved correctly, if coldly.

Following the ceremony the imperial couple and their guests adjourned to a music salon, where they had to sit through an excruciatingly boring cantata especially composed for the occasion by the aging Daniel Auber. The libretto was by the sycophantic Houssaye and he excelled himself—"The year had two springs. The heavens were rosy and they blessed the dawn of Andalusia, which had formed this flower. . . ."

That night, with another and far more grandiloquent ceremony to endure in the morning, Eugénie wrote, as ever, to her sister: "I cannot describe all that I suffered during that three quarters of an hour, seated on a throne slightly raised from the dais and facing that crowd of people. I was paler than the jasmine which I wore upon my heart."

The following day Eugénie arrived at the Tuileries at noon to join the groom for the ride to Notre Dame in the gilded coach which had taken Napoleon I and Josephine to the same destination for the same purpose in 1804. She wore another stunning gown, swathed in a cloud of transparent lace, with a diadem on her head—and this time the orange blossoms she wore in her hair were appropriate to the occasion.

A tremendous spectacle had been organized to make the match more acceptable to a skeptical public. Fleury had been appointed Grand Equerry and put in charge of the arrangements, setting up "a huge workshop with vast stores," and assembling "a vast crowd of painters, decorators, coachbuilders, saddlers and embroiderers, who worked day and night without a break." He had even sent to London for thirty-five pairs of perfectly matched horses to add to those already available.

Despite all this effort, things got off to a bad start when, just as the imperial coach moved away from the palace gates, the gilt crown surmounting it fell off. Liveried coachmen hastened to replace it, but it fell off again and the carriage had to proceed unadorned. Inevitably, some saw this as an ill omen.

The route to the cathedral was lined by infantrymen in full dress. Squadrons of splendidly accoutred cuirassiers, dragoons, and Cent Gardes clattered along ahead of and behind the carriage while bells pealed, cannons crashed, and bands played. Despite all this flash and clamor, foreign observers noted that the crowds along the route seemed less than wildly enthusiastic.

At Notre Dame many among the 2,800 people in the congregation appeared even less overjoyed. Lady Augusta Bruce, sent to report on the wedding by Queen Victoria, noted that "the object of our neighbours seemed to be to scan and criticise the dress of the Bride, and the wonderful penetration and accuracy of their eagle glances was to us something incredible!"

Gangs of workmen and interior designers had been busy all week decorating the cathedral for this event in the gaudy, overblown style that was to be characteristic of the Second Empire. Brightly painted cardboard panels concealed the ancient walls. Flowers, flags, tapers, and multicolored streamers hung from the vaulted ceiling. The pillars were swathed in blue and crimson velvet, decorated with crowns and the intertwined letters L and E. The high altar had been moved to the center of the nave and was surmounted by a velvet canopy, lined with ermine and suspended on golden cords. Fifteen thousand candles lit the church and the organ had been replaced with an orchestra five hundred strong.

Lady Augusta thought the interior of the cathedral looked "splendid." She reported to Queen Victoria that "flags and tapestries of all colours combined harmoniously with the magnificent ecclesiastical vestments, the civil and military uniforms and the beautiful gowns of the women." Hübner, whose eye was more sophisticated, proved less enthusiastic: "Crude colors, flowers and candles in profusion, lots of flags, little taste."

The orchestra played the march from Meyerbeer's opera *Le Prophète* as the bridal couple entered. The English diarist Charles Greville thought Napoleon looked "ignoble, as he must ever do." Lady Augusta was kinder: "That he is passionately in love with her no one doubts, and his countenance . . . wore a radiant and joyous expression." Eugénie, by contrast, was "pale as death," although "unable ourselves at such a distance to appreciate the details of her dress or the expression of her countenance, we saw her distinctly enough to be able to say that a more lovely coup d'oeil could not be conceived."

After the ceremony, and the crowning moment of her career as a matchmaker, Manuela suddenly found herself alone. She rode back to the Elysée tired, hungry, and deflated. The palace was practically deserted, the servants having gone out to gawk at the lights and the fireworks, and no dinner had been prepared for her.

Her only reward was to be the satisfaction that she had married off her second daughter even more magnificently than her first, for within six weeks Napoleon would settle a decent sum on her and send her packing back to Spain. "I have two incurable faults," Manuela said to Mérimée later, "I am a mother-in-law and a foreigner." But of course, her origins had nothing to do with the case. The truth was that Napoleon had never liked her and did not want her in Paris, intriguing and assuming the airs of an empress mother. Significantly, Eugénie would make no attempt to intercede for Manuela, merely advising her to leave quietly. Later, however, she would write to Paca that, "despite our unhappy relationship and the incompatibility of our characters, it grieves me to think that she will be lonely and sad."

While Manuela was dining alone, the newlyweds had rather too much company. They had been joined in their honeymoon lodge, Villeneuve-l'Etang, by the palace officials who by custom always dined with Napoleon when he came to Saint-Cloud. After the meal was over, instead of tactfully withdrawing, they stayed on, making speeches and offering endless congratulations. Napoleon grew visibly impatient for them to leave, but somehow they failed to get the message.

Finally he whispered to Eugénie to get rid of them. She hardly knew how to accomplish this and the speeches droned on. At last, sensing that her husband was about to explode, she whispered to him to walk to the door. He did so, and it was she who bade the courtiers good night before following him to her long-delayed deflowering.

That first night, and the week-long honeymoon which followed, must have been as disappointing for Napoleon as it was distasteful for Eugénie. Everything we know about him suggests that he entirely lacked the sensitivity and tenderness necessary to awaken the passions of a woman as predisposed to frigidity as Eugénie. Everything we know about her suggests that she must have been as incapable of giving sexual pleasure as of receiving it.

Pleasure apart, the forty-five-year-old Napoleon lacked the looks to make Eugénie's first full experience of sex at least aesthetically pleasing. "Noble and loving" his soul may have been, but this could hardly make the sallow, stunted emperor, with his swelling paunch and tobacco-stained teeth, seem like the beautiful youth of a maiden's romantic dreams.

As for the seasoned campaigner Napoleon, accustomed as he was to the expert ministrations of Miss Howard and others of the courtesan class, he can hardly have found the inhibited Eugénie a particularly interesting bed companion, though her beauty and remoteness may have remained a powerful lure, full of promise yet empty of fulfillment.

Napoleon was not a communicative man, and while his inner circle may have guessed the truth, the couple gave no outward sign of dissonance in the first few weeks. Indeed, courtiers remarked on their frequent—and sometimes embarrassing—attentions to each other. One court official, entering a room at the Tuileries which he believed to be unoccupied, was startled to find the emperor seated there with the empress on his knee, as he pressed hot kisses upon her. On other occasions Napoleon was heard to whisper endearments to his wife in English.

But these impetuosities were probably evidence of frustration rather than of conjugal harmony. Eugénie's attitude toward sex was summed up in the remark she made to a confidante: "But really, why do men never think of anything but *that*?" And when, some time later, Napoleon's cousin Princess Anna Murat was agonizing over whether she should agree to marry a man who was a good deal older than herself, the empress would say:

"After the first night it makes no difference whether the man is handsome or ugly. By the end of a week it's the same old thing."

Indeed, all of Eugénie's recorded observations on the subject are in the same vein. After witnessing a fight between two stags in rut in the forest at Compiègne, she exclaimed to a female companion: "Stags know what love is!" And when, toward the end of her long life, a visiting duchess observed that "men are worth very little," Eugénie took her by the arm and said: "Between ourselves, madame, they are worth nothing."

To the nightly ordeal of the boudoir was added the daily tedium of the grand salon; Eugénie soon found herself enjoying the stultifying formalities of court routine little better than she did the gross intimacies of the marriage bed.

Not that Napoleon III's court was anything like as stuffy as those of the old monarchies of Europe. By comparison it was brash, glittery, and decidedly nouveau riche. Nonetheless the pomp, protocol, and absence of privacy were sufficient to lay a leaden blanket over the headstrong spirit of the young empress.

There was a constant round of balls, levées, receptions, dinners, galas, official visits, parades, presentations, and other ceremonial duties to attend to, and although Eugénie's household staff—a grand chamberlain, two lesser chamberlains, two equerries, a secretary, a maid-of-honor, and six ladies-in-waiting—was modest by the standards of European royalty, it meant that, as she complained to Paca, she was never alone for a second.

"I have gained a crown," lamented Eugénie, "but what does that mean, other than the fact that I am the leading slave of my Kingdom?" And in a later letter: "You cannot imagine how utterly worn out I am with all the balls and ceremonies."

The Tuileries Palace, where she spent most of her time, was considerably less luxurious than it appeared on the surface. The public rooms were splendid enough, but the living quarters were ill-lit and poorly ventilated. The plumbing was primitive and noisy, even by the standards of the day. Stygian halls and endless gloomy corridors were lit day and night by guttering gas jets. And the whole layout was so impractical that armies of servants were constantly carrying wood, water, and coal up and down stairs.

Dinner, like lunch, was never informal. Chamberlains, equerries, orderly officers, the palace prefect, and the commander of the guard were always present, apart from whatever guests there might be. The diners would gather in the Salon d'Appolon at seven-thirty before moving into the Louis Quatorze Salon at eight. A periwigged lackey stood behind each diner—a gorgeously attired Nubian for Eugénie—as the chefs and footmen bustled to and fro. But although the wines were excellent, the dinner service was made of electroplated silver and the food was invariably cold by the time it arrived by dumb waiter from the kitchens deep in the palace basement.

Coffee was served after dinner in the Salon d'Appolon and conversation—which was Eugénie's strong suit—or music—for which she had no ear at all—filled the time until ten, when Napoleon usually retired. Unless his demands for her company were insistent, Eugénie would stay up until eleven-thirty or twelve, chatting some more or dancing with some of the court gentlemen to the latest tunes played on a mechanical piano.

Sometimes, when the tedium and formality got too much for her, she would break loose and insist on the company playing a game which she called "potting the candles." Footmen would bring armsful of rubber balls which Eugénie, guests, and courtiers would then kick in the direction of the candles until they had put them all out.

Such spontaneous displays of schoolgirlish energy were the product more of boredom than high spirits and were soon to be a thing of the past. Eugénie had been married six months when Baron Hübner wrote: "She is no longer the young bride, the improvised sovereign. . . . She is the mistress of the house who is conscious of her position and asserts it by her manner, by her gestures, by the orders she gives to her ladies, by the glance—a little disdainful, a little blasé, but penetrating—with which she scans the hall, allowing no detail to escape her."

Others were soon complaining of her hauteur. Said Viel Castel: "The Empress confounds dignity with superciliousness; she fears lest people should find out that she is not sufficiently an Empress and she is disdainful without reason." Said the marquise de Taisy-Châtenoy: "She played the official personage with childish satisfaction."

By this time, Eugénie had failed in her first effort to perform

A d'Orsay
fecit
1839

Napoléon Louis.

PRINCE CHARMING: Louis Napoleon, sketched by his friend d'Orsay, at the age of 31. (Mansell Collection)

IMPERIAL POMP: Napoleon III in military uniform, painting by Hippolyte
Flandrin. (Chateau de Versailles)

IMPERIAL BEAUTY: Eugenie on her wedding day, painting by Edouard
Dubufe. (Musée de Compiègne)

HORTENSE: Louis Napoleon's mother, painted about the time of her marriage by Gérard. (Mansell Collection)

"MISS HOWARD": Louis Napoleon's English mistress, 1850, artist
unknown.

EUGENIE: One of the many paintings by Winterhalter. (Metropolitan Museum of Art)

QUEEN OF HEARTS: Virginie di Castiglione in the costume that titillated
the Tuileries, gouache from a photograph by Pierson. (Sirot Collection)

PROUD FATHER: Louis Napoleon with the baby Prince Imperial, photo by
Cliché Braun. (Bettman Archive)

what she knew to be her most important function: to produce a male heir. By the end of March the court physicians had confirmed that she was pregnant, but by the end of April she had miscarried. For all her good health, vitality, and taste for vigorous exercise, Eugénie was not built to bear babies easily.

The miscarriage—apparently precipitated by an over-hot bath, taken to alleviate the pain of an accidental fall—caused much satisfaction among the likes of Mathilde and Plon-Plon and the Orléanist and Legitimist aristocracy, all of whom had reason to hope she would never produce an heir. Harriet Howard added her portion to the mountain of malice. "Her Majesty is beautiful, boring and barren," she wrote to her English friend.

The experience cast Eugénie into a deep depression. She pondered upon the fates of Mary Queen of Scots, Charles I, and Marie Antoinette—for whom she felt a growing affinity—and asked Paca: "What might have been the sad fate of my child? A thousand times I would prefer that a son of mine should wear a less brilliant but more secure crown!"

Napoleon's reaction was more robust. When Lord Cowley delivered a letter of condolence from Queen Victoria and added some regrets of his own, the emperor replied briskly that "the mistake can be rectified." Privately, he may well have begun to wonder whether he had married a woman who was sterile as well as frigid.

Another experience that contributed to Eugénie's rapid education in the realities of life as Empress of the French was an assassination plot which was foiled by Maupas's sharp-eyed secret police. It happened when she and Napoleon attended a gala at the Opéra Comique on July 5. Police agents, moving among the crowd who were waiting for the imperial arrival, spotted a wanted man and seized him and fifteen others. All of them were Italian revolutionaries and all were carrying concealed daggers. Under interrogation they admitted they had planned to kill the emperor.

To his credit, Napoleon had warned Eugénie before their marriage about risks of this kind, and Eugénie seemed to accept it philosophically. Whatever her faults, nobody ever accused her of cowardice. "If we thought about assassination all the time we should never sleep at night," she remarked to Mérimée. "The best thing is not to think about it and to trust in Providence."

For all her lively wit, quick intelligence, and forceful manner, Eugénie's sketchy formal education and limited experience of the real world had left her woefully ignorant of history, politics, science, economics, and the arts, and with no systematic knowledge of the institutions or customs of France, or of any other country for that matter. Except in the matter of dress, for which she had a genuine flair, she was something of a philistine.

Her ideas on religion were an incongruous jumble. Unlike her husband, who found it politic to profess Catholicism while remaining a freethinker, Eugénie managed to be a devout practicing Catholic while simultaneously believing in the occult. She went in for table-rapping, spirit-raising, and similar fashionable practices, and so identified herself with Marie Antoinette—whose fate she feared she would share—that she insisted on occupying the tragic queen's suite at Saint-Cloud and surrounding herself with Marie Antoinette memorabilia.

All this is not to say that she was without qualities. Hübner summed her up well. While acknowledging that her education was "superficial" and her personality "capricious and eccentric," he found that she had "great strength of will and physical courage . . . an ardent imagination and a fiery heart."

Although, like Eugénie, Napoleon had little appreciation of music, literature, or the graphic arts, he did have wide-ranging interests and was capable of sustained if not exhaustive intellectual effort. He had shown himself able to write creditable dissertations on historic, political, and economic themes, he had some advanced and extremely practical ideas about town planning, and he would in time publish a by no means contemptible biography of Julius Caesar, albeit with the aid of a formidable battery of court historians.

By contrast, Eugénie—as even one of her greatest admirers would say—"was but little moved by that power which lies in the continuity of argument, in the classification of facts, or in the logical march of thought toward a rigorous conclusion. . . . I doubt if she often read a book through from cover to cover."

While Napoleon, for a good while, remained enamored of his

difficult bride, she quickly lost her illusions about him. The Napoleonic legend with which she had grown up, thanks to her father, Mérimée, and Stendhal, the prevailing myths surrounding her husband's return from exile and ascent to the presidency, the swift decisiveness of his coup d'état, and the single-mindedness with which he had wooed her, had convinced Eugénie that—whatever his other shortcomings—she was marrying a bold man of action. The reality was rather different.

Now that his personal goal of supreme power had been achieved, the other facets of his personality had come to the fore and he was altogether too complex and cautious, too torn by the often contradictory elements in his political agenda, to conduct the affairs of France with the dash and decisiveness she had expected.

And soon there were the domestic flare-ups caused by Eugénie's discovery that Napoleon had returned to his English mistress. She might not relish her own role in the marriage bed, but she could not bear the idea of Napoleon taking his pleasure elsewhere.

As secret police files make clear, Napoleon resumed contact with Miss Howard within a few weeks of his wedding. Police Minister Maupas had been keeping her under tactful surveillance ever since the breakup, and a report to him by an anonymous society informer indicates that as early as the end of March a reconciliation with Miss Howard was in the offing.

Reporting that the English beauty had acquired an angora cat which wore a green ribbon on its tail and was attended by a servant wearing green livery, the police spy observed that "the cat and its servant are gauges of affection from the absent one." He added: "Moreover, Miss Howard uses an expression which we repeat without fully understanding what she means. 'He always was capricious,' she says, 'but he is subject to stomach aches* and I know very well that he will return to me.'"

A month later, Viel Castel was noting in his diary that "Mocquard, chef de cabinet to the Emperor, allows himself to be seen in a box at the opera with Miss Howard." Certainly Mocquard would

---

*Although she expressed herself with both elegance and irony in her native tongue, Miss Howard never mastered the French idiom. Possibly she intended to convey the idea that he suffered from hunger pangs where she was concerned, but messed up the metaphor.

not have dared to appear in public with Harriet had he not known that she was back in favor. By early July, Maupas's spy was reporting unequivocally that "Louis Napoleon has completely resumed his relations with Miss Howard, which has somewhat clouded the Imperial marriage." It certainly had. There were violent scenes and Eugénie alternated between barring Napoleon from her bedroom and threatening to leave the country.

From time to time she did both. In the first years of her marriage she made a number of incognito visits to Britain, traveling as Madame de Guzmán, or the comtesse de Pierrefonds, with one or two of her ladies. The official explanation of her absences was usually that she was visiting relatives in Scotland. Faced with such reprisals and with angry scenes, which he constitutionally could not bear, Napoleon kept promising to break things off with Miss Howard. But time after time he returned to her.

One subterfuge Napoleon employed to allow him to meet Miss Howard inconspicuously was to go to review the troops at the Satory army camp, near Versailles, where she would rendezvous with him in her carriage. "After the march-past," recalled one eyewitness some years later, "he entered a carriage that was waiting for him. It belonged to Miss Howard, with whom he would go to the Château de Beauregard. . . .

He used to change his uniform for civilian clothes in the carriage, taking off his military cap and tunic and putting on a top hat and frock coat, but keeping on his red uniform trousers and polished boots. Those who saw him going through the streets of Versailles in Miss Howard's carriage wearing this strange attire have never forgotten it. His love for the beautiful Englishwoman explained everything. . . .

In a dispatch dated September 22, 1853, Maupas's spy reported that

the Empress . . . has told her august husband that she intends leaving both Saint-Cloud and France if the Emperor has no greater regard for his dignity and the duty he owes to the wife of his choice. . . . The Emperor, always calm and gentle, even when he is in the wrong, ultimately succeeded in calming her anger by promising to break off all contact with the person in question.

*   *   *

But a month later, the spy was reporting once more that "Miss Howard is in the ascendant, to the Empress's great displeasure."

Whether it was Eugénie's unremitting pressure or Napoleon's waning passion that finally ended the affair is not certain, but in February 1854 Maupas's spy was reporting that "the old affection [had] now degenerated into friendship," and three months later he reported that Miss Howard had fulfilled her part of the separation agreement by going to London and marrying an Englishman named Clarence Trelawney.

But if Miss Howard was no longer in the picture, that was to prove no consolation for Eugénie: countless others were to take the place of "la belle Anglaise"—some for one night only, others for considerably longer periods. As Napoleon said to his cousin Mathilde: "I must have my little diversions," taking care, however, to add (perhaps for form's sake, perhaps sincerely, for Eugénie remained a potently attractive woman) that "I always return to her with pleasure."

On one occasion Eugénie caught her husband in flagrante delicto, when she made an unscheduled visit to his private bedchamber. "Sortez, mademoiselle," she commanded icily, and the emperor's doxy fled, donning her clothes as she went.

But much as she might rage, bar him from her bed, and even leave him temporarily for incognito trips abroad, Eugénie knew she could not impose the ultimate sanction—a complete cessation of all sexual relations—until she had performed her duty of producing a male heir. She had no intention of sharing the fate of the empress Josephine.

For his part, unsatisfactory though he might find her in many ways, Napoleon realized the importance of his wife's beauty, wit, and stylishness to the maintenance of his adventurous imperial image. So the mutual dissonances and disappointments were hidden behind the glossy facade of power and success. And to the world at large, Napoleon and Eugénie appeared an ideal and resplendent couple—the perfect partnership to preside over a resurgent French imperium.

12

THE EMPIRE
MEANS
WAR

ALTHOUGH NAPOLEON HAD ASSURED France and the world that "the Empire means peace," he had been on the throne a scant sixteen months before he led his country into the first major war of his reign. He would repeat the process over and over again—war with the Russians, then with the Austrians, next with the Mexicans, finally with the Prussians—until the fourth conflict would bring his regime down in ruins after less than eighteen years.

Yet he was privately a placid, even gentle, man. Here was no crude warmonger, thirsting for conquest or territorial expansion, no brilliant soldier eager to display his martial skills, nor even an intellectual militarist in the mold of Clausewitz, seeing war as a necessary extension of politics "by other means." Certainly, he was not insensitive to the sufferings of the men he sent out to die for France. On at least one occasion he would retch and weep at the carnage he saw on the field of battle. Rather, he was the confused if unresisting victim of the ineluctable dynamics of his self-created mystique.

By the circumstances of its birth and the militaristic traditions it inherited, the Second Empire could not possibly mean anything *but* war, and although he may have been quite sincere when he said, "L'Empire, c'est la paix," Napoleon must have sensed that the reverse was true. He knew, for one, that the army which had helped him to supreme power must be rewarded with opportunities for glory and advancement. He knew, too, that the imperatives of Empire would not permit a policy of *immobilisme;* during the presidency, which was a mere apprenticeship for the throne, he more than once told Hübner, the Austrian Ambassador, that he believed his predecessor Louis-Philippe had fallen through inactivity and lassitude—"because he let France fall into disrepute." "I must do something," Napoleon would say. And this, observed Hübner, "was the motive that took him to the Crimea."

The origins of the Second Empire's first war lay 2,000 miles from Paris, at the Church of the Holy Sepulchre in Jerusalem and the Church of the Nativity in nearby Bethlehem. It was on these two churches that Russia focused its ambition to enjoy exclusive guardianship of Christian interests in the crumbling and corrupt Ottoman Empire. There, on the supposed sites of Christ's birth, Crucifixion, and burial, the Orthodox and Catholic priesthoods had been engaged in a centuries-old squabble over rites, privileges, and turf, a squabble which continues to the present day.

Dividing the churches into separate sectors, chanting each other down during services, the rival priests would even descend to fisticuffs or worse while raising their hosannas in praise of the Prince of Peace—and particularly on the holiest days of the Christian calendar, when their rivalries seemed most acute. Quite often, the Muslim Turks would have to post guards with fixed bayonets to keep the peace among the warring infidels.

When Mark Twain visited the Holy Land in 1867, he found the Church of the Holy Sepulchre "scandalised by trumpery gew-gaws and tawdry ornamentation" and that the Orthodox and Catholic clergy "cannot worship together around the grave of the Saviour of the World without fighting." Even the ashes of the Latin crusader kings of Jerusalem, Godfrey and Baldwin, had been removed and their tomb coverings destroyed by "devout members of the Greek Church."

Moving on to Bethlehem and the Church of the Nativity— which was "tricked out in the usual tasteless style"—Twain found that here, too, "the priests and members of the Greek and Latin Churches cannot come by the same corridor to kneel in the sacred birthplace of the Redeemer, but are compelled to approach and retire by different avenues, lest they quarrel and fight on this holiest ground on earth."

At the time Louis Napoleon came to power in France, Holy Russia—as the leading Orthodox power, successor to the vanished glories of Byzantium, and Turkey's close and menacing neighbor—had been able to ensure that its own party was dominant and the Orthodox clergy were in firm control of the Holy Places. From all over the vast Russian Empire, pilgrims would pour into the Holy Land at Christmas and Easter, "chanting their hymns, confessing their sins, trusting in the simple precepts of the gospel [and] kneeling before the shrine of the Redeemer." One authority calculated that of the four thousand pilgrims who came to Jerusalem at Christmas 1831, all but four were Orthodox.

The French at this period did not seem to care that their Catholic co-religionists had been all but excluded from Christendom's holiest shrines. France might claim to be "the oldest daughter of the Church," but the liberal ideas that accompanied the Revolution had muted the religious zeal of the majority of French people. Few Frenchmen can have been less zealous about their religion than their new head of state. But although he must have found the confessional controversies of the Holy Land absurd if not incomprehensible, he was too shrewd a politician not to appreciate the kudos to be earned by a intervention on behalf of Rome. This would improve his standing with the clericalists in France, whose continuing support he needed; it would also serve a foreign policy that required him to assert the renewal of French power and influence.

He was still President of the Republic when he first took up the cause of the Catholics in Palestine. The Turks, quite willing to play off France against Russia, quickly agreed to reestablish equal status between the Catholic and Orthodox clergy at the Holy Places. For the Orthodox hierarchy, this seemed an intolerable erosion of hard-won rights. For example, they alone held the key to the principal door of the Church of the Nativity. Would they now have to share it, allowing the despised Latins unhindered access to the Grotto of the Nativity?

They appealed to the czar, Nicholas I, to intervene, and he, rightly viewing the picayune argument over a church key as symbolic of something a good deal more significant, wrote to the Sultan Abdul Mejid in Constantinople to say that "no changes would be allowed to take place as to the possession of those sanctuaries." To underline the point, he deployed an entire army corps on the Turkish frontier.

In February 1853, Nicholas went a step further, demanding formal recognition by the Turks that he was the exclusive protector of Christians throughout the Ottoman Empire, and threatening to invade the Turkish-ruled Danubian principalities of Wallachia and Moldavia—present-day Rumania—if his demands were not met. Turkey appealed to France and its traditional ally Britain for help. The two powers, each with its separate motive for bolstering the Turks against the Russians, sent their navies to the Dardanelles.

Austria immediately took fright at the prospect of a major war at its back door and hurriedly suggested a four-power conference in Vienna to find a peaceful solution to the problem. If only for the sake of world opinion, France and Britain agreed to take part. Throughout the rest of 1853 and into the spring of 1854 the pot simmered as the diplomats tried and failed to reach a formula agreeable to all parties.

Before ever a shot was fired, the crisis brought Napoleon one significant bonus: friendship with Britain. With all the passion of the outsider who knows he is disdained and distrusted by his contemporaries, with all the longing of the rake and parvenu for acceptance by the secure and respectable, he coveted the regard of his cross-Channel neighbor. The grandeur and stability of the British monarchy impressed him profoundly and more than anything he longed for a state invitation from Queen Victoria. Now he began to hope that the "Eastern Question" might be the key to unlock the gates of Windsor Castle.

Pragmatic, Protestant Britain's concern over the Eastern Question had little to do with who was shouting down whom in the Holy Places of Palestine and everything to do with an obsession with the balance of power, a concept that dominated the diplomacy of the time. In particular, the British viewed Russia as a voraciously expansionist power and an ever-present threat to their land links with India. For this reason, it was a constant of Whig and Tory foreign policy alike to shore up the Muslim Ottomans and undermine the Christian Muscovites.

Thus, despite their suspicions of Napoleon, the British found common cause with France and, as the Eastern Question steadily drew France and England closer, Napoleon was delighted to find his stock rising among the British press and public. Gradually, the British set aside their reservations about anyone bearing the name Bonaparte and forgot their outrage over his illegal overthrow of the French Constitution, the massacre on the boulevards, and the repression which followed.

A wry observer of the burgeoning love affair between Victoria's Britain and Louis Napoleon's France was Henry Richard Charles Wellesley, the first Earl Cowley, who had been appointed British Ambassador to Paris shortly after Napoleon's December coup. There may have been an element of puckishness on the part of the Foreign Office in sending the nephew of Wellington to keep an eye on the nephew of Napoleon, but it was a shrewd choice nonetheless.

From the outset, Cowley was urged to provide London with more than the dry bones of formal diplomatic reportage. Though determined to keep the disreputable new ruler of France at arm's length, Victoria was perversely fascinated by him and eager for all the gossip about her fellow monarch. Thus, the British Foreign Secretary (and Napoleon's old acquaintance) Lord Malmesbury asked Cowley at the end of February 1852 to "do an agreeable thing to me and to a *much higher personage*" and "write me sometimes an amusing letter about the politics and gossip." Cowley was only too happy to oblige, and for the next fifteen years his wry personal letters to Malmesbury, Lord Clarendon, and other British foreign secretaries on the affairs—amatory as well as political—of the French court provide an unusually intimate running commentary on the life of the Second Empire.

The big question confronting Cowley and his government as he presented his credentials at the Tuileries was whether this new Napoleon would prove as dangerous to the tranquility of Europe as his name might suggest. There would be no simple answer. "To fathom the thoughts or divine the intentions of that one individual," Cowley wrote in one of his first dispatches, "would sorely try the powers of the most clear-sighted.

No one's advice seems to affect him. He appears to follow, unrestrained by any one of those outward influences to which other men are subject, the aim . . . which he has set up; and who can say to where or to what this pursuit may lead him?"

Cowley added the warning: "Satisfactory as present appearances are, it would be dangerous to trust too much to them . . . Europe should be prepared." A few days later Cowley was reporting that Napoleon's character seemed to him to be "a strange mixture of good and evil." Clearly perplexed, he went on: "Few approach him who are not charmed by his manners. The patience with which he listens to those who differ from him is remarkable. I am told that an angry word never escapes him. But there is a dark side to the picture in a revengeful disposition . . . and a general want of sympathy for the feelings and affections of others."

Cowley's perplexity about Napoleon's true nature and beliefs could only have been heightened by a comment which he learned the emperor had recently made to his ambassador to Vienna. "I do not like demagogues," Napoleon had said, "but I do like moderate liberals. Although I am absolute in France, I do not wish to see absolutism flourish. It was necessary in France, where half measures were no longer possible, but I have no wish to see such coups d'état tried in other countries."

Despite these early perplexities and reservations, which were never to be completely resolved, an unusually warm relationship was to develop between Cowley and Napoleon, and the latter would lose no opportunity to demonstrate his goodwill toward Britain and its representative. The first state ball of the Second Empire, for example, began with a quadrille of honor in which Napoleon took to the floor with Cowley's wife.

In the summer of 1853, Napoleon believed the time was ripe to convert the friendly sentiments of the British press and public into a royal invitation and began laying the groundwork by planting stories in the French press and circulating rumors to the effect that a state visit to Britain was in the offing. Cowley was puzzled; he knew nothing of any such invitation and asked Clarendon, the new Foreign Secretary, if he had any information. Clarendon, equally mystified, asked the queen, whereupon Victoria squelched the idea very firmly.

She and her beloved Albert still considered Napoleon a decidedly unsavory character—a smoker, a gambler, a drinker, and a lecher, with two bastard children and a string of mistresses. "There never was the *slightest* idea of inviting the Emperor of the French," she informed Clarendon, "and Lord Cowley should take care that it should be *clearly understood* that there was and would be no *intention* of the *kind*." As for the rumors in the French newspapers, "the Queen feels sure that the Emperor has had these reports put in himself."

Despite this rebuff, Napoleon continued to woo the British with undiminished ardor. Ignoring the snub, he enthused to Cowley, "I cannot say how glad I am to find myself acting cordially with England. I desire to do so on all questions, even if this crisis passes over." And when Morny, protecting his own somewhat dubious business interests in St. Petersburg, tried to caution him against linking up too closely with the British against Russia, the emperor replied: "I cannot separate from England because the Northern Courts do not care for me. Without England, therefore, I should find myself isolated in Europe."

Napoleon had another—if trivial—reason to want to help the British take the Russians down a notch or two. When he became emperor, the czar, alone among the monarchs of Europe, had refused to address him, as protocol demanded, as "Monsieur, mon frère."

True, Nicholas had approved of Napoleon's coup d'état and his stern treatment of the "Reds." True, Nicholas entertained no philosophical revulsion against military dictatorship and, indeed, was quite prepared to accept Napoleon as a lifetime emperor. But his firm belief that only God could ordain an imperial dynasty, such as his own, made it impossible for him to accept Napoleon as a brother. "An Emperor without Divine Right is not an Emperor," scoffed Nicholas. "He will be an Emperor in fact, but never an Emperor by right."

He therefore began his letter of recognition—fulsomely enough, one might have thought—by addressing Napoleon as "Most serene, most excellent, most powerful prince, our dear friend Napoleon, Emperor of the French." But "friend," instead of "brother"! There was enormous indignation at the Tuileries.

Napoleon did his best to pass the insult off lightly, joking that while a man could choose his friends he could not choose his brothers. But the affront rankled nonetheless.

Yet the czar's snub, Napoleon's longing for friendship with Britain, his concern for the balance of power, and his desire to consolidate his image as the defender of Catholicism, may have been only contributory factors. Perhaps "I must do something" was in the end the most imperative of the impulses that drove Napoleon down the road to war with Russia. The need to establish the Second Empire swiftly as a power on the world stage was compelling. So, no doubt, was the need to reward the army with the opportunity to acquire new glory and avenge old defeats.

Just the same, Napoleon vacillated. "There is no settled policy," Cowley fumed, "one day it is peace, the next war." Napoleon was aware that war would not be popular with the public at large and he was being powerfully persuaded against it by Morny, whom Cowley was convinced was in the pay of Russia. "Is the Emperor aware of what a rascal he is and how he would sell him any day that it suited his purpose?" Cowley wrote.

A taunting reference to the first Napoleon's retreat from Moscow, made by the czar while negotiations were still proceeding, may have tipped the balance. Nicholas warned that the French would find the Russia of 1854 as formidable as the Russia of 1812, and as Cowley reported to Clarendon in mid-March of 1854, Napoleon was "now anxious that the Tsar should be duly punished for his outrageous conduct."

By the end of that month France and Britain—together with the Kingdom of Piedmont-Sardinia, which had its own distinct motives for seeking the goodwill of the French—were at war with Russia "to defend the Sultan's cause, to protect the rights of the Christians, to defend the freedom of the seas and to preserve our rightful influence in the Mediterranean," as Napoleon told his rubber-stamp parliament.

Once the British and French armies had sailed for the Crimea, Napoleon's popularity took another quantum leap upward in Britain. The formerly hostile *Times* was now full of admiration for him, crude portraits of Napoleon and Eugénie were on display all over London, and in the streets and public houses barrel organs and pianos hammered out the strains of the *Marseillaise*, the British being happily unaware that Napoleon had banned that stirring but dangerously republican anthem in favor of his mother's *Partant pour la Syrie*.

But still the longed-for invitation never arrived: to Victoria and Albert, Napoleon remained "the Beelzebub of the Boulevards." As she told Clarendon when she gave grudging permission for her cousin, the Duke of Cambridge, to accept an invitation to stay with Napoleon and Eugénie, en route for the Crimea, "she cannot mix personal friendship with a political Alliance. The former is the result of the experience of years and cannot be carried by storm."

But the pressures were building up. By the time the war was six weeks old, Victoria grudgingly consented to appear at a costume ball given by Persigny, the French Ambassador, although she insisted on appearing, and that briefly, in an ordinary dinner gown instead of fancy dress. Not long afterward Albert, having received good reports about Napoleon from two confidential emissaries, the Duke of Cambridge and his cousin, Duke Ernst of Saxe-Coburg—both of them, incidentally, quite as dissolute as the emperor—cautiously accepted an invitation to meet Napoleon at Boulogne.

Napoleon was overcome with emotion on learning of the prince's acceptance. "Tears stood in His Majesty's eyes while he expressed the pleasure which he received from this fresh proof of the cordiality of the Alliance which England proffered him," Cowley informed Clarendon.

When the royal yacht berthed at Boulogne on the morning of September 4, Napoleon was on the quayside waiting to greet his guest. Cowley, who accompanied him, noted that it was the first time he had ever seen the emperor looking nervous. If Albert was nervous, too, at the prospect of close contact with the satanic Frenchman, he concealed it well under a cloak of condescension and, since Napoleon ignored or failed to notice this, the visit was cordial from the outset.

"Everything is going on admirably," Cowley reported at the end of the second day. "His Royal Highness appears to me to have rightly appreciated the Emperor's character, giving His Majesty credit for openness and sincerity in his language, but finding an extraordinary lack of knowledge on many subjects, though he does not want for penetration and reflection."

Napoleon's undoubted charm and his penchant for shameless flattery—not to mention his residual German accent—had a lot to do with breaking down Prince Albert's reservations. He let Albert do most of the talking during their long, earnest discussions of military and diplomatic matters, and Albert returned home after five days pleased to think that his visit had been "a source of very great satisfaction" to his host, while at the same time feeling that Napoleon's mind was an odd mixture of "very sound and many crude notions."

Napoleon expressed no such reservations about the intellectual capacity of his guest, making sure that Victoria learned via Cowley and Clarendon that "in all his experience he had never met with a person possessing such various and profound knowledge and who communicated it with the same frankness. . . . He had never learned so much in so short a time and was grateful."

By now Clarendon was converted to the idea that an official invitation to Napoleon and the daughter of his former mistress would be expedient, and advised the queen accordingly. Reassured by her consort's good report, Victoria at last agreed in principle, stressing however that she "would wish that no anxiety should be shown to obtain the visit" and that "his reception here ought to be a boon to him and not a boon to us."

But nothing happened until the spring of 1855 when Napoleon, intentionally or otherwise, forced the issue by announcing that he had decided to go to the Crimea to take personal charge of the war, which had degenerated into a stalemate that was draining the resources and undermining the morale of the Allies.

The British were horrified at the idea. Supposing Napoleon, who had no military experience beyond his training at the Swiss military academy, were to lead the Allied armies to a terrible defeat? Even worse, suppose he were to lead them to a brilliant victory? "This," said Victoria with remarkable candor, "we never could bear," and Clarendon was sent hot foot to Paris to take Napoleon's mind off such a foolhardy idea by offering him a state visit.

Napoleon accepted and the dates were set—April 16 to 21. Napoleon's ministers and courtiers were perhaps even more relieved than the British that he had dropped the idea of going to the Crimea, if only for the time being. The stability of the Empire had not yet been consolidated and they were terrified of a coup or a revolution taking place while the emperor was absent at the wars.

Fog in the English Channel delayed the arrival of Napoleon and Eugénie. When the French warship *Pelican* pulled alongside the quay at Dover four hours late, the red carpets and bunting lay sodden under a gray blanket of sea mist and Prince Albert was looking equally bedraggled. The queen had wisely remained at Windsor.

Napoleon stepped ashore resplendent in a general's uniform. Eugénie looked very much the Kirkpatrick as she followed him in a tartan dress and a feathered Highland cap. Albert took her arm and the royals went off to the Lord Warden Hotel for refreshments before starting the train journey to London. A second vessel containing mountains of imperial luggage and carrying a small army of their personal servants had still not berthed by the time the royal train pulled out of Dover.

It was dusk when the imperial visitors arrived at Windsor Castle, where Victoria was waiting impatiently to greet them. Her first impressions of her guests—jotted down in her journal that night—were that Napoleon was "extremely short," with "a head and bust that ought to belong to a much taller man," while Eugénie was "very gentle, very graceful and evidently very nervous."

There was nothing gentle, though a good deal that was nervous, about Eugénie's behavior in the presence of her maids and her ladies-in-waiting as dinner time neared and her clothes—and her personal coiffeur, Félix—had still not arrived from Dover. In desperation she finally borrowed a simple gray dress, trimmed with pink ribbon, from one of her *dames d'honneur* and disguised her lack of coiffe by adorning her head with a wreath of pink flowers, taken from a vase in her bedroom. Eugénie had dress sense to the point almost of genius and Victoria was utterly charmed by her guest's simplicity and lack of ostentation. Thanks to fog in the Channel the visit had got off to an excellent start.

Napoleon and Eugénie played their parts perfectly—he the charming, modest, good-natured statesman-king without a trace of the cad and Lothario his hosts had expected; she the submissive and self-effacing, yet lively and humorous, consort and not at all the hard-headed adventuress Victoria had been warned about.

He joked and played with the royal children, a figure of avuncular jollity, and beguiled Victoria, who found "great fascination in the quiet, frank manner" of the emperor. "His voice is soft and low," she noted, "and il ne fait pas de phrases." Though Eugénie, her wardrobe restored to her, wore elaborate crinolines and diamonds at night, she dressed modestly by day, wearing little makeup and drawing her glorious red-gold hair back into a severe bun. Her conversations with Victoria centered on the bearing and rearing of babies, and she went out of her way to express approval of the high moral tone of the English court. "The dear, sweet Empress," the queen thought, was "so gentle, graceful and kind, and so modest and retiring."

These qualities made as deep an impression on Albert as they did on Victoria. The righteous prince found Eugénie perfectly captivating and flirted with her in his elephantine fashion, watched fondly by Victoria, who knew he was far too repressed for such dalliance to be anything but entirely innocent. "I am delighted to see how much he likes and admires her," she noted in her journal, while Albert starchily assured his mentor Baron von Stockmar that "our relationship rests upon an honourable and moral basis."

But it was between Napoleon and Victoria that the really intense—though again totally incorporeal—love affair developed. For all her prudishness, Victoria was always attracted to dark, exotic men and in this sense Napoleon was the forerunner of her beloved prime-minister-to-be, Disraeli. The shrewd and worldly Clarendon, observing the by-play between the queen and the emperor, commented that Victoria was "mightily tickled by it, for she had never been made love to in her life . . . and as his love-making was of a character to flatter her vanity without alarming her virtue and modesty she enjoyed the novelty without scruple or fear."

On Albert, too, Napoleon exercised a sort of seduction. He went out of his way to praise all things British—"L'Angleterre, c'est admirable. What a difference in your country, where everything is so lasting and solid." He subtly appeared to be more German than French, more serious than pleasure-loving, and as at Boulogne he listened more than he talked and flattered Albert outrageously, ever the experienced, older man impressed by the range and vigor of the younger man's intellect.

For Napoleon, the high point of the visit came on the third night at Windsor when Victoria invested him with the Order of the Garter in the Throne Room. She wore the sumptuous Garter robes; he knelt before her in white silk stocking and tights, in which, however, an eyewitness said "he did not appear to advantage." The story goes that after he had received the Garter, Napoleon murmured to the queen: "Enfin, je suis gentilhomme." It may sound apposite enough, but it seems unlikely that the newly elevated emperor said any such thing. Certainly, Victoria makes no reference to such a remark in her own account of the event.

Two more days remained of the visit and these were spent in London, where they went to the Crystal Palace and the opera and attended a Guildhall banquet, cheered wherever they went by enormous crowds of Londoners, enthusiastic for their French ally and captivated by the beauty of his empress.

After her glamorous guests had departed and life had resumed its customary gray tone, Victoria experienced a keen sense of loss. "I cannot say why," she confided to her journal, "but their departure made me so melancholy. I was near crying. . . . This visit, this great event, has passed as, alas, everything does in this world. It is a dream, a brilliant successful and pleasant dream. . . . It went off so beautifully, not a hitch nor contretemps, fine weather, everything smiling; the nation enthusiastic and happy in the firm and intimate alliance of two great countries. . . ."

Napoleon and Eugénie were no sooner home than they began planning for the return visit of Victoria and her consort four months hence. The emperor finally abandoned his idea of going to the Crimea—if indeed he ever seriously intended it—and threw himself into two pet domestic projects: the Universal Exposition which would trumpet the technological, artistic, and industrial achievements of the renascent Empire, and the rebuilding of Paris according to a master plan worked out by Napoleon and his protégé, Baron Georges Haussmann. France might be at war, and that war bogged down in bloody stalemate, but Napoleon was determined that the world should see that it had the wealth, vigor, and confidence to fight and build at the same time.

There was one unpleasant distraction: another assassination attempt by an Italian revolutionary, this time a man named Giovanni Pianori who fired two shots at Napoleon as he rode in the Bois de Boulogne. Napoleon was unhurt but Pianori, one of the Redshirts who had fought under Garibaldi against the French Army before Rome, was captured. Napoleon's betrayal of the Italian revolution he had espoused as a youth continued to be a source of danger to him and his empress.

But by the time Victoria and Albert arrived on August 18, Pianori had been tried, convicted, and guillotined, the exhibition had opened on schedule and was packing in record crowds from around the world, and the transformation of Paris was well in hand. The medieval slums had been cleared from around Notre Dame; the Palais de Justice and the Louvre had been completed; the Sainte-Chapelle had been restored; the Bois de Boulogne—once a haunt of thieves and footpads—had been tamed and prettified with ornamental gardens. Paris had never looked more impressive.

When Victoria stepped ashore at Boulogne to be greeted by Napoleon, she was the first reigning British monarch to visit France since Henry VI had come to Paris in 1431. She and Albert were accompanied by their two oldest children, fourteen-year-old Bertie, the Prince of Wales, and fifteen-year-old Vickie, the Princess Royal. For Bertie, at least, it was to be the start of a lifelong love affair with *la belle France*.

The master showman Napoleon had pulled out all the stops for this occasion. There were wild scenes of welcome at Boulogne where the route from the quayside to the railway station was lined with no fewer than 40,000 troops. The station was pure, Gallic pandemonium. Said Lady Augusta Bruce: "The confusion about luggage and attendance was quite beyond description."

Though enthusiastic about the visit, the crowds at the station were somewhat condescending over the appearance of the British queen, who clearly would not be able to hold a candle to their empress when it came to looks and style. Victoria wore a plain straw bonnet, held a green parasol, and clutched a huge handbag, embroidered with a parrot, which had been made by one of her children. The August sun beat down relentlessly and, noted Lady Augusta, "Her Majesty was not merely red but purple from the broiling heat."

The ladies-in-waiting, if not the queen herself, could clearly hear some of the comments of the crowd which clustered around as they boarded the train—"She looks nice enough, but beautiful? My God no!" and, "What a little bit of a woman!"

Cheering, waving people lined the track for much of the way to Paris, with stops for speeches and presentations at Abbeville and Amiens. In Paris, 100,000 troops and 800,000 civilians were waiting to greet the visitors, who drove in state from the Terminus de Strasbourg (now the Gare de l'Est) to the Palace of Saint-Cloud via the new Boulevard de Strasbourg, the Place de la Concorde, the Champs-Elysées, the Arc de Triomphe, and the Bois.

The cannons of the Invalides crashed out royal and imperial salutes, the crowds roared "Vive la Reine Anglaise!" and the whole city seemed transformed into a vast and splendid stage set—flags, banners, oriflammes, columns, arches and eagles and crowns and even a banner celebrating the glories of British beer: "Vive le vin de l'Ale!"

Eugénie, who was happily three months pregnant, was waiting for Victoria and Albert on the palace steps, lined with cuirassiers of the Cent Gardes in their magnificent sky blue uniforms and silver breastplates. The empress embraced her guests and their children with great warmth. The British royals responded with equal fervor.

The royal visitors' quarters—Marie Antoinette's suite, which Eugénie had relinquished for the occasion—had been extensively refurbished. In her determination to see that everything was comme il faut, Eugénie had even ordered the legs of a priceless antique table to be sawn short for the convenience of the diminutive Victoria. The queen's bedroom had been decorated and furnished to resemble the one she had left behind at Buckingham Palace. "I feel so at home," she told Napoleon.

While the arrangements for the principal guests were impeccable, all was not so smooth so far as Victoria's laides-in-waiting were concerned. Utter confusion reigned in the quarters to which they were assigned, mainly because of the absence of locks on the bedroom doors. Footmen and other male servants, consumed with prurient curiosity, kept barging in without knocking just as the prim English ladies were dressing, undressing, or bathing.

Lady Augusta describes in her diary how their frantic cries of "N'entrez pas, n'entrez pas!" were simply ignored and how she would sit in her bath, eyes glued to the door handle in case it should begin to turn.

Such elements of farce extended also to the dining room, if Lady Augusta's account is to be believed. All went smoothly at Her Majesty's end of the table, but at the other end where her ladies sat there were scenes of bizarre ineptitude—truffles served by hand, thumbs in the soup, sauces spilled over expensive gowns, wine slopped onto the tablecloth, and footmen constantly bumping into one another, with dire consequences.

Because of her condition and her fear of another miscarriage, Eugénie spent much of the visit in her quarters. Some unkind souls felt this was a stroke of luck for the dowdy English queen, who would not be damaged by the comparison between her appearance and that of her hostess. "How fortunate that the Empress should be unable to accompany the Queen everywhere," Marion Ellice wrote to Lady de Rothschild in London, for Eugénie was "so beautiful and so graceful." In another dispatch Miss Ellice was scathing about one of the royal hats: "an abominable white bonnet, with big white feathers of the most ungraceful description."

Even General Canrobert, just back from the Crimea, was amazed by Victoria's "shocking toilette," her cavernous handbags, low-heeled pumps, and crude, uncoordinated colors. Oblivious of such criticism, Victoria was happy to have the seductive Napoleon so often to herself (Albert, feeling something of an odd man out, frequently going on his own to visit the Exposition, museums, art galleries, and other improving places). "I felt—I do not know how to express it—safe with him," Victoria confided to her journal. "His society is particularly agreeable and pleasant; there is something fascinating, melancholy and engaging which draws you to him. . . . Without any personal attraction in outward appearance, he has a power of attaching those to him who come near him which is quite incredible."

For young Bertie, too, Napoleon was a mesmerically attractive figure, so different from his moralistic and constantly disapproving father that he blurted out, "I wish I were your son," as the two of them rode together in a carriage along the boulevards one afternoon. Similarly, young Vicky developed a girlish crush on Eugénie, so that when the time came to leave she burst into floods of tears while her brother begged to be allowed to stay.

The only clouds over the visit, and those small ones, were cast by members of Napoleon's own family, Mathilde, Plon-Plon, and Jérôme. Napoleon had no illusions about them and had told Cowley in advance that he wished to make Victoria's visit "more agreeable by bringing Her Majesty into as little contact as possible" with them. Clarendon, who accompanied the royal party, referred to Plon-Plon and his sister as "the assassin and the cook," but contact could not be entirely avoided.

Plon-Plon was, after all, president of the Universal Exposition and so the honor fell to him of showing the queen around the vast Palais de l'Industrie in the Champs-Elysées and the equally enormous, glass-roofed Palais des Beaux-Arts in the Avenue Montaigne. Victoria found him "rude and disagreeable in the highest degree. Il me fait peur and he has a diabolical expression . . . disagreeable and biting . . . with a smile that is quite satanic." And again, even when she invested Plon-Plon with the Order of Bath before leaving, he was "rude and disagreeable in the highest degree."

Mathilde was not disagreeable, but the very fact of her open cohabitation with Nieuwekercke made it something of an ordeal for Victoria to have to meet her. Nonetheless, the little queen bravely overcame her scruples and bussed the convention-breaking princess on both cheeks.

As for Uncle Jérôme, he made a silly fuss over protocol, claiming precedence over Albert who, not yet officially Prince Consort, was a mere princeling in his own right. When he failed to get his way, Jérôme went off in a huff to Le Havre, returning only on the last day of the visit to say his farewells—and then insisting that Napoleon reimburse his traveling expenses. Noted Viel Castel: "The old wretch does nothing without a bribe and, like a cabman, must be paid according to the distance."*

As they bade farewell on August 27, the queen gave last-minute instructions and advice to Eugénie—"such a dear, sweet, engaging and distinguished being"—on her forthcoming confinement, while Napoleon accompanied the British royals by rail to Boulogne and then some way out to sea before transferring to his own yacht and returning.

Once again, for Victoria, a bright and beautiful interlude was over. "That night when we left I felt so unhappy," she wrote to Lady Cowley on her return to Windsor. "It was with a heavy heart that I lay down in my cabin. . . . Now that those bright days are past, they seem to be only a vision or a dream, so lovely that we can scarcely believe it."

---

*Viel Castel was far from being alone in his low opinion of Jérôme. While the ex-king lay dying in 1860, the court was "engaged with all sorts of gaieties . . . with complete want of decency," according to Cowley, and at his funeral, "all Paris was on foot as on a fête day . . . people were asking where the fireworks were to take place [and] no sort of sympathy was shown by any class."

13

AN HEIR
FOR THE
EMPIRE

ON DECEMBER 29, 1855, NAPOLEON RODE OUT to meet his Imperial Guard, newly returned from Russia and reeking of blood and glory. They had achieved a victory that raised their emperor to a pinnacle of prestige and power—the storming of the Malakoff Fortress, which led to the fall of Sebastopol and the virtual end of the Crimean War.

The French assault had succeeded where a simultaneous British attack on the nearby Redan Fortress had failed, giving Napoleon, despite his warm feelings toward his ally, all the more reason for pride and gratification.

The Roman triumph he arranged for the Imperial Guards' return was one of those superbly theatrical state occasions at which Napoleon excelled. He rode out from the Tuileries on a magnificent bay charger, adorned with rich housings, conscious as always that he cut a heroic figure on horseback if not on foot.

Scorning the assassin's bomb or bullet, he insisted on remaining several lengths ahead of his escort of cuirassiers and Cent Gardes, so that—as the *Times* correspondent observed—"his worst enemy must have avowed that he became his place and that he looked the Emperor."

In the Place de la Bastille the serried ranks of the Imperial Guard and the 20th, 50th, and 70th Regiments of the Line awaited him. As Napoleon rode up to inspect them, the veterans of the Crimea raised their kepis on the tips of their bayonets and roared: "Vive l'Empereur!" After a brief and emotional speech in which he told his men that their exploits had "won for France the rank that is her due," Napoleon led the battle-stained veterans back through the heart of his capital to the Place Vendôme, past crowds even bigger and more ecstatic than those who had turned out to welcome "la Reine Anglaise."

Preceded, as *The Times* said, "by such of the wounded as were able to walk," the Foot Chausseurs, the Zouaves, the Voltigeurs, the Grenadiers, the Artillery, and the Engineers of the Guard swaggered by—regiments whose names breathed the martial poetry of Napoleonic France. Paris quivered, cheered, and wept with patriotic pride to see "those worn uniforms, the flags torn to ribands, the eagles here and there perforated with Russian bullets." But beneath the martial fervor France, like its emperor, had had its fill of war for the time being.

The Allied and Russian armies remained facing each other in the Crimean peninsula. The British government and people were keen to continue the fight, if only to wipe out the humiliation of Redan; but Napoleon wanted out. He had achieved his objectives—Czar Nicholas had been humbled (and was now succeeded by his more tractable son, Alexander II), the Second Empire had been established as a world power, and the French Army's thirst for battle honors had been temporarily slaked.

More practically, the war was becoming extremely expensive and, if allowed to drag on any longer, would soon become extremely unpopular with the French people, who in any case had never been so keen on it as the British. As Clarendon observed, "a termination of the war would be as popular in France as it would be unpopular here . . . Louis Napoleon would be applauded for [ending] it and we stoned."

Two months after the Imperial Guard's return, following an Austrian threat to join the war on the side of the Allies, the Russians agreed to an armistice and peace talks opened in Vienna. After some weeks of haggling the broad outlines of a treaty were fashioned and a Peace Congress convened in Paris, at which the details were to be finalized and the war formally ended.

But there was still some distance to travel, for the British were determined to wring as much benefit as possible out of their dubious victory while the Russians were determined to yield as little as they might. In this situation Napoleon, more anxious than the British for peace and good relations with Russia, played the backstage mediator rather than the victorious belligerent, telling the Russians they must give ground on this point and the British that they must relent on that.

As the peace conference dragged on, the time drew near for Eugénie's confinement and the French people and their emperor began to be just as much concerned with what kind of child she would produce as with what kind of treaty would emerge from the Congress. Eugénie was still not widely popular with the French public, who continued to call her somewhat dismissively "l'Espagnole." But if she were to produce the longed-for male heir her stock would certainly climb.

Yet even now, while he waited anxiously for a male heir to be produced and worried over the details of the peace settlement that threatened a rift between him and his British Allies, Napoleon could not resist the opportunity for a little low adventure. As Cowley reported: "All Paris is en émoi [aflutter] at an escapade of the Emperor, who took it into his head to go masked to a ball at Madame Le Hon's on Mardi Gras. I cannot say how much I regret it, for it has diminished the respect which I unfeignedly felt for him. He was by way of being incognito, but of course the secret was not kept, and as one might as well go to a brothel as that house. . . . I leave you to guess all that is said."

In the small hours of March 15, Eugénie's long and painful labor began and Napoleon, recalled to his domestic responsibilities, commenced his vigil in an adjoining room. As the hours passed and his wife's cries echoed through the gas-lit corridors of the Tuileries, the perhaps remorseful emperor became distraught, ordering the doctors to "use any palliative or sedative which modern science has devised" to ease her agony. During the day extra specialists were called in, one of whom told Napoleon the birth was likely to be so difficult that either the mother or child might die. Napoleon gave instructions that Eugénie, rather than the child, must be saved if it came to a choice.

According to tradition and recent legislation, ministers and members of the imperial family had to be on hand to witness the birth. Among these were Plon-Plon, not at all pleased at the prospect of being supplanted as heir to the throne. He sat scowling in an anteroom while Napoleon paced up and down, now holding his head in his hands, now drumming his fingers on the window pane.

When the time came and the accoucheurs were ready to apply their instruments, Napoleon and the official witnesses filed into the bedroom. According to one account, Plon-Plon glowered so balefully at Eugénie through his monocle that "the course of nature, to the violent torture of the poor woman, was again suspended." Finally, at three-fifteen in the morning and after twenty-two hours of labor, the child was delivered and displayed to the father and assembled witnesses around the bed.

Eugénie, drained and exhausted, murmured, "Is it a boy?" Napoleon, still distraught, replied, "No."

"Is it a girl?"

"No."

Eugénie was not too weak to display some of her customary fire. "Then what on earth is it?" she demanded.

Napoleon suddenly realized that the ordeal was over and that he had a male heir at last. He ran into the anteroom and kissed the first person he met, who happened to be a chambermaid bringing in more boiling water. In his joy, Napoleon ordered a proclamation that he and Eugénie would be godparents to every French child born in wedlock that day.

At dawn, the cannons of the Invalides began firing an imperial salute to mark the birth. Parisians, knowing that a girl would rate twenty-one guns and a boy 101, waited until they counted the twenty-second bang before applauding "the Spaniard" for giving their emperor, and France, a son.

After the birth the official witnesses had to sign the registry, confirming that they had seen the child delivered. At first the petulant Plon-Plon refused to do so. His sister Mathilde had to drag him to the book and force the pen into his hand. "Idiot," she hissed. "Do you think that by not signing you can return the child to the womb?" With ill grace, Plon-Plon did what he must, wielding the pen so angrily that he left a large blot by his name.

Within a few hours, the "Child of France" had been baptized

Napoleon Eugène Louis Jean Joseph, with the Pope as his god-father, and put on display to the elite of the Empire and the visiting delegates to the peace conference, lying in an enormous boat-shaped cradle and wearing the Legion of Honor around his neck. Clarendon, one of those who came to view the little Prince Imperial and convey Queen Victoria's congratulations, reported back that "the Emperor is enchanted with his son, dying for peace [and] does not care sixpence for the terms."*

Although the hoi-polloi could not be allowed into the palace to view the new heir to the throne, Napoleon made an exception for a delegation of market women from Les Halles who turned up with a huge bouquet. He led them personally into the empress's apartments where they cooed and clucked over the little prince. After being on display all day, the baby was handed over to the care of Miss Shaw, the English nanny sent by Queen Victoria, and the fat, jolly peasant woman from Burgundy who was to be his wet nurse.

Eugénie, physically and emotionally devastated by her suffer-ings, was so weak that it was two months before she could walk. In May, she was told by her physicians that she would repeat the experience of childbirth only at the risk of her life. This gave her all the justification she needed to banish the em-peror from her bed forever. To Mérimée, she confided: "There is now no longer any Ugénie"—Napoleon's way of pronouncing her name, which greatly irritated her—"there is only the Em-press."

This was not an inconsolable deprivation for Napoleon. His wife had, after all, given him the son he wanted; he prized do-mestic peace, and a platonic relationship might be a good deal more tranquil than what had gone before. As for sex, Napoleon had and would continue to have his "little diversions"—these despite the somber findings of an eminent British physician who arrived from London that summer to examine him and his wife.

Dr. William Fergusson of King's College Hospital, London, had been called in by Napoleon's personal physician, Conneau,

---

*Those terms, which were signed a fortnight after the baby's birth, forced Russia to demilitarize the Black Sea and cede southern Bessarabia to the Turks. The Turks were also guaranteed the protection of the other powers against Russia and admitted to the Concert of Europe.

but with a fine disregard for the principle of doctor-patient confidentiality, he had leaked his diagnoses to the British Embassy. Napoleon, now forty-eight, seemed to be suffering from "neuralgia, sciatica, dyspepsia, fatigue, irritability, insomnia, contraction of the fingers, loss of appetite and decline in sexual potency."

"The political results of this may be fearful and we may soon have to make great allowances for physical infirmity," Cowley reported to Clarendon. But whatever his reaction to the rest of Fergusson's catalogue of imperial ailments, Cowley must have been surprised by the last item, for—in his own phrase—Napoleon was at this point once more "going it" with a woman, and again the affair was the talk of the haut monde.

The emperor's new paramour was Virginie, comtesse di Castiglione, not yet nineteen years old, but reputed to be "the most beautiful woman in Europe." She seems also to have been among the most self-centered, calculating, and stupid.

She had been brought to Paris in January 1856 by her cousin, the Piedmontese prime minister Count Camillo Cavour, who was leading his country's delegation to the Peace Congress. That Congress was primarily concerned with a solution to the Eastern Question, but Cavour hoped it might also advance the cause of Italian freedom and unification. This meant wringing concessions from Austria, another participant in the Congress, and little Piedmont could only hope to do that through the French. That was why Cavour and King Victor Emmanuel had committed Piedmontese troops to the Crimean campaign and why, knowing Napoleon's susceptibility, Cavour had brought along his luscious cousin.

"I have enrolled the beauteous countess in the diplomatic service of Piedmont," he advised his foreign ministry in Turin. "I have invited her to flirt with and if necessary seduce the Emperor." To la Castiglione he said simply: "Succeed, my cousin, by any methods you like, only succeed!" Young as she was, Virginie was already experienced in the ways of randy royalty, having dallied the year before with her own monarch. As for the presence of Virginie's young husband in Paris, this was rightly considered to be no obstacle to her mission. "I am a model husband," Francesco di Castiglione told Princess Mathilde. "I never see or hear anything."

The beautiful Florentine first caught Napoleon's ever-roving eye at one of Mathilde's soirées in early January. When she was presented to him, he twirled the waxed ends of his mustache appreciatively and attempted to engage her in small talk. But Virginie seemed to be tongue-tied in the presence of such awesome imperial power and Napoleon remarked afterward: "She is beautiful, but doesn't seem to have much spirit."

She was better prepared for their next encounter, which occurred a few nights later at Plon-Plon's mansion on the Champs-Elysées. Arriving at midnight to attend a party, she met the emperor on the staircase just as he was leaving. "You are arriving rather late, madame," said Napoleon. "It is you, sire, who is leaving early," she replied pertly, and he smiled as he passed on. Later, he instructed Bacciochi to put the name of the beautiful young countess on his special invitation list.

Their third encounter came a week or so later when Virginie and her husband were invited to a ball at the Tuileries. She arrived in a shimmering silver-blue gown and all eyes were upon her as she advanced to be presented to the emperor and empress. Courtiers attuned to every nuance of imperial behavior noticed the signs of special interest displayed by Napoleon. So, no doubt, did Eugénie, and later that evening tongues were set wagging when the emperor sought out la Castiglione for a private tête-à-tête.

She and Napoleon had their next encounter at a costume ball given by the Foreign Minister in mid-February. Eugénie, heavy with child at the time and extremely irritable, watched Virginie's entrance on the arm of an elderly dandy with considerable displeasure. La Castiglione was dressed as the Queen of Hearts, but looked little like the prim figure on the playing card.

Napoleon's cousin, Princess Caroline Murat, would recall that the costume was "exceedingly décolleté," and "entirely open at the sides from the hips downwards. She wore her hair flowing loose over her neck and shoulders. Her conspicuous ornaments were crimson hearts thrown as it were at random upon the dress, some in positions that were decidedly unexpected. The Empress, congratulating her upon her achievement, added, looking at one of the symbols which was particularly conspicuous, 'But your heart seems a little low down.'"

On the occasion of another carnival ball, la Castiglione "startled the company by coming as Salambo in a costume of transparent gossamer, her bosom and ankles as bare as her beautiful arms, of which she was excusably proud."

Princess Pauline von Metternich was no less admiring than Princess Caroline, finding herself "rooted to the spot before this miracle of beauty." La Castiglione's figure, she said, "was that of a nymph. Her throat, her shoulders, her arms, her hands . . . seemed as if sculpted from pink marble. Her cleavage, however excessive, did not seem improper, for this superb creature resembled a classical statue."

With almost excessive enthusiasm, Princess Metternich went on to describe la Castiglione's face—"a delicious oval, her eyes dark green and velvety, surmounted by brows that could have been traced by a miniaturist's pencil, her small nose . . . obstinate, yet absolutely regular, her teeth like pearls." She summed up: "In a word, Venus descended from Olympus. Never have I seen such beauty, never will I see its like!"

Viel Castel, too, was waspishly appreciative of la Castiglione's beauty. "She bore the burden of her beauty with insolence," he confided to his Journal, "and displayed it with effrontery." He was particularly taken by her "truly admirable" bosom, which was "enveloped in a zephyr gauze, the eye following the contours to the last detail." Her breasts, he said, "seemed to throw out a challenge to all women."

In short, in a milieu replete with seductive women, la Castiglione had become, virtually overnight, the rage of Paris, and this could hardly fail to go to the head of a none too reflective girl of nineteen. Visiting a friend who had just given birth to a son, she picked the baby up, kissed it, and said to the mother: "When he grows up, tell him he had his first kiss from the most beautiful woman of the century." Pauline Metternich, among others, quickly found her conceit hard to stomach. "Every movement, every gesture was studied," she observed, and "she began to get on one's nerves." But as far as men were concerned, "what virtue would have been required to resist her," as Napoleon's cousin, the comtesse Tascher de la Pagerie, exclaimed.

Napoleon, of course, was without such virtue. And for all that his sexual powers were supposedly waning, Cowley was complaining to London within a month of Virginie's arrival that the emperor was "so much engrossed and occupied with the beauteous Castiglione" that it was difficult to get an appointment. "It will do his nerves no good," added the ambassador.

Alas, the affair did Cavour's cause no good, either. The Peace Congress ended without producing any of the benefits he had hoped for. But the Piedmontese prime minister knew that Italy continued to concern Napoleon, so he left Virginie in Paris to continue her mission.

Napoleon remained obsessed. Eugénie, of course, knew what was going on but suppressed her outrage, though her self-control must have been stretched to breaking point when word got back to her that la Castiglione had said to a mutual acquaintance: "My mother was a fool. If she had brought me to France before I married there would have been not a Spaniard but an Italian in the Tuileries."

For all the rage and humiliation she must have felt, the empress managed to appear serene and dignified when she and Napoleon went together to Notre Dame on June 14 for the public baptism of their son. For various reasons, Napoleon had been forced to abandon his plans for a spectacular coronation, performed by the Pope, but the baptism, as he told Eugénie, would do just as well.

It was a perfect summer's day and the sun seemed to shine especially for the Second Empire. The theaters of Paris gave free admission, at night the city sparkled with lights like a gigantic tray of diamonds, the people danced and romanced in the streets, and the parks, and multicolored rockets zoomed aloft from the Place de la Concorde. Again this emperor, who seemingly could not put a foot wrong, had given the common people a day to remember.

But to the uncommon people of the court and the fashionable faubourgs, the talk continued to be more of the emperor's raging infatuation for la Castiglione. "Even the court entourage," wrote Cowley,

> talk of a fête champêtre the other night at Villeneuve-l'Etang where a few select were alone invited and where His Majesty

rowed the said lady in a small boat alone and then disappeared with her in certain dark walks during the whole of the evening.

The poor empress was in a sad state—got excited and began to dance, when not being sufficiently strong she fell very heavily. It was a regular orgy, the men dancing with their hats on. All this is very sad. It does the Emperor an infinity of harm, politically speaking. . . .

As the affair progressed Eugénie, angry, humiliated, and bitterly aware that she could do nothing to stop it, was reduced to sniping at la Castiglione from the flank. On one occasion when the countess turned up at a palace ball wearing a dress that was extreme even by her standards, Eugénie sent her home with tart instructions to change into something more suitable. Napoleon remained enthralled. Nothing la Castiglione could do or say was outrageous enough to dampen his ardor. By January of 1857, Cowley was advising the Foreign Office that he was visiting her every night, a state of affairs which the ambassador lamented could be of no benefit to the emperor "either mentally or physically."

Certainly Napoleon could have derived no mental stimulation from the affair. Indeed, he told his cousin Mathilde that la Castiglione was "very beautiful, but she bores me to death." And at the end of April 1857, an event occurred which convinced Napoleon that he must end the affair.

He was leaving la Castiglione's mansion on the Avenue Montaigne in the small hours of the morning when two men emerged from the shadows and leaped onto his coach, while a third grabbed the harness of the lead horse and brought it to a halt. The three desperados quite clearly had murder in mind, but with great courage Napoleon's coachman laid about him with his whip, shouting and urging the horses on and scattering the assailants.

When the police caught up with the murderous trio, a few hours later, they were found once again to be Italians, two of them hired killers and the third an agent of Mazzini. Although there was absolutely no suggestion that la Castiglione was in league with them, the implications were clear: she was a lightning conductor and the affair a potential threat to the life of the emperor.

Morny, Persigny, Maupas, and other highly placed confidential advisers urged him to send her away and end the affair immediately. Napoleon was reluctant and dragged things on until August when suddenly—just before the three would-be assassins went on trial—she packed and left for London, while the emperor went off to take the waters at Plombières.

It was the end of the liaison and la Castiglione had nothing to show for it but a parting present from Napoleon, "an emerald worth 100,000 francs, the most beautiful in the world." The expenses of the affair—the clothes, the carriages, the coiffures, the servants, the rent of the mansion on the Avenue Montaigne—had eaten up her husband's modest fortune and he had finally left her. As she packed her trunks, the twenty-year-old countess confided to her journal: "I have hardly commenced my life and my role is already finished."

14

THE BOMBS OF ORSINI

ONE JANUARY DAY IN 1858, Napoleon was entertaining an official guest, Duke Ernst of Saxe-Coburg. As he proudly displayed the sights of his reconstructed capital, the conversation turned to assassination. "I fear only the dagger," said Napoleon. "In all other cases the criminal hopes to save himself by flight and that paralyzes his arm."

Having survived three assassination attempts already, Napoleon felt himself something of an expert on the subject, but he could scarcely have imagined that a spectacular fourth attempt was only hours away. As he spoke a small group of Italian terrorists, led by one Felice Orsini, was meeting in a seedy hotel in the rue Montmartre to finalize plans to kill him as he and Eugénie arrived at the opera for a gala performance that night.

Orsini was the Abu Nidal of his day, the most extreme of Italian radicals, a man with the skill, daring, and ruthlessness to perform the most outrageous crimes in pursuit of his political aims. He disdained his fellow revolutionary and exile Mazzini as a moderate whose men had bungled the attempts already made on Napoleon's life. Orsini was determined to succeed where his rival had failed.

It was not just a matter of exacting revenge for Napoleon's perceived betrayal of the Italian cause. Like the most extreme

Palestinian nationalists of today, Orsini believed his country's liberation was bound up with global revolution. He saw Napoleon's regime as the keystone of European imperialism and suppression. According to this rationale, one had only to remove him, in as spectacular a fashion as possible, and the whole edifice might collapse, allowing subject people everywhere to gain their freedom.

It was a simplistic view, which completely ignored Napoleon's undoubtedly sincere, if muddled, attachment to the principle of nationalities and his relatively liberal outlook by comparison with that of the older-established continental monarchies. The Emperor of Austria or the Czar of Russia might have seemed more logical targets, but revolutionary radicals like Orsini—as they do to this day—tend to find moderate rulers more tempting targets than outright reactionaries.

Orsini had been a leading figure in Mazzini's ill-fated Roman Republic and had spent five years in an Austrian prison before escaping to England, traditional haven for political refugees. An explosives expert, he had designed the bombs that were intended to kill Napoleon and Eugénie—fragmentation grenades packed with the most powerful explosive of the day, fulminate of mercury—and had personally smuggled them into France, via Belgium.

In Paris he had linked up with three other Italians from England, named Rudio, Gomez, and Pieri, and they had spent the past week or so observing their intended victim. Orsini had trailed the well-escorted emperor as he rode in the Bois; the others had stood in the crowds, cheering as he entered and left the Tuileries, soaking in all the details of his security arrangements. They decided to strike as the emperor and empress arrived at the opera on January 14.

A little before 8:00 P.M. Napoleon and Eugénie left the Tuileries in their state berlin, accompanied by Napoleon's aide-de-camp, General Rouguet, and escorted by a troop of lancers of the Imperial Guard, with mounted officers riding to the left and right of their carriage.

Inside the foyer of the opera house on the rue Lepelletier, Napoleon's master of ceremonies, Fleury, waited with Duke Ernst and directors of the opera for the arrival of the imperial couple; in the auditorium sat the white-tied and bejeweled social elite of the Empire.

On the sidewalk outside, crowds waited for a glimpse of the emperor and empress, among them the four conspirators. Orsini, Gomez, and Rudio stood in the entrance to a covered walkway running alongside the opera house and connecting with the Boulevard des Italiens; Pieri was submerged in the crowd some yards away in the rue Lepelletier. At that moment an off-duty police inspector spotted Pieri, recognized him as a wanted man, snapped handcuffs on him before he could take evasive action, and led him off to a nearby police station for interrogation.

Minutes later, the imperial escort clattered into view, pennants bobbing and breastplates gleaming in the gaslight. The emperor's coach pulled up alongside the red-carpeted entrance to the opera house and Napoleon and Eugénie prepared to alight. At that moment a spectator saw something he thought was a bouquet sail through the air toward the coach. It was the first bomb, thrown by Gomez.

It landed wide of the mark, exploding with tremendous force among a group of lancers, scattering men and horses in all directions. The second bomb, thrown by Rudio, landed closer to the target, causing further mayhem to men and mounts, and spewing lethal fragments of metal into the crowd.

Orsini threw the third bomb, which exploded right underneath the coach. Its force was so great that it brought down the huge chandelier inside the opera foyer. But paradoxically it caused only minor injury inside the berlin; the shock wave traveled outward rather than upward and few of the fragments penetrated the coachwork.

A policeman rushed forward to wrench open the door of the coach. Rouguet emerged first, bloodied by a superficial neck wound. Then Napoleon stepped down, his hat pierced by splinters and his nose superficially cut by a piece of flying glass. He turned to hand down Eugénie, who had escaped with nothing worse than a grazed cheek, though her white evening dress was spattered with Rouguet's blood.

The scene around them was pandemonium, the screams of wounded and dying soldiers and civilians mingling with those of the maimed and butchered horses, the air heavy with the stench of blood, fear, and smoke. But Napoleon and Eugénie were in that state of calm which often obtains before shock sets in.

The emperor's first instinct on finding himself and his wife unscathed was to go and comfort the wounded. Eugénie was more practical. "Don't be a fool," she was heard to say. "There's been enough stupidity already." And, holding him firmly by the arm, she crunched across the debris and broken glass into the foyer, surrounded by policemen looking nervously about them for signs of a further attack. The blast and the razor-sharp fragments of Orsini's bombs had killed eight people and injured 156, of whom three were blinded and at least a dozen more permanently crippled.

As Napoleon and Eugénie entered the auditorium, the orchestra struck up *Partant pour la Syrie* and the audience rose to its feet with a roar of applause. During intervals in the program a stream of notables entered the imperial box to offer felicitations on their escape.

When the Paris prefect of police, Pierre Piétri, came to do the same, Napoleon remarked sarcastically: "Your men have covered themselves with glory!" The criticism was well deserved. It transpired later that the French police had been given ample warning by their British counterparts that a group of well-known Italian revolutionaries had crossed the Channel. However, the police made up for their lapse by making Pieri talk, which enabled them to round up Orsini and his accomplices without delay.

Both Napoleon and Eugénie had behaved characteristically— and courageously—in the moments after the bombing, he with kindliness by thinking first of the wounded, she showing her sterner character by thinking first of duty and the need to show themselves to the white-tie audience. Later, as they returned to the Tuileries at midnight, huge crowds lined the streets to demonstrate relief and joy at their escape.

"L'Espagnole," until then so little liked, was the heroine of the hour. When she lowered the carriage window, showing her splendid shoulders and décolletage and waving a white handkerchief to the crowd, the cries of "Vive l'Impératrice!" were for once even more enthusiastic than those of "Vive l'Empereur!"

Within a day or two Eugénie was showing another side of her character, telling Hübner that she had seen men brandishing daggers surrounding the carriage. Even more improbably, she told Mérimée that in the chaos and confusion after she stepped from the carriage a workman had rushed up to her and kissed her bare shoulder.

One immediate consequence of the attempt on Napoleon's life was a drastic heightening of the police state aspects of his regime. The Interior Minister was fired over the security lapse that had made the bomb outrage possible and replaced by the hard-line General Espinasse, who declared: "It is time for the good to be reassured and for the wicked to tremble."

True to his promise, Espinasse rapidly brought in or reactivated a series of administrative and legislative measures that suppressed newspapers, increased penalties for "subversive" talk, and led to the deportation, without trial or even charge, of hundreds of radicals and socialists to Algeria or Cayenne, in the West Indies.

At the same time, relations with Britain took a drastic downturn in reaction to the disclosure that the would-be assassins had mounted their attempt from across the Channel. England was denounced in the government-controlled press as "a nest of vipers" and a "laboratory of crime." Foreign Minister Walewski remarked indignantly to Persigny: "Is hospitality to be given to assassins?"

The French demanded the wholesale expulsion of opponents of the regime who had found asylum in Britain. In an exchange between Napoleon and Cowley, the British Ambassador argued: "Your Majesty is convinced that Ledru-Rollin and Victor Hugo are assassins in wish if not in deed, but not the slightest proof that such has been the case has been brought forward." Just the same, Cowley reported, the emperor seemed convinced that if he named an individual as conspiring against him, it was the duty of the British government to expel him.

Under this kind of pressure, and genuinely shocked at the attempt on a friendly monarch, Palmerston's government did introduce a bill in Parliament giving it wider powers to act against foreign political exiles suspected of plotting against their home regimes. But this created a domestic crisis. There was much hostility to the legislation, which was widely seen as running counter to Britain's libertarian traditions and pandering to a foreign despot. When it came to the vote, the House of Commons rejected the bill and the government fell.

Furious over the conduct of the Commons, the ever-fanatical Bonapartist Persigny went to the Foreign Office wearing full dress uniform, drew his ceremonial sword, and fulminated: "C'est la guerre! C'est la guerre!" And indeed, as the Tory Lord Derby kissed hands with Queen Victoria and took Palmerston's place as prime minister, he predicted fearfully that war with France might be only hours away. "France seemed as if drunk with anger and hatred of England," said Hübner.

Among the angriest of the French was Eugénie, who had until recently been so enamored of all things British. When Espinasse made a barrack-room reference to the British in her hearing and then apologized for his obscene language, she replied: "Don't apologize. Say it again. That's just what the British are!" Later, when a British court acquitted a French exile named Simon Bernard, who had been accused of being an accessory to the murder of one of the victims of the Orsini bomb attempt, Eugénie sent an extraordinary personal letter to Cowley.

Eugénie said she was "filled with incredible stupefaction" by Bernard's acquittal. "Was it to defend the weak against the mighty, was it to save the liberty of the whole civilised world, that a supposedly impartial jury deemed it necessary to satisfy a frenziedly applauding mob with a verdict that can only teach that killing is no murder?" the empress enquired rhetorically. "The assassins are now strong, sanctioned as they are by England. . . . These men have your moral support; they are free at this moment to plot against us; you have given them the right to do so. . . ."

Contributing to the uproar against Britain, Morny invited the French Army to make its views about the assassination attempt known in print, through the pages of *Le Moniteur*. On this cue, the commander of the 82nd Regiment of the Line begged to be allowed to lead an expeditionary force to take revenge on "these wild beasts in their lair," while the commander of the 2nd Brigade of the First Infantry Division said his men were "ready to shed their blood anywhere in order to reach and destroy the artisans of regicide." The British press and public responded appropriately to such expressions of bombast.

Napoleon seems to have been disturbed by the outcry against Albion perfidy, but unable to stop the slide. "The French are bent on finding conspirators everywhere," he wrote to Victoria, "and I find it hard to resist all the demands for extreme measures which I am asked to take." In his cherished relations with Britain as in domestic affairs, where repression was the rule of the day, it seemed that Napoleon was again being "carried away by the current." Yet in another particular, he was preparing to swim against the tide of popular emotion and official advice.

Hübner was not alone in expecting that "this horrible crime would lead Napoleon III back into the paths of political sanity and would make him break, finally and forever, the bonds formed in his youth with the Carbonari." But instead of killing off Napoleon's lingering affection for the cause of Italian liberty, the attempt on his life seems to have revived it.

Did the attempt shock him into a realization of how far he had abandoned the cause which inspired his youth and create a determination to make up for this lapse? Or was his response the cynical calculation of a master manipulator seeking to enhance his image as a humanitarian, while increasing the bounds of his Empire and weakening the standing of a rival power? Probably a little of each.

The way Napoleon's mind was working began to show when he snubbed Austria by refusing to give an audience to Hübner, who wanted to make a formal expression of his country's pleasure at the imperial couple's escape from death. By pointed contrast, Napoleon told a Mission of Congratulation sent by Cavour that "I love Italy and will never be allied with Austria against you," and invited the Piedmontese prime minister to enter into direct correspondence with him.

Next, he sent his police chief Pietri to see Orsini in the Mazas Prison with instructions to explain that far from being the enemy of Italian freedom and unity, Napoleon was its greatest champion. The reasons for this extraordinary apologia by Napoleon to his would-be killer would become clear later.

On February 25, the trial of the terrorists began. Orsini, eloquent and handsome, cut so fine a figure in the dock that the indiscriminate bloodshed he had wreaked among entirely innocent people was all but overlooked; he and his co-conspirators were charged not with the murder of the eight who died but with the attempted murder of the emperor, who had not.

The fashionable ladies who came to watch the trial found themselves almost falling in love with the terrorist leader. "Orsini is the hero of this sad drama," observed Hübner with evident distaste. "All the great ladies . . . rage about him. They admire his beauty, his courage, his resignation. The Empress too is in raptures over this murderer in kid gloves."

There could be no denying the guilt of the accused, and Orsini's accomplices, a sorry, frightened-looking lot, could only plead that they were led astray by their leader. But when Orsini took the stand to testify in his own defense it was clear that he was pleading not for his life but for his cause.

He described the condition of Italy, under the Austrian heel, fragmented and exploited by reactionary popes; he described his sense of betrayal when French troops intervened in 1849 to destroy the Roman Republic; he told of his split with Mazzini and his growing conviction that Napoleon was the greatest obstacle to Italian freedom—"once convinced of this, I frankly confess that I resolved to kill him."

This was great courtroom drama, but the highest point was yet to come. It occurred at the end of the speech for the defense by Orsini's lawyer, the prominent liberal Jules Favre. He made no attempt to gloss over the enormity of Orsini's crime. "I am not here to glorify him, nor to justify him, any more than to save him," said Favre. "I only wish to cast some rays of light on his immortal soul."

He delivered a lengthy peroration on the travails of Italy and the sentiments of patriotic Italians. Then Favre astonished the court by producing a letter from Orsini to the emperor, which he proposed to read to the court, having received "the permission of him to whom it was addressed." This letter was the fruit of Pietri's conversation with Orsini and had been personally delivered to the emperor by the police chief.

It echoed much of what Orsini had already said from the witness box, in similar proud and measured tones. It asked not for mercy for himself but justice for Italy, and ended with the appeal: "May Your Majesty not reject the words of a patriot on the steps of the scaffold! Set my country free, and the blessings of 25 million people will follow you everywhere and forever."

There can be little doubt that Napoleon himself had engineered this coup de théâtre so that France and the world should know that he was seen by Italian patriots as the one man who could fulfill their dreams of freedom and unity. Through Pietri, he had persuaded Orsini to write the letter; by giving permission for it to be read out at the trial, he had made sure that its contents would go on the record; and by having it published in full in *Le Moniteur*, he made sure it would be picked up and reprinted in newspapers across Europe. By these means the unpredictable and ever-conspiratorial Napoleon had, in Hübner's words, "renewed his pact with the Revolution."

Whether out of genuine compassion or further calculation, Napoleon now moved to commute the death sentences inevitably passed on Orsini and his accomplices. "Orsini is not a common murderer like Pianori," said Napoleon. "He is a man and has my respect." Eugénie, who had originally been baying for the Italian's blood, concurred. Orsini was a patriot and an idealist, she said, not a vulgar criminal. She even wanted to visit him in the condemned cell, but was dissuaded.

But Napoleon's ministers were unanimous in opposing a reprieve. It would be taken as a sign of weakness, they argued, and the public would be outraged if the killers of innocent Frenchmen and women were spared. Eventually a compromise was reached: Orsini, as the leader of the conspiracy, would have to die, and with him Pieri, the next in seniority, but Rudio and Gomez would escape the guillotine and go to jail for life.

Before he went to the guillotine, Orsini wrote another letter to Napoleon, who, as before, made sure that it received the widest publicity. In it, Orsini said he was now convinced that "the hopes expressed in favor of my country find an echo in your heart, and for me, although near to death, it is no small consolation to see that Your Majesty can be moved by true Italian sentiments."

Orsini also renounced the use of assassination as a means to achieve political ends. His plot against Napoleon was the result of "a fatal mental error," he said, and he urged his compatriots to "put far from their counsel all trust in assassination." Instead, "their redemption must consist in their self-denial and unity, and in the practice of true virtue."

With such virtuous sentiments, Orsini went to the guillotine. On March 13, he and Pieri were beheaded, Orsini's last words being "Long live Italy, long live France!" It was a text for Napoleon's next military adventure.

Napoleon's plans for Italy did not involve embracing the likes of Orsini or even his less radical rival, Mazzini. The obvious agency through which France would pursue its Italian policy would remain the Kingdom of Piedmont-Sardinia, Italy's only independent constitutional monarchy and a natural leader of the Italian confederation Napoleon hoped to bring about.

Any such confederation would be under a debt of obligation to France, which Napoleon hoped would be strengthened further by a marriage between his cousin Plon-Plon and Victor Emmanuel's fifteen-year-old daughter, Marie Clotilde. Cavour and his monarch had long been hoping for an alliance with France against Austria and the time now seemed ripe, on both sides, for the deal to be struck.

Napoleon made the first move in a game that would again demonstrate his penchant for conspiracy and his predilection for farce. Without telling his Foreign Minister Walewski, he sent his physician Conneau to Turin on a secret mission to initiate talks with Cavour and Victor Emmanuel. The Italians were enthusiastic and agreed to a secret meeting with Napoleon to get down to details.

The venue was fixed for Plombières, where Napoleon would go to take the waters in July of 1858. Cavour, scarcely less conspiratorial than Napoleon, arrived there incognito on July 19 and plunged straight into negotiations with his host. Walewski, left behind in Paris, was totally in the dark.

Napoleon's idea, gleefully approved by Cavour, was to provoke Austria into a war with Piedmont, whereupon France would send an army to Victor Emmanuel's aid, drive the Austrians out of Lombardy and Venetia, and incorporate the two territories into Piedmont. The grand duchies of Tuscany, Parma, Modena, and Lucca and the papal provinces of Romagna and the Marches would be thrown in for good measure, and the augmented Piedmont would become the Kingdom of Northern Italy, easily the most powerful member of the proposed confederation. Meanwhile, to compensate for his loss of territory—and to keep the Catholics at home quiet—the Pope would become the nominal president of the confederation, but with real power in the hands of Victor Emmanuel.

But first a plausible excuse must be found for war with Austria. Cavour suggested using its refusal to sign a new commercial agreement with Piedmont as a pretext. No, no, said Napoleon, who would swallow the idea of a trade pact as a cause for war? Cavour tried again. What about demanding the withdrawal of Austrian troops from the Romagna? Good Lord, no, said Napoleon, how can you make a fuss about Austrian troops in the Romagna when I am keeping French troops in Rome?

The two conspirators hummed and hawed for a while before Napoleon came up with the solution. Cavour should send agents into Carrara to provoke an uprising against the Duke of Modena. The Austrians would warn the Piedmontese to cease and desist, Piedmont would reject their ultimatum, and the war would be on.

There was much else to discuss—how to ensure the other powers remained uninvolved; the terms of the peace treaty to be imposed on the Austrians; the shape of the proposed confederation and the precise status of the Pope within it. There was also the little matter of France's reward for helping Piedmont, for after all the game of nations was not played on the basis of idealism and altruism alone. Napoleon's price was Victor Emmanuel's French-speaking native province of Savoy and the Mediterranean county of Nice.

And then there was the matter of Princess Clotilde's marriage to the thirty-six-year-old roué, Plon-Plon. Cavour knew that his monarch was not too keen on the match, having in mind the difference in ages and Plon-Plon's unholy reputation, which was almost as notorious as Victor Emmanuel's. But Napoleon made it clear how much he would like the Franco-Piedmontese alliance to be sealed by marriage and stressed that for all his sometimes objectionable behavior, his cousin was basically a good fellow. Cavour replied that he was sure his king would raise no insuperable objection, though the final decision would be left to the princess herself.

With that, they shook hands and parted. The deal had been struck in true conspiratorial style, amid clouds of cigarette smoke and without a word committed to paper, but the meeting was far from having been the secret they had hoped. Napoleon was still talking to Cavour when his secretary brought him a telegram from Walewski saying that Cavour had been spotted sneaking into France under an assumed name at Strasbourg, his purpose and destination unknown. Others recognized Cavour in Plombières and it was not long before the news was known all over Europe that he had been there at the same time as Napoleon.

The obvious conclusions were drawn, to the particular outrage of Hübner and embarrassment of Walewski. It might have been a good deal better for all concerned if Napoleon and Cavour had been less addicted to conspiracy and had met openly; that way some innocent explanation for their talks might have seemed credible.

The revelation of Napoleon's secret diplomacy at Plombières was not the only humiliation to be inflicted upon Walewski by Napoleon at this period. While he played the game of nations behind his Foreign Minister's back, the emperor was making love to his wife almost literally under his nose.

Walewski, born in 1809, was the issue of the first Napoleon's celebrated affair with the Polish Countess Marie Walewska. He was a handsome man with an unmistakably Napoleonic cast of feature, clever and resourceful but insufferably vain and widely disliked. It was said of him that the good fairies clustered round his cradle at birth and gave him all the qualities, but that then the uninvited bad fairy turned up to decree that no one but himself would realize that he possessed them.

His wife, born Marie-Anne de Ricci, came of an aristocratic

Florentine family, like la Castiglione; unlike her predecessor, however, she was both discreet and clever. She was a blond, blue-eyed little beauty who claimed descent from Machiavelli, and quite credibly so, in view of her considerable cunning and manipulative skills. She appears, for example, to have had the knack of attracting lovers without losing the friendship of their wives.

The old court gossip, Viel Castel, called her "a real little rouée who, while going to bed with the Emperor, has managed to become the friend of the Empress." As an example of the "superb impudence" with which she handled her relations with Eugénie, Viel Castel recorded that on one occasion she went to the empress and said: "I am obliged to ask Your Majesty not to invite me to any more of your private evenings, for they accuse me of being the Emperor's mistress, and I do not want this calumny to lower me in Your Majesty's eyes." Added Viel Castel: "The Empress, much moved, kissed her and their intimacy became still closer."

Without question, la Walewska was a good deal more discreet and cunning than her predecessor. As Clarendon noted: "The uninitiated would not think there was anything between the Emperor and Madame Walewska, as all the covenances are rigidly observed." This was not always the case, though; however hard Marie-Anne tried to maintain appearances, Napoleon's urgent physical demands occasionally ruined her efforts.

On one occasion in October 1857, when the court was traveling by train to Compiègne, she and Napoleon were alone together in one compartment of the imperial carriage, while Eugénie, Mathilde, and Walewski were in the other. Suddenly the jolting of the train caused the door between the two compartments to swing open and Mathilde was amused to see her "very dear cousin sitting astride on Marie-Anne's knees, kissing her on the mouth and thrusting his hand down her bosom."

On another occasion, when the emperor went with an entourage to Cherbourg, Walewski and a court chamberlain, the marquis de Chaumont-Quitry, were together in a room adjoining the emperor's suite. Mocquard, Napoleon's chef de cabinet, entered, crossed the room to Napoleon's door, and opened it without knocking. Then, according to Chaumont-Quitry, he "reeled back in astonishment and fell in my arms. Through the open door, I could see Mme Walewska in the arms of the Emperor, and Walewski, standing next to me, must have seen what I saw."

Chaumont-Quitry was perhaps a good deal less astonished than Mocquard for, as he told Viel Castel, he quite often surprised the emperor *en bonne fortune*. In such cases, said the chamberlain, the emperor would salute him and twirl his mustache, "which he did without so much as a smile, both of us solemn as choristers chanting the Epistles."

Inevitably, Napoleon's affair with la Walewska became the subject of coarse jests in court circles. On one occasion when the emperor's mistress was among a group of ladies visiting the castle at Pierrefonds, which was being restored, she admired a lizard gargoyle. "It is very well executed," she remarked to the household minister, Marshal Vaillant, "but such a water pipe must be very expensive." "Less expensive than yours, Madame," replied Vaillant. And when one of the others present railed at him for the remark, the old soldier growled that "this drainage has cost us four million francs!"

When word of the liaison between Napoleon and Walewska reached Harriet Howard in her isolation at Beauregard, she wrote caustically to her friend in England that it seemed to be a family tradition that "each reigning Bonaparte must sleep with a Walewska."

We do not know what scenes occurred between Eugénie and Napoleon on the subject of this romance, but we get a glimpse of her state of mind at a time when the affair was at its height. "I have such a disgust for life," she wrote to her sister Paca on New Year's Eve, 1857. "Things past seem so empty, the present so full of obstacles and the future perhaps so short (at least, I hope so) that I often wonder to myself if it is worth the struggle and courage fails me."

The other injured party, Walewski, had less cause for chagrin. He benefited enormously from the affair. Although he was a conservative and a clericalist and opposed to Napoleon's Italian policies, he retained the foreign ministry long after those differences should have required his resignation. And after he was eventually pushed out, he retained a salary of 100,000 livres a year as a privy councillor, plus 30,000 a year as a senator, and rents of another 100,000 a year from land at Les Landes which Napoleon conferred upon him "for services to the Empire."

It was not an unjust verdict when, in one of his inimitable dispatches, Cowley referred to Walewski as a *maquereau*—a pimp.

15

TO WAR AGAIN

ALTHOUGH LOUIS NAPOLEON HAD NEITHER the talent nor the stomach for the bloody business of war, his conspiratorial and perversely quixotic nature once again pulled him ineluctably toward it, while the imperatives of Empire pushed remorselessly from behind. His clandestine meeting at Plombières with Cavour had set him firmly on course toward his Empire's second big power clash, and while there were moments in the succeeding months when he seemed to be wanting to apply the brakes, there was no way of stopping the momentum.

Considered coldly, on the morning after his conspirators' binge with Cavour, the risks involved in going to war for the cause of Italian unification should have seemed as daunting as the rewards were doubtful. With all its infirmities, Austria remained a military power of no small consequence. Defeat, or even stalemate, could well cost Napoleon his throne. And however successful he might be in isolating Austria diplomatically, there was always a danger that armed conflict in northern Italy could escalate into a wider European war.

The substance of Napoleon's talks with Cavour, of course, remained secret, but speculation that some kind of deal had been struck was quickly rife, causing consternation in the chanceries of Europe and skittishness on the stock exchanges. Nowhere was the consternation greater than in London, where despite past goodwill—and reciprocal visits by Victoria and Albert to Cherbourg and Napoleon and Eugénie to Osborne—the suspicion was growing that this Napoleon might well prove as great a danger to the tranquility of Europe as his uncle.

Vienna, on the other hand, was less concerned than it should have been. This was chiefly because Hübner half convinced himself and his masters that the wily Napoleon had staged the Plombières meeting as a bluff. After all, it was common knowledge that the Catholics of France—including Walewski and the increasingly devout Eugénie—were opposed to any action in Italy that could undermine the power of the Pope. And while the "Reds" might favor war with Austria, the conservative majority would hardly countenance fighting for so remote an ideal as Italian unification.

Nor did a visit to Paris by the boorish Victor Emmanuel in November 1858 seem likely to advance the Italian cause, for his crudities caused offense—or hilarity—all around. "You never saw such an extraordinary creature," Cowley wrote to Clarendon. "He sent for Walewski and began talking about his religious differences with Rome. 'Look here, my dear fellow,' he said. 'All priests are scum. If I had my way I'd have them all shot.'"

Having outraged Walewski's pro-clerical susceptibilities, Victor Emmanuel accosted one of the few virtuous ladies of the court, one Madame Mallart, and said: "There's one good thing I've discovered in Paris. The women here don't wear drawers." And to the countess Walewska, next to whom he sat at dinner, the irrepressible monarch remarked (while contemplating, as Cowley reported, "certain charms for which she is famous"): "What a lovely woman you are! Oh, how I love women! Do you rule your husband?"

Victor Emmanuel was due to visit London after Paris, and Cowley fretted that "he'll frighten the Queen out of her senses if he goes on so with her."* But Clarnedon was more amused than concerned. He found the Victor Emmanuel anecdotes

---

*In the event, the decorous atmosphere at Windsor completely cowed the ebullient Italian. "He looks like a bull, but behaves like a lamb," remarked Clarendon.

priceless. "Pray send more," he wrote. "The roars of laughter in the Cabinet just now about the caleçons [drawers] might have been heard at Westminster Bridge."

Victor Emmanuel's well-publicized gaucheries may have contributed to Hübner's continued complacency. Even Napoleon's growing personal coldness toward him failed to warn the Austrian envoy that anything really serious was afoot. At a diplomatic reception on New Year's Day, 1859, the emperor was affable to other ambassadors but frostily correct to Hübner. "I regret that our relations are not as friendly as I would wish," he said, "but please write to Vienna and say that my personal feelings toward the Emperor are unchanged."

Hübner did not appear to read any sinister significance into this remark, though given the exquisite politesse demanded by diplomatic convention, he surely should have. Indeed, others regarded it as a virtual declaration of war. Alarm bells started ringing in the chanceries, while share values plummeted on the bourses.

Meanwhile, urged by Cavour to cement the secret deal with France, Victor Emmanuel had reluctantly agreed to marry his daughter to Plon-Plon—a man, Napoleon had said, who proved himself to be an acceptable son-in-law by the kind way he treated his mistresses. "What a disgrace to Victor Emmanuel," wrote Cowley, "selling his daughter to such a man. . . . It is positively horrible to see that poor frail little creature by the side of that brute."

After the marriage in Turin at the end of January, Plon-Plon brought his plain and pious child bride back a week later to Paris, where his imperial cousin had ordered an official reception for them. Ordinary Parisians seemed less than enthusiastic as they watched the couple drive into the Tuileries. They realized all too well the implications of the match. Cowley quoted an onlooker as having said: "We do not greet the little one because she brings us war."

The Conservative British government did its best to head off that war, fearing that a French victory over Austria and the establishment of a unified Italy would upset the sacrosanct balance of power and unleash radical forces across Europe. Malmesbury therefore proposed a great power conference to settle the Italian problem and Napoleon had no choice but to agree. Possibly he believed he could achieve more at the conference table than on the battlefield, and to persuade Austria to attend he supported Vienna's demand that Piedmont-Sardinia should disarm along its frontier with Lombardy.

Cavour was outraged by what he viewed as French double-dealing and came to Paris to hold Napoleon to his secret bargain. But the emperor stood fast, reminding Cavour that he had said all along he would not go to war against Austria without adequate pretext. For this reason, he argued, he had to appear at least willing to negotiate, and Piedmont must stand down along the frontier if that was what was needed to lure the Austrians to the conference table. Cavour left in tears, threatening resignation and even suicide.

But the Austrians, certain that France would not fight, insisted on pushing their luck. Advised by Hübner that Napoleon would abandon Cavour and Victor Emmanuel in the pinch, they refused to take part in the conference if Piedmont was allowed to take its seat as a full participant. Cavour could be present, but only as an observer, Vienna insisted. Not content with this affront, the Austrians offered further provocation by giving Piedmont a five-day ultimatum to withdraw its troops and dismantle its defenses along the frontier.

Cavour and Victor Emmanuel could hardly believe their good fortune. This was the trap they had been wanting to lure Austria into all along—the very situation in which Napoleon could not fail to honor the pledges made at Plombières and since confirmed in a secret treaty. Gleefully, they rejected the Austrian ultimatum. On April 25 the French told the Austrians that if they made good their threat and crossed the River Ticino into Piedmont, they would have France to deal with. Ignoring the warning, two days later the Austrians marched.

"I seek no conquests," Napoleon assured his people, as he told them they were now at war with Austria, although in truth territorial conquest would have seemed to most of them a much better reason for war than the altruistic objective he announced—"to leave Italy mistress of itself." To allay the fears of the pious and the conservative, including his wife, Napoleon added a pledge that there would be no revolutionary disorder and that the rights of the Pope would be fully respected.

The Second Empire's second war differed from the Crimean War in at least one important respect. This time—determined to live out the Napoleonic myth—the emperor would lead his army personally into battle, just as his illustrious forebear had done. No matter that he had only theoretical experience of war, gained at the Swiss military academy in his youth, plus one brief taste of small-scale combat during the 1831 Italian uprising. No matter that, according to his aide-de-camp Fleury, he had no idea how to deploy and maneuver large numbers of troops and scarcely knew how to read a map.

In full martial panoply, his beard and mustache waxed to ferocious points, Napoleon rode at the head of the Imperial Guard to the Gare de Lyon where he was to entrain for Marseilles, en route to Genoa by sea. Patriotic crowds cheered him on his way, the most vociferous being not the bourgeoisie but the working class who saw the war as a blow to reaction and a vindication of the radical ideals which the Empire had suppressed but which they still wanted to believe Napoleon secretly harbored. "Vive l'Empereur, vive la guerre!" they shouted. Some even dared to sing the forbidden *Marseillaise*.

Eugénie, appointed regent in Napoleon's absence but having little liking for the war he was embarking on, accompanied him on the train as far as Montereau before returning to Paris. Napoleon's yacht, *La Reine Hortense*, reached Genoa on May 12 to be greeted by Cavour in the absence of his royal master, who was at the front with his troops, waiting for an expected Austrian drive on Turin.

Had the Austrians been quicker off the mark, they would have had only the 70,000-strong Piedmontese Army to contend with. But the enemy commander-in-chief, General Gyulai, allowed his Austrian uhlans and hussars, his Czech dragoons, his Hungarian grenadiers, his Croatian infantry, and his Serbian artillery to clank at a leisurely pace through the sunny Lombardy landscape as if they had all the time in the world to get to the frontier.

The French moved a good deal faster, bringing their troops up by rail—for the first time in any European war—as well as by sea, and making use of the new-fangled electric telegraph for rapid and efficient coordination of their logistical efforts. By the time the complacent Austrians were deployed for battle, a French army of 200,000 had arrived to confront them.

Even with the most brilliant generals and the most carefully wrought battle plans, war is 95 percent muddle, and there was little brilliance or proper planning on either side of this conflict. Halfway through it Gyulai would be sacked by the emperor Franz-Josef, and when it was over the victorious Napoleon would have his own field orders destroyed to remove any record of his military incompetence.

The first major battle took place almost by accident at Magenta, where 54,000 French troops more or less bumped into 58,000 Austrians who, instead of lunging into Piedmont, had timidly taken up defensive positions along a canal behind the Ticino. Faulty intelligence on both sides led Napoleon and Gyulai to believe at first that neither had encountered the other's main force, and it was with some consternation that the two commanders eventually realized they were fully engaged.

But once battle was joined, the fighting was remorseless. Throughout a long, hot June 4 the two armies clashed while Napoleon looked on, chain-smoking in the saddle, near a canal bridge that was the focal point of the battle. Whatever military virtues he lacked, physical courage was not one of them, and Napoleon was in a dangerously exposed position, clearly visible to enemy snipers for whom his golden epaulettes would have presented a tempting target.

His Imperial Guard took terrible casualties as the Austrians made repeated counterattacks to recapture the bridge. At one point the battle was going so badly for the French that Gyulai telegraphed to Vienna that the day was his. Staff officers came to Napoleon asking for orders and pleading for reinforcements. He sat expressionless, undemonstrative, and laconic as ever. "Hold on," he ordered, praying silently for General Mac-Mahon's Zouaves to turn up before it was too late.

By late afternoon MacMahon and the promised reinforcements were arriving in strength and soon the tide turned decisively. By six o'clock Magenta fell to the French in bloody and brutal street fighting. The Austrians had lost 6,000 men, the French 4,500. The Piedmontese had made no appearance on the field of battle at all, even though a large force was in the vicinity.

When Victor Emmanuel entered Napoleon's headquarters that night to congratulate him on his victory and apologize for his absence from the field of battle, he was frigidly received. "Sire," said Napoleon with chilling formality, "when one is duty bound to join forces in the face of the enemy, a scrupulous adherence to one's obligations is to be expected."

Magenta was not a victory in the brilliant style of the first Napoleon. The blind courage of the common soldier and the timely arrival of MacMahon and his Zouaves, not inspired leadership, had carried the day. Nevertheless, it *was* a victory, and an important one. Gyulai withdrew right across Lombardy to his next line of defense, the River Mincio, and four days after Magenta, Napoleon and Victor Emmanuel rode side by side into Milan as liberators.

The next objective was to storm the Mincio defenses and break through into Venetia, the second of the campaign's two territorial objectives. Napoleon set up his new headquarters in Brescia and the army awaited a decision on how Venetia was to be taken. But if Napoleon had a battle plan, he did not take his staff into his confidence; the commander-in-chief seemed to be as secretive in his strategy as he was in his diplomacy. Napoleon's style was to consult his staff, then ruminate in secret before issuing his orders—waging war "like a conspirator," as some of his officers complained.

He seemed to be in no hurry. The Franco-Piedmontese Army was moving at a leisurely pace toward the Mincio when a telegram from Eugénie in Paris spurred Napoleon out of his lethargy. The Prussian Army was massing on the Rhine, she said, and might be preparing to save the Austrians from total defeat in Italy by striking at France. The war would have to be finished—and quickly.

Meanwhile, the Austrian Army had been galvanized, too. The

young Emperor Franz-Josef had dismissed the lackluster Gyulai, taken command himself, and crossed the Mincio to do battle with the invaders. On Midsummer's Day, June 24, the two armies clashed, again almost by accident, blundering into each other along a 12-mile front south of Lake Garda, centered on the hill village of Solferino.

There were approximately 150,000 men on each side, the Austrians holding the high ground. Napoleon directed the battle from the bell tower of the village church at Castiglione, an ironically appropriate location from which to achieve the climax of his Italian adventure.

From the gray light of pre-dawn, through the glare of midday and into the haze of late afternoon the two huge armies clashed, inflicting terrible casualties on each other. From his vantage point, Napoleon looked on appalled at what he had brought about. "The poor fellows, the poor fellows," he cried at one point. "What a terrible thing war is!"

Around him lay the butts of the cigarettes he puffed and threw away non-stop throughout the battle to calm his nerves. Not for the third Napoleon the terrible indifference of the first who, surveying the corpses of his own men at Eylau, remarked: "Small change, small change. One night in Paris will soon make good these losses."

Closer to the field of battle a young Swiss observer named Henri Dunant was even more horrified by the savagery of war. "They disembowel each other with saber and bayonet," he wrote. "There is no more quarter given, it is a butchery, a combat of wild beasts, mad and drunk with blood."

By the mid-afternoon of that terrible day the French had seized the dominating heights of Solferino; an hour later the Austrian center broke and Franz-Josef's men began to retreat. As they did so a catclysmic thunderstorm erupted, overwhelming the man-made clamor of battle and reducing visibility to a few feet. By the time the storm ended and the skies cleared, the Austrians had vanished from the scene, except for the 23,000 dead and dying they left littering the sodden landscape, along with the 12,000 casualties of the French and the 5,500 of the Piedmontese.

The battle was over but not the horror. Thousands of

wounded lay unattended, their screams and moans a cacophony of fear and pain throughout the night which followed and the day which followed that. Peasants came out and robbed the dead and dying of their boots and any other items of value. Burial parties came too, and sometimes threw the wounded into mass graves along with those now mercifully beyond fresh suffering.

The Swiss observer Dunant also came to the scene, bringing with him a hastily recruited band of helpers—many of them British tourists—to succor the wounded. From his horrifying introduction to the realities of war would sprout the Geneva Convention of 1864 and its offshoot, the International Red Cross, with Napoleon as one of its sponsors.

From Castiglione, Napoleon rode past the mounds of corpses that littered the vineyards, mulberry groves, and meadows of the Solferino plain to reach his new headquarters. There, after tersely telegraphing the news to Paris—"Great battle, great victory"—he sat silent and apparently lost in contemplation while his generals refought the battle. Then he dismissed them: "Gentlemen, the day is over."

The next day he forced himself to visit a huge barn which had been turned into a field hospital, a sweltering charnelhouse where surgeons and chaplains worked under appalling conditions and amputated limbs were piled indiscriminately in a corner. He left pale and shaken, with moist and reddened eyes, stopping to vomit behind the barn before proceeding to headquarters with his staff officers.

From the Mincio, the Austrian Army retired behind the formidable defenses of the so-called Quadrilateral—Mantua, Peschiera, Verona, and Legnano—and waited for the enemy to come to it. A battle or battles even bloodier than Solferino seemed inevitable as the Franco-Piedmontese forces sought to take their final objective, Venice and its hinterland. But Napoleon was less and less inclined to see the bloody game out to the finish.

Although Britain and Russia were preserving their neutrality, the prospect of Prussian intervention grew daily more menacing in Napoleon's mind; he was bitter toward the Piedmontese for letting the French bear the brunt of the fighting and then embarrassing him by attempting to annex the papal state of Romagna; he was worried by reports of opposition to the war in France, amplified in telegrams from Eugénie, who believed its continuation could only undermine the position of the Pope and encourage socialists and other revolutionaries; above all, perhaps, he was appalled at the prospect of more bloodshed on the scale he had so recently witnessed.

A fortnight after his victory at Solferino—and, characteristically, without consulting or even informing his generals or his Allies—Napoleon sent Fleury through the Austrian lines to Verona under a flag of truce to offer an armistice. Four days later he met his fellow emperor, the twenty-eight-year-old Franz-Josef, in a house outside Villafranca.

They conferred alone, without books, maps, or documents and without interpreters, for each spoke the other's language perfectly. Within an hour, and in complete cordiality, they agreed on peace terms: Austria woud cede Lombardy to Piedmont; Venetia would remain under Austrian sovereignty with a measure of local autonomy but would join a proposed Italian confederation; the Pope would retain all his territories and would be invited to become president of the confederation; the Hapsburg rulers of the mini-states of Parma, Lucca, Modena, and Tuscany who had fled to escape popular uprisings would be restored to their thrones, and these states too would join the confederation.

The world was astonished that France should abandon its task before Napoleon had fulfilled his pledge to liberate Italy "from the Alps to the Adriatic." Cavour was so outraged that he resigned before reading more than half of the draft agreement, cabling to his supporters: "Peace made, principles sold, everything to the devil." Victor Emmanuel was philosophical and accepted the situation, but with scarce concealed bitterness. A fragment of inflamed verse by Elizabeth Barrett Browning mirrored the feelings of most Italians:

> Peace, peace, what do you say?
> What!—with the enemy's guns in our ears?
> With the country's wrongs not rendered back?
> What!—while Austria stands at bay

In Mantua, and our Venice bears
The cursed flag of the yellow and black?

Napoleon slunk back home via the Alps, more like a defeated commander than a conqueror, and retired to Saint-Cloud for a few days' rest, looking sick, exhausted and—some thought— ten years older than when he had left for Italy a mere nine weeks previously.

Well aware that the French people were far from happy with the ambiguous outcome of the campaign, he decided to deflect their discontent by staging an even bigger reception for the Army of Italy than he had done for the returning Crimean warriors. So on August 14, his great forebear's birthday, the third Napoleon's tattered Italian legions marched through Paris, swaggering twenty abreast along the grands boulevards and down the rue de la Paix to the Place Vendôme, leaving gaps in their ranks to mark the places of fallen comrades.

In the magical excitement of martial celebration, all discontent over the war's outcome was temporarily banished. As popular generals rode by, the crowd called out their names, with a special roar for MacMahon, newly created duc de Magenta, and for his Zouaves, who played a decisive role in both great battles and who now swung past with flowers in their gun barrels— "the most picturesque set of desperadoes that ever drew trigger," as the *Times* correspondent called them.

Wave after wave the proud regiments passed, calling forth the acclaim of a populace intoxicated with second-hand glory, an acclaim which included and embraced the *vivandières* and *cantinières*—those leathery female camp followers, fulfilling the functions of nurse, water carrier, cook, and prostitute, without whom no French Army of the period ever took the field.

At the head of his troops, mounted on a splendid English charger, rode their emperor, rouged and dyed to conceal the physical and mental toll which age, loose living, and the campaign itself had exacted. To the crowd he appeared, as ever, a heroic figure on horseback, and when he reined in at the Place Vendôme to take the salute and a palace servant brought the little Prince Imperial to sit on the bow of his father's saddle, the populace went wild.

Dressed in the scarlet uniform of the Imperial Guard, the three-year-old Loulou saluted solemnly, then tore his Legion of Honor and sash from his breast and threw it to the passing Zouaves, who proudly pinned it to their battle-rent colors. Did he do it on the instructions of his father, or was the act spontaneous? No matter which, it was a gesture worthy of his great-uncle—a gesture old soldiers would remember on their death-beds, the theatrical apogée of a carnival Empire.

Martial displays were one thing, political realities another. Continuing upheaval in Italy swiftly reduced Napoleon's policy there to a shambles and the deal he had struck with Franz-Josef at Villafranca, embodied into the Treaty of Zurich four months later, never came into effect.

Piedmont rapidly annexed Tuscany, the grand duchies of Parma, Modena, and Lucca, and the papal state of Romagna with the full concurrence of their respective populations and the grudging agreement of Napoleon. Franz-Josef, feeling be-trayed, reneged on his promise of home rule for Venetia. And the Italian confederation remained a chimera, which it was all along bound to be if only because nobody but Napoleon had really wanted it.

Piedmont's objective remained a united kingdom with Victor Emmanuel at its head, Mazzini and the radicals were after a united republic, while the third side of the Italian triangle, the Holy See, wished simply tó hold onto its God-ordained territories and maintain the status quo.

That Napoleon should have failed to grasp the fundamental political realities of the Italian situation is perhaps no stranger than that he should have failed to foresee the developments which forced him to abandon his military adventure halfway. What is strange is that, both in his own time and since, he should have been credited with visionary leadership or Machia-vellian cunning. The conduct and outcome of the Italian war show that he had neither quality. Here was not the scheming manipulator or the calm, wise statesman of so many historians' fancy, but simply a man totally out of his depth.

In his frustration over the Italian shambles Napoleon turned, oddly enough, to his former enemy for mutual commiseration. As in the aftermath of the Crimean War, when Napoleon had seemed almost pathetically eager to patch things up with Russia, he now thrust his attentions on the Austrians in the person of their new ambassador, Prince Richard von Metternich, who had replaced the hapless and discredited Hübner.

"This state of affairs in Italy is a hopeless muddle," Napoleon told the bemused Metternich. "I assure you I am very unhappy about it. What am I to do?" His position, he said, was "all the more terrible on account of my sincere affection for your Emperor." He even offered to help Franz-Josef "revenge himself" for his losses in Italy by proposing a campaign to occupy the Turkish-ruled principalities of Wallachia and Moldavia and put an Austrian archduke on the throne there—a proposal which Metternich found "so extraordinary that it struck me dumb."

To Cowley, Napoleon gave a similar impression of complete frustration, with one important difference: he spoke of Italy "in terms of utter despair," but at the same time "his tone is of great bitterness towards Austria." The British Ambassador added: "He is now quite at sea and does not know what to do. . . . He does not believe in the possibility of a central Italian kingdom. . . . He sighs after his confederation, which he sees going to the dogs. He does not know what to do about Tuscany, how to satisfy the Legations, how to bring the Pope to reason."

A month later Napoleon was moaning to Metternich again. "I wish the Italians would wash their dirty linen themselves," he said. "I want to withdraw my troops from Rome and Milan and have done with the concerns of the Italian nation. . . . How this business wearies me and embitters my life."

And then in an extraordinary burst of self-revelation: "It was I who awakened and detonated the revolution. My idea was grand and beautiful, my intentions pure and disinterested. By invading Piedmont you gave me a good excuse to realize a life-long ambition to restore Italy to herself. I thought I had succeeded at Villafranca; now I see that the obstacles have only increased and I am at the end of my resources."

The young Metternich, not yet as cynical and manipulative as his famous father, seemed nonplussed by Napoleon's need to confide in him. "The Emperor overwhelms me with attentions and the Empress, who has taken an immense fancy to my wife, seizes every excuse to invite us to the Tuileries," he reported in early January 1860. The Metternichs, he marveled, had been the only foreigners invited to see in the New Year at the palace, and "on the stroke of midnight the Emperor asked me to play a waltz and danced it with the Empress."

Added Metternich: "I could not help laughing inwardly at the situation. That the Ambassador of Austria should make the Emperor dance during the first moments of the New Year seemed, to say the least of it, original."

16

PROBLEMS
WITH
PLON-PLON

WHILE NAPOLEON'S SEXUAL ADVENTURISM continued to plague his relationship with Eugénie, he now found that political differences were an even greater source of domestic conflict.

Despite her ignorance of the world, or perhaps because of it, Eugénie had very decided views on all aspects of policy and was increasingly inclined to meddle in both domestic and foreign affairs. Her brief period as regent—in which role she had displayed authority and self-assurance—had given her a taste for power.

When Napoleon returned from Italy, she had not hesitated to berate him for his mistakes in the hearing of others. If the Holy Father should be driven out of Rome by the revolutionary forces her husband had recklessly unleashed, she threatened, she would follow "the godfather of my child" into exile. Napoleon's gentle reminders that it was French troops who were keeping the Pope in Rome seemed to make little impression.

But, as usual, the imperial couple put on a good show of solidarity, appearing to the world to be a supremely confident and dynamic partnership. In the summer of 1860, they embarked on a lengthy tour of the realm, first to the newly acquired territories of Nice and Savoy—Napoleon's only tangible reward for the Italian imbroglio—and thence via Toulon and Corsica to Algiers for a visit to France's most important overseas territory. It was during this leg of the tour that an incident occurred which put the imperial marriage under fresh strain.

Eugénie's beloved sister Paca had been seriously ill in hospital in Paris, suffering from a spinal ailment which defied diagnosis, and Eugénie was understandably anxious to be kept informed of her condition. Napoleon assured her that the new underwater cable from Toulon to Algiers would keep them in touch, but the cable broke while they were en route from Ajaccio to Algiers, and when they arrived in North Africa on the morning of September 17 it was in ignorance of the fact that Paca had died a few hours earlier.

The tour proceeded according to schedule, the usual round of receptions, dinners, and balls, climaxed by a splendid display of horsemanship by 10,000 Berbers, who galloped across the Metija Plain, firing their rifles in the air in salute, to rein in only feet from the viewing stand.

On the evening of September 19 the delayed cable reporting the Duchess of Alba's death was handed to Napoleon. Afraid, as ever, of emotional scenes, unwilling, as ever, to speak unpleasant truths, Napoleon withheld the news from Eugénie until the visit was over and they were on their way back to France on September 20.

Whether she accepted his explanation that the undersea cable had broken, or whether she believed he had deliberately delayed telling her for the sake of the Algerian tour, is not certain. What is certain is that Eugénie's numbing grief was mixed with acrid reproach for herself and her husband that she had been dancing and enjoying the obsequies of her Algerian subjects while her sister's body was still warm. She would recall the wretched incident with bitterness long after Napoleon's death and there can be little doubt that she felt he had been guilty once again of moral cowardice—an even worse offense in her book than his promiscuous sexuality.

The episode almost certainly had a lot to do with her otherwise inexplicable decision in November to leave Paris and travel incognita once again to England and Scotland. As soon as he heard of her plans, Cowley shot off a dispatch to London. "Various motives are attributed to this somewhat extraordinary proceeding," he wrote, "—grief, ill-health, jealousy." Cowley added that he had learned from unimpeachable sources that there had also been "terrible scenes, made by the Empress, on the subject of the papacy," in which she had threatened her husband with divine wrath.

The King of the Belgians, who found Eugénie's expedition "most astonishing," had received similar information. "She seems to have been a good deal shocked that she had been dancing in Africa when that poor sister was dying," he wrote to his niece, Queen Victoria. "Next to this there seems a difference of opinion with her master on the subject of the Pope. . . ."

Despite Eugénie's incognita, her presence in Britain soon became known to the public, who displayed a good deal of curiosity at her presence. After visits to Edinburgh, Glasgow, and Manchester, she came to London, where she stayed at Claridge's with her small retinue and was invited to Windsor Castle. Victoria was shocked to note how depressed and rundown she seemed. "She looked very pretty, but very sad," she wrote to her uncle, "and in speaking of her health and of her return from Algiers began to cry. . . . She never mentioned the Emperor. . . . It is altogether very strange. . . ."

Although Eugénie was warmly received by the British, her husband would scarcely have been a welcome visitor at that time. By 1860, old suspicions about France in general and Napoleon in particular had resurfaced. His annexation of Savoy and Nice had reawakened exaggerated fears in Britain that this Bonaparte might be as hungry for territory as his predecessor and the bonhomie of the Crimean War days was now completely dissipated.

"Much as you have been disposed to confide in him, I think you must now doubt his trustworthiness," Clarendon admonished Cowley, "and wish you had not coped with so much genius, ambition, conspiracy and fatalism. He deceives by never telling the whole truth—you never arrive au fond de son sac— there is always something in it that it does not suit him to divulge, and when you think you have reached a final point, you find it is only one from which he makes a fresh start."

Clarendon added: "He has been heaping up a pile of irritation and mistrust against himself and has now set fire to it with his own hands. With Russia crippled, Austria rotten, Prussia frightened and England growling . . . there has been no practical utility even for his own ulterior objects in acting as he has done and setting all the powers of Europe a-thinking how and when they shall be able to coalesce against him."

Clarendon spoke of the "brutal invectives" against Napoleon in the House of Commons and the "vociferous manipulation of anti-French feeling" among MPs. This, combined with "the universal Anglophobia in France," he said, made "the maintenance of friendly relations almost impossible and of peace hardly probable." As for Napoleon's ambassador, Persigny, he "seems to have gone stark mad and is doing mischief by the nonsense he talks and the menacing tone he adopts in society."

If the degree of suspicion about France in Parliament seemed almost hysterical, it was nonetheless shared by the royal family, who had so recently been charmed by the friendship of Napoleon and his consort. According to Clarendon, Prince Albert was "so rabid against the Emperor that it quite distorts his usually correct judgement. . . . He has an idée fixe about the Emperor that nothing can disturb."

As for Victoria, the possibility that Napoleon might come to London to visit the 1860 Exhibition so disturbed her that she was planning to retire to her Scottish estate at Balmoral so that she would not have to receive him. "I am no hypocrite," she said. "I can't conceal what I think, and I know I should show him that my feelings towards him are not what they were."

At this time, volunteer regiments were being raised in England to counter the perceived threat of a French invasion, and even Napoleon's former Foreign Minister, Drouyn de Lhuys, warned the visiting British economist Nassau Senior to beware of him. Napoleon, he said, "trusts to stratagem and fraud. The uncle was a lion. This man is a bear. He does not bound. He does not go straight. He crawls on slowly and tortuously, draws back if he is opposed and returns."

British animosity obviously wounded the normally phlegmatic emperor, who could not understand why so much fuss was being made about the annexation of two tiny territories, whose inhabitants had voted overwhelmingly by referendum in favor of incorporation into France.* He told Metternich that he

---

* The Niçoises voted "yes" by 25,943 to 260 with 4,743 abstentions, and the Savoyards by 130,533 to 235 with 4,610 abstentions.

was ready to make every sacrifice to maintain friendly relations with England. "But if public opinion in France, which however I shall do my best to control, should render a rupture necessary I will make war on England with such vigour and such means as shall at once put an end to the affair."

In all this, only Cowley seemed to maintain a sense of proportion. He thought the fears about Napoleon's intentions were nonsense. "There are many who think that the Emperor's policy is governed by a fixed plan," he wrote, "—that he assumed the throne with fixed ideas and that all he has done since has been in furtherance of them. Thus, I have heard it said that his plan was to reduce Europe by degrees—that he began with Russia, that he followed up with Austria, that his next step will be Germany, and that having subdued the Continent he will try his strength with England."

But, said Cowley, "I do not believe the Emperor to have any fixed policy at all. He has certain ideas and desires floating in his mind which turn up as circumstances seem favourable, but a man of less decision and character, of more indolent disposition, or more inclined to wait upon events, instead of creating them, I never came across."

Events would prove Cowley's assessment to be right on target.

When Eugénie returned to Paris from London, courtiers noticed that her attitude toward the emperor was colder than ever and that they quarreled more frequently, despite Napoleon's habit of turning away harsh words with a patient rejoinder.

This state of domestic affairs was hardly improved by the bitter enmity of Napoleon's two cousins, Plon-Plon and Mathilde, toward Eugénie. Mathilde, it seems, would never forgive Eugénie for having become the empress she herself might have been, any more than Plon-Plon could forgive her for producing the heir who ruined his chance of succession. But the feud between Eugénie and Plon-Plon was by far the more important of the two, touching as it did on matters of state.

Plon-Plon referred to her as "this simpleton of an Empress" and to her infant son as "this brat of a Prince Imperial." When Napoleon appointed her regent for the period of his absence in

Italy, Plon-Plon had exploded: "What stupidity to entrust the government to a fashion plate, for the Empress is nothing else." On one occasion he even had the temerity to refuse—in the presence of the imperial couple—to propose a toast to Eugénie at a state banquet.

To think of her as a fashion plate and nothing else was a considerable underestimation of Eugénie, for muddled and often contradictory though her views might be, Eugénie was undoubtedly effective and forceful, unmistakably a woman of the right—authoritarian, traditional, pro-Church, almost a Legitimist. By contrast, though perhaps no less muddled, Plon-Plon professed views which put him about as far to the left as it was possible to be while remaining a member of the Bonapartist establishment—libertarian, quasi-socialistic, anti-clerical, almost a republican.

Despite the more or less open personal and political warfare between his wife and his cousin, Napoleon studiously avoided taking sides. Out of family loyalty, he was inordinately tolerant of the intolerable Plon-Plon, as he was of all the Bonaparte clan—perhaps from a suppressed uncertainty about his own claim to membership.

Family sentiment apart, it suited Napoleon very well politically to be seen to be holding the middle ground between the two poles of Bonapartism, as represented on the left by his cousin and on the right by his wife. On a deeper level altogether Plon-Plon and Eugénie perhaps represented the conflicting sides of his own personality, which he must forever strive to keep in balance.

But a kindly disposition was an essential part of Napoleon's makeup, too. He seems to have had a genuine and enduring affection for his cousin, constantly forgiving his curmudgeonly behavior, defending him against his critics, finding roles for him to play, not to mention arranging the marriage which linked him to the rising Italian monarchy. The correspondence between the two cousins—the only substantial body of Napoleon's letters to survive the fall of his Empire in 1870—provides a fascinating and all too rare insight into his extraordinarily patient and forgiving personality, qualities which make Napoleon unique among despots.

In June 1848, for example, while he was still in exile in

London but hoping to return soon, Napoleon wrote to his cousin to protest, mildly enough, about a speech in which Plon-Plon had made tactless reference to the failed insurrections at Strasbourg and Boulogne. "What would you think, and what would people think of me, if in a speech while praising you I were to say that I regretted that you had paid court to Louis-Philippe?" he asked. "Be sure of this, my dear Napoleon—we must identify ourselves with each other, under pain of coming to grief otherwise."

Later that same summer, Louis had cause to caution his cousin, whose full name was Napoleon Charles Joseph Paul Bonaparte, over the way he designated himself. "You who have so much good sense and tact ought to thoroughly understand that it is rather unsuitable for you to sign yourself publicly 'Napoleon Bonaparte' with no other forename, for in this way you are signing as the Emperor signed and are giving no other name to distinguish yourself personally. . . . To sign yourself 'NB' has an air of unjustifiable pretension."

To soothe the sting of rebuke, however, Napoleon signed off: "Be sure that my friendly relations with you will never change, whatever our divergences in matters of opinion, or rather of conduct." And he meant it.

At the end of December 1848, by which time he was President of France, we find Napoleon taking his cousin to task for complaining that he had been kept in the dark about a dispute within the Council of Ministers. "I had thought you to be more logical and more reasonable," wrote Napoleon. "The ministers and I agreed to keep our difference secret [for the moment]. Therefore I had no right to tell you of it yesterday. If it came out, it was through no fault of mine. You see, therefore, that it is very bad taste to be annoyed with me for not having told you what took place in secret at my council."

In the spring of 1849, Napoleon appointed Plon-Plon ambassador to Spain, but while passing through Bordeaux on his way to Madrid Plon-Plon revealed his total unsuitability for diplomacy by saying in public that the president allowed himself to be dominated by reactionaries rather than following his own views. Where others might have revoked his appointment, Napoleon contented himself with a rebuke, whose text however he released to the press.

"You know me well enough [he wrote] to be aware that I will never submit to the ascendancy of anyone whosoever and that I shall strive unceasingly to govern in the interests of the masses and not in that of a party. . . . Every day I am receiving the most contrary opinions, but I only obey the dictates of my reason and my heart."

The pseudo-radical Plon-Plon did not enjoy being accredited to a Bourbon court. After only a few weeks in Madrid he had the gall to throw up the job and return to Paris, where he ran for parliament and took his seat on the left benches of the National Assembly. For once, Napoleon was angry enough to sever relations with his wayward cousin, and so things remained for two years. When Napoleon staged his coup in December 1851, Plon-Plon publicly opposed it and, with the dissolution of the Assembly, retired to private life.

But following the attempt on Napoleon's life in September 1852, Plon-Plon renewed contact, sending a "Dear Louis" letter in which he said that "all my feelings of brotherly friendship have been reawakened as keenly as in the past." More than ever, he said, he had come to realize that "although politics have been able to separate us, my devotion to your person remains the same." Either forgetting or ignoring his cousin's earlier admonition, he again signed himself "Napoleon Bonaparte."

This offense was apparently overlooked and Napoleon took his churlish relative to his bosom once more, giving him the rank of an imperial prince when he restored the Empire a few weeks later, making him an army general, and also giving him permanent seats in the Senate and the Council of State.

Yet by November of that year, Napoleon had cause to lecture his cousin once again for his disruptive behavior in those bodies. "When one bears our name and when one is the head of the government, there are two things which must be done," he wrote, "to satisfy the interests of the most numerous class and to attach to oneself the upper classes.

"Since you are not in authority you have only the second of these to attend to, and you should now give it your careful attention. Moreover, it is by trifles that one wins individuals, just as it is only by means of great measures that one can win the attachment of the masses. Weigh your words carefully, then, and count on my friendship."

When France went to war in the Crimea, Napoleon gave Plon-Plon command of a division which acquitted itself well at the Battle of Alma. According to the published account of a common soldier who was present, Plon-Plon "behaved very well under fire," and the commander-in-chief Saint-Arnaud, either sincerely or to please his monarch, reported officially in similar vein.

Napoleon immediately wrote to Plon-Plon to say how "very happy" he was to learn of his cousin's "fine bearing" at Alma and to award him the Military Medal, "in proof of my satisfaction as your sovereign and my affection as your cousin." By the time this letter arrived, however, Plon-Plon had left his division at the front and retired to Constantinople, suffering from what doctors diagnosed as "chronic gastroenteritis, complicated by slow fever and diarrhea, accompanied by a gradual weakening of the principal functions of the body."

"I had the satisfaction of not leaving my division until after I had taken part in the glorious Battle of Inkerman," Plon-Plon wrote to Napoleon, adding that "unfortunately I did not take a very active part in it," since most of his men were committed to the reserve.

In this letter he asked permission to return to France, arguing that the war would be virtually suspended for the winter and pleading ill-health. Napoleon's reply was a firm negative. "I can understand up to a point your returning to Constantinople to recover, but I urge you to go back to the army the moment you are able. Your conduct up to now has rallied all hearts to you . . . [but] if you were to come back now . . . you would lose in one moment all the fruits of your hardships. . . . You would be lost irretrievably in the opinion of the public. There cannot be two opinions about that."

This was a virtual command, but Plon-Plon ignored it, returning to Paris in January 1855. Amazingly, Napoleon received him without reproach, although it would seem that Plon-Plon was properly apprehensive. "Your Majesty has overwhelmed me with joy," he gushed, "in welcoming me on my return to France with a kindly affection which I am conscious I have never ceased to deserve."

Something less than kindly affection informed Napoleon's next letter to his cousin the following month. An anonymous pamphlet had been published in Brussels, sharply criticizing the conduct of the war in the east, and Napoleon had been advised—quite falsely, it seems—that Plon-Plon was the author. In a stiffly formal letter to his cousin, the emperor ordered him to "issue a flat and official repudiation of this pamphlet and the ideas it contains, otherwise I shall be compelled, to my great regret, to take the severest measures in your regard."

Plon-Plon replied with pained innocence. "How, Sire, on a mere rumor, have you been able to give credit to accusations like these? . . . I state on my honor that I am a complete stranger to a publication which I have heard of only from you." Plon-Plon demanded a court-martial so that he could clear himself, adding that even when he was vindicated, "there will remain, nevertheless, a deep wound in my heart."

Napoleon realized he had accused his cousin unjustly and, although there is no letter of apology extant, we may assume that he did apologize. Certainly, Plon-Plon was soon back in favor and allowed to give the emperor his private views of the way the war was being conducted—views which, incidentally, very much coincided with those of the anonymous pamphleteer.

The army itself never swallowed Plon-Plon's story that he had left the Crimea because of ill-health and, despite Saint-Arnaud's favorable accounts of his bearing, word began to circulate of his cowardice under fire. Soon France learned that at the front Plon-Plon had earned a new nickname—"Craint-plomb," one who fears lead. If the emperor heard these stories, he did not allow them to influence him, and he gave Plon-Plon the prestigious job of president of the 1855 Universal Exhibition, to the subsequent discomfiture, among others, of Queen Victoria.

Three years later, we find the long-suffering emperor once again taking his cousin to task, this time for failing to carry out instructions while on a delicate diplomatic mission to Czar Alexander in Warsaw. "This means that you will only serve me as long as it suits you," wrote Napoleon. "I confess that this example gives me much pain, for what confidence can I have in you in future if, when giving you an order, I am not sure whether it will be carried out?"

Again, though, Napoleon quickly forgave his cousin. The mission was, after all, a success, and a treaty of benevolent neutrality and diplomatic support was agreed between the two countries as part of Napoleon's preparation for his Italian adventure.

In January 1859, we find the rather ironic circumstance of Napoleon, who himself had married in such haste, complaining to Plon-Plon over the "precipitate" arrangements for his marriage to Clotilde. "You must obtain a delay of at least eight days to allow time for the necessary preparations," he cabled from Paris to Turin. "Such haste would give rise to a whole host of comments and criticisms."

Napoleon's concern was that if it was too obviously rushed, the marriage would be seen as a quid pro quo for the antedated secret treaty of alliance he had just concluded with Victor Emmanuel, and he wanted the wedding put off at least until February 6. But Plon-Plon cabled back to say it was too late to change; the banns had already been published for a January 29 wedding. "An adjournment would be deplorable," he said. "The King and the Princess would be dissatisfied, I should be taxed with levity and the Emperor with indecision." Plon-Plon got his way, and again Napoleon overlooked it.

Three months later, we find Napoleon once more having to warn Plon-Plon over his penchant for wild indiscretion. "Listen, I implore you, to the words of advice I wish to give you for your general good. . . . You have much intelligence but you do not possess sufficient tact in your conduct or restraint in what you say. Do you want to be a politician, upholding my authority and strengthening the throne, or merely a skeptic and a mocker, laughing at everything and sticking to nothing?"

Accusing Plon-Plon of blurting out details of the secret treaty with Piedmont, Napoleon enquired: "What confidence can I repose in you if I am not certain of your discretion, if bad advice or false reports are able to influence your conduct, or if one can no longer discuss things secretly in your presence?"

Nevertheless, when the war against Austria broke out, Napoleon had sufficient confidence in his cousin to give him command of the Fifth Army Corps. At first, this corps was assigned to assist the civil power in Tuscany and saw no action. When Napoleon eventually called it up to the front, ordering a 2,000-man garrison to stay behind in Florence, Plon-Plon moved at such a leisurely pace that he missed the entire war.

Napoleon's increasingly tart messages from the front tell the story:

June 10—"You must conform to the general exigencies."
June 12—"Endeavor to make the greatest haste possible."
June 14—"I repeat very urgently my previous orders. The Fifth Corps must join me as soon as possible."
June 18—"I hope that . . . the news of the rapid evacuation by the Austrians will have hastened your march."
June 30—(Plon-Plon's corps having completely missed Solferino)— "I am waiting for you with two-fold impatience, for apart from the pleasure of seeing you again you will greatly reinforce my army. . . . I beg you therefore to arrive as soon as possible. . . ."
July 3—"When I say a thing, I am sure of it; not only is there a bridge at Pozzolo, at a place called Molini della Volta, but there are two and I have crossed them myself. I have also had a third made this very day, a little higher up."

When Plon-Plon's corps finally did get to the front line, he received another well-deserved rocket:

July 4—"I am really angry that on the first day of your arrival you begin by not carrying out punctually the orders you have received. . . . I was firmly counting on having this morning a division on my right covering my bridges and my cavalry, and now there is not a man there."

A week later Napoleon made his decision to offer the Austrians peace, and so Plon-Plon and the Fifth Corps ended their war without having heard a shot fired in anger. This did not, however, prevent him from raising Cain when he discovered that his corps, left behind in Italy on garrison duty, would not be represented in the victory parade through Paris on August 14.

When he threatened that he and Clotilde—daughter of the war's only real beneficiary—would boycott the parade if the Fifth were not allowed to take part, Napoleon put his foot down and commanded their presence.

But Plon-Plon's gall was endless, and so apparently was Napoleon's patience. In July 1860, after ex-King Jérôme's death led Napoleon to suggest some modest cost cutting at the Palais-Royal which Plon-Plon and his father had shared until then, Plon-Plon took offense, objected that he was "unable to accept the dispositions indicated by the Emperor," and huffed that he "would prefer to go and live either at my private house or at some house that I would rent."

Napoleon replied: "I do not understand how you can distort my intentions and that a mere matter of estimating expenditure can make you entertain doubts about my regard."

Plon-Plon was determined to cast himself in the role of the put-upon relative. Telling his cousin, a few months later, that he realized he had no political future in France, he suggested going to seek a role for himself in Italy where he could "serve the Napoleonic cause and build up the Italian unity which you have made possible."

Napoleon very sensibly thought this a very bad idea indeed— as perhaps Plon-Plon hoped he might. Italian politics were "quite complicated enough without making them more confused," he replied. "I therefore oppose this proposal formally, for it could not fail to create great difficulties for me without doing you any good. . . ."

Plon-Plon, obviously angling for some major job at home in compensation, replied in hurt tones that Napoleon was "severe" toward him. Having nothing worthwhile to do in France, said Plon-Plon, he was willing to give up his civil allowance of 1 million francs a year and his status as an imperial prince to work for Italy, exchanging "a rich and lofty but humiliating position for one that would be modest, difficult and arduous but more glorious, perhaps, and more worthy of my name."

Napoleon replied the next day: "I am not severe toward you; quite the contrary. You will always find me just and affectionate, but I owe you the truth when you go astray. One cannot change one's fate at will. Anything you endeavor to take up outside your own country will do you harm instead of good. You are a general, a senator, and a councillor of state. In time of peace, what more can you want?"

Still Plon-Plon persisted, hinting that if he could not go to Italy he would like to become head of the French Navy, commander of the Imperial Guard, or at least "admitted to your counsels, as was my late father." But, he added, with a great show of hurt innocence, "since I do not enjoy your confidence, I will abandon these projects completely and Your Majesty shall never hear me speak of them again."

And so it went on throughout Napoleon's reign, each of Plon-

Plon's misdeeds dealt with firmly, patiently, and forgivingly by his cousin, each reconciliation followed by some fresh malefaction.

The correspondence tells us much about both men, but if we find ourselves warming to Napoleon for his long-suffering toleration of his obnoxious relative, we must ask whether it was entirely a virtue in a man in his position—whether the reasons of state he was so willing to invoke in other contexts did not demand that he stop wasting time and effort on so hopeless a case as Plon-Plon just because of the ties of kinship and affection.

The cliché "generous to a fault" takes on very substantial meaning when used to describe Napoleon's attitude toward his cousin.

17

MEXICAN ADVENTURE

AT THE END OF NOVEMBER 1860, while Eugénie was away in Britain, the liberal side of Napoleon's persona asserted itself in a way that took France and the world by surprise. Without prior warning he issued a decree significantly relaxing the tight grip he had hitherto kept on his rubber-stamp parliament.

For the first time, members of the Legislative Body and the Senate would be allowed actually to debate the contents of Napoleon's speech from the throne at the opening of each parliamentary session. More, the press would be free to publish reports of those debates—although only the official verbatims, which were to be provided by the presidents of the two chambers. This small but positive step toward the creation of what would become known as the "Liberal Empire" was exactly the kind of thing the paradoxical Plon-Plon had been urging and Eugénie resolutely opposing.

But Napoleon's cautious movement toward liberal domestic policies would soon be counterbalanced by a far-reaching foreign policy initiative which was anything but libertarian, either in intent or outcome. This was the Second Empire's disastrous Mexican adventure, in which Napoleon set out to create a satellite Catholic monarchy in Latin America with the aim of curbing the burgeoning power of the United States while promoting French economic and geopolitical interests in the New World. It was a thoroughly hare-brained scheme, which never had a chance of success; and it was largely inspired by Eugénie.

To be sure, Napoleon had shown himself quite capable of getting into untenable situations abroad without any prodding from his wife. But he would in all probability not have blundered into Mexico but for Eugénie's maneuvering and manipulating.

She had first become aware of the problems of Mexico during her girlhood in Madrid, where wealthy Mexican exiles of grandee descent were frequent visitors to her mother's house. After gaining independence from Spain in 1821, Mexico had been misgoverned by a bewildering succession of military dictators and civilian presidents, and had lost Texas, California, Nevada, Utah, Arizona, New Mexico, and parts of Colorado and Wyoming to the United States in the war of 1846–48. In the mid-fifties, ruling Mexican radicals had disestablished the Roman Catholic Church and begun confiscating its vast land holdings, bitterly opposed by the Church hierarchy and the landed aristocracy, who waged intermittent civil war against successive governments.

In the late 1850s, Eugénie's interest in this faraway situation was reawakened when she ran into one of the Mexicans she had known in Madrid—an elegant wastrel named Don José Mañuel Hidalgo, one of a circle of aristocratic émigrés who had been trying for some time to drum up support in Europe for the establishment of a conservative monarchy which would "save" Mexico.

Although there is no evidence either way, it is possible that this was the same Hidalgo mentioned in the anonymous description of the sexual activities of Manuela and her circle (see Chapter 9). Don José seems to fit the description of the abducted youth in certain respects. A glib charmer with preening good looks, Hidalgo was exactly the kind of man—decorative but safe—whom Eugénie liked to have around her, and he became a regular guest at the Tuileries, Saint-Cloud, Compiègne, Biarritz, wherever the court happened to be. He became such a trusted intimate that in 1860, on her return from Algeria, Eugénie gave him the doleful honor of escorting Paca's coffin back to Madrid for burial.

Eugénie would listen in horror to Hidalgo's lurid stories of life in republican Mexico—the theft of Church property, the summary execution of conservatives, the rape of nuns, the humiliation of monks, the burning and desecration of churches and convents. To her husband she pleaded Hidalgo's case that France or a consortium of powers should intervene and put a European prince onto the Mexican throne.

Napoleon would listen courteously, express sympathy, but sensibly reject the idea of intervention. "I would like to," he said on one occasion, "but it's impossible." No European power would be foolish enough to risk a war with the United States in its own backyard by violating the Monroe Doctrine of nonintervention in the western hemisphere.

But Eugénie persisted. Quite apart from her fierce loyalty to the Church and her wounded Spanish pride at the depths to which this former Spanish colony had sunk, she was driven by a consuming prejudice: unlike Napoleon, who had enjoyed his brief period in the United States, she was implacably anti-American.

With all the vehemence of a parvenu queen she disapproved of Yankee republicanism; with all the passion of a pious Catholic she disapproved of Protestant Yankee anti-clericalism; and with all the fire of a reflexive conservative she disapproved of Yankee support for liberal and radical causes everywhere. She once told Napoleon that sooner or later he would have to go to war with the United States. And she told an astonished American diplomat that, "if Mexico were not so far away and my son were not still a child, I would wish him to put himself at the head of a French army and with his sword inscribe one of the most glorious pages of the country's history." The American replied that she should thank God that Mexico was so far away and her son *was* still a child.

War with the United States was never on Napoleon's agenda, and he told Eugénie so, in his quiet fashion. But when the American Civil War broke out in April 1861, a Mexican adventure began to look a good deal more appealing. Washington would now be far too busy trying to crush the Confederacy to assert itself on behalf of Mexico. And when the Civil War had ended—as Napoleon and many other European leaders believed it would—in victory for the South, or at least stalemate and the division of the United States, the Americans would be too spent and weak to challenge a foreign incursion into their hemisphere.

Little by little Napoleon conjured up a host of apparently good reasons to take the plunge. He had, after all, been interested in Central America since his time at "the University of Ham" when he developed the idea of a canal across Nicaragua. Going to the aid of the Church in Mexico could win back the Catholic support at home which his ambivalent Italian policy had cost him. He now had a historic opportunity to reestablish a powerful commercial and strategic French presence in a part of the world from which France had been largely excluded by the Louisiana Purchase and the loss of Canada. He could indulge his insatiable appetite for plots and schemes and satisfy the imperial dynamic which demanded that he always be "doing something." And, not least, he could placate his demanding wife, whose interest in Mexico had become a shrill obsession.

In urging a French expedition to Mexico, Eugénie had an invaluable ally in Napoleon's influential half brother, Morny, who had bought a large number of Mexican government bonds at a huge discount and saw an opportunity to make a big financial killing if the French Army went in and the bonds became redeemable at face value. Morny's advice to Napoleon was reinforced by that of his friend and business associate, France's ambassador to Mexico, comte Alphonse Dubois de Saligny, whose dispatches ceaselessly sang the siren song of intervention.

The pressures on Napoleon, external and self-generated, were growing irresistible when opportunity knocked again and, just as the start of one civil war had made intervention seem feasible, the end of another now made it appear justifiable. While in America the Union was locked in battle against the Confederacy, in Mexico the radical leader Benito Juárez, a full-blooded Indian, had finally routed his conservative enemies to become president of an exhausted and bankrupt nation. One of his first actions on taking power was to declare a two-year moratorium on the repayment of massive debts to Britain, France, and Spain. And with this, the idea began to take shape in Napoleon's mind of spreading the risks of an intervention by sponsoring a three-nation invasion of Mexico to collect the debt by force.

In July 1861, he set up one of those secret meetings to which he was so addicted. This time the foreign leader who came to see him incognito was General Juan Prim, the military dictator of Spain. They met at Vichy where—as in Plombières three years previously—Napoleon had ostensibly gone to take the waters.

They discussed the possibility of a tripartite intervention, to which Prim was perfectly agreeable. But when Napoleon went on to suggest that while they were at it they should install a European prince as Emperor of Mexico, the Spanish leader was a good deal less enthusiastic. He knew that Spain was so hated in Mexico that he would be stirring up a hornet's nest if he got involved in anything more than a speedy debt-collecting operation. He also doubted very much whether Mexicans would want their country to become a monarchical island in a republican sea.

Napoleon was undeterred by the Spaniard's lack of enthusiasm, and by now so intoxicated by the idea of a Mexican adventure that he was prepared to go it alone if necessary. In Napoleon's fired-up imagination, all that was needed, now that the opportunity and the pretext for intervention existed, was to find a suitable candidate for the throne.

Apparently without telling her husband, Eugénie had already decided whom that should be. While Napoleon was at Vichy with Prim, she buttonholed Metternich at a party at Walewski's country château. She spoke with great animation about the desirability of returning Mexico to Christianity and stability under a European monarch and startled Metternich by suggesting the Archduke Ferdinand Maximilian of Austria, younger brother of Emperor Franz-Josef, as a candidate for the throne.

Metternich may have wondered whether Eugénie was floating a trial balloon for her husband, but it seems that Maximilian's name was not suggested to Napoleon until a couple of months later when he, Eugénie, and Hidalgo again discussed Mexican affairs after dinner in the Villa Eugénie, her informal seaside palace at Biarritz. Napoleon first sent Hidalgo into transports of delight by announcing that he was ready to intervene and give Mexico a king. Then the three of them began excitedly going through the roster of unemployed princes. When Maximilian's name came up, both Napoleon and Hidalgo—the latter, perhaps, in collusion with Eugénie—said that, no, he would never consider it.

But Eugénie, who was in such a state of excitement that she had remained standing throughout the conversation, even though the two men were seated, seemed to think otherwise, tapping herself on the breast with her fan and saying: "I have an intuition that he will accept."

The day after that conversation, Walewski, who was also a guest at the Villa Eugénie, sent an urgent letter to Metternich, then on leave in Vienna. In it, he reminded the Austrian Ambassador of his conversation with the empress at his château in July and added: "The Empress is again concerned with the Mexican affair . . . and a solution seems to her more than ever desirable."

Although no longer Foreign Minister, Walewski was still an important member of Napoleon and Eugénie's inner circle and was politically close to Eugénie. It seems likely that he wrote the letter at her dictation—or at least at her suggestion. "Here [at Biarritz]," he said, "they are disposed to uphold, morally of course, the candidacy of the Archduke Maximilian, if that is agreeable to Vienna." They were also ready to "take the initiative at the opportune time" with Spain and Britain. "Write me a word," urged Walewski, "so that I can, in a measure, enlighten the Empress, whose interest in the outcome of this affair never flags."

Metternich thought this insistence "very curious" and referred the matter to his Foreign Minister, Count Johann von Rechberg, who in turn consulted Franz-Josef. Metternich thought the idea absurd and expected his emperor to reject it out of hand. How could the head of the haughty Hapsburgs even consider the offer of a throne for his brother from the upstart who had lately defeated him in Italy? It seemed unthinkable. But Franz-Josef had personal reasons for wanting his tiresome brother out of the way; to Metternich's and Rechberg's surprise, he expressed cautious interest and sent Rechberg to discuss the matter with Maximilian himself.

The proposal did not entirely surprise the archduke, who had already received a tentative approach from a prominent Mex-

224 ★ IMPERIAL HEYDAY

ican exile, Hidalgo's associate José Gutérriez de Estrada. But now, with the offer coming from Napoleon and with Maximilian's imperial brother showing sufficient interest to send his Foreign Minister to discuss it, the whole thing began to seem a good deal more substantial. Urged on by his ambitious and forceful wife, Maximilian told Rechberg he would accept, on condition that he had the active backing of France and Britain and a firm invitation from the Mexican people.

Once he was notified of the Hapsburgs' agreement in principle, Napoleon made his next move. This was to send a message to the British government via his ambassador in London—now his mother's aged ex-lover, Flahault—to tell them of his plans for Mexico and to seek their support.

"It is in the common interest of the maritime powers to come to the rescue of a country disintegrating through anarchy and misrule. . . . Now is the moment for action when the war of secession makes it impossible for America to interfere," wrote Napoleon to Palmerston, the British prime minister. If properly governed, the emperor said, Mexico would serve as "a powerful bulwark against the encroachments of the United States as well as providing new markets for European commerce."

The idea had a certain appeal to the British, who—as the former Foreign Secretary Clarendon put it—were "amused to see the Emperor cocking up his leg against the Monroe Doctrine." Palmerston thought that "if the North and South are definitely disunited and if at the same time Mexico could be turned into a prosperous monarchy, I do not know any arrangement that would be more advantageous for us."

But he could not carry his cabinet with him. The entente of the fifties was now a thing of the past and the British thoroughly distrusted Napoleon. They were no keener than the Spanish to get involved in his hare-brained schemes—and perhaps that was what Napoleon expected all along. But they did want their money back and were prepared for joint action to get it, so in October the three powers signed a convention under which 6,300 Spanish, 2,800 French, and 800 British troops would jointly occupy Vera Cruz and its hinterland and stay there until the sums due were collected.

The convention specifically disavowed any intention to acquire territory or interfere in the right of the Mexicans to choose their own form of government. But for Napoleon and Eugénie this was merely a matter of form. In mid-December of 1861 a Spanish advance guard captured Vera Cruz and the game was on.

The Archduke Maximilian, a rather bloodless young man of decent liberal instincts, with the high Hapsburg forehead and the pouting Hapsburg lip, had first met Napoleon and Eugénie during a visit to Paris in May of 1856—and had not initially been too impressed.

At twenty-four, Maximilian had all the prudishness of youth, combined with the snobbishness inevitable in a Hapsburg. He therefore found the parvenu court of the Bonapartes "irresistibly comic" and "absolutely lacking in tone." At the same time, he was scandalized by Napoleon's "habit of running after every pretty woman" and especially by his open affair with la Castiglione during and after his wife's pregnancy.

In letters home to Vienna the censorious archduke described Napoleon as "not so much an emperor with a scepter as a circus ringmaster with a riding crop," a man "lacking in all nobility and breeding," with "bow legs, a sidling walk and a furtive look out of half-closed eyes."

But just as others had done before, Maximilian soon fell under the extraordinary spell of his host and of Paris in the spring. After a while the tone of his letters changed markedly. "Napoleon," he wrote, "is one of those men whose personality does not attract at first, but who improves with the knowing through his quiet charm and great simplicity of manner. . . . Once he has got over his shyness, he becomes very expansive and the more I get to know him the more I feel he trusts me."

In fact, it was the other way round: Maximilian was the one who was trusting, so much so that he seems scarcely to have noticed that Napoleon failed to give him the undertaking he had been sent to Paris to extract—a promise not to interfere in Italy—and he left believing that "we are now like old friends."

Maximilian's regard for Napoleon somehow survived even the war in Italy, one of whose minor outcomes was to leave him out of work, for he had been Viceroy of Lombardy and Venetia before Napoleon's victory stripped Austria of much of its Italian territory. Thus he was twiddling his thumbs in enforced idleness at Miramar, his idyllic retreat overlooking the Adriatic near Trieste, when Napoleon's proposition was presented to him.

Maximilian's first reaction was characteristically cautious; but just as Napoleon was prodded into action by Eugénie on the Mexican affair, so was Maximilian persuaded by his wife, Princess Charlotte of Belgium, to get involved. "For my part," as she said in a letter to her ex-governess, "I prefer a full and active life with duties and responsibilities—and even difficulties, if you will—to an idle existence contemplating the sea from the top of a rock until the age of seventy."

Just in case Maximilian should be having second thoughts, Napoleon wrote to him in January 1862, even as his troops were arriving in Vera Cruz, in terms calculated to appeal to his immature idealism and self-importance. "It is a question of rescuing a whole continent from anarchy and misery," he said, "of setting an example of good government to the whole of America, of raising the flag of monarchy, based upon a wise liberty and a sincere love of progress, in the face of dangerous Utopias and bloody disorders."

For her part, Charlotte seems to have divined that Eugénie was the driving force behind the Mexican adventure, for at about the same time she wrote to the empress saying: "Your Majesty seemed obviously marked out by Providence to initiate a project which one might call holy."

Metternich, for one, did not think there was anything holy about the project. He was amazed at how Napoleon had allowed himself to be pushed into it by the empress and to be deluded by lightweights like Hidalgo, Gutérriez, and Saligny into believing that the Mexican people would welcome a European monarch. "How many cannon shots will be required to put [Maximilian] on the throne and how many more to keep him there?" he asked. Prim made the same point in a direct warning to Napoleon. "It will be easy enough for Your Majesty to get the Archduke Maximilian crowned as Emperor," he wrote from Vera Cruz, where he was commanding the Spanish expeditionary force. "But once you recall your troops, he will not have a chance to survive."

The British warned him, too, having been told by Sir Charles

Wyke, their canny ambassador to Mexico, that although the old and wealthy families might support the French intervention, the mass of the people had very different feelings. And from Washington, Abraham Lincoln fired a verbal broadside at the allied fleet lying off Vera Cruz, warning that any European power who infringed the Monroe Doctrine would eventually have to answer for it. But Napoleon closed his ears to all this, heeding only his inner voices and those of Eugénie, Hidalgo, the other Mexican émigrés, and his shady half brother Morny.

Even Miguel Miramón, the conservative Mexican president whom Juárez had ousted, came to Paris and declared to anyone who would listen that "there is no monarchist party in Mexico." Napoleon was among those who would *not* listen, thanks mainly to the efforts of Hidalgo and Eugénie, whose intrigues effectively kept Miramón away from the Tuileries. As Metternich reported: "The Empress hates Miramón and says the Emperor will not see him."

Juárez's forces had not resisted the allied landing at Vera Cruz. Instead, they withdrew to the surrounding hills, leaving instructions to the locals not to cooperate with the invaders, and Juárez prudently began to negotiate with his uninvited guests. By mid-April, the British and Spanish had extracted a financial settlement from him and were happy to withdraw their troops and sail away. This left the field to the French, who declared war on Mexico and, with a mere 6,000 troops on the spot, set about the task of subduing a hostile country three times the size of their own.

With the blithe self-confidence of the utterly ignorant and totally arrogant, the French commander, General de Lorencez, began to march on Mexico City, 200 miles away, telling Napoleon he would be there by May 25 at the latest. He said nothing about the sullen hostility of the locals, about the guerrilla forces that were massing in the hills, about the chronic problems of supply, or about the yellow fever—the *vomito negro*—that was felling his men by the hundred.

Napoleon was delighted with his field commander's report and wrote to Miramar to tell Maximilian to start packing his bags. Lorencez's immediate objective was the city of Puebla, halfway to the capital, and once that had fallen, "the odds are that the rest will follow." The next post, Napoleon predicted, would bring "decisive news."

The next post brought nothing of the kind; instead, it brought news of a decisive and humiliating defeat. This occurred on May 5—forever after known to Mexicans as the glorious Cinco de Mayo—at a strategic hill on the approaches to Puebla, where a Mexican force cut the French to pieces and sent them reeling back toward the coast, leaving behind 500 dead.

In France the government press had already announced the capture of Puebla, complete with fulsome accounts of how the local populace had showered the French troops with flowers and kisses. The newspapers now had to report that much stiffer resistance than expected had been encountered, but that, of course, French honor would be vindicated.

To do this, though, would require a much heavier commitment of men and matériel than Napoleon had envisaged. But like the gambler he was, he had no option but to throw good money after bad. So when the chastened Lorencez said he would need an army of 30,000 to subdue the Juarists, his emperor glumly gave the order for the reinforcements to be sent.

Napoleon was now up to his armpits in the Mexican morass.

18

THE
DISTAFF
DIPLOMAT

WHILE THE MEXICAN CAULDRON SEETHED and bubbled and Maximilian and Charlotte waited at Miramar, alternately hopeful and fearful, for a formal invitation to accept the crown, Eugénie turned her attention to other foreign policy issues. "She now mixes herself up in every political question that arises," observed Cowley.

First of all, it was the perennial problem of Rome. More than ever Napoleon wanted to phase out the French military presence there while chivvying the Pope and Victor Emmanuel into a compromise agreement on the future of the papal states. The issue was enormously complicated by the intransigence of Pius IX, the deviousness of Victor Emmanuel, and the flagrant "Rome or Death!" demands of the radical Italians, Garibaldi and Mazzini. Napoleon found himself still hopelessly trapped in the coils of his own interventionism.

Edouard Thouvenel, who had replaced the pro-papal Walewski as Foreign Minister after the war in Italy, was personally committed to a policy of phased withdrawal from the Roman imbroglio. During the summer of 1863 Eugénie, superstitiously fearful that heaven would wreak vengeance on her if she allowed the Pope to be dispossessed, relentlessly pressured Napoleon to get rid of his Foreign Minister.

Eventually Napoleon conceded and decided to replace Thouvenel with the old hack, Drouyn de Lhuys. Some of his other ministers, including Morny, Fould, and Persigny, protested. Persigny, for one, believed he knew the real reason for Napoleon's dismissal of Thouvenel and told him so with a candor that seems astonishing. "You're like me," Persigny told his monarch. "You let yourself be ruled by your wife. But I only compromise my fortunes while you sacrifice your interests, your son's and the whole country's. It's almost as though you had abdicated. You're losing your prestige and discouraging the remaining friends who serve you faithfully."

Even though Napoleon frequently complained that his advisers were not as honest with him as he would like, only Persigny's long and impeccably loyal service allowed him to speak in such terms to the emperor. Napoleon did not, however, take the advice of his old comrade and Thouvenel was dismissed.

Persigny was not the only one to see his sacking as a flagrant example of petticoat politics in action. Paris society put a distinctly sexual interpretation on the affair, believing that—as Cowley noted in one of his intimate dispatches—"it was a sudden letch for the Empress when His Majesty was with her at Biarritz, which brought about the late Italian and ministerial crisis. . . . The price paid for a renewal of marital rights was Thouvenel's dismissal."

But the emperor's "sudden letch" was probably only part of the story for, quite apart from Eugénie's objections to Thouvenel, Napoleon had his own reasons for wishing to rid himself of his Foreign Minister. On the Roman question, it is true, Thouvenel merely echoed Napoleon's own long-standing wishes in wanting to withdraw French troops, but in many other respects he was too independent-minded for his master's taste. By replacing him with the pliable Lhuys, the emperor could in one stroke satisfy his own inclinations, mollify the clericalists, and placate his formidable wife.

With Thouvenel out of the way, the next issue to command Eugénie's passionate attention was the Polish question, then as now a perennial source of friction between Russia and the West. On this issue Eugénie's sympathies were for once with the underdogs, the Poles. She was intense in her condemnation of Russian brutality in putting down the latest Polish uprising and urged Napoleon to intervene—militarily, if necessary—to help a subject people whose turbulence and stubborn attachment to

Roman Catholicism struck such resonant chords in her own personality.

But more than sentiment and religious solidarity informed Eugénie's attitude toward the Polish question. It was underpinned by domestic political calculations. She knew the Polish cause was popular with all shades of opinion in France, and believed that the nation would be solidly behind intervention. As she would recall in her old age: "The whole heart of France throbbed for Poland. . . . From republicans to Legitimists, freethinkers to clericals . . . there rose the same cry of admiration for the Poles, the same horror of Russia [and] I was among the most enthusiastic. For the first and only time in my life, I found myself in complete accord with my ferocious enemy, Prince Napoleon [Plon-Plon]."

For his part, Napoleon—as with the Italian question—was sympathetic to the principle of national self-determination. But that did not mean he was willing to risk war with the Russians over Poland. More realistically than Eugénie, he realized that French admiration for Polish bravery might not go so far as to welcome a continental war on their behalf. Besides, he continued to seek close and friendly relations with Russia.

Prudently, then, he opted for quiet diplomatic pressure, in concert with Britain and Austria, to persuade the czar into more enlightened behavior toward his Polish subjects. As a by-product of this policy, he took the opportunity to humiliate the Prussians, who had been callously abetting the czar in his suppression of the Poles.

The architect of Berlin's collusion with the czar was the new Prussian minister-president, Otto von Bismarck, who saw a Polish national resurgence as a potential threat to his own plans to expand Prussian influence. In terms which would have done credit to his most notorious twentieth-century successor as Chancellor of Germany, Bismarck set out his own views on how the Polish question should be handled. "Hammer the Poles until they wish they were dead," he wrote; ". . . if we want to exist, we have no choice but to wipe them out."

It was in this spirit that, at the height of the Polish revolt, Bismarck signed an agreement with the Russians to hunt down, arrest, and hand over any insurgents who fled across the border into East Prussia. Such brutal opportunism, typical of the realpolitik which was to become the trademark of the Iron Chancellor, aroused revulsion throughout Europe, where sympathy for the Poles was practically universal.

Riding the crest of that wave of sympathy, Napoleon launched a diplomatic offensive which provoked a crisis in Berlin, forcing the angry and embarrassed Prussian king, Wilhelm I, to revoke his prime minister's agreement with the Russians, and almost causing Bismarck's dismissal. Napoleon scarcely bothered that in humiliating the Prussians and discomfiting their chancellor he might have made an enduring personal enemy of the fast-rising Bismarck.

Her husband's minor diplomatic triumph over the Prussians seems to have inspired Eugénie to a bold démarche of her own. Animated by a naive ambition to play a decisive role in the fate of Europe, she was drawn on to a breathtaking flight of diplomatic fancy—nothing less than an attempt to seduce Austria into an alliance with France against Russia and Prussia, in the pursuit of which she quite literally redrew the map of Europe. We have Metternich to thank for what we know of this extraordinary initiative, which was most probably taken without the knowledge or approval of Napoleon.

On February 21, 1863, Eugénie sent for Metternich and to his astonishment produced an atlas, opened it to the map of Europe, and—conceding that he might think her out of her mind—proceeded to "throw my hat over the windmill" and outline a master plan for Europe which she said went "even farther than what the Emperor has in mind."

First of all, she proposed, the Polish problem was to be solved by Russia, Prussia, and Austria giving up their Polish provinces so that a Polish kingdom could be reconstituted. Next, she offered a tidy solution to the fragmentation of Germany: Hanover, Saxony, and all the other principalities and duchies north of the Main would be ceded to Prussia, Silesia would be ceded to Austria, and the Rhine provinces would be handed to France.

Eugénie now turned her attention to Italy, where the Austrians would give up Venetia to Victor Emmanuel, who would in turn cede central and southern Italy to allow the setting up of a Kingdom of Central Italy and the resurrection of the Kingdom of Naples.

Finally, there was the problem of what to do about the Ottoman Empire. Under Eugénie's scheme, this not insignificant entity would be completely dismembered, Austria inheriting its Adriatic provinces, Russia the left bank of the Danube in Bessarabia, while all of Asia Minor, and the rest of Turkey in Europe, including Constantinople, went to Greece.

This fantastic exposition—according to which, Metternich noted dryly, France would cede nothing—lasted three hours. When it was over, the ambassador hastened to record all that Eugénie had said in a report to Rechberg. "What a flight," he commented, "and with what a bird!" Rechberg was hardly less flabbergasted than Metternich, but a good deal less diplomatic. He told the ambassador to convey to Eugénie and her husband that the proposals were "absolutely repugnant" to Austria, particularly those concerning the disposition of the German states, which would leave Prussia considerably stronger than Austria.

"If the imperial couple wish to seduce us," Rechberg wrote, "let them present us with a more appetizing dish; if we indulge in fantasy, let it be at least frankly favourable to us. Otherwise we prefer to remain on a realistic level."

Three days later, apparently unaware of Eugénie's initiative, Napoleon himself sent for Metternich and proposed an alliance along somewhat similar lines but with territorial proposals that were a good deal more realistic. He confined himself to the Polish and Italian questions, omitting the restructuring of Germany which the Austrians had found particularly objectionable. Most significantly, the emperor made no mention of the Rhineland reverting to France, which Metternich nevertheless took to be his principal secret objective.

On reflection, Metternich inclined to the view that Napoleon had turned Eugénie loose on him as a means of floating a trial balloon. But with historic hindsight it seems more probable that Eugénie acted on her own initiative, muddle-headedly mixing up Napoleon's privately confided ideas with some of her own, and unwittingly betraying schemes he wanted kept secret, such as the recovery of the Rhine frontier.

Whether Eugénie's démarche was authorized or not, the effect was the same. The Austrians very sensibly took fright and shied away completely from any idea of alliance with a regime whose foreign policies seemed so incongruous and unpredictable and whose diplomatic initiatives were presented in such a contradictory and undignified fashion.

There was other business outstanding between France and Austria, business relating to the unfolding Mexican affair.

A year after the humiliation of the Cinco de Mayo, things were going rather better for the French in Mexico. Their expeditionary force—now almost 40,000 strong—took Puebla after a siege lasting sixty days and advanced toward Mexico City. Juárez regrouped his forces in the north of the country, abandoning the capital to the invaders, and on June 7 Napoleon's new commanders, Generals Forey and Bazaine, rode into the city at the head of their troops to the pealing of church bells. When the news reached the Tuileries, Metternich reported, Eugénie was "radiant" and Napoleon "wept for joy."

Soon Napoleon was able to inform Maximilian by telegram that he had been proclaimed emperor by a "national assembly" and that a delegation of Mexican notables was on the way to Europe to offer him the crown formally in person. The delegates called on Napoleon and Eugénie at the Tuileries before proceeding to Miramar. But when they got there, the delegation was considerably put out by the low-key reception it received from the emperor-designate.

The fact was that Maximilian was now having queasy second thoughts about accepting the honor they were so eager to confer. Clearly, the country was by no means completely pacified and, occupied though they were with their Civil War, the Americans were still making threatening noises. "The throne of Mexico is certainly a dangerous one," Maximilian confided to his diary. And to a friend he said: "If I had heard that the whole Mexican project had come to naught, I assure you I would jump for joy."

But Charlotte was still dead set on becoming Empress of Mexico and Napoleon employed his considerable persuasive powers to reassure the wavering archduke. "Once the country is pacified both physically and morally," he wrote, "Your Imperial Highness's government will be recognized by everybody." As for the Americans, they were "well aware that since the new regime in Mexico is the work of France they cannot attack it without immediately making enemies of us."

Against his sounder instincts, Maximilian allowed himself to be convinced. Seduced by Napoleon, spurred on by his ambitious wife—and ignoring the advice of Rechberg—he eventually told the delegates that he would accept the crown and arrangements were made for him to visit Paris to negotiate the details of the military and financial guarantees he sought in order to close the deal.

By the time Maximilian and Charlotte arrived in Paris in February of 1864, Napoleon was most eager to start winding down his expensive and increasingly unpopular commitment in Mexico. The Juarists were fighting an unremitting guerrilla campaign against the invaders, costing France dearly in blood and treasure. The sooner Maximilian was installed, Napoleon reasoned, the sooner he could start raising an army to defend his throne and the sooner French troops could begin to be withdrawn.

In theory, Maximilian's final and formal acceptance of the crown depended on a successful negotiation of the guarantees he was seeking. For that reason he had wanted the visit to be private and businesslike. But Napoleon and Eugénie had other ideas. So far as they were concerned, the matter was fait accompli. So they ordered a typically lavish program of banquets and balls for their guests, with full imperial honors as though Maximilian and Charlotte were already crowned.

The Mexican flag flew above the Tuileries and street vendors were selling paper replicas of it by the thousand to the crowds who turned out in brilliant spring sunshine to welcome the archduke and his wife.

Public opinion—insofar as such a thing could be measured in a country where the press remained under control—was deeply divided on the wisdom of the Mexican adventure, but since the Central American crown of thorns was about to be passed from Napoleon's hands to Maximilian's head, even those opposed to France's involvement were happy to see the archduke and his wife in Paris.

The more knowledgeable and cynical among them referred to Maximilian as "the Archdupe," and in the negotiations that took place over a number of days he proved himself deserving of the jibe. He agreed to an arrangement whereby his regime would be financed by a 200-million-franc loan to be floated in Paris. Having no head for figures, he did not seem to realize that virtually all of this would have to be paid back to France to meet the past, present, and future costs of the expeditionary force, and that, with the economy in ruins after years of civil war, Mexico could only sink ever deeper into debt.

In the matter of military guarantees he appeared to fare better. True, there was no longer any question of British backing for his regime, as Maximilian had demanded, but Napoleon agreed to keep 20,000 troops in Mexico until 1867 and to allow 8,000 men of the French Foreign Legion to remain there at Maximilian's disposal until 1873. Moreover, a secret clause to the agreement pledged that, "whatever should happen in Europe, France would never fail the new Mexican Empire."

Seduced by the charm of the Bonapartes and the great show Paris had put on for him and his wife, Maximilian took Napoleon at his word, formally accepted the crown of Mexico, and returned home to pack. But a nasty surprise was awaiting him in Vienna.

His brother Franz-Josef, though anxious for personal reasons to get Maximilian out of the way, had all along distanced himself from the Mexican project. It was not seemly, he felt, for a Hapsburg to accept a throne from an upstart Bonaparte. More practically, he did not want Austrian prestige too closely involved in an affair which might end in disaster.

Now, through Rechberg, he presented Maximilian with the news that in becoming Emperor of Mexico he would have to formally renounce his rights of succession—and those of his heirs in perpetuity—to the throne of Austria. "If you are unable to consent to this and prefer to refuse the crown of Mexico," the emperor told his brother, "I will take it upon myself to notify the foreign countries of your refusal, and in particular the Imperial crown of France."

Although he had been given warning before leaving for Paris that something of the sort was in the offing, Maximilian was dumbfounded at this ultimatum. There was a furious scene between the two brothers in which Maximilian accused Franz-Josef of bad faith by withholding his conditions until he had committed himself. But now he would have to renege. "In the circumstances," said Maximilian, "I find myself forced to announce my withdrawal to a people who have placed their trust in me."

When the news reached the Tuileries on the evening of March 27, via Eugénie's friend Hidalgo in Trieste, Napoleon's celebrated imperturbability almost cracked under the shock. The more excitable Eugénie became quite hysterical. White with fury, she dashed off a letter for onward transmission to Maximilian which was delivered to Metternich by imperial messenger at two in the morning. It spoke of "the appalling scandal" the archduke's decision would cause to the House of Hapsburg.

"You had plenty of time to consider everything and to go into every detail, and you cannot at the very moment when the arrangements for the loan have been concluded and the convention signed, put forward a family matter of no importance, compared with the confusion into which you are throwing the whole world." Signing herself "Yours in a most justifiable bad temper," Eugénie demanded: "Let us have your last word, for this is a very serious business."

If Metternich spent a sleepless night, as one may reasonably suppose, after reading Eugénie's letter, so it seems did Napoleon. He was pale and twitchy, with bloodshot eyes, when he received the Austrian Ambassador in his private study a few hours later to deliver another broadside.

He accused the Austrian government of "deliberately prevaricating so as to place France in an impossible position." He warned that the situation would lead to "regrettable tension" between the two countries. "It really seems that I have no luck with Austria," he said, obviously still smarting under an earlier rebuff: Vienna's rejection of an alliance with France. "It looks as though I have been deliberately left in the lurch at the last moment."

Metternich tried in vain to assure Napoleon that his country was "animated by the most friendly feelings toward France." Hapsburg family tradition, Metternich claimed, forbade any member's accepting a foreign throne without renouncing rights of succession to the throne of Austria. Napoleon was not mollified. "The Archduke must have known that all along," he said. "The matter should have been settled three years ago."

Metternich could only withdraw with burning ears, "furious," as he told Rechberg, "at being dragged into a controversy before a tribunal so ill-suited to pass judgment on matters of right and wrong." He added: "The whole affair is so undignified that it makes me blush with shame."

Not content with roasting Metternich, Napoleon later that day sent his aide-de-camp to Miramar with a letter for Maximilian. "Your Imperial Highness has entered into commitments which you are no longer free to break," he admonished.

What, indeed, would you think of me if, once Your Imperial Majesty had arrived in Mexico, I were to say that I can no longer fulfill the conditions to which I have set my signature?

No, it is impossible that you should give up going to Mexico and say to all the world that you are obliged by family concerns to disappoint all the hopes that France and Mexico have placed in you. . . . It is absolutely necessary in your own interests and those of your family that matters should be settled, for the honour of the House of Hapsburg is at stake. Forgive me for this somewhat severe language, but the circumstances are so grave that I cannot refrain from speaking the plain truth.

For a man of Napoleon's notoriously mild temperament, such language was indeed "somewhat severe." More than that it was, to say the least, cynical coming from one who had admitted only a few weeks previously to the visiting Duke Ernst of Coburg that Mexico was "a bad business," and that if he were in Maximilian's shoes he would never go there. But the plot had been hatched and Maximilian assigned his role; at all costs he must be made to act it out.

For Maximilian, it was marital pressure that eventually tipped the balance. Despite the sacrifice of the rights of her children, as yet unconceived, Charlotte was still determined that he should "follow his destiny" and take the Mexican crown. Her steady insistence plus Napoleon's letter, with its carefully calculated challenge to "the honour of the House of Hapsburg," changed Maximilian's mind once again. After days of anguished vacillation, he resolved to fulfill his commitments, even though his brother's only concession was to promise vaguely that if

Maximilian was forced to return home, he would take "the necessary measures to safeguard your position in the Empire as far
as is compatible with the interests of the country."

On April 14, then, in a state bordering on nervous exhaustion, Maximilian set sail for Vera Cruz with his wife aboard the
Austrian battleship *Novara*. After a few days he seems to have
recovered, and during the rest of the six-week voyage to his
bankrupt and embattled kingdom Maximilian kept himself
busy drafting a huge compendium of rules and regulations—
down to the most arcane detail of clothing and etiquette, place-
ment and precedence—for the Hapsburg-style court he intended
to set up in Mexico City. When published it ran to six hundred
printed pages.

19

IN
LOVE
AGAIN

THE SECOND EMPIRE WAS NOW AT ITS APOGÉE. Louis Napoleon was the arbiter of Europe, propping up the Pope, inflicting humiliation on the Prussians, giving hope to the Poles, handing nationhood to the Italians, patronizing the Turks, humbling the mighty czars of Muscovy, and grandiosely bestowing a kingdom upon the scion of the haughty Hapsburgs.

His armies encircled the globe—70,000 men in North Africa, 40,000 in Mexico, 30,000 in Rome, and smaller detachments in China, Indochina, Syria, Somalia, Tahiti, Madagascar, New Caledonia, the West Indies—building a colonial empire to rival Queen Victoria's. His resplendently refurbished capital was the architectural, sartorial, commercial, cultural, culinary, and financial cynosure of the Continent.

But the moving spirit and unchallenged master of this dazzling imperium was not too exalted to let himself fall in love again. Unlike la Castiglione, la Walewska, and the string of transient bed partners who succeeded them, his latest amour had no connections with the court and not even the remotest pretension to nobility. She was a one-time circus rider and good-time girl named Marguerite Bellanger who, lacking the polish to become a *grande courtesan,* belonged to a lesser category termed *grisette.* Among an extensive circle of men friends, she enjoyed the sobriquet "Margot la Rigoleuse."

Between the end of his affair with la Walewska in 1860 and

the start of his liaison with la Rigoleuse some three years later, Napoleon's love life had consisted of brief and unsatisfactory encounters with women either procured for him by Bacciochi or recruited himself as he sidled about the grand ballroom of the Tuileries. There had never been any shortage of willing bed partners. As a memoirist noted: "All the beautiful women pay court to Bacciochi in the hope of sleeping with the Emperor."

Presumably, these eager applicants imagined themselves filling the vacant role of *maitresse-en-titre*, but they seldom lasted more than a night. And there was not even a pretense of romance to be derived from the experience; as the emperor aged, his sexuality became increasingly urgent, permitting absolutely no time to be wasted on preliminaries.

The attractive wife of one court official, seeking to advance her husband's career, sought and obtained a private audience with her monarch and, as she reported later to Mme Walewska, "did not even have time to make a token protest before he laid hold of me in an intimate place." Added this lady: "It all happens so quickly that even the staunchest principles are rendered powerless."

The marquise de Taisey-Châtenoy, another of the emperor's transient bed partners, sketched a similarly graceless picture of *l'amour napoléonienne*. After making an assignment with her in the Tuileries ballroom, he arrived in her bedroom in the early hours of the morning "looking rather insignificant in mauve silk pyjamas. There follows a brief period of physical exertion, during which he breathes heavily and the wax on the ends of his mustaches melts, causing them to droop, and finally a hasty withdrawal, leaving the marquise unimpressed and unsatisfied."

The brothers Edmond and Jules de Goncourt—no admirers of Napoleon, it is true, but too conscientious to be anything less than honest in their descriptions of life under the Second Empire—noted in their *Journal* that "when a woman is brought into the Tuileries, she is undressed in one room, then goes nude to another room where the Emperor, also nude, awaits her. [The chamberlain] who is in charge, gives her the following instruction: You may kiss His Majesty on any part of his person except the face."

Such was the perfunctory and indiscriminate sex life of the

emperor until the day in the autumn of 1863 when he met la Rigoleuse and began a prolonged relationship which, however bizarre, seems to have involved genuine affection on his part.

She was born Justine Marie Leboeuf, but because of the vulgar jokes the name inspired, she changed it some time after leaving her native village to work in Boulogne as a hotel chambermaid. With all the banal predictability of the pulp literature of her day, Justine/Marguerite soon allowed herself to be seduced by a commercial traveler and ran away with him to Paris.

There, inevitably, she was abandoned by her seducer once he had tired of her, and she joined the circus where, in training to become an acrobatic dancer and bareback rider, she learned a repertoire of tricks and contortions that were later to earn her the imperial approval. Not only was she purportedly able to leap to her feet in a flash from the prone position, but she could also perform a wide variety of functions while walking or standing on her hands. Lubricious gossip would have it that she liked to present herself to the embraces of the emperor in this unusual position.

When Napoleon first saw her, she was standing right side up, a bold and impudent twenty-five-year-old with pert blond curls and an invitingly sensual mouth. She had by now given up the circus, and while struggling none too successfully to make a career on the stage was living in a small apartment on the Boulevard La Motte-Picquet, not far from the Ecole Militaire, where she was a favorite of the young officers.

She was in the company of one of these, at an imperial hunt at Saint-Cloud, when she caught the eye of her monarch. Napoleon was immediately besotted, and before long had set her up in a house on the rue des Vignes in Passy, while for the periods when he was at his country palace she had the use of one of the villas in the grounds of Saint-Cloud.

About this affair, Eugénie found it impossible to remain complaisant. Here was no discreet woman of breeding like Marianne Walewska, but a common slut, and the affair was rapidly becoming the talk of the town and the gossip of the courts of Europe. Courtiers overheard the imperial couple quarreling furiously about it, and inevitably the British Ambassador soon received word of the latest "intestine discords in the Imperial family."

"The Emperor and the Empress are hardly on speaking terms," Cowley reported to Clarendon. "She taxes him with his present liaison to his face—calling the lady the scum of the earth—and he defends himself." Cowley was surprised to note that Eugénie had taken her grievance to the Walewskis, of all people. "Do not suppose that I have not always been aware of that man's infidelities," she told them. "I have tried everything. I have even tried to make him jealous. It was in vain, but now that he has sunk to this depth of debauchery I can stand it no longer!"

Fury and humiliation so undermined Eugénie's health that in the summer of 1864 she took her doctor's advice and left for a rest cure at Schwalbach, a spa in the German duchy of Nassau. This merely left Napoleon a free hand with la Rigoleuse, whom he took with him when he went to take the waters at Vichy. There it was noticed that the hot baths seemed to tire the emperor rather more than might have been expected.

Later that year he took Marguerite with him on yet another of his regular trips outside Paris—his annual visit to watch the army maneuvers at Châlons-sur-Marne where, she boasted to a friend, she entertained him enormously by dressing up in the uniform of a colonel of hussars.

Back in Paris, Cowley noted that as a result of this affair, Eugénie was "worrying herself to death" and suffering from "loss of appetite, nausea, etcetera." Finally, it was fear that his exertions with the athletic Marguerite might even cause her husband's death—for he returned from a visit to his mistress one day in a state of collapse—which spurred Eugénie into direct action. Recruiting the court lawyer, Amédée Mocquard,* to accompany her, she ordered up a brougham and drove to Marguerite's house in Passy.

There, Eugénie confronted Marguerite and declared: "Mademoiselle, you are killing the Emperor. This must stop. I will command you to leave. Off you go. Leave this house. . . ." Eugénie could be terrible in her wrath, but the pert Rigoleuse stood her ground defiantly. "Your husband comes here because you bore him and tire him," she told Eugénie. "If you want him

---

* The son of Napoleon's faithful secretary, the recently deceased Jean Mocquard, who had been involved in the shedding of Napoleon's English mistress, Miss Howard.

not to come here, keep him at home with your charm, your amiability, your good humor and gentleness."

Mocquard was a horrified witness to these opening shots. Then, either out of embarrassment or terror at the prospect of having to witness the full fury of the empress, he left the room and retreated up a passageway. Some time later, when the muffled sound of angry voices had subsided, he tiptoed back and cautiously opened the door of Marguerite's drawing room. There to his astonishment he saw the two women sitting side by side on a sofa, chatting together like old friends. Shortly afterward, Eugénie rose, embraced her rival, and left, with the dumbfounded Mocquard at her heels.

As soon as he got wind of it, Cowley hastened to inform London of Eugénie's expedition. Clarendon was amazed. "Spanish blood and Spanish jealousy have often begotten imprudencies," he wrote, "but I have never heard of such an imprudence as the visit of Eugénie to Marguerite. It was certain to end in miserable failure, as the damsel would feel sure of better provision from the husband than the wife. . . ."

The empress never disclosed what passed between her and her husband's doxy, and for a while the affair continued, providing Cowley and Clarendon—not to mention *le tout Paris*—with the opportunity for more delicious gossip. Reporting that Napoleon had left for a trip of one month to six weeks' duration in Algeria, Cowley wrote on May 1, 1865, that some people "connect his journey with a desire to see Mlle Bellanger more at his ease. It seems certain that she has gone to Marseilles and I hear that she is to proceed to Algiers. . . ."

Clarendon observed in reply that the emperor's "way of *carrying it on* with Mlle Bellanger was bad enough at Paris, but if he takes her to Algiers where he will be living in a lantern and everything he does at every hour of the day and night must be known, it will really be too bad." Eager for every tidbit, Clarendon added: "When next you write, pray let me know whether the Dulcinea actually crosses the sea."

Eugénie can hardly have been unaware of the gossip surrounding her husband's overseas trip, but she apparently made no attempt to discourage the journey. Indeed, it was said that she was looking forward to the exercise of power as regent in his absence. In July, therefore, Cowley was able to report that the emperor's absence "has given more confidence to the nation at large, for it has proved to them that order and tranquility can be maintained when the emperor is at a distance from the capital." What was more, said Clarendon, Eugénie's second spell as regent had "raised her in the opinion of those who had to deal with her." He added: "She rather liked the display of power, and doing 'Madame la Regente,' but this is pardonable in a woman."

Whether Napoleon actually did take la Rigoleuse with him to North Africa is unclear, but shortly after his return from Algiers the word was that the affair was over and that, as Cowley said, Eugénie was "rejoicing at having brought back the wandering sheep to a more respectable fold." Not long after that, Marguerite signed a statement declaring that a child she had borne in 1864 was not the emperor's, received a handsome cash settlement, and left Paris to take up residence in a remote country château. There she eventually settled down to married life with a Prussian named Külbach.

It was during the period of Napoleon's grand passion for Marguerite Bellanger, in the winter of 1864–65, that Harriet Howard emerged from the shadows to revisit for the last time the scenes of her brightest years as the prince-president's acknowledged mistress. Knowledgeable Parisians were astonished to see her riding down the Champs-Elysées or in the Bois, as in the days of the Second Republic, in a gleaming phaeton drawn by a pair of superb bays.

She was by now, in the words of the Countess of Cardigan, "very fat and her embonpoint increased to such an extent that the doors of her carriage had to be enlarged." Nevertheless, she was widely recognized and caused a frisson of excitement among the audience at the opera when she turned up at a gala first night also attended by the emperor and empress. Wearing "a puce silk gown, trimmed with sable, but unadorned with jewels," she spent the entire performance peering through her opera glasses into the imperial box, to the reported discomfort of its occupants.

Her behavior inspired angry comment from courtiers who thought she had gone there simply to embarrass the emperor and empress. The truth seems to have been less discreditable and a good deal more tragic. The comtesse de Beauregard, aged forty-one, knew she was incurably ill with cancer and wanted to see for the last time the man she had loved so wholeheartedly.

After her night at the opera, she returned to her château and never emerged again. On August 24, 1865, the Paris newspaper *Le Temps* reported: "Madame la Comtesse de Beauregard (Lady Howard) died on Saturday night in her Château de Beauregard after a few days' illness. . . . Shortly before her death she was converted from the Protestant religion. The curé of Chesnay-les-Versailles baptized her. In accordance with the last wishes of the deceased, her body will be taken to England. . . ."

At forty, Eugénie was an imposingly handsome woman. The years, and the trials of her life with an errant husband, had given her features a somewhat severe cast, and she was bulkier than she had been in her youth. But her Titian hair, flashing eyes, and peerless complexion—marble, shading to rose pink when she was flushed from the dance or the hunt—remained unspoiled. And she was invariably animated, with a sharp and ready wit, while her movements were graceful and assured.

"Yes," said a visiting American diplomat at this time (with some reluctance, perhaps, for he must have disapproved deeply of her part in the Mexican adventure), "she is beautiful, more lovely than words can express." Sadly, the photographs and the court portraits of the time fail to capture that beauty. The woman they portray seems insipid rather than fiery, lending weight to the lonely judgment of Disraeli that she "lacked charm, had a detestable simper and Chinese eyes"—the latter presumably a bungled reference to the peculiar upward slant of her eyebrows.

Without question, Eugénie had superb dress sense. By day she dressed simply, generally wearing woolen jackets or "Garibaldi" blouses with plain black skirts and leather belts, and a saucy little hat. By night she would appear elaborately coiffed and superb in crinoline and open bodice, revealing the creamy perfection of her bust and shoulders. But it was the flair with which she wore her clothes, not just the stylishness of the garments, that made her such a striking figure.

In other respects, though, Eugénie remained essentially philistine. She had absolutely no ear for music, was rarely seen to read a serious book, and tended to express herself in clichés (as a fervent authoritarian, "the iron fist in a velvet glove" was one of her favorites), while her taste in decor veered toward the garish. Even by the heavily opulent standards of the day, her private apartments were a riotous display of the pretentious and the overstuffed—quilted sofas, white satin curtains, and marquetry cabinets everywhere, and the walls dripping with gilt embellishments.

Another expression of Eugénie's essential naiveté may be seen in her enthusiasm for the fad of spiritualism, then current in fashionable circles. In particular, she was taken by a Scots-American medium named Daniel Dunglas Hume, who became a regular caller at the Tuileries, where he would regale and awe the imperial circle with demonstrations of clairvoyance, table rapping, levitation, and other occult tricks.

Cowley wrote to Clarendon about this strange predilection. "Have you heard of a certain charlatan named Hume," he enquired,

who pretends to raise spirits, etc? He has been here for the past month and has complete hold over the Emperor and Empress, who both believe in his supernatural powers. . . . Hertford tells a capital story that the Emperor, having asked Hume to raise the spirits of the first Emperor and Louis Philippe, and being told they were present in the room, said that he could not see or hear either. "Wait a little," said Hume, "and Your Majesty will feel their presence." Soon afterwards, H.M. felt a violent kick on an unmentionable part of his sacred person, but could never ascertain which of his predecessors had applied it.

Almost certainly, Cowley relayed this story with tongue firmly in cheek and for the amusement of Clarendon, for he could hardly have believed that Napoleon, for all his notorious good nature, would tolerate such an indignity. Nonetheless, he seemed to believe that Napoleon was taken in by Hume. "Seriously speaking," he reported, "it is impossible to conceive that such a man should be so easily gulled, and as he receives this Hume at all times, and alone, the Police are seriously alarmed."

So the palace séances continued, with Hume being allowed to return again and again. And even when Eugénie caught Hume out in some trickery she overlooked it, arguing that since age had reduced his psychic powers, he was to be forgiven for augmenting them. Only when Hume outraged her by predicting that her son would never succeed to the throne did he fall out of favor.

In all likelihood, Cowley was mistaken in his belief that Hume's hold over Eugénie extended to her husband. Napoleon was surely far too much the nineteenth-century materialist to believe in such mumbo-jumbo, and no doubt he tolerated Hume only to avoid a clash with Eugénie.

Eugénie's predilection for spiritualism may have been a symptom of her growing obsession with death and salvation. She was increasingly haunted by the fear that she would share the fate either of her sister Paca or her predecessor Marie Antoinette—or else that her son might be taken from her by a deity angered by the godlessness of the court and the scarcely disguised agnosticism of her husband. In her muddled personal theology she was able to accept every detail of Catholic doctrine while ignoring the Church's deep disapproval of spiritual parlor tricks such as those practiced by the likes of Hume.

As a good Catholic, she felt a duty to insist on her husband's continuing to maintain the Pope's temporal powers in Italy, and if that were not sufficient to guarantee the well-being of her soul, she hatched a scheme in early 1865 for the reconstruction of the Church of the Holy Sepulchre. What she had in mind was nothing less than to set up an international fund, under her own chairmanship, to pay for the demolition of the existing church buildings and the erection of a more appropriate, multi-denominational modern temple.

"Two lateral churches, one for the Latins, the other for the Greeks, might form part of the plan, while the centre nave or principal building might be open for worshippers of all denominations," reported Cowley, to whom Eugénie went with her scheme in the hope of enlisting Victoria's support. "It was proposed that all the Christian princesses should unite to facilitate the work, an appeal coming from them not likely to be refused."

Cowley felt bound to forward the proposal, while correctly surmising that Victoria would hardly feel enthusiastic about a scheme that consigned the Church of England, of which she was the head, to sharing the center nave with the ragtag of "other denominations." Predictably, Clarendon wrote back to say that "the Queen won't have the Holy Sepulchre at any price. . . . We all know the scheme was an absurdity for the benefit of the Empress' soul. . . . It is not to be and you will have to make the best excuse you can. . . ."

At about this time, the Queen of Holland also received "a strange letter from the Empress about a plan for saving her soul." It got equally short shrift, and when even the Catholic queens and princesses of Europe showed a distinct lack of enthusiasm, Eugénie had to drop the plan, and with it her hopes for a certain path to salvation.

Although preoccupied with the state of her soul, Eugénie could not escape the worldly imperatives of a court life which was seasonal, nomadic, and relentless. "One of the first duties of a sovereign," her husband used to say, "is to amuse his subjects of all ranks in the social scale. He has no more right to have a dull court than to have a weak army or a poor navy."

From mid-December to Easter the court was at the Tuileries, and most evenings were taken up with receptions, balls, concerts, and banquets on a grand scale. During spring and the early part of the summer, the court was at Saint-Cloud—the sumptuous palace which, like the Tuileries, was to be destroyed in the Franco-Prussian War of 1870—before moving on to Fontainebleau with its great forest and charming lake. In September, the emperor and empress would go to Biarritz and the informal palace known as the Villa Eugénie, where they would be accompanied only by their more intimate acquaintances and where daily life was, by imperial standards, decidedly informal.

And then, in the autumn, there were the great imperial hunting weekends at Compiègne, some 50 miles north of Paris. Parisians used to go to the Gare du Nord on Friday afternoons to goggle at the imperial couple and their guests as they entrained for Compiègne while bewigged and liveried servants loaded vast amounts of luggage on board—sometimes as many as nine hundred trunks on one train.

Cowley has left us a good description of a typical Compiègne weekend and of the personal styles of his host and hostess. Writing to Clarendon from Compiègne, he reported: "The Empress, instead of letting people alone, constantly torments herself and them by thinking it necessary to furnish constant amusement for them . . . but they are both so natural and unaffected, and there is so little ceremony and etiquette, that the life is not disagreeable for a short time."

Cowley continued:

Breakfast is at half past eleven, then there is either hunting or shooting or some expedition to go to. Horses and carriages are found for everybody who wants them and nothing can be prettier than one of their cavalcades. Dinner about eight o'clock, which never lasts more than an hour. In the evening there is dancing to a hand organ (a dreadful trial to one's auricular nerves) or charades or cards. Now and then a Company from one of the Theatres from Paris is brought down to act.

It was from one of these Compiègne weekends that Cowley sent Clarendon an intriguing account of just how unstuffy and informal Napoleon could be.

He has a constant cold upon him since we have been here, how caught you would never guess, but if your youthful reminiscences will take you back to a game called "Hare and Hounds" you will picture to yourself His Imperial Majesty, his pockets filled with little bits of paper, enacting the hare while the rest of the society of all ages follow the imperial scent. The amusement, however, ended in His Majesty catching a violent cold, from which he is still suffering.

This account moved Clarendon to reply:

The history of the imperial cold is really curious and not the least curious part is his having the taste for such puerile pastimes, and the courage to engage in them, surrounded as he knows himself to be by hostile critics. What a story the hunt would make for the newspapers, and what a subject for illustration the hare and hounds would furnish for *Punch*. Our friend is an odd little fellow, it is impossible not to like him or not to feel that he has qualities which would make him a most reliable friend if he had good advisers about him, but a man who is as ignorant and indolent as the Emperor and has as much unavoidable business to do must depend on others. . . .

Except when Napoleon and Eugénie were at Compiègne or Biarritz, most court evenings were devoted to lavish balls, banquets, and receptions. But on those evenings when the Bonapartes were en famille and not staging some grand entertainment, their diversions were simple and, to the modern sensibility, bordering on the naive. Billiards, cards, table quoits, spelling bees, blindman's buff, charades, and dancing to a mechanical piano were the favorite pastimes. Occasionally a professional theater company would come to perform a play or a noted musician would give a recital. Eugénie was particularly fond of Gounod, whose treacly piano performances rarely failed to reduce her to tears.

Very often, Napoleon would retire early to work in his study on his *Life of Julius Caesar*. Other times he would slip away for a rendezvous with his mistress-of-the-moment. But on the nights when he remained in the salon with his wife, son, and dinner guests, he was invariably the model of an amiable paterfamilias, radiating a gentle charm through the grunts and monosyllables with which he usually expressed himself.

Courtiers noted with some amusement that he was so good-natured he would let Loulou's big black dog Nero edge him off his seat. They also noticed that Napoleon was a good deal more attentive to Loulou than Eugénie was, constantly fussing over his well-being, fretting over every minor mishap and childish ailment.

20

THE
ELEGANT
MORNY

NEXT TO LOUIS NAPOLEON HIMSELF, the quintessential Second Empire man was his half brother Morny, mastermind of the December coup, a charming opportunist whose life seemed to revolve around sex, fashion, horse racing, and financial speculation, but who also revealed an unexpected talent for affairs of state.

Starting out with little but his sharp wit and good looks—and acutely conscious of his lustrous if illegitimate descent from Talleyrand on one side and the Beauharnais family on the other—he had made his first fortune in the final years of the July monarchy by speculating in sugar beet, using money lent to him by his wealthy mistress, the comtesse Fanny le Hon.

On being raised to the nobility by Louis-Philippe, Morny chose for his coat of arms a design featuring a hydrangea (i.e., a hortensia) in memory of his mother Queen Hortense, embellished with a bar sinister, a bunch of lilies, and the motto "Keep silent, but remember." Boulevard wits dubbed him "Count Hortensia," a joke which seems not to have disturbed him at all.

Until his half brother so unexpectedly became President of the Second Republic, Morny had been no Bonapartist, but a staunch supporter of the Orléans monarchy under which he had flourished. But in 1848 he adapted quickly to the new political reality and, having proved his worth in the December Days, retained a position of supreme influence, rivaling and eventually outstripping Persigny's. But while contributing much wise counsel to his half brother, he never hesitated to use his position as confidant and adviser to advance his own speculative interests.

It was Morny's business connections in Russia more than any objective strategic or political considerations that made him try to prevent Napoleon's martial venture into the Crimea. The same considerations led him to urge on his half brother an exaggeratedly conciliatory policy toward Russia, almost before the guns of Sebastopol had cooled. Similarly, it was his ownership of discounted Mexican government bonds, more than any belief in a manifest French destiny in the New World, that caused Morny to join forces with Eugénie in pushing Napoleon into his massive and misguided intervention in Mexico.

And it was the prospect of personal profit, rather than regard for French national interests, that prompted him to conspire with the British to urge Napoleon's withdrawal of support for Eugénie's cousin, de Lesseps's, daring project to build a canal across the desert at Suez. The history of the Second Empire, in short, is studded with instances of Morny intervening at the highest level to line his own pocket and those of his business associates.

To the lesser lights of finance and fashion, Morny's every move was a signpost. For his ineffable stylishness, he was often referred to as "His Elegance, the duc de Morny," and should he appear at the Bourse or at the Longchamp races wearing, for example, lemon-colored gloves, every would-be tycoon and man-about-town would follow suit within days. And if the word went around that "Morny's in it," any new stock flotation would be fully subscribed within hours.

Gossip about his succession of mistresses, his racehorses, his Old Masters, his châteaux, his haute cuisine, and his generally impeccable bon ton inspired as much admiration as the breathless accounts of his deft financial manipulations. For years it had been well known and widely admired that Morny's fortune originated in the passion he had inspired in the comtesse le Hon. And when that lady produced a baby daughter who looked more like her lover than her husband, the wits quipped admiringly that "Morny soit qui mal y pense."

Indeed, Morny seemed to have an effortless ability to derive monetary gain and sexual satisfaction at one and the same time. The worldly acclaimed his superb savoir faire when he returned from St. Petersburg in February 1857, having represented Napoleon at the coronation of Czar Alexander II, bearing not only a lucrative concession to build railways in Russia but a young, beautiful, and immensely wealthy bride. One of the very few Parisians not to have been impressed by his capture of the eighteen-year-old Princess Sophie Troubetskoi was Fanny le Hon, whose passion for Morny still burned after twenty years as his mistress. She went into mourning and received condolences as if bereaved.

In 1854 Napoleon appointed Morny president of the Legislative Body, which function Morny was able to perform with considerable subtlety and distinction while still having plenty of time for his business activities. His elevation from count to duke in 1862 confirmed the monarch's confidence in him.

As Morny's star rose, that of Persigny, his chief rival for Napoleon's ear, was sinking. From the outset—although they had joined forces to urge bold policies upon Louis Napoleon—the incompatibility of the two men had been evident. The smooth, stylish Morny had despised Persigny as a narrow and humorless ideologue, while Persigny had viewed Morny as an opportunist and Johnny-come-lately, devoid of personal loyalty to Napoleon or belief in Bonapartist principles.

In the early years of the Empire the battle between them was a seesaw. Persigny, for example, lost points by opposing the marriage to Eugénie while Morny won points by supporting it. But soon afterward Persigny's advice prevailed over Morny's in the confiscation of the Orléans property, leading to Morny's resignation as Interior Minister and Persigny's replacing him.

To a man as devoted to the Napoleonic idea as Persigny, marriage in May 1852 to the beautiful and spirited granddaughter of Marshal Ney, the resoundingly named Albine-Marie-Napoléone-Egle de la Moskowa, must have seemed a union ordained if not by Heaven, then at least by Fate. But his bliss did not last long. It soon became clear even to the none too perceptive Persigny that his bride, twenty-four years his junior, was relentlessly promiscuous. During their marriage, she bore five children, but it is quite possible that Persigny fathered none of them.

An anecdote dating from the time of his ambassadorship in London has it that for some hours Mme Persigny was missing. A search was made of the embassy and the head of chancery was heard to ask: "Have you looked carefully under all the furniture? The tables, the buffets, the secretaries?" That anecdote apart, another memento of the Persignys' time in London was Albine's fascination for all things British, which earned her the sobriquet among court wits of "Lady Persington."

One of her numerous lovers was a spectacular young rake, the duc de Gramont-Caderousse. On one occasion when Persigny was complaining loudly of his wife's infidelities, Gramont-Caderousse turned on him with silky contempt. "Sir," he drawled, "I cannot allow you talk like that about my mistress." Not only did she cuckold her husband more or less openly—on one notable occasion appearing at a palace ball with her lover's teethmarks clearly visible on her shoulder—but she was constantly berating and belittling him in company.

She would even assault him physically; more than once Persigny had to attend a cabinet meeting with the marks of her nails on his face. But he adored her and took it all meekly. Persigny's secretary observed: "His chivalrous heart forced him to hide from others his cruel inner pain."

Like his marital misfortunes, the doglike nature of Persigny's devotion to Napoleon was a joke to the more sophisticated courtiers, such as Morny. They laughed at his veritable apoplexy over the czar's refusal to address Napoleon as "mon frère." And they nodded knowingly when his behavior in the aftermath of the Orsini bomb plot—"c'est la guerre, c'est la guerre!"—so embarrassed the emperor that he was withdrawn from London for a year.

Nevertheless, Napoleon did not undervalue Persigny's services to himself and to the Empire. In mid-1856, having decided to invest his old comrade with the Grand Cross of the Legion of Honor, the highest rank of the order, Napoleon did so in a novel fashion. Persigny and his wife were at Saint-Cloud and Napoleon asked them to stay to dinner. When Persigny protested that they had no evening clothes, the emperor said that Eugénie would lend Madame Persigny a gown, while he would provide Persigny with a coat.

Subsequently, Napoleon handed Persigny an evening coat,

just taken from the imperial wardrobe, which bore a cross of the Legion of Honor on the right breast. Persigny was about to move it to the left breast where, being only a Grand Officer of the order, he was supposed to wear it. But Napoleon stopped him, saying he was herewith invested with the Grand Cross. Reporting the emperor's "very charming manner" of rewarding his old associate, Cowley observed: "I am very glad, for Persigny is one of the few honest men about H.M."

But honesty and loyalty were not enough to save Persigny when, as Minister of the Interior in 1863, he supervised parliamentary elections so ineptly that no fewer than thirty-two opposition candidates won seats in the Legislative Body. In a moment of irritation Napoleon dismissed him but, never able to turn his back completely on old friends, he shortly afterward elevated the bogus viscount to the status of a genuine duke. Despite his exalted title, though, and his continued membership of the Privy Council, Persigny was never again allowed to have the ear of his emperor.

The final removal of Persigny from his place at Napoleon's elbow signaled more than the end of a personal friendship stretching back for over thirty years; it was also a requiem for Bonapartism itself, an ideology much better suited to the attainment of power than to its exercise, and one that had been largely discarded in practice if not in theory. As Napoleon is reputed to have said at about this time: "Morny is an Orléanist, Plon-Plon is a Republican, I am a Socialist and Eugénie is a Legitimist. Only Persigny is a Bonapartist, and he is mad."

With Persigny out of the way, Morny was now unchallenged as the emperor's most influential adviser. But this, too, was not to last. Morny's death in 1865, at the age of only fifty-four and while he was at the height of his abilities, was totally unexpected and a shock to Napoleon and to France, which regarded him as vice-emperor in all but name.

When Morny first took to his bed, apparently with influenza, there was no immediate concern. But decades of high living had taken a heavy toll, and the sick man rapidly weakened and fell into a coma. Soon doctors diagnosed that his liver and pancreas were malfunctioning, conditions with which the medicine of the time could not cope. Emerging from his coma to realize that he was dying, Morny retained enough sense of posterity to order the immediate destruction of all his personal and business papers.

Napoleon and Eugénie hurried to his bedside, where the emperor held his half brother's hand, while the empress knelt in prayer. Morny was barely able to recognize them and to murmur a farewell. His young Russian wife appears to have been a good deal less affected than Napoleon and Eugénie. According to Cowley, she "behaved like a brute"—perhaps avenging herself for his many infidelities—and "to the last had dinners and parties, to the scandal of everybody." Not long after the required period of mourning was over, she remarried—her groom being the same Pépé de Alcañices, by now the Duke of Sisto, of whom Eugénie had been so madly enamored years before.

Of the departed Morny, Cowley observed that "he had it in him, if he had been honest, to have become a very great man."

If Morny and Persigny, in their very different fashions, were quintessential Second Empire men, the extraordinary Princess Pauline von Metternich was very much the Second Empire woman. Although not French, lacking the seductiveness of the court beauties, and in all probability faithful to her husband, she was the embodiment of much that characterized the Second Empire—outrageously frivolous, but with a sense of style and force of personality that masked physical and intellectual shortcomings and that also, one suspects, hid a deep anguish, for she was childless.

Pauline Metternich, wife of the Austrian Ambassador, was a classic *belle-laide*. She had pop eyes and a yellowish skin and a disarming self-mocking wit. She used to describe herself as looking like "a rather chic monkey." But by her verve and sheer ebullience, she mesmerized even those who disapproved of her.

Cowley thought her "an extraordinary young woman," though he sniffed that "things are coming to a pretty pass when the Austrian Ambassadress appears in the garb of a coachman and sings couplets in honour of the Sovereign [Napoleon] who has deprived her own Sovereign [Franz-Josef] of one of his fairest provinces."

Prosper Mérimée described her as "half great lady and half whore." She would smoke cigars, dance the can-can, and sing lewd ballads, imitating to perfection the cafés-concerts singers of the day. One night she went out for a dare onto the Boulevard des Italiens and walked the pavement with the street prostitutes until a policeman came along and demanded to see her permit.

Eugénie was inordinately fond of her, and took her advice on matters of dress and coiffeur. She even forgave her a remark which, from the lips of anyone else, would surely have been considered unforgivable. "My Empress," she said, "is a *real* Empress. The Empress Eugénie is merely Mlle de Montijo."

21

"THE FAIR IMPERIAL HARLOT"

ALTHOUGH THE WOODWORK WAS ALREADY ROTTEN, to the world at large the year 1867 appeared to be the Second Empire's annus mirabilis. It was the year of the Great Universal Exhibition of Paris, which outdid its predecessors and rivals in size and scope and which brought to the French capital—in addition to hundreds of thousands of lesser visitors—no fewer than three emperors, eight kings, one viceroy, five queens, twenty-four princes, seven princesses, nine grand dukes, two grand duchesses, and two archdukes, plus five mere dukes and two common-or-garden duchesses.

The Paris to which they flocked was a city grown legendary for its luxury and licentiousness, a city whose appeal was lyricized by the English poet Wilfred Scawen Blunt. "Paris!" he wrote, "What magic lived for us in those two syllables! What a picture they evoked of vanity and profane delights, of triumph in the world and the romance of pleasure! How great, how terrible a name was hers, the fair imperial harlot of civilised humanity!"

Poets—especially well born and fashionable poets like Blunt—do not generally consort with the dull and respectable, and Blunt may have been unaware that the great majority of Parisians, not to mention the provincial French, still lived lives of suffocating propriety. Even in court circles, there were faithful wives, loyal husbands, and wise virgins. But they did not provide the tone and texture of the city which thrilled and captivated Blunt.

Just as the drably respectable flavor of the preceding Orléanist period had been set by the buttoned-down King Louis-Philippe, so was the erotic ambience of the Second Empire determined by the example of the libidinous Louis Napoleon and his coterie of court roués, eager mistresses, and complaisant husbands.

This atmosphere of indulgence, permeating all levels of society, had made the pursuit of pleasure seem a universal preoccupation, accessible to all but the poorest. A duke or a banker might exchange a rivière of diamonds worth 50,000 francs for a few nights with one of the city's celebrated *grandes courtesans,* but a banker's clerk or a duke's valet, visiting some neighborhood *bal grisette,* could have an equally memorable time for the price of a new dress and a few drinks, with any one of an army of eager and well-versed amateurs.

Alexandre Dumas fils had coined the term *demi-monde* in the 1855 stage version of his durable and adaptable novel, *La Dame aux Camélias,* to describe the capital's parallel society of courtesans, their clients and hangers-on, and the operatives of the service industries which fed off their commerce, from restaurateurs to hairdressers and from couturiers to waiters.

At the summit of this half-world, which existed alongside the court and frequently overlapped onto it, were expensive *belles horizontales* such as Léonide Leblanc, who boasted the sobriquet "Madame Maximum" and numbered among her lovers Plon-Plon and one of Louis-Philippe's sons, the duc d'Aumale; such as Céleste Mogador—like Marguerite Bellanger, an ex-equestrienne from the Cirque Franconi—who so ensnared a foolish young nobleman that he made her the comtesse de Chabrillan; such as Cora Pearl, born Emma Crouch, the splendidly vulgar English strumpet who was famous for her toilet seat made of swansdown, her broad Cockney accent, and her sumptuous breasts, plaster casts of which she presented to her most important regular clients.

Often the clients were as extravagant and outrageous as the courtesans, and none more so than Madame Persigny's occasional lover, the seemingly insatiable duc de Gramont-

Caderousse. He was the leader of an exclusive group of one hundred or so *Cocodès*—"swells" or "sports" in contemporary English parlance—whose mirror image was the loose confederation of one hundred or so leading courtesans, known as the *Ogresses*, or man-eaters.

Gramont-Caderousse's exploits were legendary. On one notable occasion, he presented the quondam Miss Crouch with a solid silver bathtub which he filled with champagne before stripping and climbing into it, in front of a roomful of friends. At another bacchanale, he is said to have jumped a thoroughbred over a table laden with priceless Sèvres. He once paid a can-can dancer known as "Rigolboche" 5,000 francs to walk naked in broad daylight across the Boulevard des Italiens.

But his most stylish jape was performed when he knew he was about to die. He invited a dozen of his closest friends to a farewell supper party, got them very drunk, "and then, very quietly and without a struggle, expired before they had time to get sober . . . and died, as he had lived, like a clever clown."

Gramont-Caderousse was only thirty-two, having thrown away in frenzied dissipation not only his health but also a very considerable fortune. Such was the fate of many another *Cocodè*, men of seemingly inexhaustible wealth ruined by gambling and the voracious demands of irresistible vices. To these—if disease or exhaustion did not carry them off first—suicide sometimes seemed more acceptable than bankruptcy. "That pig," said Cora Pearl of a lover who shot himself in her living room. "He has ruined my lovely carpet!"

In dress and behavior, the women of the court and the "respectable" side of Parisian society all too frequently took their cue from the strumpets they looked down upon, meeting their lovers undisguised and unveiled in theaters and restaurants, riding with them publicly in the Bois, going openly to their apartments. "How astonished and horror-struck would be the great ladies of the Restoration if they could rise from their graves and behold their granddaughters emulating the demi-monde," wrote one sophisticated observer of Parisian manners and morals, the expatriate British boulevardier Captain Rees Gronow.

"The dignified, artful, proud, but perhaps not more virtuous grandmother would have been utterly disgusted, not so much at the immorality as at the bad taste displayed in such arrangements, which then existed as much as now, but were supposed to be unknown."

It was, of course, both the immorality and the bad taste of *la vie Parisienne* which shocked Captain Gronow's monarch. As a matter of diplomacy, Victoria was bound to allow the Prince of Wales to attend the 1867 exhibition, but did so with obvious misgivings. On the occasion of an intended excursion by Bertie to the French capital in 1864—even though he was to be accompanied by his wife—she had admonished him:

I am rather doubtful about your visit to Paris. If it does take place, it must be on the complete understanding that it is in real incognito, which your other visits have not been. That you stop at an hotel and do not lodge with the Emperor and Empress and do not accept an invitation to Compiègne or Fontainebleau, the style of going on there being quite unfit for a young and respectable Prince and Princess like yourselves. Of course, you might accept a day's shooting at Compiègne and dine with the Emperor and Empress, *but nothing more!*

Amid the glitter and gaiety of the Second Empire's year of marvels, Napoleon was—appropriately enough—in the thick of another love affair. Advancing age, deteriorating health, and the increasingly heavy burdens of power might have reduced his sexual powers, but the game must go on.

Socially, his latest mistress could not have been further removed from her predecessor, the cheerfully plebeian Margot la Rigoleuse. Indeed, the comtesse Louise de Mercy-Argenteau was both by birth and by marriage a member of the old aristocracy, which considered itself socially superior to the parvenu emperor and his upstart wife. Like many others in Legitimist society, the comtesse had shunned the court, and consequently it was not until the spring of 1866 that Napoleon met her.

Cowley, his ear for intrigue as finely tuned as ever, was quick to report that Napoleon was "getting up a new flirtation. . . . She is young, pretty and, being deserted very much by her husband, has taken to poetry and painting," he reported. "It is supposed that she will not surrender, but will try to convert the imperial mind from its perverted ways. . . . There is no saying what influence such a woman might gain. I shall look out for squalls on the other side of the menage."

Just before meeting Napoleon, Louise de Mercy had become the subject of scandalized gossip among her own circle when her rejected lover, the comte de Stäckelberg, committed suicide. Defiantly, she resolved to cock a snook at the high-born scandal mongers of the Faubourg-Saint-Honoré by doing something even more scandalous—taking part in an imperial charity fête in the Elysée Gardens. It was there that the emperor first saw her and, as he said as he handed her a bunch of violets he had just purchased, the effect on him was like "a thunderbolt." With an abandon that would have infuriated Eugénie if ever it had reached her ears, he told the beautiful young comtesse: "From now on, you are our Empress."

Louise de Mercy was indeed a great beauty, tall and commanding, serenely conscious of her Olympian looks, with a flawless complexion and the blond hair that was de rigueur for any society woman of the day. She was renowned for her impulsiveness and her tireless energy; it was said that she could dance all night and still appear fresh as a rose, without a grain of powder on her face. "Like Cleopatra," said a contemporary, "she would have thrown pearls into her goblet or her heart out of the window on the caprice of the moment."

She was also an accomplished miniaturist and musician, and it was not her beauty alone that drew admiring throngs of men around the piano when she sat down to play Liszt or Chopin. Her husband was a nonentity, unable or unwilling to exercise any authority over her, and her previous lovers, apart from Stäckelberg, had included the natural son of the czar, Prince Obreskow, who was a first secretary at the Russian Embassy.

After his first encounter with her, Napoleon said to Mérimée—no doubt intending it to be played back to Eugénie—that although she was beautiful, the comtesse was "too big and too strong" for his taste. "I make a point of never trying anything with a woman who looks as though she could beat me," he jested.

But very soon Louise de Mercy was a weekend guest at Compiègne, and after seeing her as Judith in a tableau vivant, Napoleon bent to kiss her hand and murmured: "Comtesse, why has such a beautiful jewel so long been kept from us?" To which she replied: "A jewel, sire! If jewel there be, it is at the service of Your Majesty."

Persigny, long since relegated to the outer fringes of the court, saw Napoleon's interest in the comtesse as a way to regain the favor of his emperor and appointed himself Cupid. At his instigation Louise persuaded her husband to buy Persigny's mansion, the former home of Madame Pompadour, at 18, rue de l'Elysée. This house was connected by an underground tunnel to the Elysée Palace, making it possible for Louise to rendezvous discreetly there with her imperial lover.

No less helpfully, Persigny arranged to meet Louise every afternoon when she went out riding in the Bois. If he wore a violet in his buttonhole, it meant that the emperor would see her in the Elysée Palace that night; at the appointed hour she would open the concealed door to the secret tunnel, which led from her boudoir to the sacristy of the Elysée where Napoleon would be waiting for her.

The affair was in all probability more sentimental and conversational than physical, for Napoleon's sexual appetite was surely waning by now. But Louise was a good deal more than merely decorative; she took a lively and intelligent interest in politics and was a good talker. Also, although Napoleon was no great lover of music, the compositions of Liszt and Chopin would not have been too demanding for his taste when played by the lovely Louise. Whatever the case, the few surviving letters from Napoleon to Louise (see Chapter 28) suggest a tenderness and warmth beyond the range of his customary libertinage.

If the emperor's example inspired Parisians of all classes to new levels of sexual activity, Eugénie's example gave similar impetus to another form of commerce for which Paris had long been famous: fashion. While disdaining sex, she was obsessed with clothes and coiffure and set the standard for all—from the haughty ladies of the old aristocracy, who disdained the parvenu court of the Bonapartes, to the *grisettes* in the neighborhood dance halls.

"It is not because the Empress Eugénie is the wife of

Napoleon III that she sets the fashion," observed Gronow. "She is considerably older and certainly not handsomer than was the duchesse de Nemours* when she left France to die in exile; but she has the chic, if I may use such a word, that the Orléans princesses did not possess; and the quietest dowager, before she ventures to adopt a coiffure, as well as the gayest lady of the demi-monde, will cast a look to see what the Empress wears."†

It was Eugénie, for example, who first popularized the crinoline skirt—a style which captured all fashionable Europe, plus America—in order to hide her pregnancy in 1855 and '56. And it was Eugénie, proud of her splendid bosom if contemptuous of the desires its display might arouse, who introduced and popularized the plunging neckline, which reached new lows during her reign. To a certain extent, she also combined politics with fashion, for example making a point of wearing gowns made of Lyon silk in order to promote the silk industry there.

The color and style of her hair set the fashion. Smart coiffeurs made a fortune persuading their customers to have their hair done à l'Impératrice, and for those who lacked the natural attributes there were wigs, plaits, *tresses chignons*, and Eugénie curls to be bought ready-made. Her wonderfully fresh complexion was also emulated and there was a booming trade in chemical preparations—some of them injurious—that were supposed to give less fortunate women something of the bloom Eugénie had received from nature.

Her eyes and her eyebrows, too, were copied by the court ladies, the bourgeoisie, and even the hoi-polloi—the brows penciled black, in the Spanish style, the eyes shadowed with blue, and the irises bathed in belladonna to make them sparkle.

As supreme arbiter of fashion, the empress assured the dazzling success of the young English couturier Charles Frederick Worth, who was to become the feared and ruthless dictator of dress for the haute monde of Paris. Worth had arrived in Paris in

---

*Daughter-in-law of King Louis-Philippe, and a noted beauty.
†In an intriguing aside, Gronow added that, "strange to say, the supreme good taste and elegance which reign in Her Majesty's toilettes were by no means conspicuous in her younger days; for, as Mademoiselle Montijo, she was voted beautiful and charming but very ill-dressed."

1846 from London, where he had been an apprentice at the clothiers Swan & Edgar. By 1857 he had established his House of Worth on the rue de la Paix, where he introduced the idea of the live mannequin to the fashion world, and where his flair and originality drew him to the attention of Pauline Metternich, who in turn drew him to the attention of the empress.

Worth was already well on the way to becoming the most sought-after fashion designer of a city besotted with style. Eugénie's patronage propelled him the rest of the way. Yet he was no charmer: according to Hippolyte Taine, he was "a little, dry, black nervous creature," who treated his rich and influential customers with utter disdain. "Carelessly stretched out on a divan, cigar between his lips. He says to them 'Walk! Turn! Good, come back in a week and I will compose you a toilette that will suit you.' "

It was not the customer who chose her clothes, but Worth, noted Taine, and he would not deign to accept a new client unless she had been introduced by another. But the ladies of Paris did not seem to mind how Worth behaved so long as he agreed to dress them. Nor did any of them seem to care that his ruderies were delivered in an execrable English accent. Worth had never made much of an attempt to master the language of his adopted country, and at a time when fashionable women changed their clothes six or more times a day he rapidly became rich enough not to care if his bitchy self-indulgence and outrageous prices* did lose him a few customers.

But just as sex had become a commodity for all but the poorest, so had fashion, and it was not only the ladies of the court, the courtesans, and the other ultra-rich clients of M. Worth who were obsessed with clothes. The bourgeoisie, grande and petite, joined in the orgy of self-adornment, helping to bring into existence the great department stores, many of which— such as Au Bon Marché, La Samaritaine, and Le Printemps— survive to this day.

In part because censorship severely limited the scope of the press to discuss more serious matters, articles on fashion oc-

---

* "He is expensive, horribly expensive, monstrously expensive," complained Princess Metternich, and Eugénie is said to have paid 100,000 to 200,000 francs for a new Worth creation.

cupied a large proportion of the newspapers and fashion writers vied with each other to promote the latest styles, fabrics, and colors, usually at exhaustive length. Fashion colors were often named after current events, such as Crimean green, Sebastopol blue, Bismarck brown, and Magenta, and—after the opening of the Suez Canal in 1869—Eau de Nil. Like color, the nomenclature of style also tended to the military or the political, as with the Garibaldi shirt and the Zouave jacket.

Never in history had a great capital been so utterly absorbed in the picayune details of fashion, and a perceptive few regarded such obsessive concern with outward appearance and embellishment as a reflection of the regime's predilection for style over substance. The ever-censorious Goncourts, who found the court "flashy and insecure, composed of parvenus with stolen titles and crude praetorians with clanking sabers," added that to society at large appearances had "never been so important, so demanding, so destructive and demoralizing."

And Gronow marveled that fashion had obtained "such a wonderful power over the French mind that it can actually transform the body so as to suit the exigency of the moment." Recalling that in former days the ideal type of Frenchwoman was a petite brunette, he commented that now it was the fashion to be "tall and commanding." Consequently, "one sees dozens of gigantic women every day that one goes out, with heels inside as well as outside their boots; perhaps even stilts under those long sweeping petticoats."

As for coloring: "Frenchwomen used to have dark hair; blondes were not generally admired, and tried by every possible means to darken their hair; but now, since the Empress has made fair hair à la mode, all women must be blondes, and what with gold powder and light wigs they do succeed. As to complexions, a dark one is now unknown; roses and lilies abound on every cheek. . . ."

Together with sex and clothes, the third leg of the triad on which Second Empire society so jauntily perched was money.

To be sure, an exaggerated materialism was no more a new phenomenon in French life than a preoccupation with sex and fashion. Orléanist France—Tocqueville's "joint stock company"—had been particularly notable for the rise of a bourgeoisie utterly preoccupied with making money. But under Louis Napoleon that preoccupation became a feverish obsession. Only in our own time, perhaps, has the acquisition and spending of wealth so completely dominated a society.

The Second Empire had been ushered in on a veritable tide of profit as share prices on the Paris Bourse soared in anticipation of the stability which the December coup promised. "L'Empire, c'est le benefice," as Napoleon might have said. And in recognition of his stimulating effect on business, a syndicate of stockbrokers went so far as to suggest erecting a statue of the emperor in front of the stock exchange.

But it was not just the well-to-do with disposable income who rushed to gamble on the stock market. By the thousands, ordinary working people scraped together their meager savings to invest in new ventures, some of them highly speculative, as when Ferdinand de Lesseps floated his Suez Canal Company in 1858 and the vast majority of the 400,000 shares on offer at 200 francs each were snapped up by 25,000 small French investors. As the London *Globe* commented (not at all kindly, for the British were much opposed to the idea of the canal), "the principal shareholders are hotel waiters . . . and petty grocery employees."

While the francs and sous of the lower middle and upper working classes were part of the tide of capital that floated France to new levels of industrialized prosperity, it was—as today—those who understood the art of channeling that flood of money in the right directions who were the big winners. As a character in Dumas fils's 1857 play *La Question d'Argent* remarked: "Business? It's all very simple; business is other people's money."

This philosophy, besides enriching people like Morny, threw into prominence financial adventurers like the brothers Emile and Isaac Pereire, who founded the Crédit Mobilier, an investment bank which sold shares to the public to raise funds for the construction of railways, roads, steamships, department stores, and hotels both in France and overseas. Although traditional bankers such as the Rothschilds looked askance at the Pereire brothers, the public had no such qualms. They snapped up Crédit Mobilier shares almost before they were issued, and their value doubled and tripled within days.

But the Crédit Mobilier proved to be, as the Rothschilds had warned, basically unsound, and under pressure from the traditional bankers it began to founder. Finally it collapsed in 1867, and with it the hopes and futures of thousands of small investors.

Then, as now, the public obsession with the acquisition of wealth attracted the opprobrium of religious leaders. In 1864 the ungrateful Pope Pius IX issued an encyclical entitled "The Syllabus of Errors" which was said to have been inspired by the spectacle of Louis Napoleon's France and which inveighed against the excessive materialism of the age. But neither the collapse of the Crédit Mobilier nor the recriminations of the Pope could quench the investment fever that gripped the country.

By 1867, any number of considerable fortunes had been made out of Napoleon's energetic and doubtless altruistic program to rebuild Paris. The medieval slums which had characterized much of the city until the middle of the century—a sea of squalor covering the Ile de la Cîté, Montmartre, the rue Saint-Denis, and lapping almost to the doors of the Louvre, the Tuileries, and Notre Dame—had been rebuilt with astonishing speed and efficiency under his direction.

Napoleon had put this work in hand almost immediately after becoming emperor at the end of 1852. By 1867, new aqueducts brought fresh, running water to districts which had previously been supplied by porters bearing barrels on their backs, while new sewers—banishing the threat of cholera that had killed 20,000 Parisians as recently as 1848—removed the effluent which had previously been drawn from reeking cesspools and taken by night cart to be dumped in the Forest of Bondy.

Gas lamps lit streets which had until recently been the Stygian haunts of footpads and cut-purses. New railway stations were the gateway from Paris to all quarters of the kingdom. The

Louvre had at last been completed after 700 years, and work was proceeding apace on the new Théâtre de l'Opéra to replace the one on the rue Lepelletier, where Napoleon and Eugénie had so narrowly escaped the bombs of Orsini.

Where pre-Second Empire Paris had possessed a mere 47 acres of unkempt gardens, it now boasted 5,000 acres of park. Splendid boulevards and broad avenues, lined with the ornate mansions of the Empire's rich and powerful, conveyed an overwhelming impression of wealth and grandeur. The road-making also had an important secondary purpose. As one ironical observer put it, "The broad new streets which drove through the town were beautifully accessible to light, air and infantry. No insurrection could have lived for an hour in those long, open avenues; and on the barricades of the future it would be difficult to do anything but die."

Gronow, who was decidedly not a critic of the emperor, ignored the security implications of the reconstruction and waxed ecstatic about the new Paris:

A beautiful, fairy-like city has replaced the crowded heaps of dingy, dark dwellings; the blind alleys and fetid courts have been exchanged for lofty and elegant mansions, wide and well-paved thoroughfares, and spacious open places. . . . Upon sites once covered with cemeteries, with sewers, with pits, and with abominations indescribable, have arisen verdant lawns, squares and gardens where at the vernal season flowers charm the eye and gratify the sense, while sparkling fountains pour forth their cool streams; spaces where the sun and air give life and animation to all around; mansions where domestic or polished society can enjoy all the luxuries and comforts which art and taste have introduced.

In cold fact, the taste in which many of the new buildings had been conceived was by no means as exemplary as Gronow imagined. The spirit of the Second Empire was frankly nouveau riche and much of the architecture of Louis Napoleon's Paris was garishly flamboyant, a wild melange of period styles—Renaissance, Gothic, Baroque, Romanesque—with little consideration given to function. Plon-Plon's gaudy mansion on the Avenue Montaigne typified the lavish vulgarity of the imperial elite, while the new opera house (not to be completed until after

Napoleon's fall) survives to this day as an example of the riotous excesses of the public architecture of the Second Empire.

The rebuilding of Paris had been entrusted to a man whom Persigny, while Interior Minister, had called "one of the most extraordinary products of our day—strong, vigorous, and energetic, yet subtle, clever, and resourceful." Georges Eugène Haussmann, whom Napoleon elevated to the rank of baron for his services, was a career civil servant and had been Prefect of Gironde until Napoleon made him Prefect of the Seine on the creation of the Empire.

Between them, he and Napoleon worked out the master plan for the refurbishment and modernization of Paris, and in 1854 the destruction of the old higgledy-piggledy capital began. It was done without raising taxes but by selling city bonds to small investors—a means of financing which, like the methods of the Crédit Mobilier, scandalized conservative bankers such as Baron Rothschild, but which seemed to appeal to the public. A bond issue of 60 million francs was entirely sold out in one day.

During the reconstruction Haussmann wielded virtually dictatorial powers and did so with some relish, for he was arrogant and impatient by nature. He also, knowingly or otherwise, allowed real estate speculators to make considerable fortunes on the basis of leaked inside information, while thousands of the Paris poor were driven out of their homes in the process of slum clearance and road widening. All this created a scandal in which the punsters of Paris joked about "Les Comptes Fantastiques d'Haussmann," and which eventually led to his disgrace and dismissal in the dying days of the Empire, when Napoleon was either too sick or too preoccupied to go to the aid of his protégé.

But visitors to Paris knew little and cared less about the seamy side of the city's reconstruction program. What they saw and rightly admired was a vital and dazzling capital, throbbing with life and pregnant with exciting possibilities. Especially in the spring, when its trees were in blossom, the atmosphere was magical, at once excitingly modern and headily romantic.

One could experience this atmosphere in its most concentrated form by visiting the Tuileries Gardens, where all the strands of Second Empire society would be represented on a spring or summer afternoon when a military band was playing. Edouard Manet, the father of Impressionism—and in his time a very controversial painter indeed—captured the scene to perfection in his canvas *La Musique aux Tuileries:* the top-hatted, frock-coated men, the crinolined women, the elaborately dressed children weaving in and out among their elders, as the brass band thumps out some popular tune of the period.

Along the boulevards, as in the parks, there was a perpetual movement of strolling idlers and hurrying *midinettes,* of swaggering soldiers and sauntering shoppers, and dispersed among the throng an army of organ grinders, flower girls, musicians, singers, ice-cream vendors, dancing bears, contortionists, escape artists, jugglers, and one-man bands. Life on the streets of Paris was a non-stop cabaret, and the most colorful of the players who performed in it were the off-duty soldiers, to be seen in greater numbers than at any time since the First Empire— chausseurs and zouaves, lancers and guides, guards and spahis and cuirassiers and hussars. "Ah, que j'aime les soldats!" went one of the latest hit songs, and all Paris seemed to agree.

The composer of that song and supreme musical interpreter of this scene of bustle and gaiety was the dandified German Jew turned Catholic, Jacques Offenbach. His music breathes the very essence of Second Empire Paris and to listen to it today is to conjure up vivid images of his time and place. Offenbach had launched his comic opera house, les Bouffes Parisiennes, in 1855, the year of the first great Paris exposition. Now, in 1867, the year of the second such exposition, he was to achieve his greatest artistic and financial success to date.

Offenbach had received his Legion of Honor in 1861, following the success of his *Orpheus in the Underworld,* a colorful satire on life in the Tuileries in which Jupiter, a thinly disguised Napoleon, spends much of his time wenching, while Juno (Eugénie) looks on in helpless rage, and the lesser gods— Napoleon's courtiers—follow his example. Unperturbed by Offenbach's subversive subtext, or perhaps unconscious of it, Napoleon had ordered a command performance of *Orpheus* and thanked the composer for an "unforgettable evening."

Opera bouffe was the perfect medium by which to satirize an empire which was itself just as much comic as grand, and it was surely appropriate that the brilliant and cynical Offenbach—the picture of a boulevardier in the well-cut clothes which adorned his knife-blade figure—should derive such critical and commercial profit from the very system he guyed. And now, at the Empire's zenith, Offenbach was presenting his boldest satire to date, subtly ridiculing the cult of war and the excesses of power in his *Grand Duchess of Gérolstein*, starring the electrifying Hortense Schneider.

During 1867, so many representatives of visiting royalty beat a path to her dressing room that the route there from the stage door of the Théâtre des Variétés became known as the Passage des Princes, a description which, of course, was also applied to a portion of Mlle Schneider's sumptuous anatomy.

But there existed another Paris, and while Offenbach breathed the musical spirit of the boulevards, it was left to a very different personality, the doomed and tortured Charles Baudelaire, to find beauty in the pestilential misery that lurked behind the city's glittering facade.

His was the Paris of the sick, the crippled, the unemployed, of the child prostitutes, beggars, ragpickers, and cutthroats who struggled to survive in the filthy back streets, some of them just off the grand boulevards, which the tourists and the bourgeoisie never entered and where even the police feared to tread. His was the Paris where, as Mark Twain noted when he visited the city that year, you could hire a man to commit murder for seven dollars, the Paris whose streets the novelist Maxime du Camp called "a cloaca* lined with nameless dens."

It was also the Paris of industrial slums—Bercy, Belleville, Les Batignolles, La Chapelle, Charonne, and Vaugirard—where the new urban working class, many of them just in from the country, slaved for 3 francs a day and blew it all on absinthe,

---

* Contemporary observers were inordinately fond of using such terminology to describe various parts of the city. Zola called Les Halles "the stomach of Paris," while Lord Hertford called the theater district in the vicinity of the Boulevard des Italiens its "clitoris."

leaving their wives and children to root for food in the garbage dumps. It was in this midden that Baudelaire grew his "flowers of evil"—the collection of poems entitled *Les Fleurs du Mal* that led to his prosecution for "offenses against public morals" when he published them in 1857.

Those poems, extracting a magic vision from the vile realities of life in the slums of Paris, have long since been recognized as a work of pure genius. But it is hardly surprising that the vain, heartless, and hypocritical society of Baudelaire's day should have found them unprintable.

Another literary work of universally recognized genius that ran afoul of the law at about the same time was Gustave Flaubert's *Madame Bovary*. This intensely realistic story of a provincial housewife's adulteries and eventual suicide outraged bourgeois sensitivities, even though its editor had made significant cuts, and even though it did not contain a single scene which by even the starchiest standards of the twentieth century could be described as erotic. Obviously, it was not the adulteries but the author's unflattering portrayal of middle-class myopia and complacency that inspired the authorities to charge Flaubert and his publisher with committing "an outrage to public morality and religion."

In the event, the prosecution case collapsed and the defendants were acquitted, even though the judgment stated that the novel deserved censure because it "failed to provoke a disgust for vice." As Flaubert observed in a letter to a friend: "The police have blundered. They thought they were attacking a run-of-the-mill novel and some ordinary little scribbler, whereas now (in part thanks to the prosecution) my novel is looked on as a masterpiece."

The prosecution of Baudelaire and Flaubert is certainly a blot on the Second Empire—but not quite such a blot as some of its critics have made it out to be. Flaubert was, after all, acquitted and by his own account the empress spoke twice in his favor, while Napoleon himself said that "they should leave him alone." (Indeed, in 1864 Napoleon received Flaubert at Compiègne and in 1866 made him a Chevalier of the Legion of Honour.) And even in our own time, in liberal-democratic Britain, books such as *Lady Chatterley's Lover* and *The Well of Lone-*

liness have been the subject of court prosecutions. It might also be noted that it was not until 1949 that six of Baudelaire's banned poems from *Les Fleurs du Mal* were permitted to be published in France.

That the Second Empire was philistine, hypocritical, corrupt, and relentlessly materialistic cannot be denied. But some of France's greatest painters, poets, composers, and novelists flourished in its time, and they were recognized no less and persecuted no more than they might have been under regimes a good deal more liberal politically.

BOOK THREE

DECLINE

AND

FALL

★

*"Nous sommes dans un pôt de chambre et on
nous enmerdera."*
—General Auguste Ducrot

22

DISASTER
AT
SADOWA

ON JULY 3, 1866, THE GREATEST BATTLE in the history of Europe up to that time, involving half a million men and fifteen hundred artillery pieces, took place on the Bohemian Plain before a nondescript village named Sadowa. No French troops and no direct French interests were involved, yet if any one event may be said to have signaled the beginning of the end for Napoleon III and his Second Empire, it was the Battle of Sadowa.

Watching the battle from high ground, a massive figure astride a red stallion, was the man who would be Napoleon's nemesis, the jackbooted and spike-helmeted Otto von Bismarck, Minister-President of Prussia. The titanic clash of arms which was to rage all day at his feet was Bismarck's doing, the climax of his ruthlessly methodical campaign to bring about a showdown between Prussia and Austria and so decide once and for all the leadership of the German-speaking people.

Bismarck was by no means confident of the outcome. Although outwardly impassive, he was somberly aware that if his side lost the battle, his own career would be finished. "I was almost as close to the gallows as to the throne," he would recall.

In the event, the disciplined steadfastness of the Prussian troops, the dour genius of their commander-in-chief, the sixty-six-year-old Count Helmuth von Moltke, and the timely arrival of reinforcements, won the day. It was a stunning victory for the Prussians, a victory that would throw the rest of Europe into a panic and, while demolishing at a stroke the mystique of Hapsburg power, cruelly deflate the diplomatic and military pretensions of imperial France.

Yet circumstances had given Napoleon plenty of opportunity to avert the clash between Prussia and Austria or, failing that, to profit from it. Instead, he had dithered and allowed Eugénie to interfere. And when, too late, he tried to intervene, he had dithered some more, serving only to undermine French prestige further and turn what might have been a golden opportunity for France into a fatal setback.

The stage was set for Sadowa in 1864, when Prussia and Austria, the two most powerful of the thirty-eight states of the Germanic Confederation, joined forces to wrest the provinces of Schleswig and Holstein from the Kingdom of Denmark. Having committed robbery with violence the thieves fell out over the spoils, Prussia seeking to annex the provinces for itself and the Austrians insisting that they should form a thirty-ninth state within the confederation.

To Bismarck, determined to drive a reluctant monarch and an uncomprehending people toward nationhood, the dispute was a perfect instrument for the execution of his plans. He was intent on relegating Austria—by war, if necessary—to a secondary place in German affairs before welding the other Teutonic kingdoms, principalities, dukedoms, and electorates into a unified reich under Prussian dominance.

A crucial factor in Bismarck's calculations was France. How would it react if Prussia's ambitions should threaten the sacrosanct balance of power? How could it be persuaded to support Prussia in a conflict with Austria, or at best to remain neutral? Bismarck did not doubt that Napoleon could somehow be bribed, manipulated, or simply bullied into acquiescence, for he had no great opinion of the Emperor of the French.

Nine years before, while still in the diplomatic service, he had visited Paris and had been singularly unimpressed by the glitter of the Second Empire. "From a distance it is stunning," he remarked, "but when you get up close there is nothing there at all." As for Napoleon himself, Bismarck's cold, Teutonic gaze had bored right through the inscrutable exterior which so bemused others and found that there was nothing there, either. To Bismarck, the emperor was merely "a sphinx without a riddle."

The junker-statesman's summing up of the country which was, after all, Continental Europe's greatest power was equally dismissive. "I look upon France," he told a confident, "as nothing more than a piece—although an essential one—upon the chessboard of politics, irrespective of who is her ruler." It was in that spirit that Bismarck conducted the diplomatic shadow play that preceded and followed his Seven Weeks' War against Austria.

Initially, Napoleon and Eugénie viewed the prospect of war between Prussia and Austria with a good deal less than alarm. As long as neither side won too overwhelming a victory, such a war could only weaken two major rivals, enhance France's own position in Europe, and perhaps give it the opportunity to claim back the Rhine provinces lost in 1815. None of this was lost on Cowley. "Whatever they may say here for decency's sake," he reported, "there is no desire to prevent a war. Perhaps I might go a step further and say that if they can they will promote one."

Eugénie confirmed the accuracy of that assessment many years later. "I must admit that the Emperor learned of the Austrian defeat without distress," she told the French diplomat and historian Maurice Paléologue, "for he desired it and had even helped indirectly to bring it about by procuring for Prussia the alliance with Italy." Her husband's motives, Eugénie said, had been to complete the work of 1859 by helping Italy to acquire Venetia, "and then, alas!, because he counted on Prussian gratitude to secure for ourselves the Rhine provinces."

As Vienna and Berlin squared up in slow motion, the ambassadors for both sides anxiously monitored the mood at the Tuileries for signs of where Napoleon's sympathies lay. He played his usual delphic game, assuring both Metternich and the Prussian envoy, Baron Robert von der Goltz, of his benign neutrality, but secretly encouraging the Prussians to strengthen their military position by making an alliance with Italy.

Nevertheless, Bismarck remained concerned that Napoleon might secretly be planning an alliance with Austria. "Our position . . . will be principally conditioned by the greater or lesser trust which we may place in the attitude of France at any given moment," he told Goltz. Bismarck instructed his envoy to sound Napoleon out in general terms on what his price would be for remaining neutral, but the emperor seemed unable to give an answer. Luxembourg, perhaps, or Belgium? suggested the Prussian. "Ah," said Napoleon, harking back to 1858 and his secret deal with Cavour, "if only you had a Savoy!"

His health was not good that year. He had an increasingly painful bladder complaint and seemed nervous and rundown. He went off on his six-week trip to Algeria, leaving Eugénie in charge once more as regent, and the Prussians noted nervously that once he was gone Metternich was spending a good deal more time at the palace.

But although Eugénie remained personally friendly toward Metternich, even promising to let him know if Napoleon should decide secretly on an alliance with Prussia, Austria's rejection of her overtures in 1863 still rankled, and she had no difficulty in complying with Napoleon's instructions to maintain the strictest neutrality outwardly, while encouraging the Prussians privately to make an alliance with Victor Emmanuel.

But the Austrians got wind of this duplicity through an intercepted and decoded diplomatic cable from Goltz, and took fright at the prospect of being engaged in a war on two fronts. Consequently, in mid-August of 1865 they backed off and compromised with the Prussians over the disputed duchies. Under the Convention of Gastein, Schleswig was to come under the rule of Prussia while Holstein was to be administered by Austria. It was only a temporary papering over of the cracks, but for a while it seemed that the threat of war had been removed, somewhat to Napoleon and Eugénie's private annoyance.

In October of 1865, Bismarck paid a private visit to France and took the opportunity to meet with Napoleon at Biarritz and later at Saint-Cloud. The atmosphere at the Villa Eugénie was, as ever, informal, and Mérimée—the perpetual house guest— played a great prank on the visiting junker by making a papiermâché model of his head and putting it into the bed of one of Eugénie's ladies-in-waiting. For all his prankishness, though, Mérimée had a healthy respect for the butt of his practical joke.

"Unfortunately," he told a friend, "there is only one great man in each century and Bismarck is the one in ours."

Napoleon and Bismarck talked at length, but the substance of their discussions remains uncertain. In fact, more is known about what Bismarck, a notable trencherman, ate and drank than what he and the French emperor said to each other. For example, they enjoyed a lunch which included turbot with a Genoese sauce of such excellence that the Prussian said: "For a sauce like that I would give twenty banks of the Rhine." From this, we may deduce that there was some discussion of Prussia's ceding the Rhine provinces in exchange for French support or neutrality.

At a further meeting a few days later, we know that Bismarck drank "a glass of madeira, ditto of sherry, one whole flask of Yquem and a glass of cognac." It seems likely that at this meeting, Bismarck suggested France might acquire the French-speaking zone of Belgium as compensation for standing aside while Prussia defeated Austria, annexed Schleswig and Holstein, and made itself master of all the German states north of the Main. Napoleon was carefully noncommittal, no doubt aware that Britain would never tolerate the dismemberment of Belgium, and the talks ended inconclusively.

Bismarck apparently came away from these meetings convinced that Napoleon was a spent force and that there was no real danger of a Franco-Austrian alliance against him. Indeed, he seemed to believe that Napoleon actually favored the Prussian cause and was ready to "dance the cotillion with us, without knowing in advance what the steps will be or when it will start." For his part, Napoleon seemed to believe that Austrian military strength was such that eventually Bismarck would have to turn to him for help and at that point he could demand what he really wanted—the lost Rhine provinces.

Napoleon later rationalized his failure to make specific demands at Biarritz or Saint-Cloud by saying that "one must not seek to shape events, but let them happen of their own accord"—astonishing words from the mouth of a Man of Destiny. More likely, he was merely rationalizing a generalized incompetence and indecisiveness greatly exaggerated by his poor state of health.

None of this inner turmoil, of course, could have been apparent to the wiseacres of Europe, who supposed that the subtle and delphic Frenchman would run rings around the ranting Teuton. The comment of Lord Napier, the British Ambassador in St. Petersburg, was typical. "We can imagine the eccentric volubility with which M. de Bismarck would develop his sanguine schemes," he wrote, "and the covert irony and silent amusement of the subtle sovereign."

As the crisis moved into its next phase, French policy appears to have been no less woolly and confused than before. Napoleon, reverting to his old obsession with Italian reunification, asked the Austrians if they would cede Venetia in return for his guarantee of neutrality—taking Rumania from the Russians, with the blessings of France, in compensation. When this idea was indignantly rejected, Napoleon turned again to the Prussians, urging them once more to seek an alliance with Italy, with Venetia as the reward for Victor Emmanuel's participation.

The Prussians, taking his advice, signed a secret treaty of alliance with Victor Emmanuel in March 1866, which was contingent upon their going to war against Austria within three months. Meanwhile, the Prussians again pressed Napoleon to declare what rewards he wanted for himself from the impending conflict.

They were now quite open about their war aims. Goltz told Napoleon that in addition to annexing Schleswig and Holstein, Prussia wanted "a closer union between the North German states," and that if any of those states seemed unwilling to accept Prussia's embrace, "it must be reduced to submission uncompromisingly." Here was as brutal an exposition of Prussian realpolitik as could be imagined, yet it seemed to leave Napoleon unperturbed.

Nor did he rise to the occasion and take advantage of Prussia's persistent prodding to say what he wanted by way of compensation. "I begged the Emperor to name any special benefits that he would be likely to claim later in order to reconcile French national feeling to this extension of Prussian power," Goltz reported. But Napoleon merely replied that "it was very difficult for him to name beforehand the compensation that he must ultimately claim for France."

Napoleon did talk, in a vague way, about Belgium but, said

Goltz, "he would hardly wish to set his hand to the disposal of Belgium at the present moment." The emperor reacted similarly when Goltz "hazarded a suggestion" that he might wish to incorporate the French-speaking cantons of Switzerland. "That is a big question," said Napoleon. "It requires much thought."

Goltz left with the impression that Napoleon's interest in the Rhine provinces "seemed to be very strong," and that in addition his sympathies were also "deeply concerned in Luxembourg." But that was as far as Napoleon would go, apart from assuring the Prussians that they had his "unalterable sympathy." Goltz's summation was that before long Napoleon would demand the pre-1815 Rhine frontier and that meanwhile he was "very anxious to encourage" Prussia's plan to go to war against Austria in alliance with Italy.

A month later, though, Napoleon was singing a very different tune to Metternich. "The Emperor said that he did not believe in war," the Austrian Ambassador reported to his Foreign Minister, Count Mensdorff, "that it was so coarse an affair that neither of the hostile powers could decide to take up arms." For himself, Napoleon again promised a strict neutrality which "he has decided to carry so far as to avoid giving advice to either Prussia or Italy." Indeed, said Metternich, Napoleon stuck firmly to his previous declaration that Italy would attack Austria "at her own risk and peril."

Unlike the Prussians, the Austrians were not prepared to discuss in any detail the benefits France might hope to derive from maintaining a benevolent neutrality. "I told the Emperor that . . . in case of success we should probably be willing to reach a friendly agreement with him and to divide the fruits of the struggle to our mutual advantage," said Metternich. Nonetheless, Metternich believed that Napoleon's word was to be trusted. "I shall believe in him until I have proof to the contrary," the ambassador reported, "for hitherto the Emperor has always spoken to me frankly. He has never deceived me."

Whether by subtle design or merely as a result of indecision, Napoleon was keeping everybody guessing. Cowley's impression at this time was that while Napoleon "would not be sorry if hostilities were to break out . . . he has done nothing, and will do nothing, to encourage a rupture." But within days Napoleon had another meeting with Metternich at which he positively egged the Austrians on to war and predicted victory. "Your position is excellent," he told the ambassador. "You will triumph over the crisis which concerns us all. . . . You will have won the greater part of Germany and you have little to fear from Italy. . . ."

Again Metternich accepted Napoleon at his word. "He will wait for the struggle to begin before he declares himself," the ambassador predicted. In the same mood of euphoria, Metternich added: "Later, the comments of the Empress led me to believe that the Emperor wants us to attack Prussia and neutralize Italy by inspiring the hope of a possible agreement over Venetia. . . . She insinuated that if we advance boldly against Prussia, France would not delay to support us morally."

By now Napoleon was stirring the pot feverishly. At the end of April he cornered Goltz at a court ball, took him to a window recess, and told him sotto voce that he had received a firm offer from the Austrians. He would prefer to make a deal with Prussia, "but he will be unable to reject the Austrian proposals unless we offer equally acceptable terms," Goltz reported. "He considers it is time that His Majesty the King made up his mind."

In view of Napoleon's repeated failure to tell the Prussians what he wanted, this remark must have tried Goltz's diplomatic patience. But the ambassador dutifully "suggested that things would be easier if the Emperor stated his objective"—and at last Napoleon came out with it. "He admitted," said Goltz, "that the eyes of France are directed toward the Rhine."

Goltz's dispatch was referred immediately to Bismarck, who by now felt sufficiently confident to reject out of hand the idea of ceding any German territory to France. This was relayed back to Goltz in Paris, and when he and Napoleon met at the following week's ball at the Tuileries for another private chat, he told the emperor as diplomatically as possible of Prussia's "utmost anxiety concerning any severance of Prussian or German territory."

To Goltz's evident astonishment, Napoleon immediately backtracked, saying that he had spoken under the impression that war was imminent, and that he had merely been drawing Goltz's attention to French popular opinion. Napoleon assured him that his personal wishes "did not lie in that direction," Goltz reported. "He wished to avoid the acquisition of territory that might be accompanied by drawbacks. He was not even sure that the population [of the Rhine provinces] even wanted to become French."

In the face of such an ignominious withdrawal by Napoleon from his former position, the Prussian Ambassador became positively patronizing. "I expressed my lively satisfaction at the Emperor's attitude," he reported. "I told him . . . he was serving not only our interests but his own by refusing to annex Prussian territory. . . . No Prussian king would ever renounce it voluntarily." For his part, Napoleon "agreed with most of my words and did not attempt to contradict them."

Goltz could not resist commenting on this "extraordinary change in the Emperor's views and inclinations." A week before, he marveled, Napoleon had "considered war inevitable and announced his extensive claims [whereas] today he has renounced these entirely." The Prussian's contempt for the Frenchman's weakness was made perfectly plain in his verdict that, bowing to French public opinion, Napoleon now desired "peace at any price."

Goltz added triumphantly: "He is ready, without war, to help ourselves and Italy to secure all that we want by means of a Congress. The result is highly favorable to ourselves and I consider it most important to take advantage of it before another change occurs. Our preparations for war must on no account be interrupted."

The Congress referred to by Goltz had just been publicly proposed by Napoleon as a way to solve the crisis. It would involve the disputants, plus France, Britain, and Russia. But things had gone too far for another European talking shop to help. The march toward war was irreversible, and Austria was now desperate to pin Napoleon down to a solemn agreement which would guarantee if not his active support then at least his benevolent neutrality.

However, Metternich was not hopeful. "I have been moving heaven and earth to find a basis on which we might reach an agreement with France," he told Mensdorff, "and I have arrived at the conviction that nothing short of the guns can bring us together. . . . I have done and said here all that is in my power to say and do."

Napoleon was now concentrating on a single issue in his talks with the Austrians—"to finish with the Italian question by the cession of Venetia." He told Metternich that "if this cession can effect peace, I will do all I can to contribute to it; if not I will profit by the opportunities which a war between Austria and Prussia may offer in this respect."

Meanwhile Eugénie was adding to the complexities of the situation by showing Metternich "marks of genuine affection and sincere compassion" and urging Austria on to bold action. "Do you not see," she said, "that the Emperor is irrevocably bound to neutrality until the first shot is fired? This is one of those moments when one must act logically. When I tell you to advance, I am not leading you into a trap. Show greater energy than you have up to now. . . . Everything combines to tell you, as I do: advance, advance!"

Quite possibly, Napoleon could not have stopped the slide to war even if he had shown the will and the competence to do so. The implacable Bismarck was set on humiliating the Austrians as part of his grand design for the unification of Germany under Prussian domination, and not even the marked reluctance of the Prussian King Wilhelm I for the pending "War of the Brothers" and the vocal opposition of much of Prussian public opinion were sufficient to deflect him.

Bismarck had at his disposal not only his own remarkable force of personality, single-minded purpose, diplomatic guile, and utter ruthlessness, but a military machine that was superbly led, extensively reorganized, splendidly equipped, and eager to be let off the leash. Looking on from the sidelines, France's professional military caste tended to discount the fighting ability of the Prussian conscript army. But one of their number, General Charles Bourbaki, had the more accurate measure of the Prussians. "Be as rude as you like about this army of lawyers and occulists," he said, "but it will get to Vienna just as soon as it likes."

By the beginning of June, time had run out for peace. The Austrians mobilized along their northern and western frontiers to meet the threat of attack and Bismarck chose to take that as a casus belli. On June 11, Prussia declared war and, taking advantage of the new railway system, Moltke performed miracles of logistics to transport his troops for deployment against the Austrians on the Bohemian frontier.

Before he followed the army in the king's private retinue, dressed in his uniform as a cavalry major, Bismarck confided to the British Ambassador, Lord Augustus Loftus, that "if we are beaten, I shall die in the last charge."

But things went well for the Prussians from the outset. After some fierce frontier engagements, the Austrians under General Ludwig von Benedek, a veteran of Solferino, fell back to a defensive line behind the River Bistritz. In numbers and esprit, they were the equal of the enemy, but Benedek was no Moltke, and the Prussian infantry had the formidable new needlegun, a breech-loading rifle capable of unprecedentedly accurate and rapid fire.

From first light to late afternoon on July 3 the lines of battle swayed to and fro as Prussian and Austrian soldiers died by their thousands in equal contest. Then, at first appearing like a line of trees on the horizon, Crown Prince Friedrich's Second Army arrived on the scene from Silesia to tip the battle decisively in favor of the Prussians and earn Friedrich the *nom de guerre* "Prince Nick-of-Time" among the ranks. The Austrians broke and ran, leaving 24,000 dead behind them. As Bourbaki had predicted, the road to Vienna lay wide open.

The following day, Bismarck went "riding alone over the dead-strewn field" and, as he told his wife, found it "a sight to freeze the blood in the veins—horrible, bloody, never to be forgotten." But his distaste for the carnage he had engineered was soon forgotten in his admiration for the spirit and discipline of the Prussian troops. "I could hug our fellows," he wrote the following day, "each facing death so gallantly, so quiet, obedient, well-behaved . . . obliging to everybody, no looting, no incendiarism, paying where they can and eating mouldy bread. There must, after all, abide in our man of the soil a rich store of the fear of God, or all that would be impossible."

Even before the full extent of the Austrian defeat was known, Cowley was cabling to London that "the consternation here at the successes of Prussia continues to be very great. . . . The Emperor is getting a little alarmed at his Frankenstein and is turning his mind a little too late to the problem of how Austria is to be saved." Thus, when Franz-Josef telegraphed a plea the day after Sadowa for his intervention as mediator, Napoleon accepted immediately.

After a late night conference with Metternich, Eugénie, and his Foreign Minister Drouyn de Lhuys, he had a proclamation rushed to the official newspaper, *Le Moniteur*, for publication the following day. It announced his mediation and made clear that it would be based on a plan he had proposed at the outbreak of hostilities. Under this plan Austria would cede Venetia to France (who would hand it over immediately to Italy), but would maintain its "great position" in Germany by continued membership of the Germanic Confederation. At the same time, while Prussia expanded north of the Main, a "third Germany" would be created by a union of the southern states, which would be under neither Prussian nor Austrian domination.

Such an arrangement, while entirely acceptable to a newly humbled Austria, would clearly not sit well with a triumphant Prussia. King Wilhelm and his generals, drunk with victory, were now all for pushing on to Vienna and dismembering the Austrian Empire. Bismarck—far more realistic than they, and having achieved his objective of cutting Austria out of the leadership of the German-speaking world—knew this would be a mistake and urged restraint. Nevertheless, he regarded the French intervention as a hostile act and muttered that "the day will come when Louis will be sorry that he came out against us."

That day came very quickly. The very publication of Napoleon's intention to mediate, without being invited to do so by the victorious Prussians, implied a French readiness to impose that mediation by force, if necessary. That was certainly the interpretation put upon Napoleon's proclamation by Metternich and by the French Ambassador in Vienna, who made it known that if the Prussians objected, "France would not be long in throwing 100,000 men on the Rhine." But when, soon afterward, the full implications of his decision became clear to him, Napoleon felt bound to rethink his position and beat a humiliating retreat.

Drained by ill-health, worried by a domestic economic crisis, by the pacific mood of French public opinion, and by the French Army's heavy commitments in Mexico and North Africa, the emperor rejected the advice of Eugénie and others to mobilize. And although the Prussians did formally accept his mediation, they showed how much importance they attached to the possibility of a French show of force by continuing their advance into Austrian territory.

Napoleon's pretensions to be the Arbiter of Europe were thus deflated in the most public fashion. The fact that Austria was given relatively easy terms in the armistice which was signed at Nikolsburg on July 27 had everything to do with Bismarck's prudent statesmanship and nothing to do with Napoleon's hasty and ill-considered intervention.

Those terms, while ceding Venetia to Italy—an acquisition Victor Emmanuel had scarcely earned, since the Austrians had roundly defeated him at Custozza—gave Bismarck the prize he had sought: the formal exclusion of Austria from the German union. Furthermore, this humiliation was to be underscored by the payment of an indemnity by Vienna to Berlin. Henceforth, Bismarck would be free to pursue his dream of a unified Germany under Prussian tutelage without interference from the effete Hapsburgs.

Napoleon now had a dangerously self-confident, expansionist neighbor on his eastern border and had made himself appear to the world as a paper tiger. The face of Europe had been changed to his detriment and as Adolphe Thiers commented: "It is France who has been beaten at Sadowa."

From London, Clarendon agreed in a letter to Cowley that "there has never yet been in recorded history such a collapse as that of Austria." The Prussian success, said Cowley, was "a triumph of political audacity and military organisation," and the Prussians were "the most swaggering robbers who were allowed to despoil their neighbours." As for France, she was "no longer the first Military Power and I doubt her recovering her place, for Prussia will take care to keep ahead of her, both in numbers and in armaments."

Bismarck would certainly have agreed with that last appraisal. He was now all but openly contemptuous of French power. When Napoleon's ambassador, comte Vincente Benedetti, suggested that France might, after all, be given the Rhine provinces and that Prussia might also compensate for annexations in North Germany by relinquishing control over the buffer states of Luxembourg and Limberg, the minister-president rebuffed him brutally. "If you want war, you can have it," he said. "We shall raise the whole of Germany against you."

Eugénie had a presentiment of what the existence of a powerful Prussia on its eastern frontier might mean for France. "With such a nation for our neighbour," she told King Wilhelm's personal envoy Prince Reuss, "we should run the risk of finding you one day in front of Paris before we had ever expected it. I should go to bed French and wake up Prussian."

On July 14, Eugénie had to leave Paris for a prearranged five-day visit to the provinces. When she returned, she noticed an alarming decline in Napoleon's already poor state of health. Receiving Metternich with tears in her eyes, she told him she had found her husband "sick, irresolute, exhausted." He could "no longer walk, no longer sleep, and scarcely eat," she said. Eugénie described Napoleon's decision to mediate on the night of July 4 as the time when "the last gleam sparkled in the Emperor's eyes." Two days later, when he realized the extent of the disaster at Sadowa, he had "relapsed into a decline which had only grown worse."

Eugénie then proceeded to make to Metternich the astonishing confession that she had urged Napoleon two days previously to abdicate and appoint her regent. He had declined her suggestion, but "I assure you," continued Her Majesty, "that we are marching to our downfall, and the best thing would be if the Emperor could disappear suddenly, at least for the time being." To Goltz a few days later, she made an even more startling—and uncannily prophetic—admission: the present situation, she said, was "the beginning of the end of the dynasty."

23

RETREAT
FROM
MEXICO

AT THE HEIGHT OF THE SADOWA CRISIS—just as he was
confronting the strategic implications of the Prussian triumph
and Bismarck's arrogant rejection of his feeble efforts to extract
some territorial rewards for his neutrality—Napoleon received
word that an unexpected and most unwelcome visitor had
turned up in France, demanding an audience. The empress Car-
lotta of Mexico, otherwise Charlotte the young wife of the
"Archdupe" Maximilian, had arrived in a desperate attempt to
save her husband's throne and, as it turned out, his very life.

There was no one, apart from Maximilian himself, whom
Napoleon can have wanted less to see; added to the pressures of
Sadowa, his miserable state of health, and his chronic aversion
to personal confrontations, there was the sense of guilt he must
have felt at having decided to abandon his commitment to his
Hapsburg protégés. At the end of 1865 he had written to Maximilian to tell him, "not without pain," that he felt compelled
to start withdrawing the army from Mexico—which meant, in
effect, abandoning the entire Mexican enterprise. And now here
was the strong-willed Charlotte, obviously intent on pressuring
him into a reversal of policy.

From the very beginning of the enterprise the auguries had
not been good. Maximilian and Charlotte had arrived in Vera
Cruz on May 31, 1864, to find that no arrangements had been
made to give them a reception in any way worthy of their sta-

tus. General Achille Bazaine, the French commander-in-chief, was absent, directing operations against the republican forces who still held out in the north and the extreme south of the country. He had left word for them that their overland journey to the capital might be hazardous because of guerrillas, but that he "had not sufficient time at his disposal to look after their safety."

An overnight storm had blown down all the decorations which had been put up in Vera Cruz to welcome Maximilian and Charlotte, adding to the overall impression of muddle and indifference. What was worse, the people of the town, a stronghold of republican sentiment, seemed far from overjoyed at the arrival of their new emperor and empress.

Indignant at the poverty of their reception, depressed by the primitive squalor they saw on all sides, the imperial couple and their entourage boarded the train that would take them on the first stage of their journey to Mexico City—a single-track railway clanking through a wild vista of marsh and desert to its terminus at Soledad, almost 200 miles short of their destination.

From there, the imperial entourage had to proceed by muledrawn carriages, a journey which Charlotte described as "ghastly beyond all words." In a letter to Eugénie, she complained that the road was "abominable" and that "the only civilized spots are the French guardhouses, with the canteens beside them." There were some brighter moments during the two-week journey to the capital, such as their warm reception at the clergy-dominated city of Puebla where all the church bells rang for them and the monsignors and silver barons seemed welcoming and respectful.

The ceremonials staged by the French military, the Church, and the aristocracy for their entry into Mexico City were certainly impressive. But when Maximilian and Charlotte entered their vast, barracks-like palace, any good feelings must have evaporated rapidly. It had not even been cleaned properly for their arrival and legend has it that there were bedbugs in the imperial suite, forcing Maximilian to spend his first night sleeping on a billiard table.

Charlotte put the best gloss she could on their situation, writing to her father, King Leopold, that "things are much less bad here than I expected," and "the French Army is full of enthusiasm for Max." If that was ever true, the enthusiasm was not to last. Bazaine, at first welcoming and avuncular, soon became irritated at Maximilian's attempts to assert his independence of the French and contemptuous of his vaguely benevolent intentions toward the Mexican peasantry. And although the middle-aged Bazaine was about to take a young Mexican beauty to wife, the majority of his officers seemed openly contemptuous of the native people, even the most exalted. One senior officer referred to the Mexican general, Juan Almonte, in Charlotte's presence, as a "nigger."

Given that kind of attitude, it is hardly surprising that Maximilian's liberal notions about elevating the peasantry inspired little respect. Nor were such notions welcome to the bishops and the well-to-do local laity, who had invited the archduke to become their emperor in the belief that he was every bit as reactionary as might be expected of a Hapsburg.

It was not long before Maximilian found himself severely at odds with the Church. Archbishop Antonio Labastida, returning from voluntary exile in Rome, obstructed all his efforts at reform, and began to clamor for the immediate and unconditional return of Church property nationalized by the previous republican regimes.

But the problem was far too delicate and complicated to be settled so crudely. To return all its vast former landholdings to the Church would mean the dispossession of scores of thousands of peasant farmers who had benefited from long-overdue land reforms. Maximilian understood this and stood out against the archbishop's peremptory demands. And although this did nothing to improve his standing with Eugénie, such a policy was in accordance with Napoleon's own advice on the subject.

While Maximilian's progressive impulses were engaged in such matters, the Hapsburg in him insisted on exerting itself. Embroiled though he was in quarrels with the Church, the army, and the aristocracy, Maximilian continued to work on his handbook of court etiquette and to upgrade the appointments and facilities of his palace to something approaching imperial magnificence.

Sarah Yorke, an American woman living in Mexico City and a frequent visitor to the court, has left us a description of the imperial couple at the time. Maximilian was "tall, slight and handsome with a certain weakness and indecision in his expression." But "he had a gift of putting people at their ease and was possessed of far greater personal magnetism than the Empress, whose strong, intelligent face was somewhat hard at times." And a courtier wrote: "The tragedy of Maximilian is that it is easy to adore him, but impossible to fear him and, in Mexico, one can only inspire respect through fear."

Bazaine neither adored nor respected, and complained to Napoleon about the amount of money Maximilian was spending on refurbishing his palace. And it was true: Maximilian was extravagant, as only a Hapsburg who had never had to handle money could be. But if the country was on the brink of bankruptcy, this was mainly because of the enormous expense of maintaining the French military presence. Maximilian was committed to paying 1,000 francs per year for each of the 38,000 French troops in Mexico, plus costs totaling 270 million francs that had accrued up to the time of his arrival in the country.

Not only had Maximilian by this time fallen out thoroughly with Bazaine, but he was also severely out of favor with the leading French civilian in Mexico, Napoleon's minister-resident, the marquis de Montholon, who joined with Bazaine in complaining of Maximilian's frivolity, instability, and general resistance to French tutelage. The puppet emperor actually thought he was entitled to behave as though he was an independent monarch!

In mid-1865 a bad state of affairs began to look considerably worse when, north of the border, the Confederates lost the American Civil War and Washington became able to turn its attentions to the situation in Mexico. From the outset, the Yankees had made it quite plain that the White House, Congress, and public opinion were totally opposed to the setting up of a monarchy in their republican backyard. Lincoln's assassination had done nothing to change that, and now the Americans were in a position, and a mood, to follow up words with deeds.

Napoleon secretly offered to withdraw his troops immediately in return for U.S. recognition of Maximilian. But Lincoln's successor, President Andrew Johnson, and his Secretary of State, William Henry Seward, left no doubt that a French military withdrawal would not suffice. The "Austrian adventurer"—as one leading American politico called Maximilian in the presence of the Austrian Ambassador—must go, too.

Recalling Napoleon's secret commitment that "France will never fail the new Mexican Empire," Maximilian asked for an increase in the French military presence. But far from contemplating the reinforcement of his forces, Napoleon was by now close to ordering an unconditional and complete withdrawal. French public opinion, the Legislative Body, and a majority of his ministers were vocally anxious to abandon the Mexican adventure. So, now, was its principal instigator, Eugénie, who for some time had been complaining bitterly that Maximilian was quarreling with the Church and defaulting on his debts.

In September 1865, Napoleon wrote to Maximilian, urging him to "use your Austrian troops* for the organization of a proper army," which Napoleon said would allow him to withdraw "the greater part" of his own forces. Deeply concerned at the implications of the letter, but unable yet to believe that Napoleon would abandon him, Maximilian wrote back begging the French emperor not to "undo in a day all the work painfully accomplished in the last few years." But at the end of December Napoleon felt constrained to draft the letter which spelled for him the end of the Mexican adventure.

"It is not without pain," he wrote,

that I find myself forced to come to a decision and put a definite term to the French occupation. The difficulties caused me by the Mexican question, the impossibility of getting further subsidies from the Legislative Body for the upkeep of an expeditionary force, and Your Majesty's own statement that you are unable to contribute to its maintenance leave me with no other choice than to withdraw my army. The evacuation, which will begin as soon as possible, will be done gradually and in such a way as not to upset public opinion or endanger the interests which we both have at heart.

Napoleon conceded that the withdrawal "may cause Your Majesty temporary embarrassment," but added that it would "have

---

* A small contingent of volunteers, who had come out from Austria, seeking adventure and fortune in the service of the Hapsburg throne.

the advantage of removing all pretexts of interference from the U.S."

In desperation, Maximilian wrote back to Napoleon to say that he could not believe that "the wisest monarch of this century and the most powerful nation in the world would give in to the Yankees in this undignified fashion." But Napoleon's mind was made up, and not likely to be changed by that kind of remark. "He thinks Maximilian wanting in decision of character and not up to the difficulties of his position," reported Cowley.

Although he was well aware that the Mexican involvement was now thoroughly unpopular in France, Napoleon was in a quandary over how to announce his decision to parliament without drastic loss of face. "The Emperor is dreadfully puzzled what to tell the Chambers," reported Cowley. And when Napoleon did make his announcement, during his speech from the throne at the opening of the parliamentary session in January 1866, Cowley's verdict was that "it was a poor affair and he seemed to feel it to be such himself. He blundered and faltered continually. . . ."

Indeed, the element of farce which seemed to dog so much of Napoleon's life almost took over as the speech ended. "His Majesty nearly came upon his nose in descending from the throne, his spur having caught in the carpet," wrote Cowley. "Supposing he had come down, what omens would have been drawn."

Back in Mexico, Maximilian was in despair. Not only was he to lose the protection of the French Army, but official American pressure had forced the Austrian Empire to ban the recruitment of any more volunteers for Mexico. Feeling utterly betrayed on all sides, his physical health failing and his mental condition becoming semi-paranoid, Maximilian wanted to abdicate and return to Europe. But the forceful Charlotte would not hear of it.

Instead, she proposed to go to Europe as his emissary. She would appeal to Napoleon's conscience and get him to change his mind; she would convince the Pope of the need to support their position and of agreeing to a concordat that would settle the points at issue between them amicably; she would arouse European statesmen to the threat posed by the United States to their interests; and she would raise money from the European banks to shore up Mexico's tottering economy.

The weak and embattled Maximilian was in no condition to gainsay his wife. In early July she left Mexico City by mule-drawn carriage with a French cavalry escort, bound for Soledad and the train to Vera Cruz, where she would catch the next packet steamer for France. A month later she disembarked at Saint-Nazaire to find that there was no official reception for her. Bazaine's cable warning Napoleon that she was coming had either been mislaid or garbled, and rumors that she was expected had been denied in the official *Moniteur*.

Deeply disgruntled, Charlotte took the train to Nantes with her aides and ladies-in-waiting. There she heard the news of the disaster at Sadowa and of the ill-health of Napoleon, who had just returned to Saint-Cloud after taking the waters at Vichy. These had done nothing to relieve the pain caused by the stone in his bladder, and when he received Charlotte's telegram saying that she wished to discuss with him "certain matters concerning Mexico," he was appalled.

His reply was blunt—"I have just returned from Vichy and am forced to stay in bed so that I am not in a position to come and see Your Majesty." Undeterred, Charlotte cabled back to say that she would be in Paris the next day. On arrival, she installed herself at the Grand Hotel, where Eugénie came to see her, hoping to fend off a demand for an audience with the emperor. The two women exchanged a "sisterly kiss," but there was little affection left between them and the interview was painful.

Charlotte wasted no breath on small talk, but plunged straight into a litany of complaints, describing the desperate situation in Mexico, the obstructiveness of Bazaine, the urgent need for continued French military and economic support. Eugénie tried in vain to steer the conversation toward safer topics—fashion, the court balls, the immense popularity in Paris of the Mexican song *La Paloma*.

Charlotte was insistent. When could she see the emperor? Alas, that would be impossible, said Eugénie. He was sick and still confined to bed. Charlotte would have none of that. She would go to Saint-Cloud the next day, she said, "and if the Emperor refuses to see me I shall break in on him."

Considerably taken aback by such blunt talk, Eugénie took her leave. That night Charlotte wrote to her husband: "I know more about China than these people here know about Mexico, where they have ventured upon one of the greatest enterprises in which the French flag has ever been involved. . . . Amid all their greatness any sort of pressure, real or imaginary, is irksome to Napoleon and his wife and they can endure it no longer. . . ."

When Mérimée heard from Eugénie that Charlotte would be coming to Saint-Cloud the next day, he wrote to a friend: "The Emperor was hoping to profit by the fine weather to enjoy a few peaceful days at Saint-Cloud, instead of which he has Her Mexican Majesty on hand. . . . They will give her a dinner, but I doubt very much if she will get any money or troops. Maximilian, I imagine, will have to abdicate. . . ."

Charlotte arrived at midday, wearing what a spiteful court lady described as "a very unbecoming hat," and was admitted to Napoleon's private suite. She, Eugénie, and Napoleon were alone together, without independent witnesses, and exactly what passed between them is not known. Charlotte said later in a letter to Maximilian that she "did everything that was humanly possible," but Napoleon "appeared to be utterly helpless, with tears pouring down his cheeks, continually turning to his wife for support."

A written memorandum previously presented by Charlotte demanded the recall of Bazaine, the retention of French forces for three more years, and a continued monthly subsidy to pay for native troops. Napoleon apparently promised to discuss these matters with his ministers before replying. He invited Charlotte to stay for lunch, but she declined and left the palace visibly agitated.

The next day she met some of Napoleon's cabinet, including Drouyn de Lhuys—who, unknown to her, was about to resign as Foreign Minister—the War Minister, Marshal Randon, and the Finance Minister, Achille Fould. But although they all made sympathetic noises, she made no impression. Charlotte also saw Metternich, who told her that Napoleon had been "degenerating mentally and physically for the past two years and is no longer capable of making a decision." Eugénie's interference, said Metternich, had done "more harm than good."

The following day, Charlotte went back to Saint-Cloud for a further confrontation with Napoleon and laid in front of him

THE BOULEVARDIER: Morny photographed on the Champs Elysees by
Tallandier. (Sirot Collection)

PLON-PLON: Louis Napoleon's difficult cousin, Prince Napoleon. (Mansell Collection)

LOYAL AIDE: The arch-Bonapartist Persigny. (Mansell Collection)

ROYAL VISIT: Napoleon and Eugenie with Victoria and Albert at Windsor, 1855. (Bettman Archive)

CHARLOTTE: Maximillian's ambitious wife, who died insane. (Mansell Collection)

THE "ARCHDUPE": Maximillian, the deluded and tragic Emperor of Mexico. (Mansell Collection)

THE MIDDLE YEARS: Napoleon and Eugenie, circa 1862, photographed by Disderi. (Bibliotheque Nationale)

AFTER SEDAN: Napoleon and Bismark outside the weaver's cottage, painted by William Camphausen. (Bettman Archive)

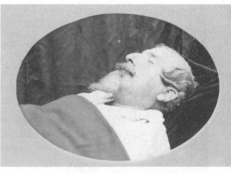

DEATH PORTRAIT: The last photograph of the deceased emperor. (Bettman Archive)

THE PRISONER: Napoleon in captivity at Wilhelmshöhe. (Bettman Archive)

THE WARRIOR: Loulou, the Prince Imperial, in his Royal Horse Artillery
uniform. (Bettman Archive)

THE WIDOW: Eugenie at her prie-dieu after the death of Loulou. (Mansell Collection)

the letter he had written to Maximilian two years before when Maximilian had been stricken by second thoughts about accepting the Mexican throne—the letter which had indignantly asked: "What would you think of me if I were to say I could no longer fulfill the conditions to which I have set my signature?"

At this, Charlotte reported later, Napoleon "wept even more than before," but Eugénie was determined to allow no more of this and got her out of the room and into another for talks with Randon and Fould. There, Charlotte began to rant about the perfidies of the French. Drawing attention to a discrepancy between the amount loaned to Mexico and the amount actually received, she demanded to know "Who are the persons whose pockets are filled with gold at Mexico's expense?" Outraged, Fould replied that the Mexicans were "dishonest, distrustful and ungrateful," and that France had already done more than enough for them.

At this, Eugénie threw a faint, the meeting broke up in chaos, and Charlotte left in hysterics. The following day the Council of Ministers voted unanimously for an immediate and total withdrawal. Meanwhile, although still far from well, Napoleon left Saint-Cloud for a visit to the army at Châlons, no doubt hoping that Charlotte would have left the country by the time he returned. But she was determined to wait him out; when he got back to Paris on August 20, she was still at the Grand Hotel and demanding a further interview.

Steeling himself, Napoleon called on her at the Grand, where to his astonishment she demanded a loan of 90 million francs, suggesting that if his ministers would not agree he should put it to the vote of the people by referendum, because "the prosperity of Mexico is the prosperity of France." Napoleon replied that the idea was impossible and that she should not indulge in any further illusions.

This stung Charlotte to the quick and she turned on Napoleon with eyes ablaze. "Your Majesty is as much concerned in this affair as we are," she said, "so it would be better if you did not indulge in any illusions either." There was nothing more to be said. Napoleon rose to his feet, gave her a chilly bow, and left.

That night, shattered by the utter failure of her mission, Charlotte cabled her husband: "Todos es inutil"—All is useless.

The next day, before leaving Paris by train on her way to Miramar, she wrote a long, incoherent letter to her husband in which it is painfully clear that her sanity was collapsing under the strain. In it, she described Napoleon as the Devil.

He was not preparing to abandon Mexico, she said, because of American threats, domestic opposition, "or for any reason whatsoever, but because he is the evil principle upon earth and wants to get rid of the good." She continued: "To me he is the Devil in person and at our last interview yesterday he had an expression that would make one's hair stand on end. He was hideous and this was an expression of his soul. . . . I have seen through him and it has left me shuddering, for the world has never known the like, nor will it. . . ."

Napoleon also wrote to Maximilian. "It is necessary for Your Majesty to come to a heroic resolution," he said. "It is henceforth impossible for me to give Mexico another écu or another soldier." He advised Maximilian to abdicate and sail for Europe with the French Army; but Maximilian defiantly—and fatally—decided to remain.

Meanwhile Charlotte was continuing her hopeless mission, now trying to enlist the help of the Pope. By the time he received her in audience on September 27, she was already in a condition of advanced paranoia. Her first words to the pontiff were that Napoleon's spies, including members of her own entourage, were trying to poison her. From that point on, her insanity deepened. Convinced that she would soon fall victim to Napoleon's poisoners, she wrote her will, leaving virtually everything she possessed to her husband.

On October 1, before leaving Rome for Miramar, she penned a farewell letter to her "dearly beloved treasure," Maximilian—"I bid you farewell. God is calling me to him. I thank you for the happiness which you have always given me. May God bless you and help you to win eternal bliss. Your faithful Charlotte."

Although God did not call her for another sixty years, she never saw her husband again. After the last French soldier left Mexico in March the following year, the republicans quickly overwhelmed Maximilian's army of 10,000 native soldiers, took the pseudo-emperor captive at Querétaro, and staged a show trial. At dawn on June 19, 1867, Maximilian and two of his generals were taken out to face a firing squad. It was a beautiful morning and on the way to the place of execution Maximilian reputedly said to his companions: "What a wonderful day! I have always wanted to die on a morning like this."

Word of Maximilian's death reached Paris by secret diplomatic cable from Washington on June 30. Napoleon burst into tears, but kept the news secret from all but Eugénie for twenty-four hours. The following day was the climax of the Great Universal Exhibition, when Napoleon was to present awards to the prize-winning exhibitors in the Palace of Industry, and the tragic news must not be allowed to cast a shadow over the occasion.

Before going with her husband to the Palace of Industry Eugénie dressed in mourning and went to the Tuileries chapel, where she prayed for an hour. One may speculate whether she prayed more ardently for Maximilian's soul or her own. Later, she and the emperor drove in state up the Champs-Elysées for the prize giving, but by the time they arrived, the news of Maximilian's execution had leaked out and half the attending foreign notables absented themselves as a mark of respect and mourning. When it was all over and they were back in the Tuileries, Eugénie collapsed and had to be carried to her bed.

Napoleon sent a cable to Maximilian's brother, Franz-Josef, saying that he and Eugénie were "plunged into grief by the terrible news." The French emperor added: "I shall never forgive myself for having, through the best intentions, helped to bring about such a calamity." Eugénie, apparently, did forgive herself. Almost forty years later, when her concern was for the verdict history would pass on her, she said: "I am not ashamed of Mexico. I deplore it, but I do not blush for it."

In an interview with Maurice Paléologue, she confirmed defiantly, even proudly, that the Mexican adventure had been her idea from the start. "I defy anyone to point to any detail that was not perfectly honorable and worthy of France," she said. "We were mistaken about the resistance and the complications in store for us. Or rather, we were misled—no doubt in good faith. But you cannot imagine the glowing vistas that were made to sparkle before our eyes." Of the fate of the unfortunate Maximilian, she made no mention.

Maximilian's widow lived on even longer than Eugénie, but without ever learning of her husband's death—perhaps without realizing she had ever had a husband. Charlotte was hopelessly insane by the time the news reached Miramar and, on doctor's orders, no attempt was made to tell her what had happened. She died at the age of eighty-six, never having recovered her sanity.

24

NAPOLEON LOOSENS HIS GRIP

WHEN COWLEY FIRST HEARD FROM GOLTZ that Eugénie had described the Sadowa setback as "the beginning of the end of the dynasty," he was inclined to dismiss the idea as the product of feminine hysteria. Given the empress's almost insane indiscretion in publicizing her husband's infirmity of purpose to the Prussian Ambassador—and through him to the courts of Europe—Cowley's reaction is understandable.

"This is exaggeration," he told the new Foreign Secretary, Lord Stanley, on August 10, 1866. "What with Mexico, what with Italy, what with his late mediation, the Emperor has no doubt fallen in prestige, but as yet there are no signs of public discontent."

Within a few days, however, the British Ambassador began to realize how wrong he was in supposing that the French people, or at least the French Army, were indifferent to the consequences of Sadowa. His military attaché, Colonel Claremont, told him he had never seen French officers "so excited upon any subject," and that "the most sensible, the quietest, and most reasonable among them say openly that it is a question of existence for the Emperor and that the aggrandizement of Prussia renders it imperative that they should again have the Rhine as their frontier line."

On August 15, therefore, Cowley felt bound to report that "if Prussia does not make some sort of concession the Emperor will

find it difficult to keep [public opinion and the army] in order."
And the following day he confessed to Stanley that "the events
of the last month have been so extraordinary that I can only
account for them by supposing that the Emperor's mind and
heart are failing him."

With unconcealed astonishment, Cowley told the Foreign
Secretary how, according to Goltz, Napoleon had made the
most abject apology to the Prussians over the French demand
for the Rhine provinces, which Bismarck had so peremptorily
rejected. As Cowley pointed out, it was impossible that the demands could have been put forward without instructions from
Napoleon himself. Yet Napoleon told Goltz that his ambassador, Benedetti, "had acted without instruction, that he had
been misunderstood by Bismarck and that he [the Emperor] requested that the whole affair of the demand should be considered 'comme nulle et sans avenue.'"

Napoleon had made this extraordinary retraction after Goltz
handed him a message from Bismarck which rejected the
French demands so bluntly that, with the instincts of the professional diplomat, Goltz found it necessary to "modify" his superior's language.

To Cowley, Goltz described Napoleon as "positively an object of pity, looking wretchedly ill and hardly seeming to know
what he was aiming at." The French emperor had agreed abjectly that Prussia was "perfectly justified in resisting his present pretensions." What was more, said Goltz, "he excused what
he had done as the result of the pressure of popular opinion,
ending by expressing the hope that it might still be possible for
Prussia to do something to alleviate his position toward the
French nation."

A few days later Benedetti delivered a set of new proposals to
Bismarck which were so secret that Napoleon had not even informed his Foreign Minister, Drouyn de Lhuys, of them. This
time Napoleon was asking for Prussia to support a French annexation of Belgium and Luxembourg in return for French consent to a federal union between the North German Confederation and the southern German states. As with the Rhine
frontier, Bismarck had no intention of acceding to the French
request. For one thing, the territories in question were not
within Prussia's gift, although Prussia could withdraw its gar-

rison from Luxembourg. For another, Bismarck was not willing to alienate the British who were guarantors of Belgium and who, for the moment, were showing great friendliness toward Prussia.

But there was everything to be gained by keeping the French hoping, so he expressed his willingness to discuss the proposal with King Wilhelm. And, supposedly to facilitate this, he asked Benedetti to put into writing the French request for Prussian collusion in the plan to annex Belgium. Such was Bismarck's extraordinary gift for persuading diplomatic antagonists of his good faith, that Benedetti complied—and the wily Prussian locked the potentially incriminating document away for future use.

As before, Napoleon seemed abjectly eager not to appear too pressing with this proposal. When Goltz saw him on August 20, the emperor took the opportunity to apologize yet again for the "peremptory and threatening" tone in which the Corsican Benedetti had presented the first demand, "which should have formed the basis of a friendly discussion." Goltz received this disavowal with some comments of his own on Benedetti's "excessive warmth," and added that the French envoy was still "displaying a greater zeal than the case justifies" in demanding an answer on the latest proposals within three or four days. "Any pressure is likely to evoke a refusal," Goltz warned. "Only if His Majesty the King is allowed ample leisure to weigh this difficult matter carefully is an agreement possible."

Again, Napoleon seemed only too anxious to propitiate the touchy Teutons. "The Emperor coincided fully with this opinion," Goltz reported to Bismarck, "and said that if M. Benedetti displayed excessive zeal, he must restrain him. There was no need for haste. The matter must be discussed in a calm and friendly spirit and all pressure should be avoided. In no case did the Emperor wish to endanger our friendly relations." Bismarck must have smiled at this, concluding that Napoleon could be kept on a string more or less indefinitely. The French, he told Goltz on October 22, "must be induced to go on hoping and, above all, to retain their faith in our goodwill without being given any definite commitment."

By the winter of 1866, French aspirations had become so worn down by the rock of Prussian resolve that Napoleon dropped the idea of annexing Belgium and reduced his timorous demands to one: possession of Luxembourg, a small, German-speaking grand duchy wedged between France, Belgium, and Germany which was, by the treaty of 1815, a fiefdom of the King of Holland. Because of its strategic position, heavy for-tifications, and Prussian garrison, Luxembourg presented a po-tential threat to French territory.

Appearing to appreciate French concerns, Bismarck expressed no opposition to French acquisition of the grand duchy, saying it was a matter for negotiation between France and the Dutch king, William III. France duly entered into secret negotiations with Holland which resulted in an offer to purchase Luxem-bourg for 300 million francs. William, hard up and eager for the means to finance an expensive love affair, accepted the offer in principle. But when news of the impending sale leaked out, in the spring of 1867, it provoked an explosion of outraged na-tional sentiment in Prussia and the smaller German states fede-rated with it.

Luxembourg had once been part of the Holy Roman Empire and a member of the German Bund. To German nationalists it was "ancient German soil, about to be torn from the Fa-therland." What was more to the point, because its defenses were garrisoned by Prussian troops, there was no way the sale could be consummated without explicit Prussian consent, ex-cept at the risk of war. Bismarck made it clear that now he cer-tainly did not consent, and the Dutch king prudently reneged on his deal with France. Thus, even as Napoleon was opening his Great Universal Exhibition, which was intended to advertise French wealth and prestige to the world, the scene was set for another humiliating geopolitical setback.

In early April, Napoleon sent for Cowley to discuss the crisis. He told the British Ambassador that he was "completely mysti-fied" by Prussian policy. "Trusting to the assurances given by Bismarck, he had gone into negotiations with Holland which had been successful, only to find that Bismarck had played him false." As a result, Napoleon told Cowley, the French people's irritation against Germany was reaching an uncontrollable level. "Alarm had got possession of the public mind, and unless some satisfaction was given to France, he could not say to what extremities it might be driven.

"He was most anxious to maintain the peace of Europe, and if the Great Powers could prevail on Prussia to give him satisfaction, or could suggest any mode of settling this question, he would be glad to adopt it." In short, Napoleon was appealing to Britain and the other major powers to get him off the hook before French public opinion drove him into an unwanted war with Prussia.

A few days later, Cowley found Napoleon even more desperate for a peaceful settlement. "My position is becoming hourly more difficult," said the emperor. "I wish sincerely to maintain peace. . . . I am now willing to abandon everything but the departure of the Prussians. Do what you like with the fortress—leave it to Holland, or give it to Belgium, neutralize it or raze it—but do what you can to obtain this concession from Prussia, or I become powerless and war is inevitable."

In the event, Bismarck was willing to allow Napoleon a minimally face-saving way out. So soon after the war with Austria, Prussia was not ready for a clash of arms with France, and Luxembourg was not a cause for which Bismarck would risk his grand design for a unified Germany, so he agreed to a British proposal for a great power conference in London. The conference convened in May and swiftly found a solution acceptable to both sides: Prussia was to withdraw its garrison from Luxembourg, the fortifications were to be destroyed, and the neutralized grand duchy would remain the property of the Dutch king. Nobody thought to enquire of the Luxembourgeois if they had any preferences.

It seemed a reasonable solution, honorable to both sides, and so it was received by the European public. But in the evolving war of nerves between France and Prussia, it was another disaster for Napoleon: to Bismarck and his colleagues in Berlin, as to the statesmen and generals of the other capitals of Europe, the Emperor of the French—whatever his earlier triumphs—had been revealed more clearly than ever as an indecisive fumbler, whose irons had to be pulled from the fire by those with steadier hands.

While Napoleon's string of foreign policy failures was undermining the Second Empire's standing abroad, an extraordinary political process was under way at home: Napoleon was attempting to reconcile the irreconcilable by turning his personal dictatorship into a parliamentary regime, but without relinquishing his ultimate grip on power.

This was more than a mere exercise in hypocrisy. One of the items in the ragbag of political, social, and economic ideas that Napoleon carried around with him all his life was an often-stated belief in the virtues of democracy. He had promised at the outset of his reign that he would eventually "crown the edifice with liberty"—that is to say, when he judged that France was mature enough to handle it without falling back into revolution and anarchy. Supporters, opponents, and onlookers alike may have regarded that pledge as little more than high-flown rhetoric, not to be taken as notice of serious intent, but Napoleon evidently meant it—in his fashion.

When he took the first tentative step toward strengthening the powers of the Chambers in 1860, there was widespread skepticism. "He can't give a little liberty and then play fast and loose with it as a cat does with a mouse," said the British Foreign Secretary, Lord Clarendon. "He can't proclaim ministerial responsibility and prevent the Chambers from making them responsible—He can't have an address to the Crown and prohibit 'les vérités dures.' . . . I am sure his opinion is, as it was his uncle's, that the French are ungovernable, except despotically."

The moderate republican Emile Ollivier, one of the handful of opposition members to have won a seat in the Legislative Body in the 1857 elections, read the signs quite differently. He recognized that in his reform decree of 1860, Napoleon had planted the fatal seed of evolution. "It is a small step, but in time it will have decisive results," Ollivier said, and when Napoleon judged the time to be right, he would "grant liberty of his own accord, which, far from weakening him as people think, will in fact consolidate his throne."

At the time, Ollivier's assessment must have appeared wildly optimistic. Although Napoleon's regime was hardly more repressive than those that preceded and were to follow it, the emperor had at his disposal a wide variety of means by which to assure that parliament remained a rubber stamp, notwithstanding its newly granted right to debate his policies and question straw ministers. There were, after all, only five opposition members in the 225-seat Legislative Body, the next elections were not due for three years, and there were ample means to ensure that when they occurred the government would retain an overwhelming majority.

Official gerrymandering was one of those means. The government practiced what it called an "active and dynamic electoral geography" to ensure that hostile urban areas were chopped up and dispersed as constituency boundaries were redrawn to accommodate population changes. More important, the government sponsored the "official" candidates whom it wanted to win and went to considerable lengths to induce the electorate to vote for them, while making life as difficult as possible for the opposition candidates.

Authorized candidates' campaigns were paid for and run by the local prefecture and assisted by an army of minor officials—policemen, schoolteachers, postmen, magistrates, and the like—while opposition candidates had to pay their own way as they battled against official intimidation, harassment, violence, and occasional arrest. Official candidates' manifestos, always printed on white paper, were posted up by the prefect or subprefect in the most advantageous locations and it was illegal to tear them down; opposition candidates had to put their colored posters up where they could find space and these could be torn down with impunity, which they frequently were.

In addition, bribery and blackmail were frequently resorted to on behalf of official candidates. The dead were resurrected to cast their ballots, while multiple voting, stuffed ballot boxes, and rigged results were commonplace.

Despite such official chicanery, the elections of 1863 produced a dramatic increase in the number of opposition members, from five to thirty-two. This outcome was not enough to pose a serious threat to the government, but after allowing such a setback to occur on his watch as Interior Minister, the faithful Persigny was dismissed from office—an action which many saw as evidence of Napoleon's true attitude toward the democratic principles he professed.

But a transforming evolutionary process was nonetheless gathering momentum. Although the government retained an overwhelming majority in the chamber, few of those who sat on the government benches could properly be called Bonapartists.

As we have seen, Bonapartism scarcely existed as an ideology any more, except in the mind of the hapless Persigny and a few others. The great majority of the members now occupying the government benches in the Legislative Body were, in fact, conservatives of various kinds—Legitimists, Orléanists, clericalists, industrialists—whose fealty to Napoleon was based only on the grudging conviction that stability under the Empire was preferable to the dangers of fractious republicanism.

Thus, the 1863 Legislative Body, for all its huge official majority, was no longer the meek servant of the regime. It quickly attained an unanticipated level of public prestige, and even among the government members there was a potential for dissent that had never been intended. At the same time the appointed Senate and Council of State, which in theory had the superior role, became progressively more sclerotic and less effective.

Not only were there now some rudiments of genuine parliamentary life, but a new combativeness was apparent in the press, and there was an increasing tendency among liberals, radicals, republicans, socialists, and other anti-establishment groups to express their views forcefully—often by means of unruly public demonstrations. The political jokesters and anonymous pamphleteers grew daily bolder and even the formerly authoritarian Morny warned his half brother in the aftermath of the 1863 elections that "only two forces remain—the Emperor and democracy. Democracy will steadily gain strength; it is urgent to satisfy it if we do not want to be swept away by it."

By conviction as by temperament, Napoleon was not the man to let that happen, and he gave Morny tacit permission to begin confidential talks with opposition leaders of all hues, except the deepest-dyed republicans, with a view to forming a national coalition administration. These efforts were brought to a halt by Morny's sudden death in 1865. The move toward liberalization languished after Morny's place as Napoleon's principal adviser was taken by the hard-nosed conservative Eugène Rouher.

By this time, however, Napoleon had made the acquaintance of Ollivier and saw in him the man to bridge the gulf between imperialists and republicans. The two men struck up an immediate if unlikely rapport. "You and I may disagree on certain questions, but basically our sentiments are identical,"

Napoleon told Ollivier. And Ollivier confided to his diary that he had been "literally charmed by the Emperor. . . . He appears to be cold, but I think from timidity rather than stiffness. One feels that he has a delicate, sensitive, feminine nature."

Ollivier had a shrewd understanding of Napoleon's ad hoc style of governing, recognizing the pragmatic improviser concealed behind the myth of the artful schemer. "You are wrong to think that the Emperor has plans," he wrote to a friend. "If he did, he would have been overthrown a hundred times already. His strength is in having none and in allowing himself to be carried along by events. He has aspirations, but not plans."

The hiatus caused by the death of Morny was suddenly ended in January of 1867, when without advance notice Napoleon took the next major step toward liberalization and bestowed on the Chambers the right of interpellation—that is, to interrupt parliamentary proceedings and demand an explanation of policy from the appropriate minister. Like Rouher and Napoleon's other old guard advisers, Eugénie was taken completely by surprise—and considerably alarmed. "I fought tooth and nail against this resurrection of parliamentarianism," she would recall many years later. "I did not understand what could have brought the Emperor to decide on such a grave innovation."

True, even she was aware that her husband's personal dictatorship could not last indefinitely and that the Constitution "would have to be slightly watered down in a democratic sense." But she was sure that "the Emperor did not think he could carry this out himself, as he was the personal incarnation of the authoritarian principle and this principle was his raison d'être." In fact, she said, Napoleon had secretly agreed with her that parliamentary rule must wait until after their son came of age and mounted the throne as a constitutional monarch, at which time she and Napoleon would retire to Biarritz.

If this had been Napoleon's intention, what made him decide to speed up the process of liberalization? Eugénie believed that because of his health, "he no longer felt capable of bearing for very long the crushing burden of supreme power." That, no doubt, was part of the answer. But Napoleon's determination to press ahead despite opposition, not to mention his own hesitations and second thoughts, may also be seen as a triumph of one side of his baffling political persona over the other.

His personal kindliness and fashionably progressive outlook, constantly at war with his authoritarian instinct, allowed him to be a despot who believed in democracy—just as his other ambivalences allowed him to be a socialist who fostered capitalism and an imperialist who supported what would nowadays be called wars of national liberation.

In this maze of paradox, he managed to strike a shrewd balance between conviction and opportunism. "March at the head of the ideas of your century," he had written, "and these ideas will follow you and support you. March behind them and they will drag you after them. March against them and they will overthrow you."

One idea system with which he flirted throughout his life was that of Saint-Simon, who believed, with an almost mystical fervor, that under state supervision industrialism could free the common man from the shackles of poverty, while science would release him from the slavery of superstition and religion. In practice, the interventionist economic policies of the Second Empire were closer to state capitalism than socialism. But they did produce some of Saint-Simon's hoped-for benefits as massive state funding and active bureaucratic encouragement stimulated basic industries, enabling France to begin to rival Britain as an industrial power.

Under Napoleon's supervision, state loans and guarantees of minimum return on capital sent railway construction surging ahead, creating in turn an enormous boom in coal, iron, steel, and heavy engineering. Investment and deposit banking mushroomed to meet the insatiable demand for funds to finance the boom. The resultant fever of technological advance and economic growth threw up a new class of industrial and entrepreneurial millionaires. And at the same time, the system allowed enough of this newfound wealth to trickle down to the masses to appear—for a while, at least—to fulfill Saint-Simon's prophecy that the rise of industrialism would remedy class conflict and sponsor political stability.

Intrigued by the unusual spectacle of the social reformer inside the skin of the imperial dictator, the literary critic Charles-Augustin Saint-Beuve admiringly dubbed Napoleon "Saint-Simon on horseback." And no less a critic of the Second Empire than Zola would acknowledge, through one of his fictional characters, that the wealth generated in large part by Napoleon's policies during this period of dizzy industrial expansion was "the manure in which the mankind of tomorrow would grow."

In one of Zola's massive cycle of novels chronicling the history of a Second Empire family, a character called Madame Caroline observes that, "without speculation, there would be no living and fertile enterprises, no more than there would be children without lust." In Madame Caroline's view, "money, poisonous and destructive, became the ferment of all social vegetation. . . . Was not money alone the power capable of razing a mountain, filling in a stretch of sea, making the earth at last a fit dwelling place for men? . . . All good came from money, which was also the source of all evil."

And, in a similar paradox, all liberty came from the emperor, who was also the source of all tyranny. Together with his 1867 reforms, which effectively gave new latitude to the Legislative Body to debate and amend the laws handed down by the Council of State, Napoleon eased the restrictive press laws and the regulations restricting the right of assembly. And while all this still left France a long way from being a true democracy, it set the stage for the parliamentary elections of June 1869, which created a momentum Napoleon could not have resisted had he wanted to.

In this election, the pro-government vote fell by almost 1 million compared with the 1863 results, while the total vote for opposition candidates rose by 1.3 million. The opposition made a clean sweep of the urban and industrial areas, and although the countryside remained solidly for the status quo, the stage was now set for the transformation of the Authoritarian Empire into the short-lived Liberal Empire.

25

BISMARCK BAITS THE TRAP

IN MID-NOVEMBER 1869, standing at the rail of the imperial yacht *l'Aigle,* Eugénie experienced one of the supreme moments of her reign. Around her as *l'Aigle* steamed into Port Said lay a fleet of fifty men-of-war, representing all the great nations of the world, dressed overall, with rails and yards manned, their guns firing a salute as the Empress of the French passed among them. Then, as *l'Aigle*'s prow turned toward the desert, the mighty fleet formed up to follow her in triumphant procession into the newly dug Suez Canal.

It was an unforgettable experience—one that seemed to reaffirm the dash and brilliance of the Empire Eugénie's husband had created and which she adorned, a moment that led her to forget the public and private turmoil she had left behind in Paris and clap her hands together in delight. "Never in my life," she was heard to exclaim, "have I seen anything more beautiful!"

The Suez Canal, lopping weeks off the journey from Europe to India and the Far East, was the most spectacular engineering feat of an age of vaulting technological advance—the nineteenth-century equivalent of the first manned moon flight. And it was an essentially French achievement. It had been created by the vision, drive, and resolve of a Frenchman, Eugénie's cousin, Ferdinand de Lesseps; it had been financed by the savings of 25,000 small French investors; and it had been encouraged by the emperor himself (and mishievously hampered by the British, who saw it as a potential threat to their hold over India).

The official opening of the canal, therefore, was very much France's—and Eugénie's—day. As Lesseps put it, she was "the cynosure of all eyes . . . all this incense and honour were offered to the Empress simply as representing at one and the same time a great country and the triumph of civilisation."

Before the multinational fleet, led by *l'Aigle*, set off on the inaugural 100-mile journey down the canal to Port Suez, the Grand Ulema of Egypt and the Archbishop of Jerusalem bestowed their benedictions in an unprecedented display of Christian-Muslim amity. Eugénie's confessor Monsignor Bauer, who was also the Apostolic Delegate to France, followed with a peroration that combined soaring hyperbole and numbing sycophancy.

"The hour which has just struck," he declared, "is not only one of the most solemn of this century, but one of the greatest and most decisive which humanity has witnessed since there has been a history here below." Then with words of praise for the "immense" part played by Eugénie in the realization of her cousin's project, Monsignor Bauer turned to the empress and said: "It is proper to your devoted soul to accomplish great things in silence, but we are under no obligation to be accomplices in this silence. . . . It is important for history to know that this great work is to a large extent yours."

Eugénie accepted this encomium with becoming grace and nodded approvingly as Monsignor Bauer went on to include some acknowledgment of Lesseps, standing at her side. "Let us declare the name of this man, who belongs to history," he said. "Let us declare to all the world that France is proud and content in her son."

As, indeed, France might be: Lesseps, not an engineer but a diplomat by profession, was a man driven by a truly magnificent obsession and willing to sacrifice everything for it—prodigiously energetic, grandiosely self-confident, and with the lack of scruple necessary to the accomplishment of great ventures. In addition to the enormous physical and technical obstacles he had surmounted to fulfill his dream, there had also been stifling Ottoman inertia and relentless British opposition* to overcome. And although France was now happy to accept the glory, Napoleon's support for Lesseps's visionary project had been far from constant over the years of struggle to complete the canal.

Eugénie, however, had unfailingly supported her cousin, and now, as her yacht led the way down the canal, she was in a fever of anxiety lest some accident or unforeseen snag should mar her hour of glory. She told her cousin that she "felt as though a circle of fire was around her head, because every moment she thought she saw *l'Aigle* stop short, the honor of the French flag compromised and the fruits of our labor lost."

These fears came to a climax over dinner when, "suffocated by emotion, she was obliged to leave the table and we overheard her sobs—sobs which do her honor, for it was French patriotism overflowing from her heart."

While Eugénie alternately reveled in and agonized over what was destined to be the last great spectacle of her husband's reign, Napoleon was in Paris, struggling to contain the dynamic forces unleashed in the wake of the June elections, which had produced such a massive opposition vote.

During the early summer, the capital had been plagued by demonstrations against the regime, often leading to violent clashes between agitators and the police. A particularly bloody confrontation took place one night in June in the rue Lepelletier, close to the opera. Inside, *le tout Paris*—in white tie, tails, and dinner gowns—was enjoying a gala performance of Gounod's *Faust;* outside, there was blood on the cobblestones as workers and mounted troopers clashed in the gas-lit street, their shouts and screams all but drowning the strains of Gounod's last-act ballet.

At one point during the summer foreign tourists fled the city, fearing that revolution was imminent. And although the post-election disturbances eventually subsided as the realization

---

* In time, of course, the British would regret they had rejected Lesseps's pleas to participate in the project and would take control of the canal for themselves, through Disraeli's purchase of the bankrupt Khedive's shares in the Suez Canal Company in 1875.

took hold that almost anything was preferable to revolution, the atmosphere remained edgy. "The fear and horror of Socialism is still the protecting god of the Empire," wrote the *Times* correspondent.

Amid all this, the emperor himself was again desperately ill, in such pain from the stone in his bladder that he had to cancel his annual summer visit to the army at Châlons. He was living on opium-based painkillers and every night his doctors drugged him to sleep, from which he would frequently awake calling the name of some long-dead companion.

From the palace of Saint-Cloud, where he was confined to his bed, officials put out the word that Napoleon was merely the victim of a bout of rheumatism, which made it difficult for him to ride his horse. But the optimistic bulletins did not allay public fears and the rumor spread that he was dying, causing a panic on the Bourse. Only when Napoleon had recovered sufficiently to be seen riding in a closed carriage along the Champ-Elysées— rouged to disguise his deathly pallor and with his gray hair dyed to a youthful brown—did the rumors subside and the Bourse edge back up.

The situation remained turbulent, but manageable. Despite the election results, the great majority of members of the Legislative Body by no means favored the overthrow of the Empire, either openly or covertly. Between the 25 "pure" republicans on the left and the 80 hard-core dynastic imperialists on the right sat a melange of 150 moderate republicans, Legitimists, Orléanists, and others. What they wanted was not revolution but, as a motion signed by 116 of them put it, to be able to "involve the country more effectively in the management of its affairs." In effect, it was a demand for the formation of a parliamentary government under a prime minister.

At first, Napoleon hesitated to move so far, so quickly, and suspended sittings of the Legislative Body. In response, there were renewed protest demonstrations and rumors began to circulate that the emperor was planning a new coup d'état to smash the impudent power of the parliamentarians. When the socialists and radicals threatened to march on the Parliament Building and force their way in, there was again talk of impending revolution and once more panic gripped the Bourse.

As Cowley had by now retired and left Paris, it was left to the

British chargé d'affaires, Lionel Sackville-West, to report to Whitehall that "the Second Empire has gone off the rails. It is no longer being guided. It is hurling itself at an accelerating speed towards the abyss."

This was an exaggeration. On October 26, the date of the planned march on parliament, troops and police were deployed in great numbers around key positions, but the threatened disturbances did not occur. That evening Napoleon received an ovation when he went to the theater, and when he finally did reconvene the Legislative Body on November 29, he promised the formation of a transitional government to serve while a consultative committee drew up a constitutional reform program.

While the interim government, under Ollivier, took office, the turbulence in the streets of Paris continued. In January 1870, *La Marseillaise*, a newspaper edited by the republican deputy Henri de Rochefort, published an attack on the Bonaparte family and, in response, one of its obscurer members—Prince Pierre Bonaparte, a ne'er-do-well cousin of the emperor—challenged Rochefort to a duel. When two of Rochefort's editorial staff called on Pierre to accept the challenge, there was a scuffle in which the prince drew a gun and shot one of them dead.

The funeral of the journalist Victor Noir turned into a massive demonstration, with more than 100,000 republican sympathizers marching to the cemetery at Neuilly. Troops were on hand to keep the peace, but there was no violence. The next day Rochefort's paper published what amounted to an open call to revolution. "For eighteen years, France has now been in the bloody hands of these ruffians, who, not satisfied with cannonading Republicans in the streets, entice them into foul snares and massacre them in their houses. People of France, do you not think that we have had enough of this?"

Rochefort was arrested, charged with insulting the emperor and his family, fined 3,000 francs, and jailed for six months. Prince Pierre was accused of murder but acquitted. Again there were predictions of mass rebellion, but again the crisis passed. The heavy deployment of troops and gendarmes in the centers of urban disaffection, the promise of constitutional reform, and the fear of Red revolution were enough to keep the situation under control.

By April, the constitutional commission had produced a plan for a hybrid form of parliamentary government in which the elected deputies would share power with the crown. Under this arrangement, both the emperor and the Legislative Body would have the right to initiate legislation; there would be a prime minister who, like the other ministers, would be chosen from among the ranks of the elected deputies and would be responsible to the chamber as well as the monarch; and the senate would be reduced to the status of a second chamber.

On May 8, Napoleon submitted these reforms to the people for their approval in the first plebiscite to be held in over seventeen years. The wording of the plebiscite cleverly sought to convey the impression that the reforms were entirely voluntary on Napoleon's part, having been "carried out since 1860 by the Emperor with the assistance of the senior institutions of State." In essence it was as much a plebiscite on the continued existence of the Empire itself as on the new Constitution, and packaged as it was, it could hardly fail to win overwhelming approval.

Napoleon rightly calculated that the French people would not cast aside the certainties of a liberalizing imperial regime for the dangers of republicanism and Red revolution. The Man of December had not lost his appeal, and when the results were in—7.35 million for and 1.53 million against—he happily recalled the outcome of the 1853 plebiscite which had confirmed him as emperor and chortled: "I'm back to my old score."

So Emile Ollivier, as leader of the parliamentary majority, became prime minister, and the Liberal Empire was born. A degree of confidence returned and the collective wisdom of the world said that, for all its air of decline, there was plenty of life in the Second Empire, which might even reinvigorate itself under its new, quasi-democratic Constitution. Certainly, no man of sense would be rash enough to predict its imminent downfall or the end of the Napoleonic dynasty. After all, the Austrian and Ottoman empires had been in decline for generations but remained major players on the world scene.

The crisis which brought these hopes to nothing burst out of a cloudless summer sky. The French economy was doing well,

the demonstrations and upheavals of recent months had subsided, and so far as foreign relations were concerned, Ollivier
felt able to tell the Legislative Body on June 30 that "in whatever direction we look abroad, we find no pressing problems."
He added: "There has never been a time in history when the
prospects of peace in Europe have looked better." Two days
later the storm broke.

Its origins lay in Madrid, where two years previously the
Spaniards had rid themselves of their corrupt and oversexed
queen, Isabella II. Since then they had been looking for a new
monarch, and one of the candidates was the young Prince
Leopold of Hohenzollern-Sigmaringen, a member of the Catholic branch of the Prussian royal family. At that time there was a
brisk market in thrones for minor European royalty: a Batten-
berg had become King of Greece, the unfortunate Maximilian
had become Emperor of Mexico, and Leopold's older brother
Karl had recently agreed to become King Carol I of Rumania.

Leopold, however, was not keen to follow his brother's example. The Spanish throne seemed to him to be dangerously unstable and, not being over-ambitious, he was quite satisfied to
remain a princeling commissioned in the Prussian Army. Nor
did the Prussian king think much of the idea. Like Leopold, he
regarded the throne as unstable and did not want to engage the
prestige of the Hohenzollern name in a project that might end
badly. If young Leo really wanted the throne, then so be it, but
Uncle Wilhelm would just as soon he turned it down.

Bismarck, however, saw things very differently: not only
would a Hohenzollern on the Spanish throne represent a powerful extension of German influence, and therefore further his realpolitik, but it would bracket France, dealing another
humiliating blow to the emperor, whom he wished to keep off-
balance.

At the secret urging of Bismarck, the Spanish caudillo,
Marshal Prim, renewed the offer which Leopold had politely rejected eighteen months previously. At the same time, Bismarck
wrote to Leopold's father, Prince Karl Anton, appealing to his
sense of duty as a Prussian to prevail on his son to accept the
throne. Karl Anton was won over; although still unenthusiastic,
Leopold succumbed to parental pressure and asked his uncle
Wilhelm for permission to accept. The Prussian king gave

this—"though with a very heavy heart"—and by the end of June the matter was settled, subject to the formal approval of the Cortes, the Spanish parliament.

Bismarck knew the French would be outraged, and was not in the least concerned. "We may see a passing fermentation in France," he wrote. "Undoubtedly, they will cry 'intrigue' and will be furious against me." But he believed that the matter would pass through the Cortes quickly and secretly, presenting Napoleon and the rest of Europe with an irreversible fait accompli.

Things did not work out so neatly, however. Because of an error in deciphering a coded message between the Spanish Embassy and Madrid, the news leaked out, and on July 2 the French realized that they were about to become the victims of what was widely seen as "another Sadowa."

They reacted even more violently than Bismarck had anticipated. The new Foreign Minister, Antoine Agénor, duc de Gramont, fumed that the Hohenzollern candidature was "nothing less than an insult to France." In a speech to the Legislative Body, he said that while the Spaniards of course had the right to choose their own monarch, their choice could not be allowed to "imperil the interests and honor of France." He called on both Spain and Prussia to renounce the Hohenzollern candidature, otherwise "we know how to fulfill our duty without hesitation and without weakness." When the text of Gramont's speech reached Berlin, Bismarck growled that it was "insolent and bumptious, beyond all expectation." He added: "This certainly looks like war."

Lord Lyons, the new British Ambassador, agreed that Gramont's words were dangerously bellicose. He took advantage of a meeting with the French Foreign Minister to tell him he thought "milder language would have been more appropriate." Gramont, anxious not to alienate the British, swallowed the rebuke.

Indeed, he told Lyons he was glad the other had raised the matter, since it gave him the opportunity to explain to the British government why he had spoken "in terms so positive." They would "understand perfectly the impossibility of contending with public opinion," he said. The French public was "so strongly roused upon the question that it could not be resisted or trifled with. . . . Nothing less than what he had said would have satisfied the public. . . . Diplomatic considerations must yield to public safety at home." Nevertheless, he appealed for British diplomatic assistance in avoiding "a catastrophe."

So far, it seemed, France was winning the propaganda war, in spite of the bellicosity of the French politicians and newspapers of all political persuasions. Even *The Times* of London, which—like most of its influential readership—was generally friendly toward Prussia and hostile toward France, called the way in which the Hohenzollern candidature had been handled a "vulgar and impudent coup d'état, in total contradiction to accepted diplomatic practice." This was true enough. By tradition, negotiations to fill vacant European thrones were conducted openly, so that all interested nations could have their say and voice their objections, if any.

At Saint-Cloud, meanwhile, Napoleon was ill again with a recurrence of his bladder trouble and suffering such acute pain that on July 1 he had been examined by a panel of five specialists who were unable, however, to agree among themselves whether an operation was necessary.* This painful condition, the heavy medication Napoleon was obliged to take, his perennial reluctance to oppose the will of his wife, the extent to which he had relinquished his personal power, and his natural tendency to vacillate, all combined to create a critical leadership vacuum as the Spanish succession crisis unfolded.

Eugénie, though now formally barred from attending cabinet meetings, was present when the enfeebled emperor met with his ministers to discuss the crisis, adding her voice to those who were spoiling for a fight—leading them, in fact. Behind her lay a history of interference in foreign affairs, over Rome, Poland, Mexico, and in her farcical venture at redrawing the map of Europe. Now she was openly thirsting for war with upstart Prussia. "Il faut en finir," she said—"We've got to finish it."

She told the Austrian Ambassador she hoped the Prussians would not back down. In fact, reported Metternich, she was "so worked up in favour of war that I could not prevent myself from teasing her a little." The prospect of war, or at least of a diplo-

---

*One of the five did put his signature to a report recommending an exploratory operation, but for reasons that have never been adequately explained no action was taken.

matic triumph over Prussia, had made her look ten years younger, he said. Members of Eugénie's household confirmed her belligerence. The comtesse de Garets, one of her maids-of-honor, recorded that "everyone here, the Empress foremost, is so desirous of war that it seems impossible we shall not have it."

A couple of days later, Metternich had a talk with the emperor and found that he, too, seemed positively to welcome the prospect of a showdown with the Prussians. "He appeared delighted, I might even say joyous, and greeted me with the phrase: 'Well, what do you think of our affair?'"

Metternich replied that he thought it was a serious matter, but that the Prussians would probably give way. But Napoleon would have none of it. "Do you really believe," he asked the Austrian, "that Berlin can give way at once, after the very strong representations which we have made to them, and which at this moment the duc de Gramont is reinforcing still more vigorously in his speech to the Chamber?"

Apparently believing war to be not only inevitable but imminent, Napoleon observed that "everything would depend on the rapidity of military preparations. . . . I believe the winner will be the one who can be ready first." Then he asked Metternich if he could count on Austria's assistance. The ambassador was evasive, saying that "it would to a great extent depend on the attitude of Russia."

To the British, the French continued to present a less bellicose face, Gramont again telling Lyons that he was "following, not leading the nation." Furthermore, he assured the ambassador that if Prince Leopold should, on the advice of King Wilhelm, withdraw his acceptance of the Spanish crown, "the whole affair will be at an end."

In fact, the French were determined to give the Prussians no such chance to withdraw from the lists. On the instructions of Gramont, approved by Napoleon and the cabinet, the French Ambassador to Berlin, Benedetti, had been sent to see the Prussian king at Ems, where he was taking the waters. Benedetti took with him a demand for a categorical statement by Wilhelm that he did not approve of Leopold's acceptance of the Spanish throne and that he was ordering him forthwith to withdraw his candidature.

Benedetti had been told to inform Wilhelm that if France did not receive a positive reply by July 12, it would be regarded as a rejection. "It will be war at once," Gramont advised Benedetti, "and in a few days we will be on the Rhine." He added with apparent approval: "You cannot imagine how excited public opinion is. It is overtaking us on every side."

Although Wilhelm was by no means willing to make the humiliating public statement demanded by the French, he was—unlike his chancellor—anxious to preserve the peace and quite prepared to urge Leopold privately to drop the matter. Accordingly, he wrote to Karl Anton, who responded, just in time to meet the July 12 deadline, by renouncing the Spanish throne on behalf of his son, who was conveniently absent somewhere in the Austrian Alps.

Given a modicum of sanity in Paris, this should have defused the crisis. But the pro-war faction had got the scent of blood and refused to be assuaged. When Napoleon suggested that Leopold's withdrawal might settle the affair honorably, Eugénie was outraged. "It's a disgrace," she snapped. "The Empire is turning into an old woman." Meeting with Napoleon and Gramont, she insisted that the Prussians must be made to give a public guarantee that there would never be a repetition of the Hohenzollern candidature, an idea that was being fervently advocated by the chauvinists in the press and parliament.

Gramont supported her and, probably against his better judgment, the exhausted and enfeebled Napoleon agreed. A telegram went to Benedetti instructing him to extract the required guarantee from the Prussian king and a formal demand was drafted for presentation to the Prussian Ambassador, Barol Karl von Werther.

The following morning, as Wilhelm strolled in the public gardens at Ems, Benedetti hurried up to him. This was a breach of protocol; Benedetti had a formal appointment with the king for later in the day and a starchier monarch might have taken offense at being approached in this fashion. But Wilhelm was in a conciliatory mood, genuinely pleased that his cousin's letter of renunciation seemed likely to end the crisis. "A stone has been lifted from my heart," he said in a note to his queen.

Accordingly, the Prussian monarch greeted the little Corsican jovially and even congratulated him on the diplomatic success of Leopold's withdrawal. Benedetti accepted the congratulations and then broached the subject of his government's latest demand. Wilhelm was taken aback by what was being asked of him, and replied—although politely enough—that such a guarantee was impossible.

But Benedetti was not to be put off. He became more urgent—"almost impertinent," Wilhelm said afterward—until eventually the king cut him short. "It seems to me, Mr. Ambassador," he said, "that I have so clearly and plainly expressed myself to the effect that I could never make such a declaration, that I have nothing more to add." With that, the king lifted his hat and walked on.

This extraordinary encounter, taking place on a fine summer morning in a fashionable spa town, occurred in full view of a crowd of elegantly dressed morning strollers.

Later that day, in a generous mood and judging that a small concession might permit the French to withdraw their preposterous demand, Wilhelm sent a message to Benedetti, via his aide-de-camp, saying that Karl Anton's formal letter of renunciation, which had just reached him, had his "entire and unreserved approval." But Benedetti was still under instructions to press for the guarantee and he sent a message back asking for another interview.

Wilhelm, however, had gone as far as he was prepared to go. His temper was definitely not improved when a message arrived from Werther in Paris, setting out, in terms a good deal more specific than Benedetti had conveyed, Napoleon's demand for "a personal letter of apology from the King to the Emperor, to pacify the French nation." Wilhelm was outraged. "Has anyone ever heard such insolence?" he exploded. "I am to appear before the world as a penitent sinner for an affair which was originated, directed and carried on not by me." The whole affair was "inconceivable," "humiliating," he said.

Before the arrival of Werther's dispatch, the king had authorized Heinrich Abeken, a Prussian Foreign Office functionary temporarily attached to his suite, to report to Bismarck on the day's events. Bismarck was in Berlin, and so furious over Leopold's renunciation and alarmed that the king might make further concessions to the French, that he was considering resignation. There seemed to be a very real danger of an outbreak of peace.

Then, as he sat gloomily at supper with the equally despondent Moltke and his War Minister, Count Albrecht von Roon, Abeken's telegram was brought to him at the table—and in it Bismarck saw the opportunity to snatch war from out of the jaws of peace.

The telegram described the day's activity accurately enough, reporting that the king had decided "not to receive Count Benedetti again, but only to keep him informed through an aide-de-camp," and that "His Majesty has nothing further to say to the Ambassador." The telegram added: "His Majesty leaves it to Your Excellency to decide whether Benedetti's fresh demand and its rejection should not at once be communicated both to our Ambassadors and the press."

Bismarck grasped immediately that with a little editing, a bad enough situation could be made to appear even worse. With a minimum of doctoring, the king's refusal to see Benedetti a second time could be made to look like an open insult to France. "His Majesty the King," read the doctored version, "thereupon decided not to receive the French Ambassador again and sent to tell him, through the aide-de-camp on duty, that His Majesty had nothing further to communicate with the Ambassador." Chuckling that this would be "a red rag to the Gallic bull," Bismarck sent his text to the *Norddeutscher Allegemeine Zeitung* and within hours a special edition was on the streets of Berlin.

Copies of the soon-to-be-famous Ems Telegram were also sent to German embassies around the world, with the intention of embarrassing the French and goading the population of both countries closer to war. And indeed, as the news spread, war fever in the French and Prussian capitals rose to new heights. "Nach Paris!" screamed the mob in Berlin. "A Berlin!" responded the superpatriots in Paris.

In the French cabinet there were some, including Napoleon, who seemed inclined to draw back from the brink. The emperor proposed an often-tried remedy by suggesting that the powers be asked to convene a peace congress. Eugénie was openly contemptuous of the idea. "I doubt whether that does justice to the feeling in the Chambers and the country," she said. Her conviction that only war could restore French honor and put the Prussians in their place was crucial in obtaining a majority vote in favor of immediate mobilization.

Later, when the Second Empire lay in ruins and the Prussian guns were pounding Paris, she would vehemently deny reports that she had ever exulted, "This is my war!" But whether she actually used those words or not, the verdict seems inescapable: together with Gramont—whom Bismarck rightly called "the stupidest man in Europe"—she was a major factor in taking France over the brink.

In the legislature the next day, the conservative politician Thiers tried to stop the slide to war. "Do you want all Europe to say that although the substance of the quarrel is settled, you have decided to pour out torrents of blood over a mere matter of form?" he asked.

But the baying of the majority of deputies overwhelmed him and even the normally sensible Ollivier was so carried away that he accepted the challenge of war "with a light heart." Despite the fevered atmosphere of the moment, that was going rather too far, and Ollivier quickly added that he had meant to say, "with a heart not weighed down with remorse—a confident heart." But the phrase would stick to him for the rest of his life.

The War Minister, General Edmond Leboeuf, followed Ollivier to boast of the army's readiness to fight—"so ready that if the war should last two years, we would not have to buy even the buttons for one gaiter." Buoyed by such assurances and carried on a wave of chauvinism, the legislature voted the credits for war by an overwhelming majority, and as the news spread, the mob ran through the lovely streets of the capital embracing each other and crying "Vive la guerre! A Berlin!"

The ban on the *Marseillaise* had been lifted and the sounds of that rousing anthem echoed down the boulevards while Offenbach's song from *The Grand Duchess of Gérolstein*, "Oh, how I love the soldiers!," enjoyed a new vogue in the crowded bars and taverns.

During the debate, Gramont had sought to allay the anxieties of a few faint-hearts that France might be going to war friendless by hinting that an alliance was in the offing with Italy and Austria. But there was never a chance of that. On the very day of the debate, Baron Vitzhum, a special envoy of Franz-Josef, had an audience with Napoleon at Saint-Cloud and told him that Austria thought Leopold's renunciation should have settled the matter. Napoleon affected a hard-line attitude. "We have gone too far to draw back now," he said, adding with his characteristic fatalism, "Providence has intervened."

He asked Austria to send an army corps to the Bohemian frontier "to prevent the whole weight of the German Army from being thrown on our backs at once," but Vitzhum was decidedly unresponsive. "A lightning conductor in the wrong place may draw the lightning rather than avert it," he said. As for an alliance, he reminded Napoleon that negotiations to that end had come to nothing and that Austria had told him it would remain neutral.

He suggested convening a congress to seek a solution to the dispute and although Napoleon seemed to favor the idea, he insisted that "it mustn't prevent us fighting." But later the same day, when Vitzhum mentioned the idea of a congress to Gramont, "the mere mention of the word so infuriated him that it was quite impossible to pursue the subject."

As for the Italians, they set a price for an alliance that Napoleon, under pressure from Eugénie and Gramont, was unwilling to pay: the withdrawal of French troops from Rome and recognition of Italy's right to occupy the papal states. "If France is to defend her honor on the Rhine," declared Gramont, "it will not be to profane it on the Tiber!"

So France did go into war without allies and without friends. The British, in particular, were totally out of sympathy with their erstwhile ally and feeling an almost brotherly affinity with the Prussians. "Words are too weak to say all I feel for you and what I think of my neighbours!" wrote Queen Victoria* to her daughter Vickie, now wife of the Prussian crown prince. "We must be neutral as long as we can, but no one here conceals their opinion as to the extreme iniquity of the war and the unjustifiable conduct of the French!"

The Times reflected a virtually unanimous national sentiment when it denounced the French declaration of war as "the

---

*Bertie, the Prince of Wales, remained faithful to his beloved France and caused something of a scandal by suggesting to the Austrian Ambassador, at a French Embassy dinner the night before the declaration of war, that Austria should join France against Prussia.

greatest national crime . . . since the days of the First Empire."
And from his lair in Chelsea, England's greatest living man of
letters, the aged and revered Thomas Carlyle, historian of the
French Revolution and biographer of Frederick the Great, contrasted "vapouring, vainglorious, gesticulating, quarrelsome,
restless and over-sensitive France" with "noble, patient, deep,
pious and solid Germany."

Just to be sure that the British did not flag in their moral
support of Prussia, Bismarck sent *The Times* a copy of the proposal Benedetti had been foolish enough to put into writing in
1867, concerning French designs on Belgium. The revelation
created a new spasm of public indignation against the perfidy of
France.

Bismarck was to boast later that in the Hohenzollern candidature crisis he laid a trap for the French, into which they
stumbled. It would be truer to say that the French dug the pit
for themselves, filled it with sharpened stakes, then marched
bravely into it, with banners flying and bands playing.

26

INTO
BATTLE,
UNPREPARED

FOR ALL HIS ASTONISHING INEPTITUDE in diplomacy and his total miscalculation of Bismarck's intentions, Napoleon had not been guilty of complacency about Prussia's military abilities. After Sadowa, he had convened an urgent meeting of his army chiefs and set up a commission to examine ways to bring the French military machine up to the standard of the Prussians'.

Through his new secretary, Francheschini Piétri, Napoleon had bombarded the French military attaché in Berlin, Colonel Eugène Stoffel, with queries about the Prussian Army, right down to such matters as: "What is the weight of the Prussian knapsack? What does it contain? What is the weight of the Prussian cavalry saddle and what weight does the horse carry beyond the weight of the rider? How is the Prussian soldier shod? Does he wear boots, or shoes and gaiters? Is the Landwehr [the reserve militia] uniform provided by the State or paid for by the man who wears it?"

Such detailed questioning must have impressed Stoffel that his emperor was a man who knew something about the nuts and bolts of soldiering, even if he was not the grand strategic thinker that his uncle had been.

Napoleon also asked Stoffel, through Piétri, for "a complete report upon a new system of mobilization adopted by Prussia, by which she will be able to put all her troops on a war footing in nine days." And he wanted a copy of the breech-loading *Zundnadelgewehr*, the needle gun which had wreaked such havoc among the Austrian lines at Sadowa. "The Emperor wishes you to do all that is possible to get one," wrote Piétri. "Let me know if you have need of means for that purpose."

Weaponry apart, the differences between French and Prussian military philosophy were huge. France adhered to the concept of a relatively small, largely professional, long-service army—at that time about 300,000 strong. Conscription was by ballot, but if one drew an unlucky number, one could pay someone else to do one's service and there was no shortage of peasants and proletarians willing, for a price, to serve in the place of a young bourgeois. By contrast, the Prussians had universal conscription for a three-year term, followed by two years part-time service in the Landwehr, which provided them with a ready force of over 1 million men.

Beyond this, there was a profound difference of esprit. Until the early 1860s, the Prussians had been considered bit players in the military scheme of things and the French—dashing, glamorous, and colorful—the true masters of land warfare, as the British were of the sea. The ruling principle of the French Army was "on se débrouille"—we'll muddle through—which the officer class laughingly designated as "System D." By contrast, the Prussian generals, a new breed of military technocrats, believed wars were to be won not by panache but by meticulous and detailed planning.

In short, war was an art to France and a science to Prussia. Where the French were Cavaliers, the Prussians were Roundheads. And they calculated, correctly, that the Second Empire's victories had been won largely because its enemies' armies had proved even more disorganized than its own in such mundane matters as supply, administration, training, and logistics.

True, Napoleon had made warfare's first large-scale use of railways to get his troops to the Italian front in 1859, but by comparison with the way Moltke used trains to catch the Austrians unprepared in 1866 that operation was slow and amateurish. Also, Napoleon and his generals had failed to follow up on the lessons of 1859 and fashion a new philosophy of warfare. Unlike Roon, Moltke, and Bismarck, the French failed to realize the extent to which modern technology had ushered in an age of total war.

Beyond the railway, enabling large numbers of troops to be conveyed swiftly to threatened frontiers, beyond the electric telegraph, permitting instantaneous communication between the generals at the front and the ministers in the capital, beyond the modern newspaper, able to whip up patriotic fervor and national solidarity with glowing dispatches from the battle zone, there was the breech-loading rifle, permitting unprecedentedly rapid and accurate firepower at far greater range, and the rifled artillery piece, permitting the heavy and accurate bombardment of the enemy's rear positions and population centers.

Although he failed to formulate a coherent philosophy around such factors, Napoleon was not blind to them. But many of his army commanders were and consequently his efforts at military reform were largely frustrated. Racked by ill-health and discredited by his foreign policy failures, Napoleon lacked the strength and prestige to impose his will on his bickering generals. At the same time, his weakening hold on parliament and toleration of greater freedom and dissent in public life had emboldened a once-obedient Legislative Body to resist and obstruct his costly plans to reorganize and rearm the military.

There was a long and rancorous debate as Napoleon's new War Minister, Marshal Adolphe Niel, battled to push his reforms through the Legislative Body. "Do you want to turn France into a barracks?" demanded an opposition deputy as Niel outlined his program. "As for you," Niel snapped back, "take care that you don't turn it into a cemetery!"

Eventually, a law was enacted in January 1868 calling for a five-year conscription, with four years of reserve service, which was intended to create a force of 800,000 by 1875. But Niel could not sell the idea of universal conscription; the ballot system remained and the better-off could still pay someone else to do their service for them. Then, in the spring of 1870, the Legislative Body, exulting in its newly won independence of the imperial will, voted to reduce the annual intake of conscripts by 10,000. Niel, however, was no longer alive to witness this setback to his plans; the previous summer he had succumbed to the same complaint that would eventually kill Napoleon—a stone in the bladder.

Perhaps the only unqualified success for Niel's and Napoleon's attempts to bring the French military up to strength and up to date was the development of a breech-loading rifle—the chassepot—which had even greater range and accuracy than the Prussian needle gun. The chassepot was hurried into production and 1 million of them would be turned out by 1870. But such limited progress in no way justified Lebouef's absurd public boast that the army was ready for war with Prussia down to the last gaiter button, nor for the French generals' equally preposterous private assurances to the emperor in the days leading up to the declaration of war.

"[They] all vouched for our victory . . . and what a victory!" Eugénie would recall in her old age. "I can still hear them telling me at St. Cloud, 'Never has our army been in better condition, better equipped, in better fighting mettle! Our offensive across the Rhine will be so shattering that it will cut Germany in two and we shall swallow Prussia at one gulp.'"

A day after France's declaration of war, Princess Mathilde hurried to Saint-Cloud to see the emperor. Absorbed as she was in her role as patroness of the arts—and barely on speaking terms with Eugénie—she was an infrequent visitor to her cousin's philistine court. But she remained fond of Napoleon and was alarmed to hear that he intended to take personal command of the army against the Prussians.

"Is it true?" she asked incredulously.

"Yes," he replied.

"But you're not in a fit state to take it! You can't sit astride a horse! You can't even stand the shaking of a carriage! How will you get on when there is fighting?"

Napoleon—his face ashen gray, his eyes dull, his shoulders bowed—tried to brush aside Mathilde's concerns. "You exaggerate, my dear, you exaggerate."

"No, I do not. Look at yourself in a glass."

Napoleon allowed himself a bitter laugh. "Oh, I dare say I'm not beautiful. I'm not very dapper!" And with a fatalistic shrug, he closed the subject.

Mathilde's concern was, of course, well founded. Although the specialists who had examined the emperor shortly before

had been unable to agree on whether he should undergo an operation for his bladder condition, Mathilde was well aware that
his health was a good deal worse than had ever been publicly
acknowledged. By contrast, Eugénie was either unaware of how
sick her husband was or else chose to ignore the evidence of his
infirmity. "I did know the Emperor was ill," she told Paléologue
long after the event, "but of the exact nature of his illness I was
totally ignorant. The doctors themselves did not know it, or at
least could not succeed in agreeing on the diagnosis."

She insisted that a report on Napoleon's condition which the
urino-genitary specialist Dr. Germaine See had handed to Conneau had not been shown to her and that Conneau only mentioned rheumatism and cystitis. "Nay, more," she said, "he
gave me no hint of any particular anxiety when the Emperor
assumed the functions of generalissimo." With more than a
hint of self-contradiction, she added however that when her
husband went off to the war, she was "careful to have packed in
his luggage all the remedies, sedatives, appliances and resources
which medicine then had at its disposal for affections of the
bladder."

Even if Eugénie did not positively urge him to go to war, she
clearly did nothing to dissuade him. And even if she had tried to
dissuade him, Napoleon would probably have overruled her. He
had always considered himself inescapably chained to his
Napoleonic destiny—a destiny which made it unthinkable that
a Bonaparte should fail to lead the army of France in person as it
marched to its most crucial battle. He remained, in any case, a
fatalist; where his star led, he must follow.

For Eugénie, in this hour of peril for the Empire, a prime objective was the preservation of the dynasty for the sake of their
son. If, heaven forbid, the emperor should die of his exertions or
be killed in battle, he would perish in a manner worthy of a
Bonaparte, inspiring a wave of popular sentiment that would
guarantee her position as regent and the eventual succession of
the young Prince Imperial. And Loulou, of course, must earn his
spurs by going to war with his father.

Although only fourteen years old, sensitive and rather puny,
he must receive the baptism of fire that would prove him to be
a worthy successor to the imperial throne. The role of soldier-

prince was, after all, the one for which he had been trained from infancy.

At the age of just nine months, "the Child of France" had been commissioned in the Imperial Guard and dressed in full ceremonial uniform, complete with bearskin. At the age of three he had sat astride his father's crupper and thrown his Legion of Honor to the passing Zouaves. From the age of five, he had gone each summer with his father to live for a few weeks amid the clatter and excitement of the vast military encampment of Châlons.

Throughout childhood, his elders had filled his head with the glories of the Napoleonic heritage. His governor, the veteran general Charles-Auguste Frossard, and his tutors forced into the boy's very fiber the deeds, dates, and places of French military glory. The elaborately structured games he played with his small circle of friends had invariably been pantomimes of battle. His fairy tales had been tall stories of the Grande Armée told by ancient generals, while veterans of more recent wars had regaled him with accounts of conquest in North Africa, the Crimea, Mexico, Italy, and the Orient.

In the enormous displays of military glitter that were so necessary to the preservation of the Second Empire's swaggering self-image, Louis had always to ride beside his father. The clatter of cavalry along the Champ-Elysées, the crash of massed bands in the Place Vendôme, the pounding of field guns on the Champ de Mars, these were the sounds of his childhood. But it may be doubted that he relished the tunes of glory as much as his elders hoped and imagined—this slight, pallid child who looks out at us from contemporary photographs with the expression more of a wistful dreamer than a budding conqueror.

True, he played the part expected of him and embellished it with a brave show of enthusiasm, but some felt bound to doubt the authenticity of his zeal. One of the great war correspondents of the age, Archie Forbes of the London *Daily News*, deplored the unreal childhood of the Prince Imperial—"a buckram boy from his swaddling clothes, poor little toy and tool of sham imperialism. No trace is discernible of him as a boy in the fashion of other boys; he is ever found a mere padded clothes horse . . . the poor, melancholy little chap."

Now, at fourteen, the "poor, melancholy little chap" was commissioned again, this time as a sublieutenant in the Voltigeurs, so that he could accompany his father to war. And no one, it seems, was prouder to see him in uniform and kepi, with his sword dangling about his ankles, than Eugénie. She had ever been the Roman mother, exhorting the child to honor and duty and the stern consciousness of his dynastic obligations. It was the tender-hearted emperor, rather than she, who had been the one to fondle him as an infant, to bounce him on his knee, and fuss over every tiny accident or trivial ailment.

"Louis is full of spirit and courage and so am I," Eugénie wrote to her mother in Madrid as her son prepared to leave for the war which she herself had promoted with such enthusiasm. "Certain names carry obligations and his are heavy, so he must do his duty, as I am sure he will. You are very fortunate to have had only daughters, for at times I feel . . . I could take my little one and carry him away to the wilderness and tear everyone who tried to lay hands on him. Then I reflect and tell myself that I would rather see him dead than dishonored."

There was a farewell dinner at Saint-Cloud for the emperor and the young Prince Imperial on July 27. The *Marseillaise*—so much more stirring than the trivial *Partant pour la Syrie*—was played in court for the first time and the atmosphere, according to a courtier, was "electric with warlike excitement . . . you may imagine the effect on an impressionable, nervous boy." Indeed, Loulou's tutor Filon heard him bawling the words of the hitherto-banned anthem—"Aux armes, citoyens/Formez vos bataillons"—and wondered where he could have learned them.

The following morning Napoleon and his son rose early to leave for general headquarters at the eastern frontier fortress of Metz. In contrast to 1859, when he rode his charger past cheering throngs through the streets of Paris on his way to lead the Army of Italy, Napoleon was to depart almost furtively. Quite apart from the painful condition which made it impossible for him to cut the heroic figure he once had on horseback, he had the gloomiest presentiments about the war. Almost alone among Frenchmen, it seemed, the emperor was not expecting a swift and decisive victory. "We are beginning a long and difficult war," he said.

So, despite the momentousness of the occasion, the emperor

felt obliged to leave, without public ceremony, from his private railway staiton on the edge of the Saint-Cloud estate.

It had been a cloudless, halcyon summer, but suddenly, prophetically, the skies turned gray and the July breeze turned unseasonably chill as Eugénie and a small group of courtiers saw Napoleon and Loulou onto the train. Eugénie traced a protective sign of the cross on the child's pale forehead as he went aboard. Then, as the train built up steam, she called out: "Do your duty, Louis." Whether she intended the injunction for her husband or her son is not clear.

As the train pulled away, the emperor suddenly remembered a minor sin of omission. "Dumanoir," he called from the window of his carriage to one of his chamberlains. "Dumanoir, I forgot to say goodbye to you."

The emperor arrived at Metz to discover his Army of the Rhine in a condition bordering on the chaotic. It was the fourteenth day of mobilization and according to Leboeuf's calculations the army should have been up to its full strength of 385,000 and ready to lunge deep into German territory from its positions along a 100-mile front from Metz to Strasbourg.

In fact, little over 200,000 men had reached their units, and many of these were without the most basic and essential items of clothing and equipment. The elaborate reforms which, in theory, Napoleon, Niel, and Leboeuf had imposed on the organization and mobilization of the army had been to no avail. Despite their best efforts, the French Army still ran according to the dictates of the traditional "System D."

Cable traffic between field commanders and the War Ministry in Paris gives some idea of the confusion. On July 21, a General Michel reported: "Have arrived at Belfort. Cannot find my brigade; cannot find the general of division. What shall I do? Do not know where my regiments are." On July 28 Michel's missing corps commander, General Félix Douay, turned up to find that, despite assurances that Belfort was "abundantly provided," his troops for the most part had "neither tents, nor cooking pots, nor flannel belts; neither medical nor veterinary canteens, nor medicines, nor forges, nor pickets for the horses—they were without hospital attendants, workmen and train. As to the magazines of Belfort, they were empty."

Scores of thousands of the missing reserve soldiers were stranded en route or else wandering aimlessly around the country, drinking, brawling, and pillaging as they tried to find their regiments; others were simply stuck in their depots, far from the war zone, the victims of impossibly clumsy mobilization procedures. These men were supposed to go from their homes to their regimental depots and then, in batches of 100, from their depots to their regiments in the field.

In one extreme case, reservists of a Zouave regiment, living in northern France, had to travel via Marseilles to their depot in Algeria, before returning to join their units in Alsace. Another group of reservists from the northeastern city of Lille spent six weeks trying to locate their regiment, by which time it had been decimated and taken prisoner at Sedan, only 80 miles from where their futile odyssey had begun.

As with men, so with supplies. The railway lines were choked as the system broke down under the strain. Where supplies did get to or near their destination, there were generally insufficient facilities to unload the wagons. With thousands of soldiers unprovided with food, shelter, proper clothing, or pay, discipline began to break down before ever a shot was fired. At the little frontier town of Froeschwiller, in Lorraine, the parish priest reported: "Everyone behaved as he wanted. The soldier came and went as he liked, wandered off from his detachment, left camp and came back as he saw fit."

As he had told Metternich in one of his intermittent moments of realism, Napoleon knew well that the side which was in a position to strike first would win. Nevertheless, he felt able to issue an order of the day on his arrival at Metz which seemed to take no account of his army's state of utter disorganization. "Whatever may be the road we take beyond our frontiers," he declared, "we shall come across the glorious tracks of our fathers. We shall prove worthy of them." Like the rest of the world, he apparently assumed, in face of all the facts, that France would invade Germany and not the other way round.

Though perplexed at the inaction of Napoleon's vaunted military machine, Britain, Austria, Russia, and the other neutral powers could scarcely imagine that France had rushed so eagerly into a war for which it was not prepared. Nor, at first, could the Prussians and the South German states—Baden, Saxony, Württemberg, and Bavaria—that were allied with them. "It may well happen," wrote the Prussian crown prince, "that for all the French saber-rattling . . . we shall be the aggressors. Whoever could have thought it?"

The war began with a very minor victory for the French Army— one so unworthy of its best traditions as to be, in its way, more shameful than the defeats that were to follow.

It came about when Napoleon, feeling the need of a little stage thunder to reassure the country that the army was in fighting trim, decided on July 30 to send a force across the frontier to seize the Prussian town of Saarbrücken. To be sure of success, and because his slipshod intelligence could give him little idea of the strength of the enemy garrison, he committed an entire army corps to the mission.

Loulou, mounted next to his father, watched in a fever of pride and excitement as the six French divisions, commanded by Frossard, his personal instructor in the art of war, advanced on Saarbrücken in splendid panoply, as though on maneuvers at Châlons. "The noise, the excitement of the soldiers and the smell of powder began to thrill me," he told a friend afterward, "and I felt as though it was a review."

Young Louis might have been less impressed had he been aware that against this formidable invasion force the Prussian defenders numbered no more than one regiment of infantry, one battery of artillery, and a few squadrons of cavalry. Nonetheless, the defenders inflicted as many casualties as they received—six French officers and eighty men killed, against four officers and seventy-nine men lost by the Prussians—before retiring in good order, according to standing instructions, when it became obvious that their position was untenable.

What Napoleon honestly thought of his army's one-sided victory we do not know, but he certainly seems to have been pleased with his son. Some spent bullets landed nearby as they watched the skirmishing on the outskirts of Saarbrücken, and in a telegram to Eugénie that evening Napoleon enthused: "Louis has just received his baptism of fire. His coolness was admirable. He was as unconcerned as if he had been strolling in the Bois de Boulogne." The doting father added that the boy had kept as a souvenir "a bullet which fell close to where he was standing," and that "some of the soldiers wept when they saw him so cool."

Characteristically, the stoical Napoleon made no mention to Eugénie of the physical agony he suffered during his jaunt to Saarbrücken. He was in such pain that after the engagement he had to be lifted off his horse and, according to an eyewitness, "had hardly the strength to walk to his carriage." After he got into the carriage, "he put his arm around his son's neck and kissed him on the cheeks, while two large tears rolled down his own."

At Saint-Cloud that night, Eugénie proudly showed Napoleon's telegram to Ollivier, who in turn lost no time in passing its contents on to the press. Paris went wild with jubilation at the news of the great victory, hailing it as the first step on the road to Berlin, and of the sterling behavior under fire of the young prince. Only later, amid the disastrous defeats inflicted by the Prussians, would the emperor's telegram become the subject of public ridicule and the hapless Loulou be derided for his childish enthusiasm as "l'enfant de la balle."

Two days later, Paris celebrated news of another "victory," even more spurious than Saarbrücken. Somebody in the Bourse, for motives that were never discovered, posted up a fake telegram which read: "Great victory: 25,000 prisoners, including the Crown Prince." The Bourse became a bedlam and the madness quickly spilled over onto the boulevards. People yelled their delight. They sang, they danced, they wept and embraced in the streets. Traffic came to a complete halt. Pedestrians climbed into the carriages of complete strangers and kissed them.

The let-down was traumatic. Within hours, Paris learned that far from defeating the Prussians, their army had taken a terrible trouncing at Froeschwiller, near the frontier in Lorraine, and that MacMahon was reeling back with heavy losses. As this unthinkable news sank in, the popular mood turned ugly and an enraged mob attacked the Bourse, demanding vengeance on the unknown perpetrator of the hoax telegram.

There was worse to come. On the same day as their defeat at

Froeschwiller, though quite coincidentally, the French suffered another disastrous setback at Spicheren, some 40 miles to the west. There, the Prussians—having easily recaptured Saarbrücken—crossed the frontier and humbled Frossard by dislodging his army corps from a commanding position and scattering them in headlong retreat.

Forced to admit these twin defeats, but hoping to obfuscate their significance, Napoleon's headquarters reported uneasily that "the enemy appears to intend attempting some movement into our territory," adding that this intrusion would, however, "give us great strategic advantages." The brutal truth was that the Army of the Rhine had been split in two and was retreating in disarray along the entire Lorraine front, leaving the way open for a massive Prussian thrust into the very heart of France.

In a coded cable to the empress from Metz, Napoleon came closer to the truth: "Marshal MacMahon has lost a battle. General Frossard, on the Saar, has been forced to fall back. The retreat is being effected in good order. All may yet be regained." The forlorn hope expressed in the final sentence did not fool Eugénie. It rang in her ears as the death knell of the Empire. Plunging from her previous high of chauvinistic overconfidence, she sank to a low from which severe setback looked to her like utter disaster. "The dynasty is lost," she cried. "We must think only of France."

That evening she drove to the Tuileries from Saint-Cloud to confer with the Regency Council. Afterward, she issued a proclamation.

Frenchmen: The opening of the war has not been favorable to us. We have suffered a check. Let us be firm under this reverse and let us hasten to repair it. Let there be but one party in the land—that of France; a single flag—that of the national honor. I come among you, faithful to my mission and my duty. You will see me the first in danger to defend the flag of France. I adjure all good citizens to maintain order. To agitate would be to conspire with our enemies.

Apparently the empress no longer believed that all was lost. Subject as she was to dramatic mood swings, her despair had given way to firm resolution. She was now convinced that with courageous leadership the Empire and the dynasty could yet be saved—and that she was the one destined to provide that leadership. She was fond of recalling that she had been born during an earthquake. "What would the ancients have said of such a presage?" she would ask rhetorically. "They would have said I was born to convulse the world." So, responding with relish to the gravity of the situation, Eugénie rose to her full stature at last—convening meetings, sending cables, issuing proclamations, inspiring hope, taking charge.

There was no shortage of admirers to see her as she saw herself. The writer Octave Feuillet put into fervent prose what many felt: "You are at this moment, madame, the living image of the motherland. On your noble forehead we can read all the sentiments which animate you, all that you suffer, all that you hope, all your anguish, all your pride, your enthusiasm, your faith. The soul of France is with you."

The day after news arrived of the twin defeats at Froeschwiller and Spicheren, Eugénie summoned the Chambers into session and, in lieu of the revolution for which many were openly calling, the newly chauvinistic left combined with the imperial right to force the hapless Ollivier out of office on a vote of no confidence. The Chambers made a second scapegoat of Leboeuf, who had boasted so insouciantly of the army's readiness. Relieved of his ministry, he went shortly afterward to the front to take command of an army corps.

In place of Ollivier, that crypto-republican who had had the temerity to demand her exclusion from cabinet meetings, Eugénie and the Regency Council appointed someone more to her liking—the staunchly imperialistic General Charles de Montauban, comte de Palikao—to head a new government and take over the War Ministry.

Palikao, whose exotic title derived from his leadership of a punitive expedition against the Chinese in 1860, was nothing if not energetic. He immediately put Paris under a state of siege, and set about raising a "citizens army" to defend it. With these changes in hand, Eugénie cabled her husband at his headquarters in Metz: "Courage, then; with energy we will get the better of the situation. I will answer for Paris."

But courage and energy, as Eugénie might have realized, were qualities that Napoleon no longer possessed. Could he still summon them up—and had he ever possessed a fraction of the first Napoleon's military genius—he might yet have regrouped his retreating forces and mounted a counterattack capable of stopping the Germans. For, as military historians have since recognized, the stunning Prussian successes to date had been due as much to good luck and brilliant opportunism as to intrinsic military superiority.

At Froeschwiller, as at Spicheren, battle had been joined by chance rather than design, for it had been Moltke's intention to avoid a major clash of arms until he had a clearer idea of the strength and location of the French forces. In fact, it had been the impetuosity—bordering on insubordination—of a Prussian corps commander at Spicheren, and the unforeseen confrontation of two large forces at Froeschwiller, that had created the situation which, brilliantly exploited by Moltke, brought about the collapse of the entire French front.

Even so, as Prussian accounts of the two battles attest, the French had fought with characteristic verve and tenacity, inflicting heavy casualties on the invaders. But now the Prussians were invested with the mystique of invincibility and the French with the stigma of defeat. Morale, such a vital factor in war, had drained away, and the commander-in-chief of the French entirely lacked the leadership qualities to restore it.

This state of affairs was all too well understood in Paris, where the republican deputy Jules Favre spoke for many when he demanded that command of the army be concentrated in the hands of one man—"but not the Emperor." In Metz, Napoleon's own aides were suggesting to him, as tactfully as possible, that his poor health made it advisable for him to relinquish command.

In fact, Napoleon was already considering returning to Paris to take over the reins of government. But the capital was in a ferment bordering on revolution and Eugénie warned him to stay away. "Have you considered all the consequences which would follow from your return to Paris under the shadow of two reverses?" she inquired by cable. Nor would she allow him to send the Prince Imperial back to the safety of the capital. As she had told her mother, Eugénie would rather see her son dead than dishonored.

By now, the public clamor for Napoleon to relinquish command was growing irresistible. The popular choice for commander-in-chief was "our glorious Bazaine" who, having risen from the ranks, was seen by the left as the saviour of France. In fact, he had few qualifications for that role, lacking the flair, decisiveness of character, and intelligence for grand strategy. He was also unappealing to his senior subordinates, possessing none of the dashing attributes of the French officer class. His vulgar habits betrayed his working-class origins, his body was corpulent and slack, his uniforms ill-cut, his face a gray pudding, and he slumped inelegantly in the saddle. Personally brave, yes, and an adequate enough officer, but François-Achille Bazaine was certainly no *beau sabreur*.

Above all, he had the mindset of the eternal number two. Had Napoleon followed his inclination and returned to Paris, Bazaine might possibly have summoned up the personal resources to take charge; in the event, the emperor's presence emasculated him. He never seemed to believe that he was really in command, and in continuing to defer to what he imagined were Napoleon's wishes, Bazaine only managed to compound his own lack of decision.

As if this were not enough, the French high command was riven with personal spite and petty jealousy. An eyewitness to one council of war at Metz, over which the emperor presided, recounted that he had "never seen anything more pitiable than the look of sheer despondency on the Emperor's face as he sat listening to the noisy and even brutal recriminations of one general after another, as he rose to defend his own movements or attack the tactics of a brother officer."

While Bazaine and his generals wrangled, the Germans were closing in on Metz. Soon, it became imperative for the French to withdraw behind the Moselle and make their way west to Verdun to avoid encirclement. As Bazaine grappled with the task, somewhat beyond his normal capacities, of orchestrating the withdrawal of 180,000 men across a flooded and inadequately bridged river, the Prussians and their allies caught up with them, severely mauling the rearguard.

Having gained the far side of the Moselle, the dispirited Army of the Rhine headed slowly westward along two congested roads, paced by reconnaissance patrols of the ubiquitous German cavalry. In the van of the retreating French, escorted by his brilliantly plumed Cent Gardes, rolled the bloated carriage train of the discredited emperor, jolting painfully down the hot, dusty road to Verdun. Sharing the emperor's carriage was Loulou, distraught and bewildered at the realization that the proud Army of France and the generals he had been brought up to revere had been soundly trounced—and that his omnipotent father was a sick and defeated old man.

As the imperial entourage made its way laboriously westward, under the hostile gaze of troops whose loyalty had evaporated with their morale, word reached Napoleon that MacMahon and the remnants of his army corps were falling back on Châlons, 50 miles beyond Verdun. Racked with pain and the realization that he was an encumbrance to Bazaine, Napoleon decided to break away and join MacMahon. At Châlons, in the setting which had been the pride of his Empire, he might regain some of his old vigor and even find a useful role to play in the crisis that threatened the destruction of everything he had lived for.

Now traveling some miles ahead of Bazaine's column, Napoleon's baggage train encountered a patrol of Prussian cavalry. The Uhlans turned tail when they realized the strength of Napoleon's escort, but the sight of even a handful of the enemy in flight so revived Loulou's flagging spirits that he cabled his mother that night: "I am very well, and so is Papa. Everything is going better and better. . . ."

Napoleon, it seems, had not the heart to deny the child's desperate need for an augury to show that the fortunes of war might yet be reversed.

For himself, Napoleon was now obsessed by the idea of reaching Châlons without delay, as though in so doing he might somehow be renewed. At Verdun, he decided to abandon his slow-moving escort and complete his journey by train. But all the harassed railway authorities could produce as a conveyance for the imperial party was a dilapidated locomotive, a third-class carriage, and a pair of cattle wagons to accommodate the emperor's retinue of aides and servants. Some moth-eaten cushions were found to protect the imperial posteriors from the rigor of the carriage's wooden benches, and in this ignominious fashion the Emperor of France set off at midnight on August 15.

Meanwhile, Bazaine had abandoned his plan to march on to Verdun. One pursuing Prussian army had cut the road ahead of him, while another was approaching from behind. Between the villages of Gravelotte and Saint-Privat, 190,000 Germans and 113,000 French fought a titanic battle in which both sides sustained heavy losses. When it was over, instead of pushing on as he might have done, Bazaine limped back to the comparative safety of Metz, where he was to remain bottled up for the rest of the campaign.

A more resolute commander, having given the Prussians as good as he had received, would have stuck to his original plan. In the event, Bazaine's withdrawal to Metz* not only removed a substantial body of fighting men from active participation in the war; it also created a political climate in Paris which would override strategic considerations, making an overall French defeat inevitable.

---

* For which he was tried by court-martial in 1872 and sentenced to life imprisonment for dereliction of duty.

27

CATASTROPHE AT SEDAN

NAPOLEON FOUND CHÂLONS, once the showcase of his Empire's martial pretensions, in a complete shambles. The tattered remnants of MacMahon's army were back, less than a month after having set out so proudly for the front. Now they were a sorry sight, physically exhausted, broken in spirit, and close to mutiny.

"It was an inert crowd," recalled one staff officer, "vegetating rather than living, scarcely moving even if you kicked them, grumbling at being disturbed in their weary sleep." There were "soldiers of the line without rifles or ammunition pouches, Zouaves in their drawers, Turcos without their turbans, dragoons without helmets, cuirassiers without cuirasses, hussars without sabretaches." As another officer noted bitterly: "Instead of the fine regiments of other days, there was a mass of beings without discipline, cohesion, or rank, a swarm of dirty, unarmed soldiers."

The fresh troops sent to Châlons to bring this shattered army up to strength were hardly more inspiring. In addition to raw recruits and depot soldiers—many so green that they could not even march in step or handle their rifles—there were eighteen battalions of the Garde Mobile from Paris whose discipline was, to put it mildly, somewhat less than ironclad. Most of these street-wise Mobiles were infected by the republicanism of the capital. They demonstrated their respect for the emperor by marching past his tent, shouting in unison: "One, two, three, shit!"

They did not want to fight, unless in defense of their homes in the capital, and when they were paraded before MacMahon they shouted, in chorus: "To Paris!" MacMahon, ever imperturbable, feigned incomprehension. "Mes enfants," he enquired in his best avuncular manner, "don't you mean 'to Berlin'?"

Despite these shortcomings in the quality of men and morale, the reconstituted Army of Châlons, by the time it was ready to take the field, was by no means a rabble but a force of 130,000 men, extensively rearmed and resupplied, which, if properly deployed, might have inflicted heavy blows on an over-extended enemy. But again the illness and vacillation of the emperor, the interference of the politicians and the empress, and the poor leadership of the generals combined to create disaster.

On August 17, the day after his arrival in Châlons, Napoleon convened a conference to discuss future plans. Among those present were MacMahon, General Louis Trochu, commander of the newly formed 12th Army Corps, General Berthaut the commander of the Gardes Mobiles, and Napoleon's irksome cousin, Plon-Plon. The emperor, drugged to deaden the agony of his bladder stone, played little part in the discussion, sitting silent and listless as the options flowed back and forth.

Plon-Plon, though scarcely a military genius himself, played a decisive role in the discussions, leading Trochu to observe later that he was the only Bonaparte who seemed to matter any more. At one point, when one of those present remarked that Napoleon should either be at the head of his troops or at the head of his government, the emperor murmured apathetically that, in relinquishing both functions, "I seem to have abdicated." Plon-Plon seized this moment of self-reproach to urge Napoleon to reassert himself and return to Paris to take over the government, however great the risk. "What the devil," he declared, "if [the Empire] must fall, let us at least fall like men."

Napoleon was not convinced. Perhaps Eugénie, as regent, should be consulted first, he said. At this, all of Plon-Plon's old resentment of Eugénie boiled to the surface. "Consult the Regent!" he exploded. "Aren't you the Sovereign? This has got to be decided at once."

Undoubtedly, Plon-Plon had a point; whatever the political

risks involved, it made sound strategic sense for the Army of Châlons to take up position in front of fortress Paris, where it had a good chance of stopping the insolent Prussians in their tracks. And if, as Plon-Plon proposed, General Trochu—a liberal soldier, popular with the republicans and socialists—went on ahead of Napoleon as the newly appointed military governor, the political risks might be minimized. Trochu's appointment, it was argued, would appease the mob. And for good measure he could take with him the fractious battalions of the Garde Mobile, whose return would also be popular.

Hesitantly, Napoleon agreed to the plan, and Trochu duly returned to Paris to take up his new post and inform the empress and Palikao that Napoleon would follow with MacMahon's army. He received a frosty reception on both counts. At the Tuileries, Eugénie was adamant. "No," she said, "the Emperor will not return to Paris. Those who inspired the decisions you talk of are enemies. The Emperor would not enter Paris alive. The Army of Châlons will make its junction with the Army of Metz." At the War Office, Palikao told Trochu: "I can't imagine why the Emperor sent you. You will only add to my difficulties."

In urgent messages to Châlons, Eugénie and Palikao all but forbade Napoleon and MacMahon to return. It was unthinkable both politically and militarily, they said, that the Army of Châlons should leave Bazaine and his men to their fate. No, MacMahon should immediately march to Bazaine's rescue. Indeed, the forces of MacMahon and Bazaine, once combined, could still defeat the Prussians in the field, leaving the capital to look after its own defense, for which it had adequate resources.

While the issue was being argued to and fro, the Prussians moved ever closer to Châlons and, since his position there was not readily defensible, MacMahon moved out—not eastward to engage the enemy, nor westward to defend the capital, but 30 miles northwest to the fortified city of Rheims. Once again reduced to total ineffectuality, the emperor tagged along, like some piece of costly but intrinsically useless baggage.

Convinced that it was impossible to rescue Bazaine, MacMahon continued to argue that he should bring his army back to the capital. Eugénie and Palikao continued to object, and MacMahon remained with his army in Rheims while the argument raged and the Prussians moved relentlessly on into the heart of France. Then an overconfident message from Bazaine settled the argument.

The message—dated August 19, but not received by Mac-Mahon until the 22nd—said that after allowing his troops two or three days' rest, Bazaine intended to break out of Metz and fight his way to the northwest, before wheeling southeast toward Châlons via either Montmédy or Sedan. On hearing this, MacMahon abandoned the idea of falling back on Paris and agreed that it would indeed be proper to march out to "join hands" with Bazaine—even though he had no idea where or when that conjunction might take place.

On August 23, with the emperor and the Prince Imperial still in tow, the hero of Magenta led his men out of Rheims, hoping to keep an appointment with the Army of Metz. Instead, it was to be an appointment with destruction.

By now one of the Prussians' ubiquitous cavalry patrols had reached Châlons, found the camp deserted, and signaled to Moltke's headquarters that MacMahon's army had redeployed at Rheims. What the Germans did not realize, and could not imagine, was that MacMahon had already marched out of Rheims and was heading east. To the Germans, conducting their own campaign on strategic considerations alone, such a move was unthinkable—too suicidal and pointless to be imagined, especially since they knew, as MacMahon did not, that Bazaine was still bottled up in Metz.

Thus, Moltke and his staff were skeptical when they learned on August 24—by way of a report in *The Times*, of all things— that MacMahon was "endeavouring to form a junction" with Bazaine.

At that point, Moltke's forces were facing due west toward Châlons, and ultimately Paris, preparing to advance along a 30-mile front stretching from Vitry-le-François to Sainté-Ménéhould. They could hardly be expected to change direction on the basis of an uncorroborated newspaper report. By the evening of the 25th, Moltke had received further information tending to authenticate the report, yet still he hesitated. It could, after all, be an elaborate deception to put him off his stride.

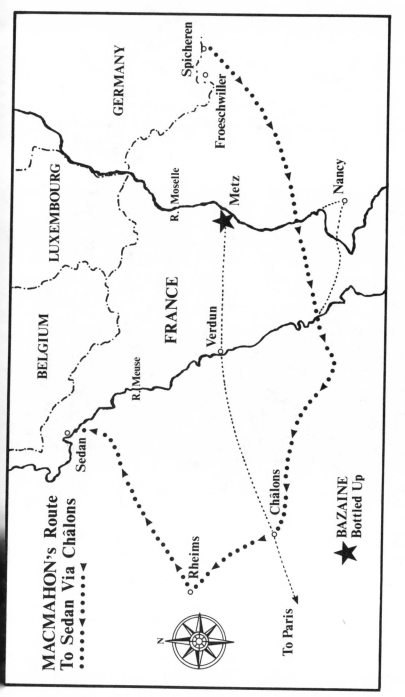

MACMAHON's Route
To Sedan Via Châlons
•••••••▾

BELGIUM

LUXEMBOURG

GERMANY

Spicheren

Froeschwiller

R. Moselle

Metz

Nancy

FRANCE

Verdun

R. Meuse

Sedan

Rheims

Châlons

To Paris

N

★ BAZAINE
Bottled Up

THE WAR ZONE:
Franco-Prussian War
of 1870

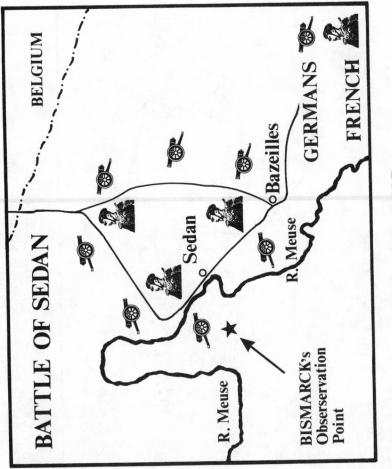

THE BATTLEFIELD:
SEDAN, August 31, 1870

For the Prussian chief of staff, as he pondered the dilemma, a moment of truth had arrived, a moment when all his brilliance and meticulousness mattered less than his instinct—and his willingness to act on it. "Don't tell me if he's a great tactician; tell me if he's lucky," the first Napoleon had once said of a candidate for promotion to general. Moltke was lucky. That night, he decided to risk everything on his intuition that the reports were true, and ordered his forces to execute a massive right wheel so that they could pursue MacMahon's army. The chase was on.

The French columns headed east in miserable conditions, with the emperor in tow—a leaden stoic, hiding his mental and physical agony behind a mask of impassivity, an object of hatred and derision to enlisted men and indifference or contempt to most of the officers. It rained incessantly, turning the country roads into a morass, soaking the weary and dispirited soldiery to the bone. Supply lines broke down and troops pillaged the countryside for food. At one point MacMahon swung his entire army to the north, so that they could obtain supplies from the rail depot at Rethel, a small blunder within a much greater one, which cost him the best part of two days' march.

By the 27th, uncomfortably aware that the enemy was hard on his heels and flanks and beginning to realize that Bazaine's breakout from Metz was illusory, MacMahon telegraphed Paris saying that since he had received no news of Bazaine's whereabouts, he must wheel north to escape the trap that was closing about him.

Palikao responded promptly. "If you abandon Bazaine," he warned, "revolution will break out in Paris and you yourself will be attacked by the entire enemy forces." He advised Mac-Mahon that he was at least thirty-six, and perhaps forty-eight, hours' march ahead of his pursuers, and that "you have nothing in front of you but a feeble part of the forces which are blockading Metz." For good measure, Palikao added: "Everyone here has felt the necessity of relieving Bazaine and the anxiety with which we follow your movements is intense."

Palikao was the victim of self-deception—willful or not, one cannot say. For three days he had been bombarding MacMahon with spurious reports of low enemy morale, of sickness and disobedience within the German ranks, of critical supply problems, and of dissension between the Prussians and their South German allies. Now he followed up his personal message to MacMahon with one carrying the full authority of the state: "In the name of the Council of Ministers and the Privy Council, I require you to aid Bazaine."

As a soldier, MacMahon could not disobey so direct an order. Canceling his plans for a wheel to the north, he prepared for a crossing of the Meuse, which lay directly ahead, beyond the Forest of Argonne.

In his tent, Napoleon heard the news with glum resignation. Despite his reduced status as an irrelevant encumbrance to the army command, he knew enough of the situation to realize that disaster lay ahead. But, emperor now in name only, he felt no more able than MacMahon to defy the orders from Paris. He had, however, sufficient spark left to take one initiative without reference to Eugénie, or anyone else in Paris.

To his own death, Napoleon was now indifferent; indeed, he longed for it. "If only I could die," he had gasped to an aide the day before as, leaning against a tree for support, he had endured the unavoidable agony of urination. But now, as the army prepared to resume its march eastward, he resolved that his son's life must be preserved at all costs. Ignoring the boy's objections, and disregarding the likelihood that if she knew about it Eugénie would insist on Loulou's remaining with the army, Napoleon ordered three of his aides-de-camp to muster an escort of Cent Gardes and take the Prince Imperial north to Mézières, near the Belgian frontier, there to await further instructions.

We have no eyewitness account of what took place as father and son parted company—for all they knew, for the last time— at the crossroads village of Tourteron. But it is not hard to imagine the depth and complexity of their feelings. On Loulou's part, fearful incredulity at the impending collapse of the world he had been born and raised to inherit; pity, perhaps combined with a guilty contempt, for the pathetic figure now cut by his once godlike father; a child's wrenching sense of loss at separation from the source of so much love and security. On Napoleon's side, fear for the boy's immediate safety and long-term future; remorse and self-hatred for having failed so miserably to live up to his son's expectations; the simple anguish of any loving parent forced to part under perilous circumstances from an only child.

At dawn on August 30, as the exhausted French slept in their bivouacs around the village of Beaumont, almost within sight of the Meuse, the Germans burst through the surrounding forest and fell on them. Though taken by surprise, the French fought back tenaciously, but the initiative was with the enemy and inevitably MacMahon's men were forced to withdraw northward, leaving behind 7,500 dead. Under remorseless artillery fire, the withdrawal turned into a rout as shattered units scrambled, amid scenes of awful destruction, to reach the river bridges at Mouzon and Villers.

Night was falling as the last of the French gained the far side of the river and continued to withdraw north along the Meuse Valley toward the picturesque little fortress town of Sedan, nestling at the edge of the Ardennes Forest, a mere seven miles from the Belgian frontier. Still unaware if Bazaine had managed to break out of Metz—and if so, where his army was—MacMahon decided to deploy his demoralized troops in defensive positions around Sedan while he pondered on his next move.

Throughout the following day, his men positioned themselves within a roughly equilateral triangle, with sides of about three miles' length, sloping up to the north of the town, like an arrowhead pointing into the Ardennes. The right-hand side of the triangle was defined by the valley of the Givonne, a small tributary of the Meuse, the left-hand by a road which crossed the Givonne at the apex of the triangle, and the base by the Meuse Valley, whose marshy terrain offered an effective barrier to a mass assault in that direction.

MacMahon seems not to have realized the desperate position he was in. His orders indicate that he believed that after a day to rest and resupply his army could break out—either west toward Metz, as Eugénie and Palikao continued to urge him in messages from Paris, or east toward Mézières, where a fresh French army corps was assembling. Apparently, he had little idea of the strength of the German forces—250,000 men with 500 artillery pieces—which were now closing in on his depleted and demoralized army of 110,000.

Moltke, poring over his maps at the field headquarters of the German Third Army on the afternoon of that last day of August, was in no doubt about the hopelessness of the French position. "Now we have them in a mousetrap," he chortled. On the heights above Sedan a few hours later, the French General Auguste Ducrot characterized the situation rather more pungently as he observed the watch-fires of the encircling enemy. "We're in a chamber pot," he said, "and they're going to crap on us."

The valley of the Meuse lay under a thick blanket of fog as the Germans began their assault before dawn on September 1. The battle began at 4:00 A.M. when Bavarian troops crossed the river to launch an assault on the village of Bazeilles, at the right-hand corner of the defensive triangle. The fighting quickly spread along the line of the Givonne, and soon the entire front was ablaze as German artillery poured round after round into the French positions.

The French were amazed and horrified at the density and accuracy of the German fire—"an avalanche of iron," as General Barthelémi Lebrun called it. MacMahon, riding out from his headquarters to review the situation along the Givonne, fell victim to the German gunners shortly after dawn. Pausing to take a sighting on the German batteries, he was hit in the leg by a shell fragment and had to be carried back to Sedan.

There, he named Ducrot to take his place as commander. Ducrot, a shrewder judge than his predecessor, could see that although the French were holding the line of the Givonne, the enemy was "only amusing us there," and that they would soon be attacked from behind, along the left-hand side of the triangle. Consequently, he decided on an immediate retreat westward, between a loop in the Meuse and the Belgian frontier, in the direction of Mézières.

Had Ducrot been able to carry out that intention before the last gap in the closing net was sealed, a good part of the Army of Châlons might yet have been saved. But at that moment an unexpected figure appeared on the scene to stop him in his tracks. General Emmanuel de Wimpffen, until recently military governor of Oran, had arrived from Paris only three days previously to join MacMahon's army as a corps commander. Before leaving

the capital Wimpffen had been given a frank assessment by Palikao of both MacMahon and the emperor.

Napoleon, said Palikao, was "in a false position and caused
the greatest embarrassment," while MacMahon "fell in too
easily with the suggestions of the Emperor." Wimpffen could
take a hint. "Send me to the army," he demanded. "I shall im-
part the required boldness and decision." This was the kind of
talk Palikao wanted to hear, and Wimpffen was the kind of man
he wanted in command of the Army of Châlons.

MacMahon could not be removed without cause, of course,
but perhaps the Germans might oblige. Palikao drafted a letter
authorizing Wimpffen to take command of the army if Mac-
Mahon should be incapacitated, and the letter was delivered to
the hero of North Africa just before he entrained for the front.

Now Wimpffen produced this letter, ordered Ducrot to hand
over command, and immediately countermanded the withdrawal. Ducrot tried desperately to convince him that a hasty
retreat to the west was the only option, but Wimpffen was not
the man to listen to the advice of others. Arrogant, overbearing,
and fairly bristling with contempt for the colleagues who had
put up such a poor showing so far against the Boche, he swept
Ducrot's objections aside. "We need a victory," asserted
Wimpffen. Replied Ducrot: "You will be very lucky if by this
evening you even have a retreat."

By now the sun had burned off the morning fog and from an
observation point on a hill south of the Meuse the killing
ground was revealed in brilliant clarity to the Prussian king,
who was accompanied by Bismarck, Roon, a scattering of Teutonic princes and grand dukes, military observers from the
United States and Britain, and William Howard Russell, the ubiquitous war correspondent of *The Times*.

Immediately in front of them, behind a sheet of flood water,
lay Sedan itself. Beyond the little town, the slopes were
crowded with the French bivouacs. Wrote Russell: "the day had
become so clear that through a good glass the movements of
individual men were plainly discernible . . . bayonets glistened,
and arms twinkled and flashed like a streamlet in the moon-
light."

On all three sides of the triangle, the German artillery batteries were now pouring fire into the French positions. The

French did not submit meekly to destruction. Time and again their cavalry charged gallantly but hopelessly against the German gun positions and their supporting infantry screens. Time and again they were driven back with hideous losses.

The Prussian king was moved to admiration of the enemy. "Ah, the brave fellows!" he exclaimed as he witnessed a particularly gallant—and futile—cavalry charge, led by the noted wit, dandy, duelist, and ladies' man, the marquis de Galliffet.*

Viewed from afar, like some splendid military review, a battle can indeed evoke sublime emotions, such as those that moved King Wilhelm. But Russell, who went onto the field of honor after the smoke had cleared, gained a somewhat different perspective. He saw "masses of coloured rags glued together with blood and brains and pinned into strange shapes by fragments of bones . . . men's bodies without heads, legs without bodies, heaps of human entrails attached to red and blue cloth, and disembowelled corpses in uniform, bodies lying about in all attitudes. . . .

"There must have been a hell of torture raging within that semicircle," wrote Russell, "in which the earth was torn asunder from all sides, with a real tempest of iron, hissing and screeching and bursting into the heavy masses at the hands of an unseen enemy."

Into that hell rode Louis Napoleon Bonaparte, courting—as eagerly as ever he had courted a woman—the death which would release him from his agonies of mind and body.

He might have remained under cover in the subprefecture of Sedan, where he had established his personal headquarters. But the Emperor of the French wanted only to die among his troops. Whether as an act of expiation or self-justification, his death in battle would surely go some way toward wiping out the stain of the inevitable defeat.

His cross was the saddle and, nailed to it by sheer will, Napoleon rode to and fro all morning across the field of carnage, smoking an endless chain of cigarettes as bullets and shell frag-

---

* Wilhelm's words of praise are carved on the memorial which overlooks the battlefield at Floing. Galliffet, the ultimate *beau sabreur*, miraculously survived the battle and, after the war, was responsible for the bloody suppression of the Paris Commune, on the orders of the government of the Third Republic.

ments sang about his ears. "What astounding heroism," a medical specialist would say later, "to sit in his saddle for five hours, holding on with both hands during the battle. The agony must have been constant. I cannot understand how he could have borne it."

On all sides of Napoleon, men fell. Two officers accompanying him were killed by a single shellburst. But the emperor remained untouched: the star he had followed all his life was not going to allow him the dignity of death in battle.

Picking his way through the grisly debris, he encountered Wimpffen and a clutch of staff officers. "Your Majesty may be quite at ease," said the new commander-in-chief as shells fell around them. "Within two hours I shall have driven your enemies into the Meuse." Amazed at Wimpffen's ability to ignore the dreadful reality of their situation, Napoleon rode on without comment. An hour later he received another message from Wimpffen, scarcely less absurd than the last. Now the general had convinced himself it would be possible to break out to the east, and he enjoined Napoleon to prepare to "place himself in the middle of his troops, who could be relied to force a passage through the German lines."

Back in Sedan, where shells were falling in the streets as panicking soldiers fell back onto the city, Napoleon resolved to end the pointless butchery. Exerting the last tatters of his authority, he ordered the white flag to be hoisted on the ramparts. But an indignant staff officer, preferring death to dishonor, immediately cut it down.

No one told the emperor, and the shelling continued unabated. An hour later, Napoleon demanded feebly: "Why does this useless struggle still go on? Too much blood has been shed." But Wimpffen, informed of the emperor's wish, refused to countenance surrender. "I will not have a capitulation!" he stormed. And the slaughter went on.

At mid-afternoon, Ducrot rode into Sedan to assess the situation within the fortress and found it "indescribable." "The streets, the squares, the gates," he recalled, "were choked with carts, carriages, guns, the impedimenta and debris of a routed army. Bands of soldiers, without arms or knapsacks, streamed in every moment and hurried into the houses and churches. At the gates, many were trodden to death."

In his room at the subprefecture, Napoleon "no longer preserved the cold and impenetrable countenance so familiar to the
world. The silence which reigned in the presence of the sovereign rendered the noise more startling." The emperor appealed to Ducrot to sign a letter asking the Germans for terms.
Ducrot declined, saying that only Wimpffen had the authority
to seek an armistice. Wimpffen, pressured to sign such a document, also declined and offered his resignation. Napoleon was
forced to refuse it; no other officer was willing to accept command in such dire circumstances.

While the French argued among themselves, the Prussians decided it was time to bring matters to a conclusion. As the official German history of the campaign would put it later, "a
powerful artillery fire directed against the enemy's last point of
refuge appeared the most suitable method of convincing him of
the hopelessness of his situation. With intent to hasten the capitulation and thus spare the German Army further sacrifices,
the King ordered the whole available artillery to concentrate its
fire on Sedan."

That did it. With German shells bursting in the garden of the
subprefecture, the emperor asserted himself again and ordered
the white flag to be hoisted once more. This time his demoralized generals—perhaps relieved that the decision had been
taken out of their hands—offered no objection. And from exile
two years later Napoleon absolved them. "I claim the entire responsibility for that act," he wrote. "I obeyed a cruel but inex-
orable fate. My heart was broken, but my conscience was easy."

From their observation point beyond the Meuse, the Prussian
king and his chief of staff saw the white flag and sent Colonel
Bronsart von Schellendorf down to the citadel to ask the French
for formal letters of surrender. Schellendorf was taken to the
subprefecture, where he was astonished to find Napoleon,
whose presence had been unknown to the Germans.

Schellendorf arrived just as Napoleon was finishing a letter to
King Wilhelm and rode back to his own lines, shouting excitedly: "Der Kaiser ist da!" Soon afterward, Napoleon's aide-de-
camp General Reille rode up the hill bearing his emperor's letter. "Monsieur, mon frère," it read. "Having been unable to die
among my troops, there is nothing left for me but to place my

sword into the hands of Your Majesty. I am Your Majesty's good brother. Napoleon."

Wilhelm's reply, written in consultation with Bismarck, read: "Regretting the circumstances in which we meet, I accept Your Majesty's sword, and beg that you will be good enough to name an officer furnished with full powers to treat for the capitulation of the army which has fought so bravely under your orders."

The Second Empire's day of reckoning was done. The guns fell silent. And as dusk settled over the scene, the strains of the Lutheran hymn "Nun danket alle Gott" rose from the German bivouac fires around Sedan.

28

THE END
OF
EMPIRE

LOUIS NAPOLEON ROSE PAINFULLY FROM HIS COT at five on the morning after the battle, intending to seek an urgent interview with the Prussian king. He hoped to persuade Wilhelm to mitigate the harsh terms laid down by Moltke and Bismarck. The Prussian warlords had rejected pleas for an "honorable capitulation," in which the French would be permitted to march out of Sedan with arms and baggage, promising not to engage in further hostilities; instead, they insisted upon an abject surrender, with the removal of the army as prisoners of war to Germany.

White-gloved, wearing the full dress uniform of a major-general, with a gold-bordered kepi on his head and his Legion of Honor decoration visible under his scarlet-lined cloak, the emperor passed in a two-horse open carriage, with a small escort, through the Torcy Gate, over the drawbridge and across the Meuse, heading for the Château Bellevue, where the Prussian king had his headquarters.

Warned of Napoleon's approach, Bismarck hurried from his own headquarters at Donchéry and rode to intercept him, "all dusty and dirty as I was, in an old cap and waterproof boots." He met the emperor on the road at Frénois and reined his horse in. "I gave the military salute," Bismarck later recalled. "He took his cap off and the officers did the same, whereupon I took off mine, although it was contrary to rule. He said, 'Couvrez-vous, donc.' I behaved to him just as if in Saint-Cloud and asked his commands."

The elaborate show of courtesy notwithstanding, Bismarck was not about to let Napoleon go over his head to his royal master. Instead, he conducted the emperor to the humble cottage of a weaver, which stood nearby. Aides brought two rush-bottomed chairs from within the cottage and for the next three quarters of an hour the two men sat side by side, conversing gravely in the early morning sunshine. Bismarck, it was observed, did most of the talking.

We have only Bismarck's version of what passed between them. Each, it seems, assured the other that he had not wanted war, Napoleon insisting that "he had been driven into it by the pressure of public opinion." On substantive matters, no progress was made. Napoleon said that in surrendering his sword he had been acting for himself, not on behalf of the government in Paris. For his part, Bismarck insisted that on a military question, such as the terms of surrender, only Moltke was authorized to speak.

At about 8:00 A.M. Bismarck took temporary leave of the emperor, who went indoors and up the narrow staircase of the tiny cottage. Mme Fournaise, the weaver's wife, overawed by such a presence, went timidly to the upstairs room to enquire of the emperor's needs. She found him sitting with his head buried in his hands. "Can I do anything for Your Majesty?" she enquired. "Only to pull down the blinds," he replied without raising his head.

Half an hour later, Napoleon emerged from the cottage and walked glumly around the flowering potato patch at the rear, chain-smoking, his hands clasped behind his back. Eyewitnesses noticed that he limped slightly, walking crablike with his left shoulder forward and his head drooping. Bismarck's press secretary, Moritz Busch, who was one of the onlookers, thought that "his whole appearance was a little unsoldierlike—the man looked too soft, I might say too shabby, for the uniform he wore."

An hour and a quarter passed before Bismarck returned, now wearing full-dress uniform, with Moltke and an escort of dragoons, to conduct the emperor to Château Bellevue. Before he left, Napoleon characteristically pressed four 20-franc pieces into the hand of Mme Fournaise. "This is probably the last hospitality I shall receive in France," he told her.

His wait at the weaver's cottage had been prolonged by the continued reluctance of Wimpffen to submit to Moltke's surrender terms. While Napoleon had been riding toward Donchéry, his generals had been conferring in an atmosphere bitter with recrimination. Wimpffen had said he would resign rather than sign such terms. Ducrot taunted him savagely. He reminded Wimpffen that he had assumed command "when you thought there was honour and profit to be gained." He could not back out now.

Harsh words were exchanged—blows, according to one account. Then a messenger from Moltke appeared in the doorway, a Captain von Zingler. "I am instructed to remind you how urgent it is that you should come to a decision," he said. "At ten o'clock precisely if you have not come to a resolution, the German batteries will fire on Sedan. It is now nine and I shall have barely time to carry your answer to headquarters."

Wimpffen said that he could not reply until he knew the outcome of the talks between Napoleon and the Prussian king. "That interview will not in any way affect the military operations, which can only be determined by the generals," replied Zingler. It was clearly useless to argue or plead with a junior officer who had been sent only to deliver a message, not to engage in debate.

Realizing that he had no option but to submit, Wimpffen accompanied Zingler to headquarters. There, with tears streaming down his face, he signed the surrender and, "my sad and painful duty having been accomplished, I remounted my horse and rode back to Sedan, with death in my soul."

Once that business was out of the way, Napoleon and Wilhelm were permitted to meet. Onlookers noted the marked contrast between the two monarchs as they greeted each other: Wilhelm tall, upright, square-shouldered, and flushed with victory; Napoleon stooped, tear-stained, decrepit, and looking smaller than his five foot five.

There were no witnesses to Wilhelm's fifteen-minute conversation with Napoleon, but later the Prussian monarch gave an account of it to his son, the crown prince, who recorded it in his diary. According to this version Wilhelm told Napoleon he realized that he had not gone to war lightly—an assurance which was "visibly welcome to Napoleon." In reply Napoleon assured the king, as he had Bismarck, that public opinion had driven him to war, to which Wilhelm courteously responded that those who had stirred up the public were more culpable than the emperor.

After Napoleon explained that he could not negotiate an end to hostilities, since this was the prerogative of the government in Paris, Wilhelm turned the conversation to Napoleon's immediate future, offering him the castle of Wilhelmshohe, near Cassel, as a residence during his captivity—"an offer which he immediately accepted."

After Wilhelm withdrew, the crown prince came to speak briefly with Napoleon, who "held out one hand, while with the other he tried to dry the tears which rolled down his face. He uttered words of gratitude to me, and for the generous manner in which the King had treated him. . . . When I expressed my regret that the war had been so terrible and so sanguinary, he said it was, alas, too true, too terrible, especially as 'they had not wanted war!'"

It was arranged that Napoleon would leave the next day for Wilhelmshohe, traveling, at his own request, via Belgium to avoid any embarrassing encounters with defeated French troops en route. Before he left, on September 3, Napoleon was permitted to send a telegram in cipher to Eugénie. Baldly and briefly, it said: "The Army is defeated and captive; I myself am a prisoner."

A thunderstorm was gathering among the thickly forested hills of the Ardennes as the incongruously splendid imperial carriage train—brought entire to Bellevue from Sedan, with its massive fourgons, its magnificent teams of draft horses, and its periwigged coachmen decked in scarlet and gold—set out on the first stage of the journey to Wilhelmshohe. Onlookers remarked on the contrast with Wilhelm's modest equipage as the victorious Prussian monarch set off in the opposite direction, toward Paris, to join his advancing armies.

En route to the Belgian frontier, it was impossible to avoid encountering columns of French prisoners, marching somberly in the mist and rain, toward "le Camp de la Misère," the temporary holding camp set up for them on a peninsula formed by a deep loop in the Meuse. Recognizing the emperor's train, the prisoners shook their fists and hurled obscene abuse at the man who had led them to their present plight.

Slowly, the imperial wagons jolted and lurched toward Verviers where, on the morning of September 5, the emperor and his suite were to entrain for Cassel. As he boarded the train, Napoleon heard the cry of a newspaper boy, selling his wares on the platform—"Fall of the Empire! Flight of the Empress!"

For days before the catastrophe at Sedan, Eugénie's mood had been swinging from stoic determination to black despair and back again. She had received no news of the emperor or the Army of Châlons since the end of August, though she knew that the Prince Imperial had been sent for safety to Mézières. At night she dosed herself with chloral in a vain attempt to induce sleep. By day, adrenaline fueled her febrile energies.

"She is worn out with fatigue and emotion," reported Metternich. "The day before yesterday, she said to me that all night long she had been telling herself she was mad, that all this was not true, was only the working of a disordered brain. The conviction was so strong that on waking she shed tears of despair to find she was not mad."

When, finally, Napoleon's telegram from the Château Bellevue reached the Tuileries on the afternoon of September 3, she snapped. Her acting secretaries, Filon and Conti, were together in the empress's study when she appeared at the head of a staircase leading down to her private apartments. "She was pale and terrible," Filon recalled. "Her eyes were hard and brilliant with anger, her face distorted by emotion."

"Do you know what they are saying?" she demanded incredulously. "They are saying that the Emperor has surrendered, that he has capitulated!" Her voice rose to a shriek as she stared accusingly at the two secretaries: "Surely you do not believe that abomination!"

Filon and Conti gazed at her speechless. "You do not believe it!" she demanded again, a statement rather than a question, as if she were willing them to reassure her that the news was false. Conti tried feebly to calm her. "There are circumstances, Madame, when even the bravest . . ." She cut him short.

What followed, as described by Filon, was an experience that clearly haunted him for life. "Her soul, stirred to its innermost depths, poured forth its agony in a torrent of incoherent and mad words," he wrote. "What she said then, Conti never repeated to anyone and I shall die, like him, without repeating it. . . . It lasted five long, terrible minutes. The Empress then left the room and went down the little staircase. We remained speechless and stunned, like men who have lived through an earthquake."

Thirty-eight years later, in conversation with Maurice Paléologue, Eugénie would say no more about the incident than that "everything that lay on my heart burst out." But quoting another source, "which I regard as having the value and stamp of a direct confession," Paléologue adds the detail that

With convulsed features and haggard eyes, like a Fury she screamed her distracted words: "No, the Emperor has not surrendered! A Napoleon never surrenders! He is dead! Do you hear me? I tell you he is dead and they're trying to hide it from me." Then, contradicting herself: "Why didn't he kill himself? Why didn't he have himself buried under the walls of Sedan? Could he not feel he was disgracing himself? What a name to leave to his son!"

That evening, crowds gathered on the boulevards and converged on the Place Vendôme, singing the *Marseillaise* and shouting "Vive la République!" and "Vive la France!" The shouted slogan "la déchéance!"—dethronement—was also heard, and by the next morning that cry drowned out all others. When the Chambers met in emergency session at noon, the mob streamed into the Palais Bourbon and demanded the proclamation of a republic.

Meanwhile a crowd some 200,000 strong was surrounding the Tuileries, where the flag flying from the masthead indicated that the empress was in residence. The mob tore imperial eagles from the lamp standards and gate posts and the cry of "la déchéance!" rose to a menacing roar.

Inside, courtiers were begging Eugénie to flee. But although she had long feared that one day she would suffer the fate of Marie Antoinette, she refused. Her mood had swung again and now she entertained the illusion that if she hung on, the politicians might be inspired to close ranks around her in the nation's hour of peril. She said as much to a parliamentary delegation, which came to ask her to hand over executive power. But it was too late. Following the defection of Trochu, the military governor of Paris, the Republic was declared at the Hôtel de Ville.

Although the mob still milled around outside the Tuileries, they seemed by now to be good-natured enough and little inclined to break in. Nonetheless, their mood could suddenly change, and Metternich, accompanied by the Italian Ambassador, Constantine Nigra, hurried to the palace at mid-afternoon to urge Eugénie to leave immediately. Now, with the Republic proclaimed, there seemed no point in staying, and Eugénie at last agreed.

"I had no fear of death," she would say later in an extraordinarily revealing moment of reminiscence. "All I dreaded was falling into the hands of viragos, who would defile my last scene with something shameful or grotesque, who would try to dishonor me as they murdered me. I fancied them lifting my skirts, I heard ferocious laughter—for, you know, the *tricoteuses* have not died out."

Because of the mob, it was unwise to try to leave by the Place du Carrousel, so Eugénie led the way along a private passage, through the palace museum to the Louvre, and thence out into the rue Saint-Germain l'Auxerrois, where they passed unnoticed. Metternich hailed a passing cab and handed Eugénie and her lady-in-waiting, Mme Lebreton, into it. Just then, a street urchin cried out, "There's the Empress!" Nigra cuffed him into silence and the cab drew away.

What made Eugénie decide to turn to so prosaic a figure as her dentist at a moment of such high drama we do not know. But it turned out to be a wise decision. When Dr. Thomas Evans, an American who had been caring for the empress's dental health for some years, returned to his house on the Avenue de l'Impératrice late that momentous afternoon, he was astonished to find Eugénie and Mme Lebreton waiting for him. When the empress asked him to help her escape to England, he agreed immediately.

The next day Evans took Eugénie and her lady-in-waiting in his carriage to Deauville, on the Channel coast, where his wife was vacationing. En route, Eugénie became philosophical. "It has sometimes seemed to me," she said, "that the French set up their heroes, so to speak, on pillars of salt, so that when the first storm strikes them they tumble down to lie forever in the mud." Eugénie was also able to tell a wry joke against herself: "Only a few days ago, I said that I would never leave the Tuileries in a cab like Louis-Philippe. Well, that is exactly what I have done."

At Deauville, Evans left the two women with his wife at the Hôtel de Casino while he went to the harbor, looking for a skipper who would take them across the Channel. There, he found the *Gazelle*, a 42-ton yacht owned by Sir John Burgoyne, a retired British Army officer who had fought in the Crimea. At first, Burgoyne seemed inclined to take Evans's story for some kind of practical joke, but Lady Burgoyne persuaded him that it rang true. At midnight, still accompanied by the faithful dentist, Eugénie and Mme Lebreton boarded the boat surreptitiously to avoid being spotted. With high tide at dawn, the *Gazelle* slipped its moorings and headed out into the Channel.

It was a terrible crossing. Violent squalls, high seas, and driving rain buffeted the yacht ceaselessly and Eugénie was "sure we were lost." But, as she told Evans the next day, "I did not feel alarmed in the least. I have always loved the sea and for me it had no terrors. Were I to disappear, I said to myself, death could not have come more opportunely nor give me a more welcome grave."

When the *Gazelle* reached the safety of Ryde, on the Isle of Wight, after almost twenty-four hours at sea, they learned that a warship commanded by Burgoyne's cousin had sunk in the same storm that night with all hands. They also learned that the Prince Imperial, having reached Dover two days before from Belgium, was now in a hotel at Hastings, only a few miles away. Mother and son were reunited that evening.

A poignant surprise awaited Napoleon when he arrived at Wilhelmshohe, in torrential rain, on the evening of September 5. The château had been the residence of his uncle Jérôme when the latter had been King of Westphalia and it contained many Napoleonic souvenirs—among them a portrait of Napoleon's long-dead mother, Queen Hortense, as a young woman.

It must have seemed to Napoleon that his life had come full circle. Here he was, as he had begun, in exile and without a throne; and there on the wall, to remind him of his youth and of life's transience, hung the image of the mother he had loved so dearly.

The governor of the château, and Napoleon's principal jailer, was an upright old Prussian general, Count Karl von Monts. Somewhat stiffly—for he regarded Napoleon as "the instigator of this bloody war"—Monts introduced himself and the officers commanding the detachment of troops who would keep a round-the-clock guard on the château and its new residents.

Napoleon was accompanied by a personal suite of military aides, plus his physician Conneau, his valet Thélin, and his secretary Piétri. In addition there were more than a hundred grooms, valets, and other servants to look after the members of the suite and their eighty-five horses. Wilhelmshohe, with its great lake, its fine old trees, and its splendid park, was to be a considerably more luxurious prison than Ham.

As Monts reported:

A post and telegraph office was provided at the château for the use of the prisoners, who were allowed to send even cipher messages. . . . Cooks from the palace at Berlin prepared the meals of the Emperor and his suite; those for the domestics were supplied by the hotelkeeper, Schombart. The prisoners were given great liberty and permitted to visit, unaccompanied, Cassel, Wilhelmstahl [a château between those two places], and the environs of Wilhelmshohe, either on foot, on horseback, or in carriages; but they were not allowed to sleep out.

With Prussian thoroughness, Monts reported also that "Queen Augusta took the greatest interest in the prisoners and sent them games of every kind. A billiard table was specially provided for them and of this they made good use." But, Monts noted disapprovingly, "they read very few of the French books in the fine library."

The meticulous Monts has also left us a detailed and in some ways surprising physical description of Napoleon at the time of his captivity. "Scarcely any gray hairs are visible," he reports, in contrast to many who described Napoleon's hair as being nearly white during the campaign; possibly the imperial barber had dyed it to the sandy color which Monts noticed. And although others have described Napoleon's complexion as "waxen" or "ashen," Monts found it "healthy, that of a man of a certain age, well preserved"; a judicious application of makeup, perhaps.

Even more surprisingly, Monts insists that Napoleon showed no sign of bladder trouble at Wilhelmshohe and that he often went horseback riding for pleasure, sometimes remaining in the saddle for more than two hours at a stretch. Medical experts can account for this only by saying that Napoleon's stone must have broken up by itself and have been voided—apparently the third time that this had occurred since the trouble first manifested itself in the mid-60s.

Napoleon's first visitor was Lady Cowley, the British Ambassador's wife with whom he had danced the first quadrille of the first state ball of his reign, almost seventeen years before. "Finding herself in Frankfort," her husband explained in a letter to his old friend, Granville, "she did not like to go on without going to see him. He was delighted to see her, but quite overcome at first. . . . When he came to describe the battle of Sedan his feelings gave way completely."

Unlike Monts, Lady Cowley thought Napoleon looked ill. She also reported his complaint that "he can hold no communications with anyone, except by permission, and all letters pass through the Prussian authorities there." The provision of a post and telegraph office was perhaps not just an act of kindness by the Germans. Furthermore, Napoleon complained to Lady Cowley that "he cannot stir beyond the grounds, as he is at once exposed to insult, and it seems that his journey through Germany was most disagreeable, as he was hooted and jeered at wherever he stopped."

For the first fortnight of his captivity, Napoleon did not hear from Eugénie and was "much grieved" by her silence. Then, on September 17, three letters arrived together. Eugénie had heard of his vain attempts to find death on the battlefield and had apparently repented of her outburst on the palace staircase. Indeed, her mood had now swung over to one of intense ardor.

"My tenderness and love for you only grow," she wrote.

To be together at last, that is all I wish for. The more the world falls away from us, the more closely shall we be attached, and hand in hand we shall await the judgment of God. . . . Poor, dear friend, if only my devotion can bring you an instant's forgetfulness of the trials through which your great soul has passed. Your adorable long-suffering makes me think of Our Lord. You, too, believe me, will have justice one day. . . .

What Napoleon made of such effusions we do not know; phlegmatic though he was by nature, he must surely have been startled to find his wife comparing him with the Saviour. Sensibly making no attempt to match her in hyperbole, he replied that "the affectionate expressions in your letters have done me a world of good. . . . Your letters are a wonderful consolation and I thank you for them. To what can I attach myself if it is not your affection and that of our son?" Allowing himself to lapse into pure bathos, he wrote in a subsequent letter: "When I am free, I want to come and live with you and Louis in a little cottage with bow windows and creepers."

On October 30, Eugénie arrived in person—without prior warning—to visit him. Monts, who did not live on the premises, hastened to the château when informed of her presence. She and Napoleon were already in conversation by the time Monts arrived and joined them in the emperor's study. It seems clear that, despite the worshipful tone of her letters, she was as peremptory as ever.

"All her manner convinced me that she had always known how to impose her views on her husband's policy," Monts recalled. "She . . . displayed throughout great assurance in her observations. I derived the absolute impression that she was accustomed not only to make herself listened to, but to have the last word. She affected a certain superiority over the Emperor, a sort of tutorship; and if it is true that she had been at the head of the war party in Paris I fully understand that her opinion was the decisive one."

However, the stern and upright Prussian noted with approval that Eugénie was by no means the foolish, vain, and extravagant creature of legend and gossip. She had been "so heavily struck and tried by Fate that no one could imagine her to have been a frivolous and superficial person. The events of the last weeks had undoubtedly given more gravity to her character." Writing some years after the event, Monts added:

Today still, when I think of her I see a woman possessing maturity of mind, acquired late, perhaps; sure of herself, sagacious, combining agreeable manners with the intelligence of the woman who has made the interests of the public her own. My feelings concerning the poor woman were those of deep compassion, increased by the thought that she must be conscious of having been the cause of the punishment.

It seems a scrupulously fair judgment.

By now, Monts had warmed considerably toward Napoleon, too—"his features express kindliness and goodwill, and his voice does not belie that impression"—and had concluded that far from being a war criminal, he was a humane man who had unfortunately given way to political pressures which he should have resisted.

As Monts surmised, Eugénie's visit had political as well as personal motives. Bismarck was anxious to put a speedy end to the war and the Siege of Paris, whose starvation and bombardment of civilians was beginning to tarnish the Germans' reputation as an essentially peaceful, God-fearing nation forced into a war it never wanted. But the republican Government of National Defense refused to negotiate peace so long as the Germans insisted on France's ceding the provinces of Alsace and Lorraine, and Bismarck had therefore been toying with the idea of dealing with a resurrected imperial regime.

He had sent feelers to Eugénie, in exile in England, hinting that Bazaine's 125,000-strong Army of the Rhine, still bottled up in Metz, might be allowed to act as a shield behind which the Empire—to which Bazaine still formally owed allegiance—could be restored. Unwilling to be party to the dismemberment of France, Eugénie had refused the bait, appealing directly to King Wilhelm to "offer terms which your defeated enemy can accept." Wilhelm had replied, courteously but firmly, that Germany was demanding Alsace and Lorraine not for territorial aggrandizement, but for its security—"to push back the point of departure of the French armies which, in the future, will come to attack us."

It was on learning of the surrender of Bazaine and his troops on October 27 that Eugénie had come so precipitately to Wilhelmshohe, bringing only enough luggage for a few days. Despite her refusal to connive at the cession of Alsace and Lorraine, she had apparently hoped to the last minute that the Germans would help resurrect the Empire. "You see," she told Monts, "if the King of Prussia had restored the French Army to us, we should have been able to make an honorable peace and restore order in France."

What she meant by an "honorable peace" we do not know, and possibly neither did she, but certainly Napoleon seems to have approved entirely of her position on Alsace and Lorraine. "A thousand times better," he said, "to live forgotten and miserable than to owe our elevation to the abandoning of our dignity or the interests of the country."

Eugénie remained at Wilhelmshohe for only three days, leaving for England on the evening of November 1. But she continued to dream vainly of a restoration of the Empire, which would then proceed to wrest from the Germans far better peace terms than they were prepared to offer to the Republic. Those hopes were shattered when, at the end of January 1871, the Government of National Defense capitulated and the German Empire—officially proclaimed ten days before at the Palace of Versailles—extracted the price it wanted: Alsace, Lorraine, and indemnities totaling 5 billion francs.

After the armistice was signed Napoleon was visited by an enterprising German-Jewish journalist, Mels Cohen, to whom he gave a novel, and oddly contradictory, interpretation of the crisis that led up to the declaration of war. He insisted that far from being opposed to the Hohenzollern candidature, he would have been happy to see Prince Leopold on the Spanish throne.

"He is doubly related to me," said Napoleon, "as the great grandson of Caroline Bonaparte and the grandson of Stephanie Beauharnais. . . . His relationship with the King of Prussia is lost in obscurity; it is actually disputed; his relationship with me dates from yesterday." However, Leopold's accession to the Spanish throne would have been a danger to France, because "at the end of two or three years he would infallibly fall from the throne and then Prussia would inevitably intervene in Spain. . . . It is this consideration which has guided me in the affair."

Napoleon went on to tell Cohen that if the Empire had not been overthrown, "peace would have been signed within a month. . . . On what terms? No matter. At all events, on better terms than those to which we had to submit later." The emperor then launched into an apocalyptic forecast of the future facing France. "Horrible things will happen after the peace," he said. "Revolution, in spite of the appearance of deceptive calm, will be continuous. . . . Suppressed in one place, it will break out in another, like a cancer.

"Finally, wearying for a moment, it will stop, and the ignorant and foolish who guide the state will believe that they have conquered by moderation what they call legality. The fools! And then the awakening! What before would have seemed 'Terror' will be mere child's play. . . . And then, though it will be too late, they will demand a coup d'état."

Napoleon also offered his often-muddled view of events to his last mistress, Louise de Mercy-Argenteau, who corresponded with him regularly during his six months' internment at Wilhelmshohe. His letters to her make it seem that, like Eugénie, he still harbored the impossible dream of restoration.

If he were in Wilhelm's place, he said in a letter dated February 4, he would "enter Paris at the head of my army; I would scatter the demagogues who have usurped power; I would decline to treat with any but the legitimate government; I would propose to that government a less onerous peace than that offered to the Assembly and an alliance based upon an equitable appreciation of the interests of both countries."

In another letter he railed against "the eagerness with which the neutrals have recognized the sovereignty of M. Thiers," newly elected President of the Third Republic. It was, he said, "proof of the little dignity which animates the foreign Courts." In yet another letter he asked: "How can one fail to be discouraged in the presence of the conditions of peace imposed upon France? I admit that we were the aggressors; I admit that we were defeated and that, therefore, we were compelled to pay the cost of the war or abandon part of our territory; but to condemn us to make both sacrifices is very hard."

Napoleon's letters to Louise were scattered with intimacies that would surely have infuriated Eugénie had she known of them. "I am writing to you as if you were my Minister for Foreign Affairs," he wrote on March 2, "but I find it a consolation, in the midst of the preoccupations which beset me, to open my heart to you." On February 25: "I send you the line that you

wanted. It is a pale reflection of my sentiments towards you."
On February 4: "The attachment to me of which you give evidence touches me deeply." And on February 23, after she had been to see him at Wilhelmshohe: "Need I tell you of the sweet remembrances and regrets that your visit has left?"

Louise had traveled to Wilhelmshohe from her husband's château near Terwagne, in Belgium. Napoleon received her in the salon where Hortense's portrait hung over a marble fireplace. Gesturing toward the painting, Napoleon said: "My mother was here, waiting for me." In a corner of the room, by the french windows which looked out onto the grounds of the château, was a grand piano on which stood a vase of hortensias.

Louise opened the piano, sat down, and began to sing to her own accompaniment: "Plaisir d'amour ne dure q'un moment . . ." Napoleon stretched out on a sofa and closed his eyes. After the last notes of the song had died away, Louise knelt by him and laid her head on his shoulder. He put one arm around her and so they remained, unspeaking, the defeated emperor at peace in the presence of his last love and his first. It was their final meeting.

The next morning, as Louise was leaving, Thélin handed her a farewell gift from his master—a string of pearls that had belonged to Hortense.

29

DEATH
IN
EXILE

WHEN NAPOLEON WAS RELEASED from captivity in March
1871, along with all the other French prisoners of war, he
crossed the Channel to England to rejoin his wife and son. They
met him at Dover where, in a piquant reversal of the events of
1848, he crossed paths with members of the Orléans family, on
their way to board the ferry back to France.

The Bonapartes went straight on to the rented country property, half an hour by rail from central London, which they now
called home. There Napoleon received a surprise almost as
poignant as the discovery of his mother's portrait at Wilhelmshohe: he had visited this house, Camden Place—at
Chislehurst, in Kent—during his first youthful exile in Britain,
when it had belonged to a wealthy builder named Henry
Rowles, whose daughter, Emily, Napoleon had unsuccessfully
courted.

Even more curious—and certainly no coincidence—its present owner, a financier named Nathaniel Strode, had been an acquaintance of Napoleon's and Harriet Howard's during their
days together in London in the 1840s. After Napoleon's separation from Harriet, Strode had remained on friendly terms with
both, and indeed Harriet had appointed him executor of her will
when she realized that she was dying. There is evidence, too,
that Napoleon used Strode as a conduit by which to pay his
former mistress—by then the comtesse de Beauregard—consid-

erable sums of money between 1862 and 1864, when she was in financial difficulty.

Eugénie was presumably unaware of this connection, or her pride would surely have forced her to refuse Strode's offer, made during Napoleon's internment in Germany, to lease Camden Place to her at a nominal rent for as long as she wished. The motive behind Strode's generosity is not clear. He may have felt he was discharging a sentimental obligation to the emperor on behalf of the departed Miss Howard; he may merely have sought the gratification of playing benefactor to such celebrated refugees.

Whatever Strode's motivation, it must have seemed to Napoleon once again that his life was coming full circle as he rode through the great ornamental gates of Camden Place. Even these had an association with his past: they had adorned the entrance of the Great Universal Exhibition of 1867, Strode having purchased them at auction after the exhibition closed.

Though scarcely imperial, the house was not the creeper-covered cottage of Napoleon's spasm of maudlin imagination.* It was big enough to accommodate the emperor, the empress, the Prince Imperial, a "court" of thirty-seven, including secretaries, doctors, and Loulou's tutor, as well as ladies- and gentlemen-in-waiting, and twenty-three household servants. It stood in several acres of well-tended grounds adjoining Chislehurst Common, and—one other reason why it had commended itself to the pious Eugénie—was just a short walk from St. Mary's Roman Catholic Church.

One of Napoleon's first visitors at Camden Place, Malmesbury, was deeply moved by "the quiet calm and dignity" that Napoleon displayed in such adversity. The emperor greeted his old friend with "that remarkable smile that could light up his dark countenance," displaying "the grandest example of human moral courage that the severest Stoic could have imagined."

A week later Napoleon and Eugénie traveled to Windsor to see Victoria, who found him "grown very stout and grey . . . but otherwise there was the same gentle, pleasing and gracious manner." Like Malmesbury, she was impressed by the "meek-

---

* At the time of writing, Camden Place is the headquarters of the Chislehurst Golf Club. The ornamental gates were melted down to make munitions in World War II.

ness, dignity and patience" with which Napoleon bore his misfortunes. For her part, Eugénie was clearly irritated at times by her husband's calm acceptance of his fate. Unlike him, she would rail endlessly against the republicans who had ousted them, at the erstwhile supporters who had betrayed them, and at those of all persuasions who now hurled scurrilous accusations against them, until at one point Napoleon was moved to utter wearily: "Eugénie, you do not possess an idea; the idea possesses you."

In later years, Eugénie would put a rather different gloss on things, professing admiration for the way in which, "when disaster overwhelmed us, [Napoleon] carried his stoicism and his meekness to the point of sublimity. . . . Never one word of complaint, of blame, of recrimination!"

Often, Eugénie told Paléologue, she used to beg him to defend himself. "But he would reply meekly, 'No . . . there are some catastrophes so painful to a nation that it has a right to fling all the blame on its chief, even unjustly. . . . For a sovereign, there are no excuses, no extenuating circumstances. It is his highest prerogative to assume himself, and himself alone, every responsibility incurred by those who served him—or betrayed him.'"

"Those were noble words, sir," said Eugénie, "and I shall never forget them. They have been my support and my light for thirty years."

Although they were in drastically reduced circumstances, the imperial couple were by no means indigent. Eugénie had taken the precaution of entrusting her jewelry to the Metternichs, and had sold some of it since coming to England. At the same time Napoleon had been able to sell some real estate he owned in Italy. They were therefore spared the humiliation of poverty, and if Filon is to be believed, there was by now also a "perfect sympathy and understanding" between Napoleon and his wife.

But regrets, boredom, and exile, accentuated by the atrocious English climate, took their inevitable toll. "The days were sad indeed under the misty sky in that great kingdom of fog and rain," recalled Marie de Larminat, one of Eugénie's faithful maids-of-honor. "By degrees, we began to rasp on each other's nerves." Given her irascible temperament, Eugénie probably felt the tensions more keenly than the others. "Here we are on the raft of the *Medusa*," she said in a letter. "There are moments when we feel like eating each other."

Napoleon—perhaps at peace with himself, now that he had nothing left to lose—seemed oblivious to much of this tension, shutting himself away in his small, overheated first-floor study, chain-smoking as he worked on his apologias for the conduct of the war: *The Military Forces of France*, which was published in 1872, and *The Campaign of 1870*, published posthumously a year later. Deeply wounded though he was at being characterized as "the coward of Sedan," he seemed unable to write about the campaign with force and coherence. His style was no doubt cramped by the fact that, as he told Filon, "I wish to justify myself without accusing others."

In the midst of these labors, Napoleon received word from France that Persigny was seriously ill. Like many other leading personalities of the Empire, Persigny had fled to Britain at the fall. But he did not remain long. In the summer of 1871, risking the wrath of a republican regime that was looking for scapegoats, Persigny had returned home, full of bitterness that despite their proximity in exile there had been no reconciliation between him and the emperor.

This was not Napoleon's fault; he was an infinitely forgiving man and he had much for which to thank Persigny. But because of Eugénie's unremitting hostility, the most fanatical of all the Bonapartists was persona non grata at Camden Place. Even thirty years later, Eugénie could speak of Persigny only with cold rancor.

"From the very day of my marriage I was honoured with his hatred," she told Paléologue. "He sometimes forgot himself so far as to call me 'the Spanish woman,' 'the foreigner!' Taking advantage of the distinguished services he had rendered the Napoleonic cause, he would endure nobody to come between the Emperor and himself: the Emperor and the Empire were his sole property; it was he who had created them; and so he deemed himself the sole person qualified to advise the one and govern the other. It is incredible what kindliness my husband needed to put up with the furies and tantrums of Persigny. Imagine a boiler that was perpetually blowing up!"

At the end of 1871, his flighty duchess having gone on a pleasure trip to Egypt and the Levant, Persigny suffered a stroke at his home in Seine-et-Oise. "Lady Persington" was enjoying herself too much to return to his side, but Napoleon penned a brief letter:

> My dear Persigny,
> I learn with pain the state of your health. I hope that you will be able to triumph over this illness; but while awaiting your recovery I must tell you that I forget what it was which divided us in order to remember only the demonstrations of devotion that you gave me for many years. Believe in my sincere friendship.
> Napoleon.

The letter was dated January 12, 1872. Persigny died before it reached him.

Despite everything, Napoleon professed to believe that the Empire would eventually be restored. And, indeed, as republican France found the robust economic legacy of the Empire equal to the payment of its war debt and contemplated the horrors of the 1871 Paris Commune and its bloody suppression, a nostalgia for the "good old days" began to gain ground. Not just old Bonapartists, but foreign diplomats, journalists, and other disinterested observers sensed a growing sentiment for a return to Empire, and Bonapartist agents flitted clandestinely between Paris and Chislehurst with all kinds of schemes to suggest to the tired old man of Camden Place.

The black-coated republicans in Paris evidently feared that Napoleon would, indeed, attempt a comeback. They kept his residence under discreet surveillance, and Napoleon had only to leave Chislehurst for a somewhat joyless visit to Torquay in the summer of 1871 to inspire scare headlines in the Paris press of "a second return from Elba." It was even rumored that he had a life-size wooden horse, on which he was practicing to enter Paris in appropriately heroic imperial style.

Plon-Plon came to Chislehurst from his exile in Switzerland with a plea for Napoleon to prepare himself to return. And on this point, if on no other, the imperial cousin found himself in agreement with Eugénie. Napoleon's response was characteristically ambivalent. His health was such, he said in a letter to a friend, that "I am neither able nor willing to attempt a coup d'état." Shortly after that, his mood appeared to have swung.

"My health will never stand in the way," he declared. "I will do my duty."

This pose of quiet resolve did not last. In mid-December 1872, the journalist Mels Cohen visited Napoleon at Camden Place for a second interview and found that although his host asserted that the restoration of the Empire was "a historical necessity," he would do nothing to hasten it. "It would be wrong," said Napoleon. "The rivers which flow most slowly are the most beneficent."

He was particularly dismissive of the idea of a military coup. "If today I give to a general the right to restore me to the throne," he said, "in six months' time I cannot deny him the right to depose me. . . . At a single word from me the flag of the Empire would be raised in fifty places at once from one end of France to the other. . . . But I will never speak that word!"

And yet Napoleon continued to stress his belief that the Empire would be restored, with or without him. It was as certain, he said, as that the fog which shrouded the Kentish countryside that day would "be followed by clear and brilliant sunshine." The old man was clearly troubled by the English fogs. "They are the cause of all my discomfort," he complained to Cohen. "They stifle me."

But a good deal more than the fog was causing Napoleon's discomfort. Cohen observed that talking tired him, and as they parted company Napoleon said au revoir "in a voice so low that it showed that life was weary in him and drawing to a close."

Indeed, it was. After a couple of years of quiescence, his bladder complaint had flared up again. Either hoping to make himself fit to return to France or because he could endure the pain no longer, Napoleon consented to an examination by a panel of doctors headed by the leading British urologist, Sir Henry Thompson, which was conducted on Christmas Eve.

On the 26th, Sir Henry performed an exploratory operation and found a stone as big as "a full sized date" in the emperor's bladder. Napoleon gave his reluctant consent when Thompson and the other doctors decided that the stone should be removed. The chosen method was to be a procedure known as lithotitry, in which the stone would be crushed by a plier-like device inserted into the bladder, rather than by the older and more dangerous method of simply cutting the stone out.

Such was the size of the stone and the uncertainty of the patient's general condition that Thompson and his colleagues agreed on a series of relatively brief operations, to crush the stone little by little. On January 3, 1873, Napoleon underwent the first bout of surgery under chloroform. The operation successfully got rid of half the stone and in a second operation on January 6 more of the stone was removed. A final operation was scheduled for January 9. But on the afternoon of the 8th, Napoleon—who had been drifting in and out of consciousness for days, and may have been given an inadvertent overdose of chloral—began to sink.

Surfacing briefly from his coma, he asked the whereabouts of his son, who by this time was a cadet at the Royal Military Academy at Woolwich. "He has gone back to Woolwich," replied Eugénie. "Do you want him?" "No," replied the emperor. "No, he is working and I do not want him disturbed." His next—and last—coherent words were uttered the following morning, when Conneau came to his bedside. "Ah, is that you, Conneau?" said the dying man. "You were at Sedan, were you not?"*

Realizing that Napoleon was sinking fast, the doctors sent for Father Goddard, the Chislehurst parish priest, and for Eugénie, who was just about to drive to Woolwich to fetch her son. Sending comte Clary to Woolwich in her place, she hurried to her husband's bedside. "Louis is coming, dear," she said. Napoleon was not able to summon any words in reply, but according to Fleury, at the mention of his son, "a slight smile and an expression of joy immediately spread over his white face."

Fleury continues:

At this moment Father Goddard entered the room and administered extreme unction. The Empress noticed the hard breathing, but did not imagine that the end was so near. Father Goddard gently drew her away. She thought that he wished to remain alone with the Emperor. The doctors evidently perceived that the Em-

---

*Some accounts give the emperor's last words as "Ah, it's you, Conneau. It's true, isn't it, that we were not cowards at Sedan?" But though this version is more poetic, Conneau himself never avowed it, and neither did Fleury, the only other courtier at the deathbed to have given a description of the scene.

press did not realize the real situation, so they told her that the Emperor was dying. She then returned to the bed, everybody fell on their knees, and the emperor Napoleon passed quietly away.

Half an hour later, young Louis arrived from Woolwich. As he rushed into the house, he encountered Father Goddard, in tears, and guessed the worst. The prince hurried up the stairs to his father's bedroom, to be met by his mother on the landing. "I have nothing left but you, Louis," she sobbed. At his father's bedside, the sixteen-year-old Prince Imperial sank to his knees and prayed. Then he took the head of the dead emperor in both hands and kissed it.

"Our friend is an odd little chap. It is impossible not to like him."

Only an English aristocrat of the Victorian establishment could have rendered so loftily condescending a verdict on the most powerful living monarch of Continental Europe. But if lofty condescension were the style for the headstones of the mighty, Clarendon's observation would make a good epitaph. It says all that can be said with any certainty about the character of its subject; 115 years after his death, virtually anything else one can say about Louis Napoleon Bonaparte remains open to controversy.

That there was something compellingly likable about him even his traducers concede—Karl Marx and Victor Hugo excepted. That he was "odd" seems equally undeniable: a dictator with democratic leanings, an imperialist who championed self-determination, a capitalist with socialist tendencies, a militarist who retched at the sight of a battlefield on the morning after. The list of contradictions and paradoxes is endless. Among comparably important historical figures of recent times, Louis Napoleon is uniquely baffling. As fast as one part of his personality comes into focus, another part starts to blur, and historians of our time have been as mystified by "the sphinx of the Tuileries" as were his contemporaries.

"To fathom his thought or divine his intentions would try the powers of the most clear-sighted," sighed Cowley. "What a singular man!" exclaimed Hübner. "What a mixture of opposites! Calculating and naive, pleasure-loving and fond of marvels, sometimes sincere, sometimes impenetrable, ever a conspirator."

Louis Napoleon concealed his personal feelings as compulsively as he obfuscated his policies and obscured his objectives. "If I had married him," said Princess Mathilde in a moment of exasperation, "I swear I'd have broken his head open to see what was in it!"

The best efforts of scholarship in the generations since Louis Napoleon's death have only served to deepen his mystery and sharpen the conflicting opinions about him. A major reason for this scholarly disarray is that so little documentation survives. Napoleon III's administrative and personal records were largely destroyed in the fall of the Second Empire and the suppression of the Paris Commune in the following year, while his surviving correspondence—much of it trivial—scarcely fills one volume. By comparison, the letters of his uncle, the first Napoleon, fill sixty-four volumes.

Nor was Louis Napoleon a talker. ("How can one understand a man who spoke so little and wrote even less?" complains Theodore Zeldin, one of the most recondite of Second Empire historians.) He raised personal concealment to the level of an art form; for diplomats such as Cowley, who lamented that "the Emperor will not trust anyone with the secret of his real feelings and intentions," Napoleon-watching had many of the attributes of Kremlinology in our own time, pre-Gorbachev, involving much reading of entrails and inspired guesswork.

As we have seen, some contemporary observers took the emperor's silences as a cover for wisdom and sagacity, while others believed they concealed a ruthless amorality. His nemesis, Bismarck, considered them to be merely a mask for inner emptiness. To him, Louis Napoleon was "a sphinx without a riddle."

One point that impressed virtually all his contemporaries—but that seems, deliberately or otherwise, to have been overlooked by many of his later critics—was that, for a self-proclaimed Caesar, he seemed entirely untouched by megalomania. He had at his disposal all the powers of ruthless dictatorship, but exercised them only at moments of crisis, and then reluctantly, and generally reversed their effects—where they were reversible—as soon as he felt able to. Victor Hugo, from his self-imposed exile, may have thundered maledictions upon Louis Napoleon's crimes against humanity, but by the standards of later dictators they seem mere misdemeanors. As the French Academician Alain Decaux has neatly put it, Louis Napoleon hid a velvet fist in an iron glove.

However, some historians and biographers, anxious to redress the balance after the battering Louis Napoleon's reputation underwent in the early years of the Third Republic, seem to have gone too far. They appear to have been so impressed by his undoubted personal kindliness—and by his avowal of progressive liberal ideas, such as social justice at home and national self-determination abroad—that they have minimized his undoubted misdeeds and deficiencies and portrayed him as a misjudged reformer and statesman of rare vision, brought down in the end only by ill-health and the inadequacy of his ministers.

The Franco-American historian Albert Guérard surely went a little overboard in describing Louis Napoleon as "profoundly devoted to the cause of the masses, the inarticulate, the humble, the forgotten . . . a better European than Bismarck or Gambetta and a better socialist than Karl Marx." So, too, did his pseudonymous British colleague, Robert Sencourt, who claimed the French Second Empire to have been more important than the First, and detected in Louis Napoleon (a man, it should be remembered, who led his country into four quite unnecessary major wars in sixteen years) "a warm and deep benevolence: a regard not only for his people and his country, but also for Europe, if not for the world. . . ."

At the other extreme, however, Louis Napoleon has been portrayed either as a proto-Fascist, obsessed with order and discipline and trampling on elementary human rights, or else as a cynical looter of his country's wealth. Some have discerned uncomfortably close parallels between the rise of Louis Napoleon and the style of his regime and the Fascist dictatorships of the twentieth century; others believe with A. J. P. Taylor that the system which claimed to care for the masses was run by the most dishonest politicians in French history. "All of them, even Napoleon himself," says Taylor, "were convinced that the Empire would not last; and they plundered France while the opportunity lasted."

There is, of course, a middle range of opinion, which sees Napoleon III as neither saviour nor criminal, but merely as an amiable incompetent—an essentially directionless and indecisive improviser, vaguely well meaning but without any consistent policy or cohesive ideology beyond a superstitious and mystical belief in his own destiny. Philip Guedalla, the most stylish member of this school, described Louis Napoleon's career as "the tragedy of an arriviste who arrived," and Louis himself as "a man of one idea; and when it was accomplished he was without one." In similar vein, but less sympathetically, Lewis Namier called Napoleon III "a dreamer, entertaining vast, nebulous schemes, but vacillating, confused and therefore complex and ineffective."

Should a writer without pretensions to scholarship—a journalist, not a historian—venture into this maze of contradictions? In the search for the essential Louis Napoleon, it may just be that a seasoned journalist's inveterate curiosity, and his experience of the world and the men and women who shape it, can provide a compass.

For example, academic historians and scholarly biographers have tended to gloss over two aspects of Louis Napoleon's life—his doubtful paternity and his insatiable sexuality—as though they were of little relevance and, indeed, beneath the consideration of a "serious" writer. On the contrary, these two questions seem to this author to be central to an understanding of Louis Napoleon's complex personality. Indeed, reluctance to delve into such matters, either out of Anglo-Saxon prudishness, or Gallic pseudo-sophistication, or ignorance of modern psychology, may be the reason why Louis Napoleon has been so little understood.

Guérard rightly called him a "damaged soul," but failed to suggest the cause of the damage. Like other biographers of Napoleon III, he seems to have overlooked the possibility that his subject was one of those men of power whose eventual downfall is inevitable because they subconsciously engineer it. And yet the theme of the heroic protagonist destroyed by a fatal character flaw is not exactly a new-fangled idea. It comes to us from Greek tragedy; contemporary psychiatric theory has merely provided a scientific rationale for an ancient literary concept.

Seen through this prism—but without venturing too far into the realm of psychobiography—Louis Napoleon looks very much like what psychologists nowadays would call a pathologically narcissistic personality: a man with a relentless drive for political power and sexual conquest, offset by an unconscious desire to fail. Certainly, a desire to fail would explain the otherwise inexplicably self-destructive policies that caused the collapse of the Second Empire.

Such a desire, according to current theory, arises out of a deep-seated sense of worthlessness, a feeling that one's success is undeserved and must therefore be sacrificed as an act of self-punishment. If this was indeed Louis Napoleon's daemon, it most probably originated in his doubts about the authenticity of his claim to be a Bonaparte.

It is entirely unrealistic to imagine that he was unaware of the rumors about his paternity, which were rife throughout Europe, and which must have been given substance in his mind by his official father's rejection of him during much of his youth and early manhood.

Louis Napoleon may or may not have dismissed the rumors as malicious gossip. He may have remained unaffected by such cruel jibes as that of Victor Hugo in *Les Châtiments:* "This child of chance . . . whose name is a theft and whose birth a fraud." But it seems unlikely. Although this secretive man has not left the merest hint of his feelings on the matter, his very silence surely tells us something. It must be significant that there is not a single instance on record of his ever having referred to the subject—either verbally or in writing, seriously or in jest.

We may reasonably surmise that on a conscious level he could not bring himself even to acknowledge the existence of such doubts about his paternity. Thus, when his uncle Jérôme Bonaparte sneered "you have nothing of HIM about you," Louis Napoleon essentially ducked the issue, turning the thrust aside with the smart riposte: "Perhaps, but I have his family about me."

But if Louis Napoleon's life may be seen from one perspective as Greek tragedy, from another it looks remarkably like a combination of bedroom farce and opera bouffe—libretto by Sophocles and Feydeau, musical score by Offenbach!

His sexual appetite was prodigious and one must not be deterred from delving into his lovelife by the disdain of those critics who maintain that a ruler's behavior in the bedroom has no relevance to his conduct of affairs. This was not, after all, a case of a head of state allowing himself an occasional diversion, or a long-term mistress, to relieve the tedium of a dynastic marriage. This was a matter of a tireless and indiscriminate womanizer who, as Princess Mathilde put it, "runs after every alley cat he sees."

True, none of Louis Napoleon's numerous extramarital encounters and affairs—not even the one with Count Cavour's seductive and not-so-secret agent, Virginie di Castiglione—had any discernible effect on the policies of the Second Empire. But he spent an inordinate amount of time and effort on the business of the boudoir that might better have been devoted to affairs of state. And, brief encounters apart, it is clear that his love for two particular women—Harriet Howard and Eugénie de Montijo—had a profound influence on his life, and therefore on his times. But for the generosity of the first he might never have gained an empire; but for the self-absorption of the second, he might have been able to overcome his urge to throw it away. Eugénie's frigidity, her nagging, and her intolerance of his personal deficiencies can only have added to his lack of self-worth and—together with her compulsive meddling in foreign policy—contributed to the downfall of his Empire.

Spurned in the marriage bed, nagged in the parlor, Louis Napoleon continued his relentless pursuit of the perfect orgasm long past the point where chronic ill-health* would have made a less driven man desist, and he did so in an indiscriminate and reckless manner that left him open to ridicule in the courts of Europe. Such behavior can hardly be dismissed as unimportant. Indeed, it may be seen as another manifestation of Louis Napoleon's desire for self-punishment and failure. It must surely have been a factor, for example, in the way he was viewed by Bismarck, who made not a moral but a political value judgment when he plotted the destruction of the Second Empire in a spirit of such contempt for its ruler.

---

* Not including syphilis, incidentally, despite his promiscuousness and the prevalence of the disease in an age without antibiotics.

And when Bismarck triumphed, permitting Louis Napoleon to expiate the "crime" of his illegitimacy by losing his Empire, the defeated emperor seemed strangely at peace, astonishing all comers by his resignation and composure. As Malmesbury observed: "His quiet and calm dignity and absence of all nervousness and irritability were the grandest examples of human moral courage that the severest stoic could have imagined." Or, as Eugénie would recall: "He carried his stoicism and his meekness to the point of sublimity."

His complexities and his call upon our understanding do not end there, of course. Although he was born in the first decade of the last century, Louis Napoleon was essentially a man of our time. And 1848, Europe's "mad and holy year" of revolution—the year he came to power, the year Marx published the Communist Manifesto—was in many ways Year One of the modern world. Anyone reading the pamphlets and newspapers of that year, studying the speeches of its politicians, observing the maneuvers of its statesmen, must feel very much at home.

For all the technological, scientific, medical, and social advances that have been made since then, the issues that concerned 1848—terror versus law-and-order, national self-determination versus big-power oppression, democracy versus dictatorship, socialism versus capitalism, free trade versus protection, religion versus science—equally concern the late 1980s. And although Louis Napoleon came to power by evoking memories of a time past—the era of his uncle, the first Napoleon—he was an essentially forward-looking, surprisingly modern politician. It may be disputed whether he was a profound thinker, but unquestionably he grasped the political potential of the emerging technologies; he virtually invented the campaign tour, the whistle-stop, the media event, and the calculated leak, not to mention the modern version of the ultimate political weapon, the coup d'état.

Beyond that, he had an instinctive understanding of populist dynamics and was thus able effortlessly to outsmart the radicals and socialists on one hand, and the stuffed-shirt establishment politicians on the other, who tried to block his path to power. He understood that his countrymen—above all the peasantry and the bourgeoisie, big and small—traumatized by the fear of revolutionary bloodshed and chaos, wanted the illusion of freedom and the reality of authority. So he restored the universal franchise the politicians had whittled away, believing correctly that the people would subsequently use their votes to endorse his seizure of supreme power from the parliamentarians.

Throughout his twenty-two years in office—four as prince-president, eighteen as emperor—he was a sort of despot and a kind of democrat, in a way no leader had been before and perhaps only his compatriot Charles de Gaulle has been since. And while it is true that he blazed a trail for the Fascist dictators of the twentieth century, he also put up some signposts for the less malevolent. His concept of a Caesarian leader embodying the will of the people was copied, consciously or otherwise, by Hitler and Mussolini, but his concept of government as theater and sleight-of-hand—a business to be conducted conspiratorially behind the back of parliament—also showed the way to a breed of democratic leader which found its transatlantic apotheosis over a century later in Ronald Reagan. His immense popularity and apparent purposefulness during his early years in power, contrasted with the drift, detachment, and defeat of his final years, are also eerily reminiscent of the Reagan presidency.

But to pursue the parallels between Napoleon III and the politicians of our own century, however beguiling an exercise, does not help to unravel his mystery. Nor is it his "relevance for our time," or some such pomposity, that makes him such a compelling and, in the end, appealing figure. Rather, it is the unusually vivid way in which his life illustrates the truth propounded by Carlyle, Emerson, and others that (to use T. S. Eliot's phrase) "the lengthened shadow of a man is history."

This was never truer than in the case of Louis Napoleon and his era. He *was* the Second Empire. It was entirely his invention and quite inconceivable without him. Its character mirrored his own—spendthrift, dissolute, showy, muddle-headed, insubstantial, yet humane, audacious, brave, well intentioned, inventive, and wickedly congenial.

The reign of Louis Napoleon saw a reduced France rise to a position of Continental pre-eminence as a military and industrial power and its capital transformed into the "City of Light" which it remains to this day. Even after its crushing defeat in 1870—and the trauma of the Commune in the following year—France remained economically strong enough to pay off its crippling war reparations and resume its great power status in astonishingly short order.

Louis Napoleon must surely take a good deal of the credit for that, even though it is true that the industrialization of France, albeit encouraged by his sensible economic and fiscal policies, would have occurred anyway, and even though the military and diplomatic predominance of the Second Empire was a grand illusion, as Bismarck so brutally demonstrated when it became clear to him that its downfall was necessary for the rise of the German Empire.

Still, all that is buried under the massive landslides which engulfed Europe in the first half of the twentieth century, so that virtually all that remains to remind us of Louis Napoleon's glory days is the enduring visual splendor of the present-day French capital (plus Les Halles, but minus such later landmarks as the Eiffel Tower, the domes of Sacré-Coeur, and the Pompidou Center). That and the strangely melancholic gaiety of those Offenbach compositions which have survived into the repertoire of the modern concert hall and opera house.

The rest of the Second Empire's achievements are confetti, blown to the wind, and to capture the unique personality of its creator may ultimately be as impossible as to retrieve all those gaily colored scraps of paper, flying off in different directions. But the chase itself has been exhilarating and as Fleury said after the dust had settled on the ruins of Saint-Cloud and the Tuileries: "It wasn't a proper empire, but we had the devil of a good time."

P O S T S C R I P T :

T H E   L O N G   T W I L I G H T

"Heavens! How dearly we paid for our splendors."
—EMPRESS EUGÉNIE

WHILE THE SPLENDID BOULEVARDS and avenues of present-day Paris, and much of that city's architecture, implicitly memorialize the third Napoleon, it is left to a modest back road in a leafy London suburb to commemorate the young man who might have become the fourth.

Few of the present-day inhabitants of Chislehurst know why one of the thoroughfares crossing their common is called Prince Imperial Road, and fewer still seem aware of the story behind the 20-foot-tall granite cross, partly hidden by foliage, which stands between the road and the bridle path that runs alongside it.

Indeed, the monument embodies an irony more sublime than anything a writer of fiction could invent: erected in 1880 by popular subscription of the residents of Chislehurst, it commemorates the paradox—all but forgotten nowadays—that the only son of Napoleon III and his empress, and as such the last slender hope of a Bonapartist restoration, met his death wearing the uniform of a lieutenant of the Royal Horse Artillery while taking part in a British colonial war in far-off Zululand.

The impulse that led young Louis to seek glory under the

Union Jack in a war so remote from French interests may suggest that he inherited his father's streak of romanticism. In fact, it was an act of almost pure political calculation, another of his father's tendencies. The circumstances of young Louis's death, however, under the assegais of a Zulu war party, show that he failed to inherit a third of his father's attributes—his phenomenal luck.

Young Louis never thought of himself as a permanent exile. Almost from the moment of his reunion with his mother after the fall of the Empire, he was buoyed up by the belief that sooner or later the fickle French would want the Bonapartes back.

That the dynasty might be restored was more than just a private fantasy of the Bonaparte family and a few diehard supporters. The belief was widely held throughout Europe, and was even shared by Queen Victoria. Following the death of the emperor, she declared that she did not think his passing would damage the Bonapartist cause. "On the contrary, she thinks the reverse. For the peace of Europe, she thinks that it would be best if the Prince Imperial were ultimately to succeed."

It was with this in mind that Louis had been sent to learn the art of war at Woolwich. A Bonaparte must have a military background and it was no coincidence that the Prince Imperial— "the P.I.," as he was popularly known to the British, who traditionally have a soft spot for refugee royalty—was to be trained in the specialty of the Bonapartes: artillery. He was serious about his studies and, far from seeking the privileges of his princely status, proved to be an energetic and avid student, determined to excel and to make himself popular with his fellows.

Although a fine horseman, young Louis was short and slight, with his father's disproportionately long torso. Unlike his father, he showed no more than a polite interest in the opposite sex. Indeed, he seems to have been almost painfully virtuous. In a private prayer—found inside the pages of his missal after his death—he asked God to visit all sorts of tests and hardships upon him and concluded by praying that he would "never have to blush for my inmost thoughts."

It was widely rumored that he might marry Victoria's youngest daughter, Princess Beatrice, but despite Victoria's friendship for Eugénie and the Bonapartes' frequent visits to Windsor and

Osborne, that can never have been more than a popular fiction. As head of the Anglican Church, Victoria could never seriously have considered marrying her daughter to a Roman Catholic; as Pretender to the throne of France, Louis could never seriously have contemplated defecting to the Church of England.

On his eighteenth birthday, March 16, 1874, Bonapartists flocked to Camden Place from France to celebrate Louis's coming of age. In a marquee set up on Chislehurst Common, he told the faithful—and a sizable contingent of French secret policemen—that he was willing and eager to return as Napoleon IV if the people of France should call him back in a plebiscite.

The aging Plon-Plon, still with ambitions of his own, tried to persuade the Bonapartists that he, and not Loulou, was the legitimate heir, but his politics were too left-wing and his temperament too explosive to win them over. Some Bonapartists, it is true, thought it improper that their future monarch should be training with the British Army, but Louis considered his education at Woolwich to be a necessary preparation for his succession to the throne.

Indeed, after his graduation he considered participation in a suitable war to be another rite of passage he must undertake to prove himself fit to assume the throne. "When one belongs to a race of soldiers, it is only sword in hand that one gains recognition," he wrote in a letter to a friend. "Eagerly he scanned the face of the earth, the sword burning in his hands," wrote Marie de Larminat.

At one point, Louis wrote to the emperor Franz-Josef, asking to be allowed to serve in the Austrian Army of occupation in Bosnia and Herzegovina. But the Hapsburgs had had quite enough of the Bonapartes for the moment and his request was politely refused.

Like his father, Louis was haunted by the disgrace of Sedan, and the jibes of the republicans against "l'enfant de la balle" continued to rankle. He kept with him, as a constant reminder of the need to prove himself in battle, a newspaper clipping containing a reference to the embarrassing incident at Saarbrücken.

Adding to Louis's unrest was the fact that Eugénie was keeping him short of funds. This made it impossible for him to keep up with his fashionable English friends and, unable to repay their hospitality, he found himself compelled to refuse country house invitations. Louis was sinking into gloom, boredom, and frustration, when a shattering event in South Africa seemed to offer a way out.

This was the battle of Isandhlwana, in Zululand, in which the impis of King Cetewayo fell upon a British punitive force on January 22, 1879, and wiped it out, massacring 800 British troops and 500 of their black auxiliaries. The blow to British pride and prestige was enormous, and in a fever of patriotic excitement, an expeditionary force was immediately raised to go and teach the black savages a lesson.

Louis's classmates from Woolwich, now officers of "E" Battery, the Royal Horse Artillery, volunteered to a man, and Louis, without his mother's knowledge, wrote to the Duke of Cambridge, the army commander-in-chief, begging to be allowed to join them. He wept when his request was rejected. The reasons were political: Cambridge had mentioned the matter to Disraeli, then prime minister, who had replied that he had "never heard of anything more injudicious" than allowing a foreign prince—albeit an exile—to risk his life in a British colonial war.

When Eugénie learned of the affair, she was at first relieved that Louis's quixotic offer had been spurned. But he was so distressed at the rejection, and so persuasive in his argument that he needed to prove himself to the French as a soldier, that eventually she went in person to Cambridge to urge him to reconsider. She did not want her son to risk his life, she said, but could he not go to South Africa "in the role of a spectator"?

Cambridge had no objection, and when he mentioned the matter to Victoria, she made it clear that if this was what her friend Eugénie wanted, she had no objection either. So Disraeli's objections were overwhelmed and permission was granted. "Well," Disraeli told a friend, "my conscience is clear. I did all I could to stop his going. But what can you do when you have two obstinate women to deal with?"

The night before he sailed for South Africa, Louis wrote his will, a prudent enough measure to take before going to a war zone and not one that would necessarily indicate any real expectation of death. Yet the document reeks with a foreboding that is in marked contrast to Louis's outwardly insouciant manner.

"I die in the Roman Catholic Apostolic faith, in which I was born," he wrote.

I desire my body to be laid by that of my father, until such time as both are transferred to the resting place of the Founder of our house, in the bosom of the French people. . . .* My last thought will be of my country: it is for my country that I should wish to die. When I am no more, I trust that my mother will keep for me the loving remembrance I will keep for her until my last moment. I shall die with a sentiment of profound gratitude for Her Majesty the Queen of England and all the royal family, and for the country where I have received eight years of such cordial hospitality.

The next day, Eugénie accompanied her son to Southampton where he boarded the S.S. *Danube,* bound for Capetown and Durban. The news that Louis had angled so desperately to be allowed to fight alongside his classmates was enormously appreciated by the British press and public, and the crowds who turned up at the dockside to speed the redcoats on their way had a special cheer for the popular "P.I." The *Danube* even flew the Tricolor alongside the Blue Ensign, an unprecedented honor.

Louis's arrival in South Africa presented the British commander-in-chief, the bumbling Lord Chelmsford, with something of a problem—and after the disgrace of Isandhlwana, Chelmsford already had problems enough on his mind. Told to be sure that Louis was kept out of harm's way, he found him a job on headquarters staff with the hope that his staff officers would keep an eye on him.

Louis had other ideas. He took advantage of his position at headquarters to get to know field officers as they came and went to and from their forays beyond the Blood River and made a name for himself as a keen and likable young chap. He also made a good impression on a young French journalist named Déléage, who was on assignment from *Le Figaro* to cover the campaign. Although a convinced republican, Déléage found the Prince Imperial "a Frenchman with all the qualities of his race—a true child of Paris, with the accent of the boulevards."

Without Chelmsford's knowledge, Louis accompanied a

---

* Their remains have never returned to France, much less to Les Invalides, and remain interred at Farnborough Hill in Hampshire.

scouting force deep into enemy territory and distinguished himself by his recklessness and his practice of deliberately courting discomfort to prove his manliness. He traveled without a blanket and found the nights so cold on the high veldt that he could not sleep. Instead, he walked around all night, singing military songs and chatting to the sentries.

He must have had an inexhaustible supply of adrenaline. Far from suffering from sleeplessness, when the force encountered a small group of Zulus, who immediately took flight, Louis rode so far ahead of his comrades in pursuit of them that he had to be peremptorily called back by the officer in command. Later, he took part with great relish in an attack on a Zulu kraal, whose inhabitants all fled without a fight, and was boyishly delighted when the spot was named "Kraal Napoleon" in his honor.

It all seemed wonderful sport, and Louis excitedly told an older officer: "I've no desire to be killed, but if I had to fall I should prefer an assegai to a bullet. It would prove I'd been at close quarters."

Back at headquarters, Chelmsford angrily forbade him to go out on patrol again and ordered him to remain in camp on staff duties. But shortly after that, the order was given for headquarters to move forward across the Blood River, and in the ensuing confusion Louis found another opportunity for "adventure."

As the army lumbered into Zululand, a river of scarlet and white winding slowly across the tawny high veldt, Louis found himself assigned to the staff of the quartermaster-general, Colonel Harrison. From Harrison he got permission to accompany a mapmaking patrol, led by an acting captain named Carey, which was to look for a camping site for the Second Division. It was considered a safe enough operation—so safe that it consisted of only six troopers and a Basuto guide, plus the two officers.

They set out on the morning of June 1 and at four that afternoon, they were resting by the bank of the Imbazani River, their horses picketed and a pot of coffee brewing on a wood fire. Their resting place was surrounded by man-high kaffir corn, which came to within ten yards of the riverbank.

They had barely finished their coffee when one of the pickets spotted the head of a Zulu, bobbing above the kaffir corn on the other side of the stream. "Hurry, get mounted!" ordered Carey as the patrol got to their feet and raced for the horses. The Zulus had guns and let loose a crackle of poorly aimed rifle fire as they rushed forward. A horse was hit and fell, bringing its rider down.

By this time, Carey and the rest of the patrol, except for Louis and one trooper, were mounted and riding away. Louis's horse, a big ugly gray named Fate, was frightened and skittering in circles around its picket peg. When Louis drew the peg, Fate pulled away, trying to follow the other horses. Louis ran to catch him up, intending to vault into the saddle—a trick at which he was expert.

"Get mounted, sir, for God's sake get mounted!" shouted the remaining trooper as he rode past. Louis had hold of Fate's holster strap and was about to leap into the saddle. Then the strap broke, leaving him sprawling face down.

His right arm was injured in the fall. He had lost his sword in the scramble. He was alone, without even covering fire to give him a chance to escape. Louis drew his revolver with his left hand and turned to face the oncoming Zulus—thirty of them. They stopped as he walked toward them. He managed to fire three shots before he fell under a hail of assegais.

When Louis's corpse was recovered the next day it had eighteen assegai wounds, any one of which might have been fatal, and all in the front of his body. Unlike the bodies of two troopers who were killed in flight, his had not been mutilated—a sign of respect for his courage by the Zulus. One of them, when captured later, told the British that the young Prince Imperial had died "like a lion."

When the news of Loulou's death reached Eugénie at Camden Place, a friend who was present recorded that "she sat as white and motionless as a statue for some hours . . . before tears happily came to her relief." Later, said the friend—the wife of Sir Lintorn Simmons, governor of the Woolwich Military Academy where Loulou had been a cadet—Eugénie "threw herself on my shoulder, clasped me tightly with both arms round my waist and lay there, sobbing convulsively."

Queen Victoria, who hurried to Chislehurst to convey her condolences, found "the dear Empress's conduct beyond all praise." In a letter to Disraeli, the queen noted that "her resignation, her unmurmuring, patient submission to God's will, her conviction that it could not be otherwise, and the total absence of all blame of others, are admirable."

How little she understood Eugénie. Revealing the true strength of a character which, for all its shortcomings, would never submit meekly to the blows of fate, the bereaved empress told her mother: "My grief is savage, unquiet, irascible. I am in no way resigned and . . . I don't want to be consoled, I want to be left in peace." And in a later letter, hurling her defiance at the gods: "I still live, for grief does not kill."

Her son's remains were brought back from South Africa for a funeral at Chislehurst which—despite the British government's attempts to play it down in deference to its relations with the prickly Third Republic—was something of a state occasion, with the Queen, the Princess of Wales, and Princess Beatrice among the mourners, and the Prince of Wales, the Duke of Cambridge, and the Duke of Connaught among the pall bearers.

Plon-Plon arrived from Switzerland to pay his last respects to "the brat" he had always hated and discovered he had even better cause for dislike than he realized. Loulou's will, read out just before the funeral, cut Plon-Plon out of the succession and named Plon-Plon's eldest son, Victor, as head of the family and the putative Napoleon V. At the end of the service, Plon-Plon abruptly left, without a word to the grieving mother.

She and Plon-Plon were to remain unreconciled to the day of his death in 1891. But as she characteristically said: "Although I detested him, I never despised him."*

No doubt Eugénie did despise Captain Carey, the officer who had abandoned her son to the mercies of the Zulus, yet in her attitude toward him she displayed great generosity of spirit. Carey was court-martialed and cashiered for cowardice, but when his case came up for review, Eugénie appealed successfully for his exoneration. "Let no one suffer, either in his reputation or in his interests," she wrote. "I, who can desire nothing more on earth, ask it as a last prayer."

In March 1880, accompanied by a retinue of friends and retainers, Eugénie embarked on a pilgrimage to South Africa and Ityotosi, the scene of her son's death. From Durban, where they

---

* Plon-Plon could never forgive his son for having become head of the family. "I leave nothing to Victor," he said in his will. "He is a traitor and a rebel. I do not wish him to be present at my funeral."

disembarked, Eugénie and her party made a fifty-day trek by train and horse-drawn wagon to Ityotosi and stayed a week, so as to be there on June 1, the anniversary of Loulou's death. The British had erected a cross on the fatal spot and Eugénie spent the night of June 1 alone beside it, praying and meditating.

It was an airless night and the candles placed around the foot of the cross burned steadily. Just before dawn, Eugénie said afterward, they flickered as if blown by a nonexistent wind, and she cried out: "Is it you? Do you want me to go away?"

The next day she and her party commenced their return journey to the coast and thence to England.

In her grief over Loulou's death, Eugénie had written to her mother: "I had only him. I have only one idea; to rejoin him." Yet she was to live on for another forty-one years, an increasingly imperious and formidable old nomad flitting about Europe and as far afield as Ceylon, cruising in her private yacht, entertaining or being entertained by the mighty, encouraging the aspirations of the doggedly persistent Bonapartists, and turning her new home at Farnborough Hill, Hampshire, into a Napoleonic shrine.

She purchased Farnborough Hill in 1880 from Thomas Longman, the London publisher, partly because Chislehurst held too many unhappy memories and partly because the modest Roman Catholic church there was not grand enough to serve as the last resting place for her husband and son.

The estate she acquired, on both sides of the Portsmouth Road, included several hundred acres of farm and woodland; there, on a hill facing the big house, she built a grandiose priory and mausoleum to house her son's and husband's remains and eventually her own. It also housed a small order of Premonstrian monks who would sing masses for the repose of their souls.

As the years went by and scar tissue grew over the wounds left by the Second Empire, the French government gradually allowed Eugénie to recover much of her personal property, which went to embellish her lavish quarters at Farnborough, including family portraits by Winterhalter and other court painters, a set of Gobelins panels, Louis XVI chairs, Sèvres vases, and the like.

In return, Eugénie donated an important collection of First Empire memorabilia, bequeathed to her husband by his mother, to the national museum at Malmaison.

Both at Farnborough, and at her second home, the Villa Cyrnos on the Côte d'Azure at Cap Martin, between Menton and Monte Carlo, she lived in great style. Said a frequent visitor: "Her servants, the food, the whole entourage recalls a Court." But, eschewing the luxury of her homes on dry land, Eugénie liked to spend a good deal of time at sea on her small, rather uncomfortable and none too stable steam yacht, the *Thistle*.

"I never feel so well on earth as when on top of a wave," Eugénie remarked happily, oblivious to the distress of her entourage, many of whom were prone to seasickness. "The sea is my element, it is the cure, par excellence, for every physical and moral sickness." But as the *Thistle* pottered about the Mediterranean to Naples, Venice, Athens, and Constantinople, and back via Alexandria, Tangier, and Gibraltar, Eugénie's ladies begged to be excused, referring to her beloved *Thistle* as "that awful skiff," and wishing she would stay on terra firma.

On her frequent trips from Farnborough to Cap Martin, Eugénie traveled via Paris with the blessings of a Third Republic now sufficiently self-assured to consider her presence in the capital to pose no kind of threat. While there she always stayed at the Hotel Continental, where she kept a permanent suite of rooms directly facing the Tuileries Gardens. Some wondered how she could bear to look out on the empty space between the two wings of the Louvre where her palace had once stood.

But Jean Cocteau, who visited her in her suite, thought such a notion "stupid." "What could remain from the past but habit to affect a woman who had died several times?" he asked. "The habit of living in a certain district which is stronger than any other." From Cocteau we receive a characteristically vivid impression of a woman still magnetic in her late seventies. As he took his leave and she invited him to return, he recalls, "I saw a flash of youth illuminate her whole face and her whole frail, mourning-clad figure, like the lightning flash of the salamander which gives life to ruins."

Cocteau also remarks on how the "heavenly blue" of her eyes contrasted with the black eye shadow underlining them, which "recalled the tattooed eyes of young sailors who are released from prison when they are old. In these old men you find to your surprise the indelible signs of angry beauty."

The poet had been introduced to the empress by a special favorite of hers, Alphonse Daudet's son Lucien, a brilliant, attractive, but essentially dilettantish young painter and littérateur, one of a circle of homosexual aesthetes that included Marcel Proust as well as Cocteau. Eugénie was aware of Lucien's essential ineffectuality—"you must work, work, work," she chided him—but she adored him nonetheless, calling him "Lucien," "Luciano," and even "mon cher enfant," an amazing concession in one so conscious of protocol and her own status.

Knowing of Lucien's intimacy with the empress, an enterprising Paris publisher commissioned him to write a book about her which, as Lucien told her in seeking her permission, would be "without indiscretions or anecdotes, a kind of written portrait which would provide, as it were, the psychological and moral references for those who would later on read books about Your Majesty and who will form ideas, sometimes correctly, sometimes not."

Eugénie replied that she could not prevent him, but that she would stick to her resolution not to provide any information about her past life, and that "you must be just and say what you think of me—not only the things which would be agreeable for me to read." Knowing that the devoted Lucien was hardly likely to risk losing her affection, she added: "Do not speak too well of me, nor too ill either, of course."

When Lucien's book, *L'Inconnue, l'Impératrice Eugénie,* was published in 1912, he came to Farnborough and read it to her in two sittings and then, kneeling in front of her, waited fearfully for her reaction. She said nothing but, her eyes full of tears, registered her approval with a warm embrace. As she told a friend, she was "amazed that all this could have been written without containing one word of injury." For the first time she has read a book about herself in which not one phrase displeased her.

But Lucien was a featherweight. Hoping to ensure that posterity would judge her favorably, she chose a heavyweight to be the receptacle of the political confidences she denied to her young admirer. Her choice was Paléologue, the historian, diplomat, and member of the Académie Française, whose acquaintance she made through Princess Mathilde, with whom in later life she had become reconciled.*

Said Mathilde to Paléologue: "She has read your books; I have sometimes told her about you; and she is curious to make your acquaintance." Paléologue took the bait and during Eugénie's next sojourn at the Continental, in June 1901, he called on her.

"Despite her seventy-five years," Paléologue noted,

she still retains the traces of her former beauty. The face has kept its fineness, with the modelling of the features clean-cut, as on a medal. The brow gives a hint of its height beneath her white hair, a brow manifestly predestined for the diadem. The lively, close-set eyes shine with a hard, sombre gleam. . . . Her shoulders, held rigid and erect, do not so much as touch the back of the armchair. The hands, still extremely delicate, are of a pale amber colour, as if they had been steeped in some balm. From her person, in fact, there springs a curious impression of majesty, of something hieratic, and of ruin.

After some initial circumlocutions and discussion of contemporary political affairs, Eugénie made clear to Paléologue what was on her mind ("How will the future judge us? That's what I'm burning to know"), expressed the hope "that our intercourse will not end with your visit today," and launched into a description of her late husband's "selflessness and magnanimity."

As they parted, she said: "I have only one favour to ask of God now—that old as I am, I may yet live long enough to see France find in her heart more justice towards us." Unless we are to discount Paléologue altogether, remarks such as this, and others made during subsequent meetings,† surely give the lie to those admirers of Eugénie who claim that she disdained to dignify her critics by answering their charges.

---

* "Her nature is very proud and very courageous and it has been greatly ennobled by misfortune," Mathilde said of Eugénie in recommending her to Paléologue. "You know how very different we were from each other in character, tastes, opinions—and everything else," said Eugénie of Mathilde after the latter's death in 1904. "But I never felt her less of a trusty friend, and of a noble and very generous heart."

† "Promise me that one day when I am gone you will tell this story" . . . "I am constantly brooding on the verdict which the tribunal of history will bring in" . . . "Promise not to forget my protestations and to spread it abroad when I have left this world of sorrows"; and so forth.

True, she turned aside all pleas that she write or dictate her memoirs. Nevertheless, her series of interviews with Paléologue between 1901 and 1919 surely amounts to her political testament; perhaps, in her view, a more convincing one than her own account might prove to be, given that she could convince her prestigious interlocutor of her honesty and sincerity. Fortunately for posterity, Paléologue, while respectful and even admiring—she had "a pride and nobility of spirit beyond the common," he observed—remained unconvinced by at least some of her interpretations and recollections.

Quite apart from their historic value, Paléologue clearly enjoyed his conversations with Eugénie, which covered contemporary politics, in which she was passionately interested, as much as events of the past. In January 1905, he "found her more stirred than ever by the great problems of foreign policy . . . talking of them with such ease and clarity that she seems to have a map all the time before her."

A year later, two weeks before Eugénie's eightieth birthday, Paléologue observed: "The stiffness of her movements is more pronounced and her face has become thinner. But she has lost nothing of her fine carriage; not a line of her figure has failed; her eyes, with their black pencilling beneath them, retain their hard flash; and her speech has remained clear, sonorous, unhesitating and crisp."

On June 26, 1909, Paléologue found Eugénie in a highly emotional state, "her voice quavering, her breath hardly sufficing her, and on the pale mask of her face, two great tears flowing down the furrows." The fiftieth anniversaries of Magenta and Solferino had just passed, unmarked by the Third Republic, and she was outraged by the deliberate omission.

"I bear the French people no grudge," she said,

because, under the shock of defeat, on the morrow of Sedan, they overwhelmed my husband and myself with the full flood of their wrath, . . . They were so abruptly surprised by the catastrophe; and we had inspired them with such faith in the grandeur and power of France! They fell from so high! But now thirty-nine years have passed. Thirty-nine years—more than a third of a century! And the injustice persists! The brilliant and glorious achievements of our reign are systematically forgotten. . . . Is it not abominable? Will the hour of justice and recompense never strike for us?

Paléologue's last meeting with Eugénie occurred in December 1919, on his return to Paris after six momentous years as French Ambassador to Russia, and although he found her in advanced decline physically, "this wrecked frame was still dominated by a spirit at once energetic, tenacious and proud."

She had reason to feel proud: the German Reich, created out of the wreckage of her husband's Empire, had been defeated and the lost provinces of Alsace and Lorraine had been restored to France. "Today," Eugénie told Paléologue, "I can understand why God has made me live so long. . . . Our dead of 1870 . . . are at last requited for their sacrifice."

Despite her fall from power, Eugénie maintained her connections with European royalty. Following the death of Queen Victoria she remained on close terms with Victoria's son Bertie, now Edward VII, and his queen, and was a frequent visitor to Windsor, Osborne, and Sandringham. She was on intimate terms with the Dowager Empress of Russia. And she seemed to exercise a curious fascination over the German Kaiser, Wilhelm II. He called on her at Farnborough in 1894 when he came to inspect the nearby British Army Headquarters at Aldershot, and went out of his way to call on her again in 1907 when Eugénie was cruising on the *Thistle* in the Norwegian fiords.

Wilhelm arrived at the same anchorage at the same time in the battleship *Hohenzollern* and asked permission to visit her aboard her yacht. After being piped aboard and introduced to the members of Eugénie's entourage, he had a two-hour private talk with her in her stateroom, before returning to his own ship. A friend who was aboard the *Thistle* at the time wrote that "the empress rather likes him and says he is always most agreeable and charming to her." Eugénie, however, put a very different gloss on the encounter when she described it to Paléologue five years later. She told him that Wilhelm's ranting against England and France had "left me with a disturbing recollection."

Whatever her true feelings about the Kaiser, Eugénie was obviously enchanted by her three-day visit to the Austrian Emperor Franz-Josef at Ischl in the summer of 1906. A Legitimist at heart, as her husband and others had often observed, Eugénie had always been enormously impressed by the mystique of the Hapsburgs and their ancient lineage. At dinner with Franz-Josef, wrote her English friend Isabel Vesey, who accompanied her, she looked beautiful, despite her eighty years, "in her black silk dress with its long sweeping train, her white hair crowned with a jet diadem, her lovely neck and shoulders." In such exalted company, attended by the courtly old Franz-Josef—who with exquisite tact wore only one decoration, the Legion of Honor— Eugénie could not but blossom. "I feel that I am enveloped in a dream," she said.

The respectful attentions of powerful rulers like Wilhelm and Franz-Josef and the frequent presence at Farnborough of European statesmen and ambassadors—and influential journalists, like Wickham Steed of *The Times*—could only whet Eugénie's appetite for politics and diplomacy, despite the disastrous effects of her past dabbling on the fortunes of the Second Empire.

Lucien Daudet told his mother that Eugénie "talks almost exclusively politics these days." Her memory was "incomparable" and her experience "unique," he thought, and "every incident reminds her of something analagous in the past." When he rhapsodized to her about her political sagacity, Eugénie replied: "Bah! I am like an old bird that makes a noise without meaning whom nobody listens to." Not to be put down, however archly, Lucien replied: "Yes, madame, the prophet bird."

When World War I broke out, Eugénie directed all her enthusiasm to the Allied cause, both as a patriotic Frenchwoman— for all the country's republicanism—and as a guest and admirer of the British. She immediately pressured all her male servants of military age to volunteer, at the same time offering the *Thistle* to the Admiralty and turning Farnborough Hill into a hospital for wounded officers, which for a while was commanded by the wife of Sir Douglas Haig, commander-in-chief of the British Army in France.

But she was not at all happy when the United States entered the war and began influencing Allied policy. She had never been able to accept her husband's support for "the principle of nationalities"—"it was that, and that alone, which was our undoing," she told Paléologue—and consequently she was utterly opposed to Woodrow Wilson's fourteen-point declaration in favor of self-determination, which was adopted as an Allied war aim.

"All these talks and speeches and theories of Wilson's are

most dangerous and more dangerous to England than anyone else and are also dangerous to France," she said to a confidant, Colonel Willoughby Verner. "This 'League of Nations.' What folly! This 'self-determination of nations.' What madness!"

She seems to have been almost beside herself. "You, you, you English," she demanded of Verner, "what are you about? Why should you run risks by creating nations such as Czechoslovakia and I know not what?"

And yet she was right about the disastrous consequences of the Versailles Treaty which the victorious Allies imposed on Germany in 1919. "What have you done?" she demanded rhetorically of her friend, Dr. Wilfred Attenborough. "This is no peace. These are the seeds of a future war!"

In June 1920, aged ninety-four, Eugénie made a last visit to Spain, where she stayed with her relatives, the Albas, at the Palacio de Lira. During her visit she underwent an operation to remove a cataract which had been the cause of her near-blindness and seemed to take on a new lease of life as she was able to see objects and faces that in recent years had been a blur to her.

But on July 10 she suddenly sickened. It soon became plain that she was not going to recover, and a priest was called to hear her confession and give her extreme unction. "I am tired. It is time for me to go away," she murmured to a relative. The following day she died in the bed of her beloved sister, Paca.

According to her instructions, her body—dressed in the habit of a nun—was returned to Farnborough for burial, and again a Bonaparte funeral turned into something of a British state occasion without the endorsement of the government. King George V and Queen Mary and a host of other monarchs, reigning and deposed, attended, but because of the protests of the French government the twenty-one-gun salute due to a sovereign was not fired. And in a solecism of which republican France must surely have approved, the military band from Aldershot played not *Partant pour la Syrie* but *La Marseillaise*—the republican anthem which had been banned throughout all but the last few weeks of the Second Empire.

Almost seventy years after her death, what should be the verdict on Eugénie? An objective reading of the evidence suggests that for all her faults, she was never quite the vindictive, self-centered, priest-ridden reactionary of republican legend—and that for all her virtues, she was never quite the strong, loyal, long-suffering, and misunderstood heroine portrayed by revisionist historians.

Rather, she was an unfulfilled, neurotic woman, of limited talents though fiery spirit, of great style, and commanding presence, who was unable to love and therefore desperate to dominate—a woman whose beauty and ambition won her great position but little happiness.

Like her husband—to borrow Guedalla's phrase—hers was the tragedy of an arriviste who arrived.

BIBLIOGRAPHY

THIS IS NOT A WORK OF ORIGINAL SCHOLARSHIP. My intent was not to unearth lost or hidden documents that might cast new light on the character of my subject. Even assuming such evidence to exist, only a professional historian with a substantial grant and unlimited time would have had the resources to find it. Rather, my purpose was to re-examine and reassess, in the light of the copious evidence already available, a fascinating and important figure who has been strangely neglected and, it seems to me, little understood. My thanks are due, therefore, to all those historians, biographers, memoirists, diarists, journalists, archivists, and letter writers, living and dead, on whose work I have drawn.

Among those who, while their books are not in the public domain, have nevertheless been especially generous in allowing me to quote them are Sir Michael Howard, author of *The Franco-Prussian War* (London: Rupert Hart-Davis, 1961); Ivor Guest, author of *Napoleon III in England* (London: British Technical and General Press, 1952); Simone André Maurois, author of *Miss Howard and the Emperor* (New York: Alfred A. Knopf, 1957, translated by Humphrey Hare). My particular thanks are due to them.

ALBRECHT-CARRIE, René, *Adolphe Thiers or the Triumph of the Bourgeoisie.* Boston: Twayne, 1977.
ALLISON, John M. S., *Monsieur Thiers.* London: Allen & Unwin, 1932.
d'AMBÈS, Baron (pseud.), *Intimate Memories of Napoleon III* (ed. and trans. A. R. Allinson), London: St. Paul, 1912.
ARONSON, Theo, *The Fall of the Third Napoleon.* Indianapolis: Bobbs-Merrill, 1970.

————, *Queen Victoria and the Bonapartes.* Indianapolis: Bobbs-Merrill, 1972.

AUBRY, Octave, *The Second Empire.* New York: Lippincott, 1940.

————, *Eugénie, Empress of the French* (trans. F. M. Atkinson), London: Cobden-Sanderson, 1939.

BAGEHOT, Walter, *Collected Works* (ed. Norman St. John Stevas). Vol. 4, Cambridge, Mass.: Harvard University Press, 1968.

BARKER, Nancy Nichols, *Distaff Diplomacy: The Empress Eugénie and the Foreign Policy of the Second Empire.* Austin, Tex.: University of Texas Press, 1967.

BARTHEZ, Dr. Ernest, *The Empress Eugénie and Her Circle.* London: Fisher & Unwin, 1912.

BEATTY, Charles, *De Lesseps of Suez.* New York: Harper, 1956.

von BISMARCK, Otto, *The Memoirs* (trans. A. J. Butler). New York: Fertig, 1966.

BONAPARTE, Louis Napoleon, *Political and Historical Works.* New York: Fertig, 1972.

————, *Oeuvres.* Paris: Plon, 1869.

BROCKETT, L. P., *The Year of Battles.* New York: Goodspeed, 1871.

BRODSKY, Alvin, *Imperial Charade.* Indianapolis: Bobbs-Merrill, 1978.

BURCHELL, S. C., *Imperial Masquerade.* New York: Athenaeum, 1971.

CARETTE, A., *Recollections of the Court of the Tuileries.* New York: Appleton, 1890.

CORLEY, T. A. B., *Democratic Despot: A Life of Napoleon III.* New York: Potter, 1961.

CORNU, Hortense, "Louis Napoleon Painted by a Contemporary," *Cornhill Magazine.* London (January–June 1873).

CORTI, Count Egon Caesar, *Maximilian and Charlotte of Mexico.* New York: Knopf, 1928.

COWLEY, 1st Earl (ed. Frederick Arthur Wellesley), *The Paris Embassy During the Second Empire.* London: Butterworth, 1928.

CRANKSHAW, Edward, *Bismarck.* London: Macmillan, 1981.

DANSETTE, Adrien, *Les amours de Napoleon III.* Paris: Fayard, 1938.

————, *Louis Napoleon à la conquète du pouvoir.* Paris: Hachette, 1961.

————, *Du 2 Décembre au 4 Septembre.* Paris: Hachette, 1972.

————, *Naissance de la France moderne.* Paris: Hachette, 1976.

DAUDET, Lucien, *L'Inconnue, l'Impératrice, Eugénie.* Paris: Plon, 1922.

————, *Dans l'ombre de l'Impératrice Eugénie. Lettres intimes addressées à Mme. Alphonse Daudet.* Paris: Plon 1935.

DECAUX, Alain, *La Castiglione, dame de coeur de l'Europe.* Paris: Perrin, 1953.

————, *L'empire, l'amour et l'argent.* Paris: Perrin, 1982.

DUFF, David, *Eugénie and Napoleon III.* London: Collins, 1978.

EUGÉNIE, Empress, *Lettres familières* (ed. 17th Duke of Alba and G. Hanotaux). Paris: Le Divan, 1935.

EVANS, Dr. T. W., *Memoirs.* New York: Appleton, 1905.

FILON, Pierre Augustin, *Memoirs of the Prince Imperial.* London: Heinemann, 1913.

———, *Souvenirs sur l'Impératrice Eugénie.* Paris: Calmann-Levy, 1929.

FLAUBERT, Gustave, *Madame Bovary* (trans. Alan Russell), Harmondsworth, Middlesex: Penguin, 1950.

———, *Sentimental Education* (trans. Robert Baldick) Harmondsworth, Middlesex: Penguin, 1964.

FLEISCHMANN, Hector, *Napoleon III and the Women He Loved.* London: Holden & Hardingham, 1915.

FLEURY, Count, *Memoirs of the Empress Eugénie.* New York: Appleton, 1920.

FORBES, Archibald, *The Life of Napoleon the Third.* London: Chatto & Windus, 1898.

FRASER, Sir William, *Napoleon III (My Recollections).* London: Sampson Low Marston, 1896.

des GARETS, Comtesse (née Marie de Larminat) *Auprès de l'Impératrice Eugénie.* Paris: Plon, 1928.

GEER, Walter, *Napoleon III.* London: Cape, 1921.

de GONCOURT, Jules and Edmond, *Journals.* Paris: Charpentier, 1888–96.

GOOCH, G. P., *The Second Empire.* London: Longmans, 1960.

GREVILLE, Charles (ed. Lytton Strachey and Roger Fulford), *The Greville Memoirs.* London: Macmillan, 1938.

GRONOW, Rees Howell, *Reminiscences and Recollections.* New York: Scribners, 1900.

GUEDALLA, Phillip, *The Second Empire.* London: Constable, 1922.

GUÉRARD, Albert, *Napoleon III.* Cambridge, Mass.: Harvard University Press, 1943.

GUEST, Ivor, *Napoleon III in England.* London: British Technical and General Press, 1952.

HASLIP, Joan, *Imperial Adventurer: Emperor Maximilian of Mexico and His Empress.* London: Weidenfeld & Nicolson, 1971.

HASWELL, James M., *The Man of His Time.* London: Hotten, 1871.

d'HAUTERIVE, Ernest (ed.), *The Second Empire and Its Downfall: The Correspondence of Napoleon III and Prince Napoleon* (trans. Herbert Wilson). New York: Doran, 1927.

d'HÉRISSON, Maurice d'Irisson, *Journal of a Staff Officer in Paris During the Events of 1870 and 1871.* London: Remington, 1885.

HOOPER, George, *The Campaign of Sedan: The Downfall of the Second Empire.* London: Bell, 1909.

HORTENSE, Queen (ed. J. Hanoteau) *Mémoires.* Paris: Plon, 1927.

———, *Lettres.* Paris: Revue des Deux Mondes, 1933.

HOWARD, Michael, *The Franco-Prussian War.* London: Hart-Davis, 1961.

HÜBNER, Baron, *Neuf ans de souvenirs d'un ambassadeur d'Autriche à Paris.* Paris: Plon, 1904.

HUGO, Victor, *Napoléon le petit.* London: Vizetelly, 1852.

————, *Histoire d'un crime*. Paris: Calmann-Lévy, 1877.

JERROLD, Blanchard, *The Life of Napoleon III*. London: W. H. Allen, 1874–82.

JOHN, Katherine, *The Prince Imperial*. New York: Putnam, 1939.

KINGLAKE, A. W., *The Invasion of the Crimea*. London: Blackwood, 1899.

KURTZ, Harold, *The Empress Eugénie*. London: Hamish Hamilton, 1964.

LACAPRA, Dominick, *"Madame Bovary" on Trial*. Ithaca, N.Y.: Cornell University Press, 1982.

LEGGE, Edward, *The Comedy and Tragedy of the Second Empire*. London and New York: Harper, 1911.

————, *The Empress Eugénie and Her Son*. London: Grant Richards, 1916.

LOLIÉE, Frederic, *The Gilded Beauties of the Second Empire*. London: John Long, 1909.

LORD, R. H., *The Origins of the War of 1870*. Cambridge, Mass.: Harvard University Press, 1924.

MALMESBURY, Earl of, *Memoirs of an ex-Minister*. London: Longmans Green, 1885.

MARX, Karl, *The 18th Brumaire of Louis Bonaparte* (trans. Daniel de Leon), Chicago: Kerr, 1907.

MASUYER, Valérie, *Journal*. Paris: *Revue des Deux Mondes*. 1914–15.

MAUROIS, Simone André, *Miss Howard and the Emperor* (trans. Humphrey Hare). New York: Knopf, 1958.

MEDLICOTT, W. N., *Bismarck and Modern Germany*. London: English University Press, 1965.

de MERCY-ARGENTEAU, Comtesse Louise, *The Last Love of an Emperor*. London: Iris, 1916.

MERIMÉE, Prosper, *Correspondance Générale de Prosper Merimée*. Paris: Le Divan, 1941–64.

MONTS, Karl von, *La captivité de Napoleon III en Allemagne*. Paris: Pierre Lafitte, 1910.

MURAT, Princess Caroline, *My Memoirs*. London: Eveleigh Nash, 1910.

NEVILL, Ralph (ed.), *The Reminiscences of Lady Dorothy Nevill*. London: Nelson, 1910.

PACKE, Michael St. John, *The Bombs of Orsini*. London: Secker & Warburg, 1958.

PALÉOLOGUE, Maurice, *The Tragic Empress* (trans. Hamish Miles). New York: Harper, 1928.

PALMER, Alan, *Bismarck*. London: Weidenfeld & Nicolson, 1976.

PAYNE, Howard C., *The Police State of Louis Napoleon Bonaparte, 1851–60*. Seattle: University of Washington Press, 1966.

PEARL, Cyril, *The Girl with the Swansdown Seat*. New York: Bobbs-Merrill, 1955.

PERSIGNY, duc de, *Mémoires*. Paris: Plon, 1896.

POTTINGER, E. Ann, *Napoleon III and the German Crisis, 1865–66*. Cambridge, Mass.: Harvard University Press, 1966.

RICHTER, Werner, *Bismarck* (trans. Brian Battershaw). London: Mac-Donald, 1964.

RIDLEY, Jasper, *Napoleon III and Eugénie*. London: Constable, 1979.

de SAINT-AMAND, Imbert, *Louis Napoleon and Mlle de Montijo*. New York: Scribner's, 1897.

————, *Napoleon III at the Height of His Power*. New York: Scribner's, 1900.

SCHONFIELD, Hugh J., *The Suez Canal*. Miami, Fla.: University of Miami Press, 1969.

SENCOURT, Robert (pseud.), *The Life of the Empress Eugénie*. London: Benn, 1931.

SENIOR, Nassau, *Conversations with Distinguished Persons During the Second Empire*. London: Hurst & Blackett, 1880.

SIMPSON, F. A., *The Rise of Louis Napoleon, 1808–1848*. London: Longmans Green, 1909.

————, *Louis Napoleon and the Recovery of France*. London: Longmans Green, 1923.

SMITH, W. H. C., *Napoleon III*. London: Wayland, 1972.

SNYDER, Louis L. *The Blood and Iron Chancellor*. Princeton, N.J.: Van Nostrand, 1967.

de SOISSONS, Comte, *The True Story of the Empress Eugénie*. London: Bodley Head, 1920.

STODDART, Jane, *The Life of the Empress Eugénie*. London: Hodder & Stoughton, 1906.

STOECKL, Baroness, *When Men Had Time to Love*. London: John Murray, 1953.

THOMPSON, J. M., *Louis Napoleon and the Second Empire*. New York: Norton, 1967.

TISDALL, E. E. P., *The Prince Imperial: A Study of His Life Among the British*. London: Jarrold's, 1959.

de TOCQUEVILLE, Alexis, *Recollections*. New York: Meridian, 1959.

TROUBETZKOY, Alexis, *The Road to Balaklava: Stumbling into War with Russia*. Toronto: Trafalgar Press, 1986.

TURNBULL, Patrick, *Eugénie of the French*. London: Michael Joseph, 1974.

VICTORIA, Queen, *Letters of Queen Victoria*. London: John Murray, 1907–32.

————, *Leaves from a Journal*. London: Andre Deutsch, 1961.

de VIEL CASTEL, Comte Horace, *Memoirs*. London: Remington, 1888.

VIZETELLY, Ernest Alfred, *Court Life of the Second French Empire*. New York: Scribners, 1907.

WELLESLEY, Sir Victor, and SENCOURT, Robert, *Conversations with Napoleon III*. London: Benn, 1934.

WILLIAMS, Roger L., *The Mortal Napoleon III*. Princeton, N.J.: Princeton University Press, 1971.

————, *The World of Napoleon III*. New York: Free Press, 1967.

ZELDIN, Theodore, *Emile Ollivier and the Liberal Empire of Napoleon III*. Oxford: Clarendon Press, 1963.

————, *The Political System of Napoleon III*. London: Macmillan, 1958.

NOTES

8   "I WOULD GIVE ALL MY HERITAGE," Simpson, *The Rise of Louis Napoleon.*

9   "A COLD RESERVE," Hortense, *Mémoires.*

13 "I WISH YOU WERE A MAN," Thompson, *op. cit.*

13 LN's "FURIOUS ITALIAN PASSIONS," Cornu, *Louis Napoleon Painted by a Contemporary.*

13 "NO MORE TALK OF CHIVALRY," Dansette, *Les amours de Napoléon III.*

15 "THE MESSIAH OF THE PEOPLE," Hortense, *op. cit.*

15 "LOUIS IS NOT ATTRACTIVE ENOUGH," Dansette, *Amours.*

16 "A WILD, HARUM-SCARUM YOUTH," Malmesbury, *Memoirs of an ex-Minister.*

CHAPTER 2

18 "WE HAVE ACCEPTED ENGAGEMENTS," Simpson, *The Rise of LN.*

19 LN rescued by his mother, Hortense, *Mémoires,* and Masuyer, *Journal.*

21 "HE WAS A DIFFERENT MAN," Corley, *Democratic Despot.*

22 "I RECEIVE HARD WORDS FROM YOU," Simpson, *op. cit.*

23 "AH, MY DEAR PRINCE," Dansette, *Amours.*

24 "LOVE IS LIKE A SICKNESS," *ibid.*

24 "I HAVE NO GREATER WISH," *ibid.*

25 "LOUIS DEVOURED HER WITH HIS EYES," *ibid.*

CHAPTER 3

28 "ALL THE WORLD WILL TAKE ME FOR A FOOL," Simpson, *The Rise of LN.*

28 "WHAT CARE I FOR THE CRIES OF THE MOB," *ibid.*

30 "IN CASE IT SHOULD NOT SUCCEED," Geer, *Napoleon III.*

30 "I DO NOT REPROACH MYSELF," Simpson, *op. cit.*

31 "HOW SAD I AM, ALONE IN LONDON," Saint-Amand, *Louis Napoleon and Mlle de Montijo.*

31 "THE PRINCE KISSED HER LOVINGLY," Ambes, *Intimate Memories of Napoleon III.*

32 "NEVER TIRE OF CLAIMING," Geer, *op. cit.*

32 "OUR TURBULENT NEIGHBOURS," Guest, *Napoleon III in England.*

32 "IN LEAVING VOLUNTARILY," Jerrold, *The Life of Napoleon III.*

34 LN's lifestyle in London, Guest, *op. cit.*

34 "I AM ALWAYS AFRAID TO WRITE TO YOU," Simpson, *op. cit.*

35 "SOCIETY DID NOT VIEW THIS PRINCE," Nevill, *Reminiscences of Lady Dorothy Nevill.*

35 "FURNISHED WITH A LUXURY AND SPLENDOUR," Greville, *The Greville Memoirs.*

CHAPTER 4

40 "AFTER TOMORROW OUR EAGLES WILL HAVE TRIUMPHED," *The Times,* August 7, 1840.
41 LN's men go ashore, *ibid.*
41 "GOOD MORNING, MY BRAVE FELLOW," *ibid.*
42 "I DREW MY SABER," *ibid.*
42 The subprefect "ADDRESSED THEM ENERGETICALLY," *ibid.*
43 "MY GOD, HOW MISTAKEN," *ibid.*
44 "I HAD A PEEP," *ibid.*
44 "WOMEN, ALWAYS TENDER," *ibid.,* August 8.
45 "I REPRESENT A PRINCIPLE," Saint-Amand, *LN and Montijo.*
45 "THE SWORD OF AUSTERLITZ IS TOO HEAVY," *ibid.*
45 "HIS COUNTENANCE SEEMED TO US," *ibid.*
45 "IS ANYTHING IN FRANCE PERPETUAL?" Simpson, *Napoleon III.*
46 "I HAVE NOT YET WRITTEN," Saint-Amand, *op. cit.*
46 "FROM YOUR SUMPTUOUS CORTEGE," Bonaparte, *Political and Historical Works.*
47 "NO ONE KNOWS BETTER THAN I," Simpson, *op. cit.*
48 "A LITTLE COPPER, ZINC AND ACID," *ibid.*
48 "THE YEARS ROLL ON," *ibid.*
48 "YESTERDAY I HAD THE FIRST REAL JOY," *ibid.*
48 "THE NAPOLEONIC CAUSE GOES TO THE SOUL," *ibid.*
49 "THE GOVERNMENT WHICH HAS RECOGNIZED," Bonaparte, *op. cit.*
50 LN's escape from Ham, Dansette, *Conquête du pouvoir.*
50 LN "DETERMINED NOT TO ENDURE THE RIDICULE," Simpson, *op. cit.*

CHAPTER 5

52 LN's London lifestyle, Guest, *Napoleon III in England.*
53 Rachel and Plon-Plon were making love, Dansette, *Amours.*
56 Harriet Howard's background, Maurois, *Miss Howard and the Emperor.*
56 "I AM COLLECTING ALL MY BOOKS," Simpson, *Napoleon III.*
57 "HE HAS A THOUSAND GOOD AND AGREEABLE QUALITIES," Gronow, *Reminiscences and Recollections.*
57 LN as a "MAN OF DESTINY," Bonaparte, *Political and Historical Works.*

58   Miss H. "LACKED NEITHER GENEROSITY . . ." Fleury, *Souvenirs.*

CHAPTER 6

60   "A JOINT STOCK COMPANY," Tocqueville, *Recollections.*
60   LN "UNDER THE FLAG OF THE REPUBLIC," Merimée, *Correspondance Générale. Napoleon III and Eugénie.*
61   "EVERYBODY PAID LIP SERVICE," Flaubert, *Sentimental Education.*
62   "SOCIETY WAS CUT IN TWO," de Tocqueville, *Recollections.*
65   "IN SPITE OF THE MOST HUMANITARIAN LEGISLATION," Flaubert, *op. cit.*
66   "THIS COMMON LITTLE GENTLEMAN," Merimée, *Correspondance Générale.*
66   Cavaignac "CLEARING THE WAY FOR" LN, *ibid.*
68   LN "SEEMS TO BE WELL MEANING," Simpson, *Louis Napoleon and the Recovery of France.*
69   "IF I SHOULD SUCCEED," Albrecht-Carrie, *Adolphe Thiers or the Triumph of the Bourgeoisie.*
71   "WE WILL GIVE HIM WOMEN," Simpson, *op. cit.*
71   "FRANCE MADE TWO MISTAKES," Allison, *Monsieur Thiers.*

CHAPTER 7

72   "I SHALL REGARD AS ENEMIES," Bonaparte, *Political and Historical Works.*
73   LN "PRODUCES ON ME THE EFFECT OF A WOMAN," *The Times,* January 21, 1837.
74   Morny's existence a shock to LN, Masuyer, *Journal.*
75   Lanjuinais on LN's laziness, Senior, *Conversations with Distinguished Persons During the Second Empire.*
76   Cornu on the same subject, *ibid.*
76   "MY SINCEREST FRIENDS," Bonaparte, *Oeuvres.*
76   "IT WOULD BE PRESUMPTUOUS," *ibid.*
77   "HAVE WE RETURNED," Maurois, *Miss Howard.*
77   LN's letter to Barrot, Bonaparte, *op. cit.*
81   "THE VILE MULTITUDE," Ridley, *op. cit.*
84   "WHEN THEY ARE HANGING," Cornu, "Louis Napoleon Painted by a Contemporary."
84   "THE NAME NAPOLEON," Bonaparte, *op. cit.*

CHAPTER 8

90   "IF THERE IS A CLEAN SWEEP," Dansette, *Conquète du pouvoir.*

90   "WELL, GENERAL, WE WOULD HAVE LIKED," *ibid.*

91   "IT ATTACKED THE POWER," *The Times,* December 3, 1851.

91   "SOLDIERS, I DO NOT SPEAK," *ibid.*

94   "THE IDÉE FIXE OF THE NEPHEW," Marx, *The 18th Brumaire of Louis Bonaparte.*

95   "I WILL FORGIVE HIM," quoted in Ridley, *Napoleon III and Eugénie.*

96   LN "WORE DECEMBER 4 LIKE A HAIR SHIRT," Paléologue, *The Tragic Empress.*

96   "LIBERTY, EQUALITY, FRATERNITY," Marx, *op. cit.*

98   "A STRICT AND SLENDER . . . BUDGET," Payne, *The Police State of Louis Napoleon Bonaparte.*

99   "WHEN IT IS BETTER TO OVERLOOK," *ibid.*

101   "IF THE MODEST TITLE OF PRESIDENT," Bonaparte, *Oeuvres.*

101   "IT SEEMS THAT FRANCE DESIRES," *ibid.*

102   Guards dance the can-can, Cowley, *The Paris Embassy During the Second Empire.*

CHAPTER 9

106   "I FEEL YOUR DEAR CHILD," Victoria, *Letters of Queen Victoria.*

106   "SOME HIDEOUS GERMAN PRINCESS," Maurois, *Miss Howard.*

106   "AT ABOUT HALF-PAST TEN," Viel Castel, *Memoirs.*

106   "HER ATTITUDE CHANGED," Fleury, *Memoirs of the Empress Eugénie.*

107   LN meets Eugénie, Filon, *Souvenirs sur l'impératrice Eugénie.*

108   "I SAID TO HIM," *ibid.*

109   "HER DAINTY FIGURE," Turnbull, *Eugénie of the French.*

109   "HOW CAN I REACH YOU?" Stoddart, *The Life of the Empress Eugénie.*

110   "VERY WELL, THEN," Duff, *Eugénie and Napoleon III.*

112   Monks hacked to death, Ridley, *Napoleon and Eugénie.*

113   Stendhal's cryptic messages, *ibid.*

114   "DADDY, HOW I WANT TO KISS YOU," Eugénie, *Lettres.*

115   "HE WAS SAUNTERING IN THE PRADO," Duff, *op. cit.*

116   "MY END DRAWS NEAR," Eugénie, *Lettres.*

116   "THE YOUNG DUCHESS IS THOUGHT," Ridley, *op. cit.*

117   "HER SLENDER BODY," Stoddart, *op. cit.*

117   Eugénie riding bareback, *ibid.*

118   The man under Eugénie's bed, Ridley, *op. cit.*

118   "AN UGLY LITTLE FAT MAN," Malmesbury, *Memoirs.*

119 "For me to remain in my post," Sencourt, *The Life of the Empress Eugénie*.
119 "Like Achilles' spear," Duff, *op. cit.*
120 "She knew how to keep men at a distance," Turnbull, *op. cit.*
120 "Found her nose rather forbidding," quoted in *ibid*.

CHAPTER 10

121 "He will go and look for a flower," Eugénie, *Lettres*.
122 "Louis will marry," Brodsky, *Imperial Charade*.
122 "When the walls would be breached," Hübner, *Neuf ans de souvenirs d'un ambassadeur d'Autriche à Paris*.
122 LN "going it finely," Cowley, *The Paris Embassy*.
122 "My dear fellow, I am already taken," Ridley, *Napoleon and Eugénie*.
123 Mme Fortoul's protest, Filon, *Souvenirs*.
123 LN begged her to be calm, *ibid*.
123 "One does not marry," Loliee, *The Gilded Beauties of the Second Empire*.
123 Mathilde begs LN on her knees, Stoddart, *Life of Eugénie*.
124 "To hear the way in which," Cowley, *op. cit.*
125 A "foreign adventuress," Filon, *Souvenirs*.
126 A private audience, *ibid*.
126 She would leave in the morning, *ibid*.
126 "One can say," Hübner, *Neuf ans*.
126 LN's proposal of marriage, Eugénie, *Lettres*.
127 "The dates do not fit," Corley, *Democratic Despot*.
127 "I wish to be the first," Eugénie, *Lettres*.
127 "If the fair Infanta," Maurois, *Miss Howard*.
128 Begged her to go to London, *ibid*.
129 "I could easily," *ibid*.
129 "A terrible scene," Aubry, *The Second Empire*.
131 Empress by election, Merimée, *Correspondance*.

CHAPTER 11

132 "This is a sad time," Eugénie, *Lettres*.
133 "She never loved the Emperor," Soissons, *The True Story of the Empress Eugénie*.
133 Eugénie's telegram to Alcañices, Ridley, *Napoleon III and Eugénie*.
133 "I know all about that," Sencourt, *Life*.
134 "My longing to help the depressed," Eugénie, *Lettres*.
134 "The very summit," Hübner, *Neuf ans*.

135 "YOU WILL SEE THE SCANDAL," Dansette, *Amours.*
135 "I CANNOT DESCRIBE ALL THAT I SUFFERED," Eugénie, *Lettres.*
136 "THE OBJECT OF OUR NEIGHBOURS," Aronson, *Victoria and the Bonapartes.*
136 "FLAGS AND TAPESTRIES," *op. cit.*
136 "CRUDE COLORS," Hübner, *op. cit.*
137 LN looked "IGNOBLE," Greville, *Memoirs.*
137 "THAT HE IS PASSIONATELY," Aronson, *op. cit.*
137 "I HAVE TWO INCURABLE FAULTS," Dansette, *Amours.*
138 "BUT REALLY, WHY DO MEN NEVER THINK," Maurois, *Miss Howard.*
139 "AFTER THE FIRST NIGHT," Cowley, *The Paris Embassy.*
139 "BETWEEN OURSELVES, MADAME," Dansette, *op. cit.*
139 "I HAVE GAINED A CROWN," Eugénie, *Lettres.*
140 "SHE IS NO LONGER THE YOUNG BRIDE," Hübner, *Neuf ans.*
141 "HER MAJESTY IS BEAUTIFUL, BORING," Maurois, *op. cit.*
141 "WHAT MIGHT HAVE BEEN," Eugénie, *op. cit.*
142 "GREAT STRENGTH OF WILL," Hübner, *op. cit.*
142 "WAS BUT LITTLE MOVED," Filon, *Souvenirs.*
143 An angora cat which wore a green ribbon, Maurois, *Miss Howard.*
143 "MOCQUARD, CHEF DE CABINET," *ibid.*
144 LN "HAS COMPLETELY RESUMED HIS RELATIONS," *ibid.*
144 "AFTER THE MARCH-PAST," *ibid.*
144 "THE EMPRESS . . . HAS TOLD," *ibid.*
145 "I MUST HAVE MY LITTLE DIVERSIONS," *ibid.*

CHAPTER 12

147 "I MUST DO SOMETHING," Hübner, *Neuf ans.*
148 "CHANTING THEIR HYMNS," Troubetzkoy, *The Road to Balaklava.*
149 "NO CHANGES WOULD BE ALLOWED," *ibid.*
150 "DO AN AGREEABLE THING," Cowley, *The Paris Embassy.*
150 "TO FATHOM THE THOUGHTS," *ibid.*
151 "I DO NOT LIKE DEMAGOGUES," *ibid.*
152 "THERE NEVER WAS THE SLIGHTEST IDEA," Victoria, *Letters.*
152 "AN EMPEROR WITHOUT DIVINE RIGHT," Troubetzkoy, *op. cit.*
153 "THERE IS NO SETTLED POLICY," Cowley, *op. cit.*
154 "TEARS STOOD IN HIS MAJESTY'S EYES," *ibid.*
154 "EVERYTHING IS GOING ON ADMIRABLY," *ibid.*
155 "IN ALL HIS EXPERIENCE," Cowley, *op. cit.*
157 "GREAT FASCINATION IN THE QUIET," Victoria, *Leaves from a Journal.*
157 Victoria was "MIGHTILY TICKLED," Cowley, *op. cit.*
158 "I CANNOT SAY WHY," Victoria, *Leaves . . .*
159 "THE CONFUSION ABOUT LUGGAGE," Aronson, *Victoria and the Bonapartes.*

161 "N'ENTREZ PAS!" *ibid.*
161 "I FELT—I DO NOT KNOW," Victoria, *Leaves* . . .
162 "I WISH I WERE YOUR SON," Merimée, *Correspondance.*
162 "THE ASSASSIN AND THE COOK," Cowley, *op. cit.*
162 "RUDE AND DISAGREEABLE," Victoria, *Leaves* . . .
163 "THE OLD WRETCH," Viel Castel, *Journal.*
163 "THAT NIGHT WHEN WE LEFT," Victoria, *Leaves* . . .

CHAPTER 13

165 "A TERMINATION OF THE WAR," Cowley, *The Paris Embassy.*
166 "ALL PARIS IS EN ÉMOI," *ibid.*
166 "USE ANY PALLIATIVE," Legge, *The Comedy and Tragedy of the Second Empire.*
167 "THE COURSE OF NATURE," Sencourt, *Life.*
167 "IS IT A BOY?" Dansette, *Amours.*
168 "THERE IS NOW NO LONGER ANY UGÉNIE," Maurois, *Miss Howard.*
169 "THE POLITICAL RESULTS," Cowley, *op. cit.*
169 "I HAVE ENROLLED THE BEAUTEOUS COUNTESS," Decaux, *La Castiglione, dame de coeur de l'Europe.*
170 "SHE IS BEAUTIFUL, BUT . . ." *ibid.*
170 "YOU ARE ARRIVING RATHER LATE," *ibid.*
170 "EXCEEDINGLY DÉCOLLETÉ," Murat, *My Memoirs.*
171 "ROOTED TO THE SPOT," Decaux, *op. cit.*
171 "SHE BORE THE BURDEN," Viel Castel, *Memoirs.*
171 "WHEN HE GROWS UP," Dansette, *op. cit.*
171 "EVERY MOVEMENT, EVERY GESTURE," Decaux, *op. cit.*
172 "MY MOTHER WAS A FOOL," Dansette, *op. cit.*
172 "EVEN THE COURT ENTOURAGE," Cowley, *op. cit.*
174 "AN EMERALD WORTH 100,000 FRANCS," Maurois, *op. cit.*
174 "I HAVE HARDLY COMMENCED," Decaux, *op. cit.*

CHAPTER 14

175 "I FEAR ONLY THE DAGGER," Packe, *The Bombs of Orsini.*
177 Bomb plot details, *ibid.*
178 "DON'T BE A FOOL," Sencourt, *Life.*
179 "YOUR MAJESTY IS CONVINCED," Cowley, *The Paris Embassy.*
180 "C'EST LA GUERRE," Corley, *Democratic Despot.*
180 "DON'T APOLOGIZE," Hübner, *Neuf ans.*
180 Eugénie's "INCREDIBLE STUPEFACTION," Cowley, *op. cit.*
181 "THE FRENCH ARE BENT," Cowley, *op. cit.*
181 "THIS HORRIBLE CRIME," Hübner, *op. cit.*

182 "ORSINI IS THE HERO," *ibid.*

182 "I AM NOT HERE TO GLORIFY HIM," Packe, *op. cit.*

183 Orsini "NOT A COMMON MURDERER," Aubrey, *Second Empire.*

183 "THE HOPES EXPRESSED IN FAVOR," Packe, *op. cit.*

187 "A REAL LITTLE ROUÉE," Viel Castel, *Memoirs.*

187 Walewska's "SUPERB IMPUDENCE," Soissons, *True Story.*

187 LN "ON WALEWSKA'S KNEES," Viel Castel, *op. cit.*

188 "IN THE ARMS OF THE EMPEROR," Decaux, *L'Empire, l'amour.*

188 LN "EN BONNE FORTUNE," *ibid.*

188 "LESS EXPENSIVE THAN YOURS," Soissons, *True Story.*

188 "EACH REIGNING BONAPARTE MUST SLEEP," Maurois, *Miss Howard.*

188 "I HAVE SUCH A DISGUST FOR LIFE," Eugénie, *Lettres.*

CHAPTER 15

191 "YOU NEVER SAW SUCH AN EXTRAORDINARY CREATURE," Cowley, *The Paris Embassy.*

192 "PRAY SEND MORE," *ibid.*

192 "I REGRET THAT OUR RELATIONS," Hübner, *Neuf ans.*

192 "WHAT A DISGRACE," Cowley, *op. cit.*

194 Workers cheer the war, Viel Castel, *Memoirs.*

195 LN has field orders destroyed, Corley, *Democratic Despot.*

196 "WHEN ONE IS DUTY BOUND," *ibid.*

196 "LIKE A CONSPIRATOR," *The Times*, June 25, 1859.

197 "THEY DISEMBOWEL EACH OTHER," Ridley, *Napoleon III and Eugénie.*

198 "GENTLEMEN, THE DAY IS OVER," Corley, *op. cit.*

202 "THIS STATE OF AFFAIRS," Wellesley/Sencourt, *Conversations with Napoleon III.*

202 "IN TERMS OF UTTER DESPAIR," *ibid.*

202 "I WISH THE ITALIANS," *ibid.*

202 "THE EMPEROR OVERWHELMS ME," *ibid.*

CHAPTER 16

204 "THE GODFATHER OF MY CHILD," Cowley, *The Paris Embassy.*

205 "VARIOUS MOTIVES," *ibid.*

206 "SHE SEEMS TO HAVE BEEN," Victoria, *Letters.*

206 "SHE LOOKED VERY PRETTY," *ibid.*

206 "MUCH AS YOU HAVE BEEN DISPOSED," Cowley, *op. cit.*

207 "BRUTAL INVECTIVES," *ibid.*

207 Prince Albert "SO RABID," *ibid.*

207 "I AM NO HYPOCRITE," *ibid.*

207 "Trusts to stratagem and fraud," Senior, *Conversations*.
208 "But if public opinion," Cowley, *op. cit.*
208 "There are many who think," *ibid.*
209 Plon-Plon refuses toast, Viel Castel, *Memoirs*.
210 "What would you think?" (and passim), d'Hauterive, *The Second Empire and Its Downfall: Correspondence of Napoleon III and Prince Napoleon.*
213 "Craint-plomb," Viel Castel, *op. cit.*

CHAPTER 17

220 "I would like to," Haslip, *Imperial Adventurer: Emperor Maximilian of Mexico and His Empress.*
220 Sooner or later, he would have to go to war, Corti, *Maximilian and Charlotte of Mexico.*
220 "If Mexico were not so far," Wellesley/Sencourt, *Conversations.*
223 "I have an intuition," Sencourt, *Life.*
223 "The Empress is again concerned," Corti, *op. cit.*
224 "It is in the common interest," Wellesley/Sencourt, *op. cit.*
224 "Amused to see the Emperor," *ibid.*
225 "Habit of running after every pretty woman," Haslip, *op. cit.*
225 "Not so much an emperor," *ibid.*
226 "For my part I prefer," *ibid.*
226 "It is a question of rescuing," Corti, *op. cit.*
226 LN "marked out by Providence," *ibid.*
226 "How many cannon shots?" Wellesley/Sencourt, *op. cit.*
227 "The Empress hates Miramón," *ibid.*
228 "The odds are," Haslip, *op. cit.*

CHAPTER 18

229 "She now mixes herself up," Wellesley/Sencourt, *Conversations.*
230 "You're like me," Legge, *Comedy and Tragedy.*
230 "It was a sudden letch," quoted in Wellesley/Sencourt, *op. cit.*
231 "The whole heart of France," Paléologue, *Tragic Empress.*
231 "Hammer the Poles," Crankshaw, *Bismarck.*
232 Redrawing the map, Wellesley/Sencourt, *op. cit.*
233 "If the imperial couple wish," *ibid.*
234 Eugénie was "radiant," *ibid.*
234 "The throne of Mexico," Corti, *Maximilian and Charlotte.*
234 "Once the country is pacified," *ibid.*
236 "Whatever should happen in Europe," *ibid.*
236 "If you are unable," *ibid.*

237 "The appalling scandal," Wellesley/Sencourt, *op. cit.*
237 "Deliberately prevaricating," *ibid.*
238 "Furious at being dragged," *ibid.*
238 "Your Imperial Highness has entered into," *ibid.*

CHAPTER 19

241 "All the beautiful women pay court," Dansette, *Amours.*
241 "Did not even have time to protest," *ibid.*
241 "When a woman is brought," Goncourts, *Journals.*
242 Bellanger's background, Dansette, *op. cit.*
242 "Intestine discords," Cowley, *The Paris Embassy.*
243 "Mademoiselle, you are killing the Emperor," Kurtz, *The Empress Eugénie.*
244 "Spanish blood and Spanish jealousy," Cowley, *op. cit.*
244 "Connect his journey," *ibid.*
245 "Has given more confidence to the nation," *ibid.*
245 Harriet by now "very fat," Murat, *Memoirs.*
245 "A puce silk gown," Maurois, *Miss Howard.*
247 "Have you heard of a certain charlatan," Cowley, *op. cit.*
248 "Two lateral churches," *ibid.*
249 "The Queen won't have the Holy Sepulchre," *ibid.*
249 "One of the first duties," Fleury, *Memoirs.*
250 The empress "constantly torments herself," quoted in Wellesley/Sencourt, *Conversations.*
250 LN "has a constant cold," *ibid.*
250 "The history of the imperial cold," Cowley, *op. cit.*

CHAPTER 20

255 "Have you looked carefully," Williams, *The World of Napoleon III.*
255 "Sir, I cannot allow you," Decaux, *L'Empire, l'amour.*
255 "His chivalrous heart," *ibid.*
256 Persigny's Grand Cross, Cowley, *The Paris Embassy.*
256 "Morny is an Orléanist," Gooch, *Second Empire.*
257 Morny's wife "behaved like a brute," Cowley, *op. cit.*
257 "An extraordinary young woman," *ibid.*
257 "Half great lady and half whore," Merimée, *Correspondance.*
258 "My Empress is a *real* Empress," Aubrey, *L'Impératrice Eugénie.*

CHAPTER 21

261 "AND THEN, VERY QUIETLY . . . EXPIRED," Legge, *Comedy and Tragedy.*
261 "THAT PIG," Pearl, *The Girl with the Swansdown Seat.*
261 "HOW ASTONISHED AND HORROR-STRUCK," Gronow, *Reminiscences and Recollections.*
262 "I AM RATHER DOUBTFUL ABOUT YOUR VISIT," Cowley, *The Paris Embassy.*
262 "GETTING UP A NEW FLIRTATION," *ibid.*
263 "YOU ARE OUR EMPRESS," Dansette, *Amours.*
263 "LIKE CLEOPATRA," Legge, *op. cit.*
263 "TOO BIG AND TOO STRONG," Merimée, *Correspondance.*
264 "WHY HAS SUCH A BEAUTIFUL JEWEL," Dansette, *op. cit.*
265 Eugénie "SETS THE FASHION," Gronow, *op. cit.*
267 "FLASHY AND INSECURE," Goncourts, *Journal.*
267 "SUCH A WONDERFUL POWER," Gronow, *op. cit.*
268 "THE PRINCIPAL SHAREHOLDERS ARE HOTEL WAITERS," Beatty, *de Lesseps.*
270 "THE BROAD NEW STREETS," Guedalla, *Second Empire.*
270 "A BEAUTIFUL, FAIRY-LIKE CITY," Gronow, *op. cit.*
274 "THE POLICE HAVE BLUNDERED," LaCapra, *"Madame Bovary" on Trial.*

CHAPTER 22

279 "I WAS ALMOST AS CLOSE," Crankshaw, *Bismarck.*
280 "FROM A DISTANCE, IT IS STUNNING," Burchell, *Imperial Masquerade.*
281 "I LOOK UPON FRANCE," Lord, *The Origins of the War of 1870.*
281 "WHATEVER THEY MAY SAY HERE," Cowley, *Paris Embassy.*
281 "I MUST ADMIT THAT THE EMPEROR," Paléologue, *Tragic Empress.*
282 "OUR POSITION . . . WILL BE PRINCIPALLY," Pottinger, *Napoleon III and the German Crisis, 1865–66.*
283 "FOR A SAUCE LIKE THAT," *ibid.*
283 LN ready to dance, Crankshaw, *op. cit.*
283 "ONE MUST NOT SEEK," Palmer, *Bismarck.*
284 "WE CAN IMAGINE THE ECCENTRIC VOLUBILITY," Medlicott, *Bismarck and Germany.*
284 Prussia wanted "A CLOSER UNION," Wellesley/Sencourt, *Conversations.*
284 "I begged the Emperor," *ibid.*
285 LN "SAID THAT HE DID NOT BELIEVE IN WAR," *ibid.*
285 LN "WOULD NOT BE SORRY," *ibid.*
285 "I TOLD THE EMPEROR," *ibid.*

286   "Your position is excellent," *ibid.*
286   "He will wait," *ibid.*
286   LN receives a firm offer, *ibid.*
288   "Marks of genuine affection," *ibid.*
288   "Be as rude as you like," Howard, *The Franco-Prussian War.*
289   "If we are beaten," Crankshaw, *op. cit.*
289   "Riding alone," Snyder, *The Blood and Iron Chancellor.*
289   "I could hug our fellows," *ibid.*
289   "The consternation here," Wellesley/Sencourt, *op. cit.*
290   "The day will come," Crankshaw, *op. cit.*
291   "It is France who has been beaten," *ibid.*
291   "There has never yet been," Cowley, *Paris Embassy.*
292   "If you want war," Crankshaw, *op. cit.*
292   "With such a nation for our neighbour," Wellesley/Sencourt, *op. cit.*
292   LN "sick, irresolute, exhausted," *ibid.*
292   "The beginning of the end," *ibid.*

CHAPTER 23

294   Bazaine "had not sufficient time," Haslip, *Imperial Adventurer.*
294   "Ghastly beyond all words," *ibid.*
296   "Tall, slight and handsome," quoted in *ibid.*
297   "Use your Austrian troops," Corti, *Maximilian and Charlotte.*
297   "It is not without pain," *ibid.*
298   "The wisest monarch of this century," *ibid.*
298   "He thinks Maximilian wanting in decision," Cowley, *Paris Embassy.*
298   LN's speech "a poor affair," *ibid.*
299   "And if the Emperor refuses," Corti, *op. cit.*
300   "I know more about China," *ibid.*
300   "The Emperor was hoping," Merimée, *Correspondance.*
300   "Did everything that was humanly possible," Haslip, *op. cit.*
300   LN "degenerating . . . for the past two years," *ibid.*
301   LN "wept even more," *ibid.*
301   "Who are the persons?" Corti, *op. cit.*
301   "Todos es inutil," *ibid.*
302   "Or for any reason whatsoever," *ibid.*
302   "I bid you farewell," *ibid.*
303   "I shall never forgive myself," Sencourt/Wellesley, *op. cit.*
303   "I am not ashamed," Paléologue, *Tragic Empress.*

CHAPTER 24

305 "THIS IS EXAGGERATION," Wellesley/Sencourt, *Conversations*.
305 Never seen French officers "SO EXCITED," *ibid*.
306 "THE EVENTS OF THE LAST MONTH," *ibid*.
306 LN disavows "PEREMPTORY," Benedetti, *ibid*.
306 "POSITIVELY AN OBJECT OF PITY," Cowley, *The op. cit.*
307 The French "MUST BE INDUCED TO HOPE," Crankshaw, *Bismarck*.
308 "ANCIENT GERMAN SOIL," Richter, *Bismarck*.
308 LN "COMPLETELY MYSTIFIED," Wellesley/Sencourt, *op. cit.*
309 "MY POSITION IS BECOMING HOURLY," *ibid*.
310 "HE CAN'T GIVE A LITTLE LIBERTY," Cowley, *op. cit.*
310 "IT IS A SMALL STEP," Zeldin, *Emile Ollivier and the Liberal Empire of Napoleon III.*
312 "YOU AND I MAY DISAGREE," *ibid*.
313 "LITERALLY CHARMED BY THE EMPEROR," *ibid*.
313 "YOU ARE WRONG TO THINK," *ibid*.
313 "I FOUGHT TOOTH AND NAIL," Paléologue, *Tragic Empress*.

CHAPTER 25

316 "NEVER IN MY LIFE," Beatty, *de Lesseps*.
317 She was "THE CYNOSURE," Turnbull, *Eugénie*.
317 "THE HOUR WHICH HAS JUST STRUCK," Beatty, *op. cit.*
318 "FELT AS THOUGH A CIRCLE OF FIRE," Schonfield, *The Suez Canal*.
320 "THE SECOND EMPIRE HAS GONE OFF THE RAILS," Ridley, *Napoleon III and Eugénie*.
320 "FOR EIGHTEEN YEARS, FRANCE," *ibid*.
323 "WE MAY SEE A PASSING FERMENTATION," Lord, *The Origins*.
323 "INSOLENT AND BUMPTIOUS," *ibid*.
323 "MILDER LANGUAGE WOULD HAVE BEEN MORE APPROPRIATE," Wellesley/Sencourt, *Conversations*.
324 "WE'VE GOT TO FINISH IT," Barker, *Distaff Diplomacy*.
324 "SO WORKED UP," Wellesley/Sencourt, *op. cit.*
325 "EVERYONE HERE . . . IS SO DESIROUS OF WAR," Barker, *op. cit.*
325 "HE APPEARED DELIGHTED," Wellesley/Sencourt, *op. cit.*
326 "IT WILL BE WAR AT ONCE," Howard, *Franco-Prussian War*.
326 "IT'S A DISGRACE," Barker, *op. cit.*
327 Benedetti "ALMOST IMPERTINENT," Lord, *op. cit.*
328 Decided "NOT TO RECEIVE COUNT BENEDETTI," *ibid*.
328 "I DOUBT WHETHER THAT DOES JUSTICE," Ridley, *op. cit.*
329 "DO YOU WANT ALL EUROPE TO SAY," Howard, *op. cit.*
329 "WITH A LIGHT HEART," *ibid*.
329 "SO READY THAT IF THE WAR," Corley, *Democratic Despot*.
330 "WE HAVE GONE TOO FAR," Wellesley/Sencourt, *op. cit.*

330 "WORDS ARE TOO WEAK," Aronson, *The Fall of the Third Napoleon*.
331 "VAPOURING, VAINGLORIOUS . . . FRANCE," *The Times*, November 11, 1870.

CHAPTER 26

332 "THE WEIGHT OF THE KNAPSACK," Legge, *Comedy and Tragedy*.
332 "A COMPLETE REPORT UPON . . . MOBILISATION," *ibid.*
334 "DO YOU WANT TO TURN FRANCE," Howard, *Franco-Prussian War*.
335 "ALL VOUCHED FOR OUR VICTORY," Paléologue, *Tragic Empress*.
335 "IS IT TRUE?" *ibid.*
336 "I DID KNOW THE EMPEROR WAS ILL," *ibid.*
337 "A BUCKRAM BOY," Forbes, *The Life of Napoleon the Third*.
338 "LOUIS IS FULL OF SPIRIT," Eugénie, *Lettres*.
338 "ELECTRIC WITH WARLIKE EXCITEMENT," Filon, *Memoirs*.
339 "I FORGOT TO SAY GOODBYE," Aronson, *The Fall*.
339 "HAVE ARRIVED AT BELFORT," Hooper, *The Campaign of Sedan: The Downfall of the Second Empire*.
340 "EVERYONE BEHAVED AS HE WANTED," Howard, *op. cit.*
341 "IT MAY WELL HAPPEN," *ibid.*
341 "THE NOISE, THE EXCITEMENT," Aronson, *op. cit.*
342 LN lifted off his horse, Forbes, *op. cit.*
343 "MARSHAL MACMAHON HAS LOST A BATTLE," Brockett, *The Year of Battles*.
343 "THE DYNASTY IS LOST," Filon, *Souvenirs*.
343 "FRENCHMEN: THE OPENING OF THE WAR," Brockett, *op. cit.*
344 Eugénie born during an earthquake, Filon, *op. cit.*
344 "YOU ARE AT THIS MOMENT, MADAME," quoted in Kurtz, *Empress Eugénie*.
345 "HAVE YOU CONSIDERED," Howard, *op. cit.*
346 "NEVER SEEN ANYTHING MORE PITIABLE," Legge, *op. cit.*

CHAPTER 27

349 "IT WAS AN INERT CROWD," d'Hérisson, *Journal of a Staff Officer in Paris During the Events of 1870 and 1871*.
350 "ONE, TWO, THREE, SHIT!" *ibid.*
350 "I SEEM TO HAVE ABDICATED," Howard, *Franco-Prussian War*.
351 "THE EMPEROR WILL NOT RETURN," John, *The Prince Imperial*.
353 "IF YOU ABANDON BAZAINE," Howard, *op. cit.*
354 "IN THE NAME OF THE COUNCIL OF MINISTERS," *ibid.*
356 "NOW WE HAVE THEM IN A MOUSETRAP," *ibid.*
356 "WE'RE IN A CHAMBER POT," *ibid.*

357　"Send me to the army," Forbes, *Life.*
357　"We need a victory," Howard, *op. cit.*
357　"The day had become so clear," quoted in Hooper, *Campaign of Sedan.*
358　"Masses of coloured rags," *The Times,* September 6, 1870.
359　"What astounding heroism," Evans, *Memoirs.*
359　"Your Majesty may be quite at ease," Forbes, *op. cit.*
359　"Why does this useless struggle," Hooper, *op. cit.*
359　The streets "were choked," *ibid.*
360　"I claim the entire responsibility," Legge, *Comedy and Tragedy.*
360　"Having been unable to die," *ibid.*
361　"Regretting the circumstances," *ibid.*

CHAPTER 28

362　"All dusty and dirty," Hooper, *Campaign of Sedan.*
363　LN "driven into it," *ibid.*
363　LN and the weaver's wife, Forbes, *Napoleon III.*
363　"His whose appearance . . . unsoldierlike," Legge, *Comedy and Tragedy.*
364　"When you thought there was honour," Howard, *Franco-Prussian War.*
364　"I am instructed to remind you," Hooper, *op. cit.*
364　"My sad and painful duty," *ibid.*
365　An assurance which was "visibly welcome," Legge, *op. cit.*
366　"She is worn out," John, *Prince Imperial.*
366　"She was pale and terrible," Filon, *Souvenirs.*
367　"With convulsed features," Paléologue, *Tragic Empress.*
368　"I had no fear of death," Evans, *Memoirs.*
369　"It has sometimes seemed to me," *ibid.*
369　"I did not feel alarmed," *ibid.*
370　"A post and telegraph office," Monts, *La captivité de Napoleon III en Allemagne.*
371　Lady Cowley's visit, Legge, *The Empress Eugénie and Her Son.*
371　"My tenderness and love for you," Eugénie, *Lettres.*
372　"All her manner convinced me," Monts, *op. cit.*
374　"If the King of Prussia," Monts, *op. cit.*
374　"A thousand times better," Eugénie, *op. cit.*
375　Mels Cohen interview quoted in Wellesley/Sencourt, *Conversations.*
375　LN's letters to Louise, Legge, *op. cit.*
376　Louise visits Wilhelmshohe, Dansette, *Amours.*

CHAPTER 29

378 "QUIET CALM AND DIGNITY," Malmesbury, *Memoirs.*
378 "GROWN VERY STOUT AND GREY," Victoria, *Letters.*
379 "WHEN DISASTER OVERWHELMED US," Paléologue, *Tragic Empress.*
379 "THE DAYS WERE SAD INDEED," des Garets, *Auprès de l'impératrice Eugénie.*
380 "I WISH TO JUSTIFY MYSELF," Filon, *Souvenirs.*
380 "FROM THE VERY DAY OF MY MARRIAGE," Paléologue, *op. cit.*
382 "A HISTORICAL NECESSITY," quoted in Wellesley/Sencourt, *Conversations.*
383 LN's operation details, Williams, *The Mortal Napoleon III.*
384 LN's death, Fleury, *Memoirs.*

POSTSCRIPT

394 "ON THE CONTRARY, SHE THINKS THE REVERSE," Victoria, *Letters.*
394 Prince Louis's prayer, John, *Prince Imperial.*
395 "WHEN ONE BELONGS," Tisdall, *Prince Imperial.*
395 "EAGERLY HE SCANNED," des Garets, *Auprés de l'impératrice.*
396 "MY CONSCIENCE IS CLEAR," *ibid.*
397 Prince Louis's will, *ibid.*
397 "A FRENCHMAN WITH ALL THE QUALITIES," John, *op. cit.*
398 "I'VE NO DESIRE TO BE KILLED," *ibid.*
399 Died "LIKE A LION," Tisdall, *op. cit.*
399 "SHE SAT AS WHITE AND MOTIONLESS," Kurtz, *Empress Eugénie.*
399 Eugénie's conduct "BEYOND ALL PRAISE," Victoria, *Letters.*
400 "MY GRIEF IS SAVAGE," Eugénie, *Lettres.*
400 "LET NO ONE SUFFER," John, *op. cit.*
401 "IS IT YOU?" Kurtz, *op. cit.*
401 "I HAD ONLY HIM," Eugénie, *op. cit.*
402 "HER SERVANTS, THE FOOD," Stoeckl, *When Men Had Time to Love.*
402 "I NEVER FEEL SO WELL," *ibid.*
402 "WHAT COULD REMAIN?" quoted in Kurtz, *op. cit.*
403 "WITHOUT INDISCRETIONS," Daudet, *L'inconnue, l'impératrice Eugénie.*
403 "AMAZED THAT ALL THIS," *ibid.*
404 "SHE HAS READ YOUR BOOKS," Paléologue, *Tragic Empress.*
404 "HOW WILL THE FUTURE JUDGE US?" *ibid.*
405 "FOUND HER MORE STIRRED THAN EVER," *ibid.*
405 "THE STIFFNESS OF HER MOVEMENTS," *ibid.*
405 "I BEAR THE FRENCH PEOPLE NO GRUDGE," *ibid.*
406 "THIS WRECKED FRAME," *ibid.*
406 "THE EMPRESS RATHER LIKES HIM," Kurtz, *op. cit.*

406 "Left me with a disturbing recollection," Paléologue, *op. cit.*

407 "In her black silk dress," Kurtz, *op. cit.*

407 "Talks almost exclusively politics," Daudet, *Dans l'ombre de l'impératrice Eugénie.*

408 Woodrow Wilson's dangerous policies, Kurtz, *op. cit.*

408 "What have you done?" *ibid.*

INDEX